Essentials of WJ IV®
Cognitive Abilities Assessment

Essentials

of WJ IV® Cognitive Abilities Assessment

Fredrick A. Schrank
Scott L. Decker
John M. Garruto

WILEY

Published by John Wiley & Sons, Inc., Hoboken, New Jersey.
Published simultaneously in Canada.

For general information on our other products and services, please contact our Customer Care Department within the U.S. at 800-956-7739, outside the U.S. at 317-572-3986, or fax 317-572-4002.

Wiley publishes in a variety of print and electronic formats and by print-on-demand. Some material included with standard print versions of this book may not be included in e-books or in print-on-demand. If this book refers to media such as a CD or DVD that is not included in the version you purchased, you may download this material at **http://booksupport.wiley.com**. For more information about Wiley products, visit **www.wiley.com**.

Library of Congress Cataloging-in-Publication Data:

Names: Schrank, Fredrick A. (Fredrick Allen), author. | Decker, Scott L.,
   author. | Garruto, John M., 1973- author.
Title: Essentials of WJ IV cognitive abilities assessment / Fredrick A.
   Schrank, Scott L. Decker, John M. Garruto.
Description: Hoboken, New Jersey : John Wiley & Sons Inc., [2016] | Includes
   index.
Identifiers: LCCN 2015050975 | ISBN 9781119163367 (pbk.) | ISBN 9781119163381
   (epub) | ISBN 9781119163374 (epdf)
Subjects: LCSH: Woodcock-Johnson Tests of Cognitive Ability.
Classification: LCC BF432.5.W66 S367 2016 | DDC 153.9/3–dc23 LC record available at
   http://lccn.loc.gov/2015050975

Cover Design: Wiley
Cover image: © Greg Kuchik/Getty Images

Printed in Singapore

FIRST EDITION

PB Printing   10 9 8 7 6 5 4 3 2 1

CONTENTS

Four How to Interpret the WJ IV COG 144

Fredrick A. Schrank

Robert Walrath, John O. Willis, and Ron Dumont

The Essentials of WJ IV Cognitive Abilities Assessment
is dedicated to the memory of our colleague, teacher, and friend
Dr. Raymond S. Dean,
who championed the idea that intellectual assessment
can be especially meaningful
when it results in the objective identification of
functional limitations in cognitive abilities.

SERIES PREFACE

I n the *Essentials of Psychological Assessment* series, we have attempted to provide the reader with books that deliver key practical information in the most efficient and accessible style. The series features instruments in a variety of domains, such as cognition, personality, education, and neuropsychology. For the experienced clinician, books in the series offer a concise yet thorough way to master utilization of the continuously evolving supply of new and revised instruments as well as a convenient method for keeping up to date on the tried-and-true measures. The novice will find here a prioritized assembly of all the information and techniques that must be at one's fingertips to begin the complicated process of individual psychological diagnosis.

Wherever feasible, visual shortcuts to highlight key points are utilized along-side systematic, step-by-step guidelines. Chapters are focused and succinct. Topics are targeted for an easy understanding of the essentials of administration, scoring, interpretation, and clinical application. Theory and research are continually woven into the fabric of each book, but always to enhance clinical inference, never to sidetrack or overwhelm. We have long been advocates of "intelligent" testing—the notion that a profile of test scores is meaningless unless it is brought to life by the clinical observations and astute detective work of knowledgeable examiners. Test profiles must be used to make a difference in the child's or adult's life, or why bother to test? We want this series to help our readers become the best intelligent testers they can be.

The *Essentials of WJ IV® Cognitive Abilities Assessment* is designed to be a helpful reference to all examiners, whether they are experienced with the WJ III or just learning the WJ IV. The authors and contributors, all experts on the popular and widely used WJ IV, have detailed important points of administration, scoring, and interpretation that will assist in building competency with the WJ IV COG. In addition, Schrank and colleagues go beyond the interpretive guidance provided in the examiner's manual by clarifying what is measured by each test and cluster through operational definitions. Importantly, they relate the underlying cognitive processes tapped by each of the tests to internal and external neurocognitive research evidence. Their whole approach is to suggest links to evidence-based interventions for examinees who demonstrate limitations in performance on the tests and to provide models for using and interpreting results of the WJ IV COG in contemporary practice.

Alan S. Kaufman, PhD, and Nadeen L. Kaufman, EdD, Series Editors
Yale Child Study Center, Yale University School of Medicine

ACKNOWLEDGMENTS

The *Essentials of WJ IV Cognitive Abilities Assessment* could not have been written without the help and support of our friends, colleagues, students, and family. **Melanie Bartels Graw** came to our rescue and accepted responsibility for writing the administration and scoring chapters of this book. **Nancy Mather** and **Barbara Wendling** graciously reviewed manuscript content and provided insightful feedback that both clarified and strengthened the final work you are now reading. **Kevin McGrew** could be consistently counted on to keep us abreast of the latest research studies that form the neurocognitive basis for interpretation that is found in Chapter 4 and the case studies in Chapters 6 and 7. In Chapter 5, **Robert Walrath**, **John Willis**, and **Ron Dumont** provided their independent perspective on the strengths and weaknesses of the WJ IV COG. **Joseph Ferraracci** helped collect case study data and **Michael Eason** provided support with data management. **Erica LaForte** provided measurement support and helped secure the necessary permissions to include relevant data and content from the WJ IV. Finally, and perhaps most important, our spouses and children provided us with the emotional support and degrees of freedom to undertake such an important and ambitious project. Thank you, sincerely.

Fredrick A. Schrank
Scott L. Decker
John M. Garruto

One

OVERVIEW

The *Woodcock-Johnson IV Tests of Cognitive Abilities* (WJ IV COG: Schrank, McGrew, & Mather, 2014b) is a battery of carefully engineered tests for measuring cognitive abilities and intellectual level. The WJ IV COG was conormed with the *Woodcock-Johnson IV Tests of Oral Language* (WJ IV OL; Schrank, Mather, & McGrew, 2014b), the WJ IV *Tests of Achievement* (WJ IV ACH; Schrank, Mather, & McGrew, 2014a) to form the complete *Woodcock-Johnson IV* (Schrank, McGrew, & Mather, 2014a). The three batteries can be used independently or together in any combination. When the entire system is used, comparisons can be made among an individual's cognitive abilities, oral language, and achievement scores. Normative data was obtained from a large, nationally representative sample of 7,416 individuals ranging in age from 2 to 90+ years of age. Although primarily recommended for use with school-age children, adolescents, college students, and adults, some of the WJ IV COG tests can be used selectively with preschool children. A conormed but separate battery of tests called the *Woodcock-Johnson IV Tests of Early Cognitive and Academic Development* (WJ IV ECAD; Schrank, McGrew, & Mather, 2015b) is recommended for use with preschool children of ages 3 through 5 or with children of ages 6 through 9 who have a cognitive developmental delay.

The WJ IV COG is based on an update to the Cattell-Horn-Carroll (CHC) theory of cognitive abilities as described by Schneider and McGrew (2012) and McGrew, LaForte, and Schrank (2014). Cognitive complexity has been infused within several new tests, and interpretive emphasis has been shifted to the most important abilities for learning, interventions, and accommodations.

This book is intended to help you understand the essentials of cognitive ability assessment using the WJ IV COG. Although interpretation of the WJ IV COG can be complex, this book is presented in an easy-to-read format. In one small guide, administration, scoring, and interpretation are addressed in simple language. The clinical and psychoeducational case report chapters are intended to help you understand the use and interpretation of the WJ IV with practical examples and illustrations. Throughout the book, important points are highlighted by "Rapid Reference," "Caution," and "Don't Forget" boxes. At the end of Chapters 1 to 5, "Test Yourself" sections will help you assess your understanding of what you have read.

This chapter begins with a discussion of how the Woodcock-Johnson cognitive tests have evolved to become the most comprehensive battery of contemporary cognitive tests available to assessment professionals. The chapter ends with a summary of the technical characteristics of the WJ IV COG and a list of suggested resources for more information on the WJ IV COG.

HISTORY AND DEVELOPMENT

The WJ IV COG represents the fourth generation of the cognitive tests that originally formed Part One of the *Woodcock-Johnson Psycho-Educational Battery* (WJPEB; Woodcock & Johnson, 1977). Initial work on the WJPEB begin in 1973, although some of the tests were developed prior to that date. The first revision, the *Woodcock-Johnson Psycho-Educational Battery–Revised* (Woodcock & Johnson, 1989a), was published in 1989. The *Woodcock-Johnson III Tests of Cognitive Abilities* (Woodcock, McGrew, & Mather, 2001b) was published in 2001. The WJ IV COG was published in 2014.

1977: The Woodcock-Johnson Psycho-Educational Battery

The WJPEB began as one battery that consisted of three parts: Tests of Cognitive Ability, Tests of Achievement, and Tests of Interest Level. Initially, no overriding theoretical model guided development of the cognitive tests. Historically, test development began with a number of controlled experiments for measuring learning abilities. The first test constructed was Visual-Auditory Learning (Woodcock, 1958). Visual-Auditory Learning was the result of Woodcock's (1956) doctoral dissertation at the University of Oregon. Employing a set of reading rebuses, he developed the test to predict the ability to learn to read using a visual-auditory association, encoding, and retrieval experiment. Later, the Analysis-Synthesis test was developed to predict an individual's ability to learn mathematics. Additional cognitive tests were developed to create a heterogeneous mix of broad and complex cognitive abilities. In the end, 12 tests were included in the cognitive portion of the battery representing both verbal and nonverbal functions (a common interpretive construct of the era).

Level	Broad Function	Subtest	Broad Function

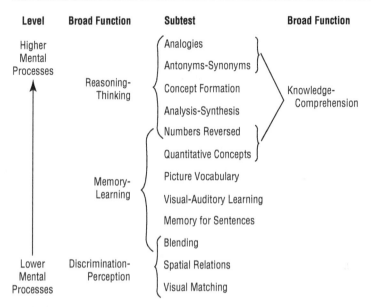

Figure 1.1 Broad functions, level-of-processing, and 12 cognitive tests from the 1977 WJPEB

Additionally, the abilities were designed to fall on a continuum from lower mental processes (simple operations) to higher mental processes (complex operations) as shown in Figure 1.1. Test-level analysis on the continuum from lower mental processes to higher mental processes has remained a useful model for interpreting test performance in all succeeding generations of the Woodcock-Johnson batteries.

WJPEB test construction followed a scientific-empirical method. Following the battery's norming (which occurred in 1976 and 1977), factor and cluster analyses were constructed to help define a small number of broad functions measured by the battery. Four functions were identified and labeled as Knowledge-Comprehension, Reasoning-Thinking, Memory-Learning, and Discrimination-Perception. In the 1970s, the term intelligence quotient and its abbreviation, IQ, were viewed somewhat negatively by many in the professional community. However, an overall cognitive score was viewed as a necessity. As a consequence, the term *Broad Cognitive Ability* (*BCA*) was introduced. In deriving the BCA, the 12 cognitive tests were differentially weighted to give a statistically better estimate of an individual's overall cognitive ability than would be obtained by weighting the tests equally.

1989: The Woodcock-Johnson Psycho-Educational Battery–Revised

In 1985, John Horn made a presentation at a conference honoring Lloyd Humphreys, who was one of his mentors. Horn's presentation fostered insight into the structure of human intellectual abilities and laid the theoretical foundation for the *Woodcock-Johnson–Revised Tests of Cognitive Ability* (WJ-R COG; Woodcock & Johnson, 1989c). The WJ-R COG interpretive model was closely associated with Horn's thesis and came to be described as an operational representation of *Gf-Gc* theory (Horn, 1991).

Kevin McGrew conducted much of the statistical work for the WJ-R and served as the primary author of the *WJ-R Technical Manual* (McGrew, Werder, & Woodcock, 1991). Following Horn's 1985 presentation, McGrew synthesized all of the extant exploratory and confirmatory factor analyses of the 1977 WJPEB. He developed a table similar to that found in Figure 1.2 that served as a blueprint for planning and organizing the revision to approximate *Gf-Gc* theory more closely.

Ten new tests were developed and added to the WJ-R COG. In the 1990s, the WJ-R COG became the primary battery of tests for measuring seven broad abilities identified in *Gf-Gc* theory: Long-Term Storage and Retrieval (*Glr*), Short-Term Memory (*Gsm*), Processing Speed (*Gs*), Auditory Processing (*Ga*), Visual Processing (*Gv*), Comprehension-Knowledge (*Gc*), and Fluid Reasoning (*Gf*). An eighth factor, Quantitative Ability (*Gq*), was available when using the WJ-R *Tests of Achievement* (Woodcock & Johnson, 1989b). **Rapid Reference** 1.1 outlines these eight abilities.

Gf-Gc theory was soon applied to the analysis and interpretation of other intelligence tests. In a groundbreaking analysis, Woodcock (1990) showed that

≡ *Rapid Reference 1.1 Eight* Gf-Gc *Abilities Measured by the 1989 WJ-R*

Long-Term Storage and Retrieval *(Glr)*
Short-Term Memory *(Gsm)*
Processing Speed *(Gs)*
Auditory Processing *(Ga)*
Visual Processing *(Gv)*
Comprehension-Knowledge *(Gc)*
Fluid Reasoning *(Gf)*
Quantitative Ability *(Gq)*

WJPEB Subtests	COGNITIVE FACTORS							
	Glr	Gsm	Gs	Ga	Gv*	Gc	Gf	Gq
Visual-Auditory Learning	●							
Memory for Sentences		○				○		
Numbers Reversed		○						
Spatial Relations**			●					
Visual Matching			●					
Blending				●				
Picture Vocabulary						●		
Antonyms-Synonyms						●		
Analysis-Synthesis							●	
Concept Formation							●	
Analogies						○	○	
Quantitative Concepts								●
Word Attack				○				
Calculation								●
Applied Problems								●
Science						●		
Social Studies						●		
Humanities						●		

Glr—Long-Term Retrieval
Gsm—Short-Term Memory
Gs—Processing Speed ● High Loadings
Ga—Auditory Processing ○ Moderate Loadings
Gv—Visual Processing
Gc—Comprehension-Knowledge
Gf—Fluid Reasoning
Gq—Quantitative Ability

* There are no measures of Gv in the 1977 WJPEB.

** Spatial Relations is a highly speeded test in the 1977 WJPEB.

Figure 1.2 Cognitive factors measured by the 1977 WJPEB

Gf-Gc theory describes the factor structure of other intelligence test batteries when their sets of tests are included in studies with sufficient breadth and depth of markers to ensure that the presence of all major factors could be identified. His article became widely cited in psychological and educational literature. As a consequence, *Gf-Gc* theory gained support as a major descriptor of human intellectual abilities and as a standard for evaluating tests of intelligence (McGrew & Flanagan, 1998).

2001: The Woodcock-Johnson III

In 1993, John Carroll published *Human Cognitive Abilities: A Survey of Factor Analytic Studies*. The thesis of this book is often described as Carroll's three-stratum theory (Carroll, 1993, 1998). Carroll said that human cognitive abilities could be conceptualized in a three-stratum hierarchy. Through his analysis of 461 data sets, Carroll identified 69 specific, or narrow, cognitive abilities (stratum I), similar to the Well Replicated Common Factor (WERCOF) abilities identified by Horn (1968, 1991) and associates (Ekstrom, French, & Harmon, 1979). In addition, Carroll grouped the narrow abilities into broad categories of cognitive abilities (stratum II) that are similar, in most respects, to the broad *Gf-Gc* factors described by Horn and his associates. Stratum III represents the construct of general intellectual ability (*g*) (Carroll, 1993, 1998). Figure 1.3 is a visual representation of Carroll's three-stratum theory.

The integration of these two independently and empirically derived theories has come to be called CHC theory. CHC theory provided the blueprint for the WJ III and subsequent support for interpretation of the WJ III COG. The primary difference between Carroll's three-stratum model and Horn's *Gf-Gc* model is the meaning of the general intellectual ability (*g*) factor at stratum III. Horn was emphatic that he did not believe *g* was an entity. The presence of a psychometric *g* was never the subject of debate; Horn suggested that *g* was merely a statistical artifact rather than a quality of cognitive functioning. However, because many assessment professionals expressed a need for a general intellectual ability score in the WJ III COG, the first-principal component (*g*) score was made available via computer scoring. The score was called General Intellectual Ability (GIA). Inclusion of this score on the WJ III can be traced to the influence of Carroll.

The primary emphasis in interpretation of the WJ III COG was the broad factors from stratum II. Kevin McGrew and Nancy Mather joined Richard Woodcock on the WJ III author team (Woodcock, McGrew, & Mather, 2001a, 2001b). The authors developed the model of two qualitatively different tests for each of the broad CHC factors so that interpretation of the ability would be as broad-based as possible. During the decade that followed publication, the WJ III COG became one of the most widely used tests for measurement of intellectual ability and differential cognitive abilities.

2014: The Woodcock-Johnson IV

When the time came to complete work on a fourth edition of the *Woodcock-Johnson*, Richard Woodcock had retired from active participation and a team of scientist-practitioner authors consisting of Fredrick Schrank,

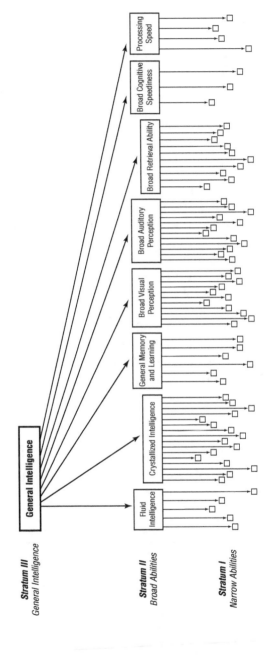

Figure 1.3 Carroll's three-stratum theory

Stratum III
General Intelligence

Stratum II
Broad Abilities

Stratum I
Narrow Abilities

General Intelligence

Fluid Intelligence

Crystallized Intelligence

General Memory and Learning

Broad Visual Perception

Broad Auditory Perception

Broad Retrieval Ability

Broad Cognitive Speediness

Processing Speed

Kevin McGrew, and Nancy Mather ushered in the new era of Woodcock-Johnson cognitive abilities assessment. Several new tests and interpretive procedures were created. One of the authors' goals was to move beyond the initial specification of CHC theory and base the WJ IV COG on the current status of contemporary research into human cognitive abilities. Impetus for this goal can be traced to a suggestion by John Carroll at the University of Virginia in 1994 when he offered a self-critique of his three-stratum theory. Among other considerations, he cautioned that the specifications in his theory were based on considerable subjectivity in sorting and classification of factors from independently derived data sets. He noted that his specification of abilities was based primarily on scores from psychometric tests and that cross-validation of the proposed constructs was needed from other data sets and other forms of scientific research. In the WJ IV, CHC theory has evolved beyond the initial specifications through both simplification and elaboration (McGrew et al., 2014; Schneider & McGrew, 2012). In Chapter 4 of this book, other sources of research are reviewed to cross-validate, modify, add to, or clarify some of the theoretical constructs posited by Cattell, Horn, Carroll, Woodcock, and others.

The interpretive model for the WJ IV reflects the most contemporary reflection of CHC theory at the time of publication. Analysis of the WJ-R, WJ III, and WJ IV standardization samples (which were not analyzed by Carroll) provided three large, multi-ability data sets to either confirm or revise initial construct specifications. Support for changes to the interpretive constructs was gleaned from other sources of neuroscience research. Perhaps the most significant changes to the WJ IV COG broad abilities were derived from contemporary research in the domains of working memory and phonological processing. See **Rapid Reference** 1.2.

≋ Rapid Reference 1.2 Broad and Narrow CHC Abilities Measured by the WJ IV COG

WJ IV COG Test	Primary Broad CHC Ability *Narrow Ability*
1 Oral Vocabulary	Comprehension-Knowledge (*Gc*)
A: Synonyms	*Lexical knowledge* (VL)
B: Antonyms	*Language development* (LD)
2 Number Series	Fluid Reasoning (*Gf*)
	Quantitative reasoning (RQ)
	Inductive reasoning (I)

WJ IV COG Test	Primary Broad CHC Ability *Narrow Ability*
3 Verbal Attention	Short-Term Working Memory *(Gwm)*
	Working memory capacity (WM)
	Attentional control (AC)
4 Letter-Pattern Matching	Cognitive Processing Speed *(Gs)*
	Perceptual speed (P)
5 Phonological Processing	Auditory Processing *(Ga)*
A: Word Access	*Phonetic coding* (PC)
B: Word Fluency	*Speed of lexical access* (LA)
C: Substitution	*Word Fluency* (FW)
6 Story Recall	Long-Term Storage and Retrieval *(Glr)*
	Meaningful memory (MM)
	Listening ability (LS)
7 Visualization	Visual Processing *(Gv)*
A: Spatial Relations	*Visualization* (Vz)
B: Block Rotation	
8 General Information	Comprehension-Knowledge *(Gc)*
A: Where	*General (verbal) information* (K0)
B: What	
9 Concept Formation	Fluid Reasoning *(Gf)*
	Inductive reasoning (I)
10 Numbers Reversed	Short-Term Working Memory *(Gwm)*
	Working memory capacity (WM)
11 Number-Pattern Matching	Cognitive Processing Speed *(Gs)*
	Perceptual speed (P)
12 Nonword Repetition	Auditory Processing *(Ga)*
	Phonetic coding (PC)
	Memory for sound patterns (UM)
	Auditory memory span (MS)
13 Visual Auditory Learning	Long-Term Storage and Retrieval *(Glr)*
	Associative memory (MA)
14 Picture Recognition	Visual Processing *(Gv)*
	Visual memory (MV)
15 Analysis-Synthesis	Fluid Reasoning *(Gf)*
	General sequential (deductive) reasoning (RG)
16 Object-Number Sequencing	Short-Term Working Memory *(Gwm)*
	Working memory capacity (WM)
17 Pair Cancellation	Cognitive Processing Speed *(Gs)*
	Perceptual speed (P)
	Spatial scanning (SS)
	Attentional control (AC)
18 Memory for Words	Short-Term Working Memory *(Gwm)*
	Auditory memory span (MS)

Another primary goal for the WJ IV COG was to incorporate cognitive complexity into several of the tests and clusters. One interpretive model that has remained constant throughout all editions of the Woodcock-Johnson is the analysis of test requirements via level of cognitive complexity (see Figure 1.1). By deliberate design, the WJPEB, WJ-R, and WJ III all included tasks that fall on a continuum from simple cognitive operations to complex cognitive processes. In the WJ IV, a concerted effort was directed to increase the number of tests with cognitive complexity requirements to provide greater ecological validity and interpretive relevance for the test or cluster scores. In the WJ IV COG, increased cognitive complexity is most clearly evidenced in the composition of the tests that compose the auditory processing cluster. The tests that comprise the WJ IV COG Auditory Processing cluster are designed to measure cognitively complex, ecologically relevant processes that involve auditory processing abilities. Each test is based on a combination of narrow abilities that spans one or more other broad abilities. The two new tests are COG Test 5: Phonological Processing and COG Test 12: Nonword Repetition. More information on the interpretation of the auditory processing tests can be found in Chapter 4.

The new author team had many other goals in mind as well. To select the tests that compose the GIA score (the core tests), those that are included in the standard battery, and the tests that compose each cognitive cluster, the authors drew heavily on their experiences as psychologists and educators. Their aim was to select tests that would provide the most important information for professional practice needs. As a result, the composition of the GIA score and most of the broad CHC factor scores changed dramatically from the WJ III. New tests, such as Test 3: Verbal Attention, were developed to assess working memory in an ecologically valid format so that test results would more effectively mirror the typical working memory requirements often required in classroom and occupational performance. Another example is Test 4: Letter-Pattern Matching, which was developed to assess visual perceptual speed for orthographic pattern recognition, a foundational function that underlies reading and spelling performance.

Perhaps one of the most innovative features of the WJ IV COG is the *Gf-Gc* Composite, a measure of intellectual level that is derived solely from four academically predictive tests representing the two highest-order (*g*-loaded or *g*-saturated) factors included in the CHC theory of cognitive abilities (McGrew, 2005, 2009; McGrew et al., 2014; Schneider & McGrew, 2012). The *Gf-Gc* Composite is highly correlated with general intelligence (*g*) as measured by the WJ IV COG GIA cluster score as well as by other global indices of general intelligence. By design, only *Gf* and *Gc* ability measures are included in the calculation of this intellectual development score. Conceptually, the *Gf-Gc* Composite is analogous to the Wechsler General Ability Index (GAI), a composite score developed to remove the influence of working memory capacity (WM) and processing speed (*Gs*) when estimating intelligence (Wechsler, 2008). Additional information on the *Gf-Gc* Composite and its use in the identification of specific learning disabilities can be found in **Appendix** of this book.

The WJ IV is now part of a three-battery configuration that also includes the WJ IV *Tests of Oral Language* and the WJ IV *Tests of Achievement*. The batteries are all conormed and can be used independently or in any combination. The new configuration recognizes the importance of oral language abilities as important correlates of cognitive and academic functioning. Some of the oral language clusters can be included in an analysis of intra-cognitive variations, including a Speed of Lexical Access cluster that represents a new contribution to CHC theory. The entire WJ IV system provides the most contemporary model for measuring a wide array of cognitive abilities that are described in CHC theory.

Finally, the WJ IV COG is easier to administer, score, and interpret than any of the predecessor batteries. The first seven tests are considered the core tests for analysis of strengths and weaknesses at the test level. Additional tests are available for cluster-level interpretation, and, as with previous editions of the Woodcock-Johnson cognitive batteries, selective testing remains an option for specific assessment needs. For example, there are new academic domain-specific Scholastic Aptitude clusters in the WJ IV COG that allow for more efficient comparisons to current levels of academic achievement.

Although much of the WJ IV is new, the authors sought to retain the focus on psychometric quality that has been associated with the previous editions Woodcock-Johnson batteries. This was achieved by providing a new, large, and nationally representative standardization sample of the US population; by updating items and simplifying test administration and interpretation procedures; by augmenting the underlying scaling of speeded tests; and by utilizing state-of-the art test development and data analytic methods as models to facilitate progress in the field of applied test development. **Rapid Reference** 1.3 lists the key innovative features of the WJ IV COG.

≡ Rapid Reference 1.3 Key Innovative Features of the WJ IV COG

Reflects updated CHC theory
Core tests provide most important information
Increased cognitive complexity
Gf-Gc Composite
A comprehensive assessment system with WJ IV OL and WJ IV ACH
Ease of administration, scoring, and interpretation

Standardization Sample and Psychometric Properties. The WJ IV norming sample was selected to be representative of the US population from age 24 months to age 90 years and older. The *Standards for Educational and Psychological Testing* (American Educational Research Association [AERA], American Psychological Association, & National Council on Measurement in Education; 2014) were followed carefully (Reynolds & Niilesksela, 2015). Normative data were based on a total sample of 7,416 individuals who were administered selected cognitive, oral language, achievement, or preschool tests. The preschool sample (2–5 years of age and not enrolled in kindergarten) was composed of 664 individuals. The kindergarten to 12th-grade sample was composed of 3,891 individuals; the college/university sample was composed of 775 undergraduate and graduate students. The adult nonschool sample (14–95+ years of and age not enrolled in a secondary school or college) was composed of 2,086 individuals. These individuals were drawn from geographically and economically diverse communities in 46 states and the District of Columbia.

Data from the 7,416 norming subjects were summarized for each test and cluster. Age norms are provided at 1-month intervals from as young as age 2 years 0 months (2–0) (for some tests) to 18 years 11 months (18–11) and at 1-year intervals from age 19 through 95+. Grade norms are provided at 1-month intervals from K.0 to 17.9. Two-year college norms (grades 13 and 14) are also available for use with technical and community college students. Complete information on the WJ IV test design, development, and standardization procedures is described by McGrew et al. (2014).

Reliability. Reliability statistics were calculated for all WJ IV COG tests across their range of intended use. The reliabilities for all but the speeded tests were calculated for all norming subjects using the split-half procedure (odd and even items) and corrected for length using the Spearman-Brown correction formula. The reliabilities for the speeded tests (Letter-Pattern Matching, Number-Pattern Matching, Pair Cancellation) were calculated from a 1-day-interval test-retest study across three age groups (ages 7–11; ages 14–17; and ages 26–79) ($n = 146$). The retest interval in this study was set at 1 day to minimize (but not entirely eliminate) changes in test scores due to changes in subjects' states or traits. **Rapid Reference** 1.4 reports the median reliability coefficients (r_{11} for nonspeeded tests and r_{12} for speeded tests) obtained using the procedures just described. Most numbers are .80 or higher, which is a desirable level for an individual test. **Rapid Reference** 1.5 reports median reliabilities for the clusters across their range of intended use. These reliabilities were computed using Mosier's (1943) formula. Most cluster reliabilities are .90 or higher.

≡ Rapid Reference 1.4 WJ IV COG Median Test Reliabilities

Test	Median Reliability
Standard Battery	
Test 1: Oral Vocabulary	.89
Test 2: Number Series	.91
Test 3: Verbal Attention	.86
Test 4: Letter-Pattern Matching	.91
Test 5: Phonological Processing	.84
Test 6: Story Recall	.93
Test 7: Visualization	.85
Test 8: General Information	.88
Test 9: Concept Formation	.93
Test 10: Numbers Reversed	.88
Extended Battery	
Test 11: Number-Pattern Matching	.85
Test 12: Nonword Repetition	.91
Test 13: Visual-Auditory Learning	.97
Test 14: Picture Recognition	.74
Test 15: Analysis-Synthesis	.93
Test 16: Object-Number Sequencing	.89
Test 17: Pair Cancellation	.89
Test 18: Memory for Words	.97

≡ Rapid Reference 1.5 WJ IV COG Median Cluster Reliabilities

Cluster	Median Reliability
General Intellectual Ability	.97
Brief Intellectual Ability	.94
Gf-Gc Composite	.96
Comprehension-Knowledge (Gc)	.93
Comprehension-Knowledge-Extended	.94
Fluid Reasoning (Gf)	.94
Fluid Reasoning-Extended	.96
Short-Term Working Memory (Gsm)	.91
Short-Term Working Memory-Extended	.93
Cognitive Processing Speed (Gs)	.94
Auditory Processing (Ga)	.92
Long-Term Storage and Retrieval (Glr)	.97
Visual Processing (Gv)	.86
Quantitative Reasoning (RQ)	.94
Auditory Memory Span (MS)	.90
Number Facility (N)	.90
Perceptual Speed (P)	.93
Cognitive Efficiency	.93
Cognitive Efficiency-Extended	.95
Reading Aptitude A	.89
Reading Aptitude B	.90
Math Aptitude A	.89
Math Aptitude B	.89
Writing Aptitude A	.89
Writing Aptitude B	.90

Validity. Validity is the most important consideration in test development, evaluation, and interpretation. The WJ IV COG is based on several sources of validity evidence. Chapter 4 of this book includes a discussion of the relationships among the WJ IV tests, CHC theory, and related neurocognitive research. Chapter 4 also provides information on *consequential validity*, that is, how the WJ IV COG tests are aligned with evidenced-based interventions that may enhance cognitive and/or academic performance and/or accommodations for limitations in cognitive abilities.

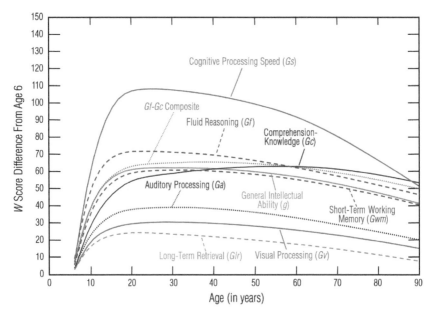

Figure 1.4 Plot of seven WJ IV COG CHC factors, GIA, and *Gf-Gc* Composite *W* scores differences by age

The existence of divergent growth curves among the broad and narrow CHC abilities is another type of evidence for the existence of unique abilities (Carroll, 1983, 1993). Figure 1.4 presents the growth curves for ages 6 to 90 years for the broad CHC factors measured by the WJ IV COG. The figure also includes a curve for the GIA score and a curve for the *Gf-Gc* Composite, showing how these two clusters develop in parallel until about age 15 and then differentiate.

Figure 1.5 is a plot of the WJ IV COG narrow CHC abilities (including the curve for Cognitive Efficiency) with the General Intellectual Ability (GIA) score as a referent. Figures 1.4 and 1.5 illustrate that the unique abilities measured by the WJ IV COG follow different developmental courses or trajectories over the age span from childhood to geriatric levels. These pictographic patterns of growth and decline are based on cross-sectional data, not longitudinal data. Therefore,

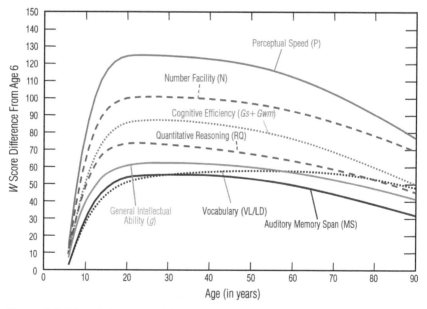

Figure 1.5 Plot of six WJ IV COG narrow CHC factors (including Cognitive Efficiency) and GIA W scores differences by age

they portray the rise and decline of median performance across age for the general population in the WJ IV norm sample, not performance changes in an individual over time.

The patterns of test and cluster score intercorrelations presented in the *WJ IV Technical Manual* (McGrew et al., 2014) support the interpretation of the growth curves and provide both convergent and discriminate validity evidence for the WJ IV COG clusters. The typical range of test and cluster intercorrelations is .30 to .60. Together, the growth curves and intercorrelations provide support to the concept that the cognitive tests and clusters measure intellectual abilities that are distinct from one another. In addition, confirmatory factor analyses presented in McGrew et al. demonstrate that the relationships among the WJ IV tests conform to the cognitive ability constructs derived from CHC theory (AERA et al., 2014; Campbell & Fiske, 1959).

The WJ IV intellectual ability scores correlate very well with the overall scores from other intelligence test batteries (such as IQ or composite scores), including the *Wechsler Intelligence Scale for Children®–Fourth Edition (WISC®*-IV) (Wechsler, 2003), the *Wechsler Adult Intelligence Scale ®–Fourth Edition* (WAIS®-IV) (Wechsler, 2008), the *Kaufman Assessment Battery for Children–Second Edition* (KABC-II) (Kaufman & Kaufman 2004), the *Stanford-Binet Intelligence Scales, Fifth Edition* (SB-5) (Roid, 2003). **Rapid Reference** 1.6 presents correlations for the WJ IV COG General Intellectual Ability (g; GIA), Brief Intellectual Ability (BIA), and *Gf-Gc* Composite cluster scores with the composite measures of general intelligence (g) from the other measures. The .72 to .86 correlations for the WJ IV GIA cluster with the general intelligence total scores from the other intelligence batteries support the conclusion that the WJ IV GIA is a strong and valid measure of the complex set of abilities that constitute general intelligence. The magnitude of the correlations between the WJ IV BIA cluster and the general intelligence scores from the other batteries support the validity of the BIA cluster as a valid screening measure of general intelligence.

The high correlations between the WJ IV *Gf-Gc* Composite and the WISC–IV, WAIS–IV, and SB– Full Scale IQ scores, in contrast to the noticeably lower correlation between the WJ IV COG *Gf-Gc* Composite cluster and the KABC–II Mental Processing Index, support the interpretation of the WJ IV COG *Gf-Gc* Composite cluster score as a valid alternate measure of intellectual level that is less influenced by cognitive processing abilities than is the WJ IV COG GIA score. By design, when compared to the GIA cluster score and other full scale intelligence scores, an obtained *Gf-Gc* Composite cluster score may be less attenuated by the

≡ Rapid Reference 1.6 WJ IV COG GIA, BIA, Gf-Gc Composite Correlations with Other Intellectual Ability Scales

Other Intellectual Ability Scale	GIA	BIA	Gf-Gc
WISC–IV FSIQ	0.86	0.83	0.83
SB–5 FSIQ	0.80	0.79	0.82
WAIS–IV FSIQ	0.84	0.74	0.78
KABC–II Mental Processing Index	0.72	0.67	0.57

FSIQ = Full Scale IQ

effects of a cognitive processing or cognitive efficiency disability for some individuals, particularly for many individuals with a specific learning disability. This makes the *Gf-Gc* Composite a particularly valuable alternative measure of intellectual level in an evaluation for a specific learning disability (see **Appendix** of this book).

As reported by McGrew and colleagues (2014), the patterns of mean WJ IV COG scores for gifted individuals, individuals with intellectual disabilities, and individuals with specific learning disabilities in reading, math, and writing were generally consistent with expectation for those groups. For example, the standard score ranges for individuals with giftedness and individuals with intellectual disabilities differed markedly. The gifted group typically scored above 115; the individuals with intellectual disabilities typically scored in the 50 to 60 range of standard scores. The individuals with specific learning disabilities displayed mean test and cluster standard scores that were in the 80 to 89 range for achievement tests in areas of disability. Score patterns also are reported for individuals with language delay, attention-deficit/hyperactivity disorder, head injury, and autism spectrum disorders.

Further Information on the WJ IV COG. The WJ IV *Technical Manual* (McGrew et al., 2014) is the most comprehensive source for information on the WJ IV, including the WJ IV COG. Detailed information on the purposes, design, standardization, reliability, and validity of the WJ IV COG can be obtained from this manual, which is supplied as part of the WJ IV COG test kit. The *Technical Manual* also includes an appendix with the most contemporary ability specifications of CHC theory. The *WJ IV Technical Abstract* (LaForte, McGrew, & Schrank, 2015), an extensive summary of the information provided in the *Technical Manual*, can be downloaded without cost from the publisher's website, http://www.riversidepublishing.com/products/wj-iv/pdf/Woodcock-Johnson_IV_Assessment_Service_Bulletin_2.pdf. Other topical bulletins on the WJ IV are also available from the publisher's website at no cost.

The *Examiner's Manual* (Mather & Wendling, 2014) for the WJ IV COG includes the basic principles of individual clinical assessment, specific information regarding use of the tests, and suggested procedures for learning to administer, score, and complete the interpretive options for the WJ IV COG. The *WJ IV Interpretation and Instructional Interventions Program* (WIIIP; Schrank & Wendling, 2015a) is an online program option designed to help professionals interpret the WJ IV. The program also links limitations in performance on the WJ IV tests and clusters, including the WJ IV COG, to evidence-based instructional interventions and/or accommodations. The WIIIP also includes a number of checklists for gathering and documenting background information and observations that can be used to interpret test performance. Mather and Jaffe's (2015) *Woodcock-Johnson IV: Recommendations, Reports, and Strategies* includes a wide variety of WJ IV reports written by contributing assessment professionals that also include recommendations and instructional strategies based on a student's school-related difficulties. See **Rapid Reference** 1.7.

≡ Rapid Reference 1.7 Components of the WJ IV Tests of Cognitive Abilities

Woodcock-Johnson IV Tests of Cognitive Abilities

Authors: Fredrick A. Schrank, Kevin S. McGrew, & Nancy Mather

Publication Date: 2014

What the Battery Measures: General Intellectual Ability (g); Brief Intellectual Ability; Gf-Gc Composite (intellectual level); Scholastic Aptitudes; Comprehension-Knowledge (lexical knowledge/language development, general [verbal] information; Fluid Reasoning (quantitative reasoning, deduction, induction); Short-Term Working Memory (working memory capacity, auditory short-term memory); Cognitive Processing Speed (perceptual speed); Auditory Processing (phonetic coding, speed of phono-lexical access; word fluency; memory for sound patterns); Long-Term Storage and Retrieval (listening ability; meaningful memory; associative memory); Visual Processing (visualization, spatial relations, visual memory); Cognitive Efficiency (perceptual speed and working memory capacity)

Administration Time: Varies; approximately 5–10 minutes per test; about 1 hour for Standard Battery

Qualification of Examiners: Graduate-level training in cognitive assessment

What the Battery Includes: Standard and extended test books; 25 test records; online scoring and reporting with purchase of test records; examiner's manual; technical manual; scoring templates for selected tests

WJ IV Interpretation and Instructional Interventions Program

Authors: Fredrick A. Schrank & Barbara J. Wendling

Publication Date: 2015

What the WIIIP Provides: Comprehensive narrative reports, instructional interventions and accommodations related to test performance, checklists (Reason for Referral Checklist, Parent's Checklist, Teacher's Checklist,

Classroom Observation Form, Self-Report Checklist: Adolescent/Adult;
Writing Evaluation Scale).

Publisher, All Components:

Houghton Mifflin Harcourt/Riverside Publishing Company
One Pierce Place
Suite 900W
Itasca, IL 60143

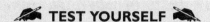

🐾 TEST YOURSELF 🐾

1. **The WJ IV COG is based on the Cattell-Horn-Carroll (CHC) theory of human cognitive abilities. True or false?**
   a. True
   b. False
2. **Who is credited with distinguishing two types of intelligence—fluid and crystallized?**
   a. Richard Woodcock
   b. John Horn
   c. Raymond Cattell
   d. John Carroll
3. **Who is credited with expanding *Gf-Gc* theory to include multiple cognitive abilities?**
   a. Richard Woodcock
   b. John Horn
   c. Raymond Cattell
   d. John Carroll
4. **Who is credited with developing the three-stratum theory of human cognitive abilities?**
   a. Raymond Cattell
   b. John Horn
   c. John Carroll
   d. Elaine Crampfoot
5. **Which of the following broad CHC factors is not included in the WJ IV COG?**
   a. Comprehenion-Knowledge (*Gc*)
   b. Fluid Reasoning (*Gf*)
   c. Short-Term Working Memory (*Gwm*)
   d. Cognitive Processing Speed (*Gs*)

   e. Auditory Processing (*Ga*)
   f. Long-Term Retrieval (*Glr*)
   g. Visual Processing (*Gv*)
   h. None of the above (all are included)
6. **Which of the following tests is new to the WJ IV COG?**
   a. Visual-Auditory Learning
   b. Phonological Processing
   c. Numbers Reversed
   d. Concept Formation
7. **Perceptual Speed (P) is considered a broad cognitive ability. True or false?**
   a. True
   b. False
8. **What is the total norming sample for the WJ IV COG?**
   a. 4,783
   b. 7,416
   c. 9000+
   d. 6,359
9. **The *Gf-Gc* Composite is a measure of intellectual level. True or false?**
   a. True
   b. False
10. **Who are the authors of the *WJ IV Interpretation and Instructional Interventions Program* (WIIIP)?**
   a. Nancy Mather, Kevin McGrew, and Fredrick Schrank
   b. Nancy Mather and Barbara Wendling
   c. Nancy Mather and Lynne Jaffe
   d. Fredrick Schrank and Barbara Wendling

Answers: 1. True; 2. c; 3. b; 4. c; 5. h; 6. b; 7. False; 8. b; 9. True; 10. d

Two

HOW TO ADMINISTER THE WJ IV COG

Melanie A. Bartels Graw

Although the administration procedures for the WJ IV COG are not unduly complex, they do require advance training, practice, and preparation on the part of the examiner. Interpretation of administration results requires a higher degree of knowledge and skill than what is required for administering and scoring the tests. **Rapid Reference** 2.1 includes pertinent professional standards from the *Standards for Educational and Psychological Testing* (American Educational Research Association [AERA], American Psychological Association, & National Council on Measurement in Education, 2014) that speak to the necessity of proper training.

≣ *Rapid Reference 2.1*

Selected Standards from the *Standards for Educational and Psychological Testing*

Standard 10.1: Those who use psychological tests should confine their testing and related assessment activities to their areas of competence, as demonstrated through education, training, experience, and appropriate credentials. (p. 164)
Standard 10.3: Professionals should verify that persons under their supervision have appropriate knowledge and skills to administer and score tests. (p. 164)
Standard 12.16: Those responsible for educational testing programs should provide appropriate training, documentation, and oversight so that the individuals

who administer and score the test(s) are proficient in the appropriate test administration and scoring procedures and understand the importance of adhering to the directions provided by the test developer. (p. 200)

Source: AERA et al., 2014.

The goal of standardized testing is to discern how well a person can respond to a set of stimuli when given instructions that are identical to those presented to participants in the norm sample. The best way to become familiar with the WJ IV COG to ensure standardized administration is to review the content of the testing material and then practice administering the tests. This chapter provides a head start in this process by presenting information about the testing materials, general assessment procedures, and test-by-test administration instructions.

GENERAL TESTING INFORMATION

Testing Materials

To administer the WJ IV COG, you need the following materials: the two Test Books, the corresponding Test Record and Response Booklet, and at least two sharpened pencils. For timed tests, you need a stopwatch, a digital watch, or a watch or clock with a second hand. For tests requiring an audio presentation, audio equipment—preferably with headphones or earbuds—and the audio recording CD are also necessary. Obtaining derived scores for the WJ IV COG requires access to the *Woodcock-Johnson Online Scoring and Reporting* (Schrank & Dailey, 2014) or the optional *WJ IV Interpretation and Instructional Interventions Program* (WIIIP; Schrank & Wendling, 2015a). More about the specific use of the scoring program is included in Chapter 3.

Tests Using the Response Booklet. The Response Booklet includes test material that the examinee uses to complete tests requiring written responses. Letter-Pattern Matching, Number-Pattern Matching, and Pair Cancellation require the use of the Response Booklet for administration. The Response Booklet also includes a blank worksheet for the examinee to use if he or she needs to work out the logic of an item in Number Series. There are specific directions in the Test Book

> **DON'T FORGET**
> ....
> Control access to the Response Booklet. Present it as directed in the Test Book.

about how to present the Response Booklet when providing instructions to the examinee. You must control access to the Response Booklet and should not leave it lying on the table while you give directions. Provide the examinee with the booklet and a sharpened pencil when directed to do so in the Test Book. At the end of each test, collect the pencil and booklet immediately.

Timed Tests. Several of the WJ IV COG tests are timed: Letter-Pattern Matching, Phonological Processing—Word Fluency, Number-Pattern Matching, and Pair Cancellation. The time limit for each timed test is indicated in the Test Book and Test Record. A stopwatch is preferred for administering these tests; however, a watch or clock with a second hand may be used if a stopwatch is not available. It is important that you monitor the time the examinee uses for a test. If the examinee finishes early, you must enter the *exact* finishing time in minutes and seconds on the Test Record because examinees who do well and finish early will receive a higher ability score than individuals who work for the full time. For all timed tests, do not allow the examinee to take the time to erase a response he or she wishes to change. Instead, tell the examinee to cross out (X) the response he or she does not want.

DON'T FORGET
....
Timed tests require strict adherence to the time limits. Record the examinee's exact finishing time in minutes and seconds.

In addition to the timed tests, some tests have instructions to proceed to the next item if the examinee has not responded within a specified period of time or to expose the stimulus for a specific amount of time. The stopwatch or watch with a second hand is needed in these cases as well.

Tests Using the Audio Recording. Use the standardized audio recording to present Verbal Attention, Phonological Processing—Word Access, Phonological Processing—Substitution, Story Recall, Numbers Reversed, Nonword Repetition, Object-Number Sequencing, and Memory for Words. When administering these tests, use good-quality audio equipment and headphones or earbuds. The audio equipment must have a good speaker, be in good working order, and produce a faithful, clear reproduction of the test items. In addition, you need a single earphone, or earbud, and a splitter that allows both the earbud and the headphones to be plugged into the audio player. This arrangement makes it possible for you to monitor the audio recording as well as the examinee's responses.

Although some tests may be presented orally, it is recommended that you use the audio recording and headphones unless the examinee resists wearing headphones or has difficulty paying attention to the audio-recorded presentation.

If you must present a test orally, attempt to say each item in the same manner that it is presented on the audio recording. Please note that Items 23 through 46 of Nonword Repetition should not be administered without the use of the audio recording.

To facilitate locating starting points or specific items when obtaining the basal, refer to the track list included with the audio CD, which identifies the first item number at the beginning of the track. Track numbers also are included in "Suggested Starting Points" tables and next to corresponding starting point items in the Test Book.

Before you begin testing, adjust the volume of the headphones to a comfortable level for the examinee. Make sure the audio recording is set to start at the correct item for that examinee's level of testing. Generally, when administering an audio-recorded test, look away from the examinee while the test item is being presented. After the double beep, look at the examinee expectantly to encourage a response.

The audio recording was designed to give adequate time between items for the examinee to respond. Do not repeat or replay any items unless the Test Book states that it is permissible to do so. Generally, this would occur only on sample items.

> **DON'T FORGET**
> ....
> Follow audio-recorded test procedures. Look away from the examinee while the item is being presented; after the double beep, look at the examinee expectantly to encourage a response.

Testing Environment

When you set up the testing environment, be sure you have all necessary material and equipment to ensure smooth and quick test administration. Select a testing room that is quiet and comfortable and has adequate ventilation and lighting. If possible, you and the examinee should be the only two people in the room. The room should have a table or desk and two chairs, with one chair being an appropriate size for the examinee. The best seating arrangement is one in which you and the examinee sit diagonally across from each other at one corner of the table. If that arrangement is not possible, you can sit directly across the table, although in this scenario, the table must be low and narrow enough for you to see over the upright Test Book easel to observe any examinee's pointing responses and to comfortably point to the examinee's test page when necessary. In any case, the seating arrangement should allow adequate space for you to view both sides of the Test Book, point to all parts of the examinee's page and the Response Booklet, operate the audio equipment, and record responses out of the examinee's view.

The examinee should be able to view only the examinee pages in the Test Book and Response Booklet. When the Test Book easel is set up for administration, it acts as a screen allowing you to shield the Test Record and record responses out of the examinee's view. When equipment such as the stopwatch or audio equipment is not in use, place it out of the examinee's sight.

DON'T FORGET

- Have all necessary testing material and equipment available and in the testing space prior to beginning testing.
- Select an appropriate location for the testing session.
- *Standard 6.4:* The testing environment should furnish reasonable comfort with minimal distractions to avoid construct-irrelevant variance (AERA et al., 2014, p. 116).

Establishing Rapport

In most instances, you will have little difficulty establishing a good relationship with the examinee. Do not begin testing unless the person seems relatively comfortable with the testing situation. If he or she does not feel well or does not respond appropriately, do not attempt testing. One way of establishing rapport is to begin the testing session with a short period of conversation while you complete the "Identifying Information" portion of the Test Record. You may also preface the test using the "Introducing the Test" section that is provided in the front of each Test Book to help make the examinee feel more at ease. It is unnecessary to provide a lengthy explanation of the test.

TIP

When completing the identifying information for young examinees, verify the date of birth using school records or with a parent.

Prior to test administration, confirm whether the examinee should be wearing glasses or a hearing aid and that the individual has them for testing.

Smile frequently throughout the testing session and call the person by name. Between tests, let the examinee know that he or she is doing a good job, using such comments as "I like the way you are working" or "You are making a good effort." Encourage a response even when items are difficult. Be careful that any comments you make do not reveal the answers as correct or incorrect (except as required by specific test directions)—for example, do not say "Good" only after correct responses or pause longer after incorrect responses before proceeding to the next item.

CAUTION

....

- Do not reveal correct answers except as required by specific test directions.
- Do not provide clues or an indication whether responses are correct or incorrect.
- Provide encouragement consistently throughout test administration, not just when the examinee responds either correctly or incorrectly.

Accommodations

The WJ IV COG tests were designed to be useful with individuals from a wide range of abilities and backgrounds. Several administration features allow individuals with disabilities to participate more fully in the evaluation process. Use a separate room for test administration incorporating noise buffers, special lighting, special acoustics, and special furniture as necessary to minimize distractibility. You may take frequent breaks and even spread the testing procedure out over several days to maximize interest and performance. Except for controlled learning tests and tests that are intended to measure processing speed or fluency, you also may allow additional time for examinees to complete the testing tasks. The oral instructions have been kept at a sufficiently simple level of complexity and vocabulary to avoid many language comprehension barriers. These instructions may be repeated verbally (or signed, for an individual with a hearing impairment, although scores should be interpreted cautiously on certain tests; see Mather & Wendling, 2014, for more information) as necessary. Audio-recorded tests may be amplified and presented at a volume that is comfortable for the examinee. The use of large print, fewer items per page, and increased space between items helps prevent examinees from being overwhelmed by the test pages. Visual magnification devices and templates to reduce glare also can be incorporated into the assessment without affecting validity.

Accommodations should be made only to respond "to specific individual characteristics ... in a way that does not change the construct the test is measuring or the meaning of scores" (AERA et al., 2014, p. 67). Because of the standardized nature of the WJ IV COG, modification to the testing procedure can fundamentally alter the results and validity of the tests. "For norm-based score interpretations, any modification that changes the construct will invalidate the norms for score interpretations (p. 61). If possible, try to select tests that do not require modifications. Make note of and describe any deviations from the standardized administration on the Test Record. Be sure to answer the question, "Were any modifications made to the standardized test procedures during this administration?," located at the bottom of the front of the Test Record. If you check "Yes," continue by completing this sentence: "The following modifications were made: _____." In addition, always include a statement of the modified testing conditions in the Score Report or the Comprehensive Report produced by the online scoring program (Schrank & Dailey, 2014) or the WIIIP (Schrank & Wendling, 2015a).

The broad classes of examinees who often require some type of accommodation in the assessment process include young children; English language learners; individuals with attentional and/or learning difficulties; and individuals with hearing, visual, or physical impairments. When testing an individual with special needs, consult a trained professional with expertise in that particular area. For an examinee with a hearing impairment, this may mean hiring a certified sign language interpreter; for an examinee with attention-deficit/hyperactivity disorder, it may mean speaking with a clinical expert about the nature of the disorder. In any case, it is essential that you be sensitive to the limitations that different impairments or conditions may place on an individual's abilities and behavior.

Order of Administration

Rarely is it necessary, or even desirable, to administer all 18 tests contained in the WJ IV COG. Instead, most examiners select the tests that will elicit the most relevant and appropriate information for the purposes defined by the referral needs. A selective testing table for the WJ IV COG is contained in the first few pages of each Test Book and in the WJ IV COG *Examiner's Manual* (Mather & Wendling, 2014). This table is reproduced in **Rapid Reference** 2.2.

≡ Rapid Reference 2.2 Selective Testing Table for the WJ IV COG

Column groups:
- **Cognitive Composites:** General Intellectual Ability (GIA), Brief Intellectual Ability, Gf-Gc Composite
- **CHC Factors:** Comprehension-Knowledge (Gc), Fluid Reasoning (Gf), Short-Term Working Memory (Gwm), Cognitive Processing Speed (Gs), Auditory Processing (Ga), Long-Term Retrieval (Glr), Visual Processing (Gv)
- **Narrow Ability and Other Clinical Clusters:** Quantitative Reasoning (RQ), Auditory Memory Span (MS), Number Facility (N), Perceptual Speed (P), Vocabulary (VL/LD), Cognitive Efficiency

Battery	Test	Name	GIA	BIA	Gf-Gc	Gc	Gf	Gwm	Gs	Ga	Glr	Gv	RQ	MS	N	P	VL/LD	Cog. Eff.
Standard Battery	COG 1	Oral Vocabulary	■	■	■	■											■	
Standard Battery	COG 2	Number Series	■	■	■		■						■					
Standard Battery	COG 3	Verbal Attention	■	■				■										□
Standard Battery	COG 4	Letter-Pattern Matching	■						■							■		■
Standard Battery	COG 5	Phonological Processing	■							■								
Standard Battery	COG 6	Story Recall	■								■							
Standard Battery	COG 7	Visualization	■									■						
Standard Battery	COG 8	General Information			■	■												
Standard Battery	COG 9	Concept Formation			■		■											
Standard Battery	COG 10	Numbers Reversed						■						■				■
Extended Battery	COG 11	Number-Pattern Matching													■	■		□
Extended Battery	COG 12	Nonword Repetition								■								
Extended Battery	COG 13	Visual-Auditory Learning									■							
Extended Battery	COG 14	Picture Recognition										■						
Extended Battery	COG 15	Analysis-Synthesis					□						■					
Extended Battery	COG 16	Object-Number Sequencing						□										
Extended Battery	COG 17	Pair Cancellation							■									
Extended Battery	COG 18	Memory for Words												■				
Oral Language Battery	OL 1	Picture Vocabulary				□											■	
Oral Language Battery	OL 5	Sentence Repetition												■				

■ Tests required to create the cluster listed.
□ Additional tests required to create an extended version of the cluster listed.

One of the revision goals was to organize the WJ IV COG for ease of administration; the sequence of the WJ IV COG tests is purposeful. Many examiners will administer the tests in numeric order, discontinuing testing at preferred stopping points. Administering a small subset of tests, such as Tests 1 through 7, provides the most important information in the least amount of testing time. For most evaluation purposes, the best place to begin is at the beginning—Test 1: Oral Vocabulary—and administer the tests in the order that they appear. However, you may administer the tests in any order deemed appropriate and discontinue testing at any time. Keep in mind that the tests have been organized to alternate between different formats (e.g., timed versus untimed) to achieve optimal attention and interest.

An examiner can go as deep into the battery as desired. As more tests are administered, breadth of assessment data increases. **Rapid Reference** 2.3 outlines six example evaluation purposes, suggests a set of WJ IV COG tests to administer, stipulates the approximate time needed for testing, and lists the outcome measures and analyses obtained from the set of tests administered.

≡ Rapid Reference 2.3 Six Example WJ IV COG Evaluation Purposes, Tests to Administer, Time Required for Evaluation, and Outcome Measures and Analyses

Evaluation Purpose	Tests to Administer	Time Required	Outcome Measures and Analyses
To obtain a brief measure of intelligence	Tests 1–3	20 minutes	Brief Intellectual Ability (BIA)
To obtain the standard measure of general intelligence	Tests 1–7	40 minutes	General Intellectual Ability (GIA)
To determine any relative strengths and weaknesses among the core cognitive tests			Evaluation of relative strengths and weaknesses among Tests 1–7

Evaluation Purpose	Tests to Administer	Time Required	Outcome Measures and Analyses
To include a broad or narrow CHC cluster in the intra-cognitive variation procedure	Tests 1–7 plus the additional test to create the cluster	Varies by number of tests administered (45–120 minutes)	General Intellectual Ability (GIA); evaluation of relative strengths and weaknesses among Tests 1–7 and the broad CHC cluster obtained
To obtain a standard cognitive evaluation	Tests 1–10	60 minutes	General Intellectual Ability (GIA) Comprehension-Knowledge (Gc) Fluid Reasoning (Gf) Short-Term Working Memory (Gwm) Evaluation of relative strengths and weaknesses among tests and the Gc, Gf, and Gwm clusters Gf-Gc Composite Cognitive Efficiency Comparison of Cognitive Efficiency and Gwm to the Gf-Gc Composite
To compare cognitive processing clusters, cognitive-linguistic competencies, and/or achievement levels to the Gf-Gc Composite	Tests 1, 2, 8, 9 plus any cognitive, oral language, and achievement tests that create target clusters for the Gf-Gc/Other Ability Comparison	Varies by number of tests administered: 30–120 minutes for cognitive tests, additional time for oral language and achievement tests	Evaluation of cognitive processing, cognitive-linguistic competency, and/or achievement strengths and weaknesses relative to the Gf-Gc Composite

Evaluation Purpose	Tests to Administer	Time Required	Outcome Measures and Analyses
To determine if an individual's achievement is at levels that would be predicted from normative data of others with a similar profile of closely related cogntive abilities	Tests included in specific Scholastic Aptitude cluster and selected target achievement areas	20–25 minutes for Scholastic Aptitude cluster; additional time for achievement clusters	Evaluation of the level of concordance between cognitive ability and acheivement; not a traditional ability/achievement discrepancy model

If only a brief measure of intellectual functioning is needed, administer Tests 1 through 3. These three tests create the Brief Intellectual Ability (BIA) score and are ideal for some assessment purposes, such as to rule out an intellectual disability or to determine if a student qualifies for participation in a program for individuals with intellectual giftedness.

Core Tests Administration. The first seven tests are the core tests of the WJ IV COG. These seven tests also create the General Intellectual Ability (GIA) score. Each test was chosen by the authors to represent the best and most predictive measure of the respective broad CHC ability. For example, Number Series was selected for inclusion in the core tests—and for calculation of the GIA—because it is the single best fluid reasoning measure among all the WJ IV COG tests that were normed in the battery's standardization. This is true for each of the first seven tests; each of the seven tests is the authors' first choice for a single test to represent a broad CHC ability.

Administering the core tests yields the necessary scores to use the intra-cognitive variation procedure. When WJ IV COG Tests 1 through 7 are administered, the online scoring and reporting program (Schrank & Dailey, 2014) automates the analysis to determine if any relative cognitive strengths or weaknesses exist at the test level.

When an additional cognitive test is administered, the test and any created cluster is included in the same variation procedure. **Rapid Reference** 2.4 lists the core (required) tests for the intra-cognitive variation procedure and any other tests from the WJ IV COG, the WJ IV OL, or the WJ IV ACH that can be included in the same analysis. Regardless of any additional tests included in the procedure, the intra-cognitive variation procedure is always based on a comparison to a predicted score that is based on six of the first seven tests in the WJ IV COG. The target test, and any related test from the same broad ability, is not included in the calculation of the predicted score. In addition, note that Cognitive Efficiency is not included as a target cluster in this analysis because the cluster contains tests from two different broad CHC abilities (Short-Term Working Memory and Cognitive Processing Speed).

≡ Rapid Reference 2.4 Required and Optional Tests and Clusters in the WJ IV Intra-Cognitive Variation Procedure

Required from WJ IV COG	Optional from WJ IV COG/Obtained Cluster	Optional from WJ IV OL or WJ IV ACH/Obtained Cluster
Test 1: Oral Vocabulary	*Compared as Oral Vocabulary* Test 8: General Information/ Comprehension-Knowledge (*Gc*)	*Compared as Oral Vocabulary* OL 1: Picture Vocabulary Vocabulary (LD/VL) Comprehension-Knowledge (*Gc*)–Extended OL 2: Oral Comprehension Oral Language
Test 2: Number Series	*Compared as Number Series* Test 9: Concept Formation Fluid Reasoning (*Gf*) Test 15: Analysis-Synthesis Fluid Reasoning–Extended Quantitative Reasoning (RQ)	*Compared as Number Series* ACH 13: Number Matrices
Test 3: Verbal Attention	*Compared as Verbal Attention* Test 10: Numbers Reversed Short-Term Working Memory (*Gwm*) Test 16: Object-Number Sequencing Short-Term Working Memory–Extended Test 18: Memory for Words	*Compared as Verbal Attention* OL 5: Sentence Repetition Auditory Memory Span (MS) OL 6: Understanding Directions

Required from WJ IV COG	Optional from WJ IV COG/Obtained Cluster	Optional from WJ IV OL or WJ IV ACH/Obtained Cluster
Test 4: Letter-Pattern Matching	*Compared as Letter-Pattern Matching* Test 11: Number-Pattern Matching Perceptual Speed (P) Test 17: Pair Cancellation Cognitive Processing Speed (Gs)	*Compared as Letter-Pattern Matching* OL 4: Rapid Picture Naming OL 8: Retrieval Fluency Speed of Lexical Access (LA)
Test 5: Phonological Processing	*Compared as Phonological Processing* Test 12: Nonword Repetition Auditory Processing (Ga)	*Compared as Phonological Processing* OL 3: Segmentation OL 7: Sound Blending Phonetic Coding (PC)
Test 6: Story Recall	*Compared as Story Recall* Test 13: Visual-Auditory Learning Long-Term Retrieval (Glr)	
Test 7: Visualization	*Compared as Visualization* Test 14: Picture Recognition Visual Processing (Gv)	

Standard Battery Administration. The 10 tests that are included in the Standard Battery are considered a standard WJ IV COG administration. Because many examiners, school districts, or agencies adopt a standard protocol as a minimum cognitive assessment battery for a comprehensive evaluation, the authors sought to select tests for the Standard Battery that would yield the most critical scores for evaluation purposes and provide the most important comparisons between clusters that is possible within a standard administration format and an approximately 1-hour administration window. Consequently, a standard evaluation yields the BIA and GIA scores and provides the test-level evaluation of relative strengths and weaknesses. In addition, a Standard Battery protocol yields three important CHC factor scores that also enter into the intra-cognitive variations analysis: Comprehension-Knowledge (*Gc*), Fluid Reasoning (*Gf*), and Short-Term Working Memory (*Gwm*). Two additional cluster scores are also obtained: the *Gf-Gc* Composite and Cognitive Efficiency. A useful comparison of Cognitive Efficiency and Short-Term Working Memory (*Gwm*) to the *Gf-Gc* Composite is also obtained. **Rapid Reference** 2.5 lists the tests, clusters and variation procedures that are obtained when all of the tests in Standard Battery are administered.

≡ Rapid Reference 2.5 WJ IV Standard Battery Tests, Clusters, and Variation Procedures

WJ IV COG Standard Battery Tests	WJ IV COG Standard Battery Clusters	WJ IV COG Standard Battery Variation Procedures
Test 1: Oral Vocabulary Test 2: Number Series Test 3: Verbal Attention Test 4: Letter-Pattern Matching Test 5: Phonological Processing Test 6: Story Recall	Brief Intellectual Ability	
Test 7: Visualization	General Intellectual Ability	Variations for Tests 1–7
Test 8: General Information	Comprehension-Knowledge (*Gc*)	Variations for Tests 1–8 plus *Gc*
Test 9: Concept Formation	Fluid Reasoning (*Gf*) *Gf-Gc* Composite	Variations for Tests 1–9 plus *Gc* and *Gf*
Test 10: Numbers Reversed	Short-Term Working Memory (*Gwm*) Cognitive Efficiency	Variations for Tests 1–10 plus *Gc*, *Gf*, and *Gwm* *Gf-Gc* Composite Compared to *Gwm* and Cognitive Efficiency

One of the design objectives of the WJ IV was to include the *Gf-Gc* Composite, a measure of intellectual level derived solely from tests of fluid reasoning and comprehension-knowledge, and a related *Gf-Gc* Composite/Other Ability comparison procedure for evaluation of within-individual strengths and weaknesses among cognitive processing, cognitive-linguistic competencies, and areas of academic achievement in relation to the *Gf-Gc* Composite. An extensive set of cognitive, oral language, and achievement clusters can be compared to the *Gf-Gc* Composite. The **Appendix** of this book includes a detailed description of this cluster and its suggested use in the evaluation of individuals with suspected learning disabilities.

Extended Battery Administration and Selective Testing. The tests that are included in the Extended Battery can be particularly useful for focused, selective testing based on an individual's needs, on the referral question, or to investigate a hypothesis that the examiner may have generated during the course of administering the tests in the Standard Battery. Or they can be administered as an extension to a Standard Battery or core test (Tests 1–7) administration when more information is needed or desired. For example, adding Number-Pattern Matching to an evaluation will yield the Perceptual Speed (P) cluster, which may be an important ability to evaluate when questions of accommodations for extended time in classroom assignments or high-stakes testing are a focus of concern. (Adding Number-Pattern Matching will also yield the Number Facility cluster.) Adding Nonword Repetition will produce the Auditory Processing (*Ga*) cluster, which may be of particular interest in determining the presence and nature of language-related disabilities. Adding Visual-Auditory Learning to a core test or Standard Battery administration will yield the Long-Term Retrieval (*Glr*) cluster; adding Pair Cancellation will produce the Cognitive Processing Speed (*Gs*) cluster.

Other special-purpose clusters can be obtained by selective testing, including extended (three test) versions of the fluid reasoning (Fluid Reasoning–Extended) and short-term working memory (Short-Term Working Memory–Extended) clusters. A Comprehension-Knowledge–Extended cluster can be obtained by adding the Picture Vocabulary test from the WJ IV OL, which will simultaneously yield a narrow ability Vocabulary (LD/VL) cluster. A narrow Auditory Memory Span (MS) cluster can be obtained (and included in the intracognitive variations) by administering Memory for Words in conjunction with the Sentence Repetition test from the WJ IV OL.

Some examiners may prefer to utilize one or more focused Scholastic Aptitude selective testing options, which are outlined in **Rapid Reference** 2.6. The WJ IV Scholastic Aptitude scores yield information about an individual's

≡ Rapid Reference 2.6 Scholastic Aptitude Selective Testing Table for the WJ IV COG

		Target Tasks for Scholastic Aptitude/ Achievement Comparisons														
		Reading						Mathematics				Writing			
		Reading	Broad Reading	Basic Reading Skills	Reading Comprehension	Reading Fluency	Reading Rate	Mathematics	Broad Mathematics	Math Calculation Skills	Math Problem Solving	Written Language	Broad Written Language	Basic Writing Skills	Written Expression
Standard Battery	COG 1	Oral Vocabulary	■	■	■	■	■	■	■	■	■	■	■	■	■	■
	COG 2	Number Series							■	■	■					
	COG 3	Verbal Attention			■										■	
	COG 4	Letter-Pattern Matching														
	COG 5	Phonological Processing	■	■	■	■	■	■					■	■	■	■
	COG 6	Story Recall									■	■				■
	COG 7	Visualization							■	■	■	■				
	COG 8	General Information														
	COG 9	Concept Formation	■	■		■	■	■								
	COG 10	Numbers Reversed									■					
Extended Battery	COG 11	Number-Pattern Matching	■	■	■	■	■	■					■	■	■	■
	COG 12	Nonword Repetition														
	COG 13	Visual-Auditory Learning														
	COG 14	Picture Recognition														
	COG 15	Analysis-Synthesis									■					
	COG 16	Object-Number Sequencing														
	COG 17	Pair Cancellation							■	■	■					
	COG 18	Memory for Words														

predicted performance in reading, mathematics, or written language and provide optimal and efficient prediction of expected achievement in each domain by administering a small set of tests that is highly related to each area of achievement (McGrew, LaForte, & Schrank, 2014).

When used in conjunction with the WJ IV ACH, these clusters are useful for a brief and focused determination of whether an individual, such as a student, is performing academically as well as would be expected, based on his or her performance on closely related cognitive tests. Unlike a traditional ability/achievement discrepancy procedure, proper interpretation of any WJ IV scholastic aptitude/achievement comparison involves examining the consistency between ability and achievement scores. In other words, a person with a low mathematics aptitude would be expected to have low math skills, whereas a person with high math aptitude would be expected to have more advanced mathematics skills.

Time Requirements

Although administration time will vary depending on your purpose for testing, you can estimate your testing time by calculating 5 minutes for each test you plan to administer. In general, allow 35 to 40 minutes to administer the core tests (tests 1–7), 50 to 60 minutes to administer the Standard Battery (tests 1–10), and 90 to 105 (or more) minutes to administer the tests in both the Standard and Extended Batteries. It is important to note that very young examinees or individuals with unique learning patterns may require more time.

Suggested Starting Points

Suggested starting points are based on your estimate of the examinee's level of ability for the skill being assessed. "Suggested Starting Points" tables generally are located within the first few pages at the beginning of each test in the Test Book. Timed tests and controlled learning tests do not include suggested starting points because all examinees begin with sample items and/or an introduction and proceed through the test until the time limit or a cutoff has been reached. Additionally, some tests include more than one "Suggested Starting Points" table. Typically this occurs when all subjects begin with a sample item to introduce the task and then are routed to another sample item of appropriate difficulty based on their estimated ability. Utilizing the suggested starting points with basal and ceiling guidelines helps to reduce testing time and, subsequently, examinee fatigue.

Basal and Ceiling Criteria

Many of the WJ IV COG tests require you to establish a basal and a ceiling. The purpose of basal and ceiling requirements is to limit the number of items administered but still be able to estimate, with high probability, the score that would have been obtained if all items had been administered. Eliminating the items that would be too easy or too difficult for the examinee also serves to minimize testing time while maximizing the examinee's tolerance for the testing situation.

Basal and ceiling criteria are included in the Test Book for each test that requires them and are also shown in an abbreviated fashion on the Test Record. For some tests, examinees begin with Item 1, which serves as the basal, and continue until they reach the ceiling level. When other tests are administered, the basal criterion is met when the examinee correctly responds to the specified number of consecutive lowest-numbered items. If an examinee fails to meet the basal criterion for any test, proceed by testing backward until the examinee has met the basal criterion or you have administered Item 1. Do not fill in scores on the Test Record for unadminstered items below the basal, but count those items as correct when calculating the number correct.

The best practice is to test by complete pages when stimulus material appears on the examinee's side of the Test Book. In this way, examinees do not see any additional testing material and are essentially unaware that there

> **DON'T FORGET**
> ....
> Test by complete pages when stimuli are visible to the examinee.

are other items on the test. If an examinee reaches a ceiling in the middle of a page and there is no stimulus material on the examinee's page, you may discontinue testing. However, if the examinee reaches a ceiling in the middle of a page that does have stimuli visible, you must complete that page. If the examinee responds correctly to any item administered while completing the page, you must continue testing until a ceiling is reached.

Scoring

The correct and incorrect keys in the Test Books are intended as guides to demonstrate how certain responses are scored. Not all possible responses are included in these keys, and you may have to use your professional judgment in determining an item's score. In cases where the examinee's response does not fall clearly in either the correct or incorrect category, you may wish to write the response on the Test Record and come back to it later. Do not use an unscored item in determining a basal or ceiling. If, after further consideration, it is still not clear how to score several items, balance the scores by scoring one item 1 and the other item 0. If you have several questionable responses, you should seek advice from a professional colleague who may be able to help you make a determination. As a general rule for all WJ IV COG tests, do not penalize the examinee for mispronunciations resulting from articulation errors, dialect variations, or regional speech patterns.

If an examinee asks for more information, use your judgment as to whether it is appropriate to answer his or her question; however, if the examinee requests information that you are not allowed to provide, respond by saying something like "I'm not supposed to help you with that." Even after testing has been completed, do not tell the examinee whether his or her answers were correct or incorrect or explain how to solve any items. Doing so invalidates the test.

You may have to query the examinee on certain items when his or her response is not clear. Some items in the Test Books have query keys that provide guidance for eliciting additional information from the examinee if he or she produces a particular response; use professional judgment when querying responses that do not appear in these keys. If the correctness of a response is still unclear following a query, the response should be recorded as given and scored after the testing session.

When an examinee provides multiple responses to an item requiring a single response, the general principle to follow is to score the last answer given. The last response, regardless of its correctness, is used to determine the final item score. Follow this procedure even if the examinee changes an earlier response much later in the testing session. In situations where the examinee provides two conflicting answers, query the response by asking the question "Which one?" or by directing the examinee to "Give just one answer."

Test Observations

Although the WJ IV COG tests are designed to provide accurate quantitative information about an examinee's abilities, it is also important that you observe and record the examinee's reactions and behaviors in a test-taking situation. The "Test Session Observations Checklist," located on the front of the Test Record, can help you document these observations. The checklist includes seven categories: (1) level of conversational proficiency, (2) level of cooperation, (3) level of activity, (4) attention and concentration, (5) self-confidence, (6) care in responding, and (7) response to difficult tasks. Use the checklist immediately after the testing session, marking only one response for each category and noting any other clinically interesting behaviors. If the category does not apply to the individual, leave that item blank. The checklist is designed so that it is easy to identify a typical rating in each category. For example, typical examinees are cooperative during the examination, seem at ease and comfortable, are attentive to the tasks, respond promptly but carefully, and generally persist with difficult tasks. Remember that what is typical for one age or grade level may not be typical for another; you should be familiar with the behaviors that specific age and grade groups exhibit. For some age or grade levels, ratings such as "appeared fidgety or restless at times" could be included within the range of behaviors deemed "typical for age/grade" rather than in a separate category.

Be sure to answer the question "Do you have any reason to believe this testing session may not represent a fair sample of the examinee's abilities?" located after the checklist on the Test Record. If you check "Yes," continue by completing this sentence: "These results may not be a fair estimate because _____." Examples of reasons for questioning validity include suspected or known problems with hearing or vision, emotional problems that interfere with the examinee's concentration, and certain background factors (e.g., a case in which English is not a well-established second language).

TEST-BY-TEST ADMINISTRATION PROCEDURES

When administering the WJ IV COG tests, strive to be precise and brief. Practice administering the test several times to familiarize yourself with the testing formats and procedures. The WJ IV test kit includes the WJ IV COG *Examiner Training Workbook* (Wendling, 2014) and Appendix B in the WJ IV COG *Examiner's Manual* (Mather & Wendling, 2014) includes a reproducible test-by-test training checklist. These materials are designed to help you build competency with WJ IV COG test administration.

Testing might proceed slowly at first until the administration becomes more fluent, but make sure to follow the instructions and script exactly. The examiner pages include specific information for item administration. The directions include the script to be read to the examinee (printed in bold blue text) and applicable pointing and pausing instructions (printed in black text). The examiner pages may also include shaded boxes with supplemental administration and scoring information. Always use the exact wording and instructions presented in the Test Book for item presentation and corrective feedback and, when necessary, to elicit more information.

After the initial practice sessions, try to maintain a brisk testing pace. A rapid testing pace, without interruptions, shortens administration time and keeps the examinee from becoming restless or fatigued. The first page after the tab for each test in the Test Book provides general information and instructions specific to that test. Review this information frequently. This page usually includes scoring information, suggested starting points, basal and ceiling requirements, and information about the materials required to administer the test.

DON'T FORGET

Exact Administration

- Bold, blue text on the examiner's page in the Test Book presents the directions the examiner reads to the examinee.
- The text read to the examinee includes additional administration directions to the examiner (e.g., when to point or pause).
- The examiner's page may include special instructions presented in shaded boxes.

Brisk Administration

- Do not interrupt testing to "visit" with the examinee.
- Proceed to the next item immediately after the examinee responds.
- Maintain a quick testing pace to enhance rapport and help keep the examinee's attention.

In most cases, WJ IV COG tests should be administered in the order that they appear in the easel Test Books, beginning with the Standard Battery. Following are descriptions of the WJ IV COG tests and their administration procedures including common errors examiners make when administering the test. The Rapid Reference boxes pertaining to each test description provide essential information about the test, including starting point, equipment needed, and basal and ceiling criteria. It will be useful to refer to the material in the Test Books and Test Record while reviewing the following test descriptions and administration procedures.

Test 1: Oral Vocabulary

Oral Vocabulary (**Rapid Reference** 2.7) consists of two subtests: Synonyms and Antonyms. In the Synonyms subtest, the person is provided with a word and is asked to respond with a synonym. In the Antonyms subtest, the person is provided with a word and is asked to respond with an antonym. You must administer both subtests to obtain derived scores for this test.

Administration. The test requires the administration of sample items or training items to ensure that the examinee understands the task requirements. Therefore, it is important to follow all pointing directions and to provide the corrective feedback allowed during the administration of sample or training items. The supplemental information in shaded boxes on the right side of the examiner's page contains the additional administration instructions for corrective feedback. It is important to be familiar with this information and follow the directions.

Know the correct pronunciation of all items before administering the test. For some of the more difficult items, a pronunciation key is provided with the item in the Test Book; you also may consult any standard dictionary. If the examinee responds in a language other than English, say, "Tell me in English." Remember to complete, as needed, any query included in an item scoring key.

Unless noted, only one-word responses are acceptable. If a person provides a two-word response, ask for a one-word answer. If an examinee responds to an Antonym item by giving the stimulus word preceded by "non-" or "un-," ask for another answer unless otherwise indicated in the scoring key.

All examinees begin with a sample item for Synonyms and Antonyms. Because there is stimulus material on the examinee's page, test by complete pages for both subtests.

Item Scoring. Score correct responses 1, incorrect responses 0. Responses are correct when they differ from the correct response only in verb tense or number (singular/plural), unless otherwise indicated by the scoring key. For example, on Synonyms Item 10, "roads" is correct. On Synonyms Item 13, the responses "gobble," "gobbles," or "gobbled" are all correct. A response is incorrect if the examinee substitutes a different part of speech, such as a noun for a verb or an adjective, unless otherwise indicated by the scoring key. Count all unadministered items below the basal as correct, but do not fill in the scores on the Test Record. Do not include sample items when calculating the number correct.

Common Examiner Errors. Errors examiners commonly make include:

Reading from the Test Record rather than the Test Book (missing queries).
Mispronouncing the words when administering the items.
Not testing by complete pages.
Not including items below the basal in the calculation of the raw score.

≋ Rapid Reference 2.7 Test I: Oral Vocabulary

Materials needed:

Standard Battery Test Book, Test Record

Starting point:

Administer sample items first as indicated in the Test Book, then use the "Suggested Starting Points" table in the Test Book

Basal (for each subtest):

6 consecutive lowest-numbered items correct, or Item I

Ceiling (for each subtest):

6 consecutive highest-numbered items incorrect, or last item

Tips:

Administer both subtests.

Know the correct pronunciation of each item.

Remember to complete any necessary additional item query.

Accept responses that differ in tense or number.

Do not accept responses that are a different part of speech.

Request one-word responses unless otherwise noted.

Do not penalize for mispronunciations resulting from articulation errors, dialect variations, or regional speech patterns.

Test by complete pages.

Do not include sample items in the number correct.

Test 2: Number Series

Number Series (**Rapid Reference** 2.8) presents a series of numbers with one or more numbers missing. The examinee must determine the numerical pattern and provide the missing number in the series.

Administration. This test requires the administration of sample items to ensure that the examinee understands the task requirements. Follow all pointing directions and provide the corrective feedback allowed during the administration of sample or training items as indicated in the shaded boxes on the right side of the examiner's page.

Administer Sample Item A to all individuals; then, based on the person's estimated ability, select a starting item using the suggested starting points. Provide the examinee with the worksheet in the Response Booklet or a sheet of paper and a pencil when directed to do so in the Test Book, or if the examinee requests it prior to the direction in the Test Book. Test by complete pages. Each item has a timing guideline of 1 minute. If the examinee has not responded after 1 minute and does not appear to be trying to solve the problem, encourage a response and then move the examinee to the next item. However, if the examinee is still actively attempting to solve the problem, more time is allowed. On this test, it is permissible to uncover one item at a time for individuals who are confused by more than one item appearing on the page.

Item Scoring. Score correct responses 1, incorrect responses 0. Some items require two numbers, and both must be given to receive credit. These answers are indicated in the Test Book with the word *and*. Some items have more than one possible answer, but only one of the responses is required to receive credit. These answers are indicated in the Test Book with the word *or*. Count all unadministered items below the basal as correct, but do not fill in the scores on the Test Record. Do not include sample items when calculating the number correct.

Common Examiner Errors. Errors examiners commonly make include:

Forgetting to provide paper and pencil to examinee.
Not administering sample items correctly.
Using item timing guideline as a rule even though examinee is actively solving.
Not testing by complete pages.

≡ *Rapid Reference 2.8 Test 2: Number Series*

....

Materials needed:

Standard Battery Test Book, Test Record, Response Booklet Worksheet or blank paper, pencil, stopwatch

Starting point:

Sample item, then use the "Suggested Starting Points" table

Basal:

5 consecutive lowest-numbered items correct, or Item 1

Ceiling:

5 consecutive highest-numbered items incorrect, or last item

Tips:

Encourage a response after 1 minute, but allow more time if the examinee is still
   trying to solve.
Test by complete pages.
Do not include sample items in the number correct.

Test 3: Verbal Attention

Verbal Attention (**Rapid Reference** 2.9) requires the ability to hold information
in immediate awareness to answer a specific question about the sequence of presented information. In this test, the examinee listens to a series of intermixed
animals and numbers presented from the audio recording and then answers a
question about the sequence, such as "Tell me the first number and then the
animals in order."

   Administration. This test requires the use of the CD and good-quality audio
equipment. Before beginning the test, determine the starting point, and then cue
Sample Item B or Sample Item C on the audio recording and adjust the volume to
a comfortable level on the examinee's headphones. Present Sample Item A orally.
Present all other sample items and test items from the audio recording. You may
pause or stop the recording if an examinee needs more time. Except for the sample
items, do not repeat or replay any test items. The error correction procedure for
the sample items allows for item repetition to ensure the examinee understands
the task requirement.

   In rare cases, the items may be presented orally. In such cases, attempt to say
each item in the same manner that it is presented on the audio recording—in
an even voice at a rate of exactly one animal or number per second. Your voice
should drop slightly at the end of the series to signal to the examinee that the
series has ended.

   If beginning with Sample Item A and the examinee responds correctly to
no more than two items through Item 8, discontinue testing. However, if the

examinee responds correctly to three or more items, continue to Sample Item C. Testing may be discontinued when you reach the ceiling because this test has no visual stimuli for the examinee. There is no need to test by complete pages.

Item Scoring. Score correct responses 1, incorrect responses 0. When an item requires a particular response order (e.g., "Tell me the first and then the last animal."), the examinee's response must be in the requested order to be counted correct. Count all unadministered items below the basal as correct, but do not fill in the scores on the Test Record. Do not include sample items when calculating the number correct.

Common Examiner Errors. Errors examiners commonly make include:

Failing to pause the recording if the examinee needs more response time.
Giving credit for correct identification but wrong order of items when order is specified.
Not applying basal and ceiling guidelines correctly.
Testing by complete pages.

≡ *Rapid Reference 2.9 Test 3: Verbal Attention*

Materials needed:

Standard Battery Test Book, Test Record, audio recording and audio equipment

Starting point:

Sample item A or C for all examinees (refer to the "Suggested Starting Points" table in the Test Book)

Basal:

6 consecutive lowest-numbered items correct, or Item 1

Ceiling:

6 consecutive highest-numbered items incorrect, or last item, except when beginning with Sample Item A. In that case, if the examinee responds correctly to two or fewer items on Items 1 through 8, discontinue testing.

Tips:

Except for Sample Item A, use the audio recording to administer the test.

Do not repeat or replay any test items—only sample items.

Pause the recording if the examinee needs more response time.

Do not penalize for mispronunciations resulting from articulation errors, dialect variations, or regional speech patterns.

Test 4: Letter-Pattern Matching

Letter-Pattern Matching (**Rapid Reference** 2.10) requires the examinee to find and mark two identical letter patterns in a row of distractor letter patterns within a 3-minute period. The matching letter patterns are common orthographic patterns, whereas the distractors are less frequent or impossible letter strings.

Administration. This test requires the use of the Response Booklet, a pencil, and a stopwatch or watch with a second hand. All examinees begin with the sample items and complete the Practice Exercise to ensure that they understand the task before attempting the test items. When administering these training items, follow all directions carefully to ensure examinee comprehension. The supplemental information in shaded boxes on the right side of the examiner's page contains the additional administration instructions for corrective feedback. It is important to be familiar with this information and follow the directions. If the examinee scores 3 or fewer after the error-correction procedure on the Practice Exercise, discontinue testing and record a score of 0 for the test.

Do not allow the examinee to study the items while you are presenting the directions. If necessary during completion of the test, remind the examinee not to erase but to cross out (X) any incorrectly marked pair. Do not provide the examinee with a card or paper to block the items on this test. Remind the examinee to proceed row by row if he or she begins skipping around in the test.

Because examinees who do well and finish in less than the maximum allowable time will receive a higher ability score than individuals who work for the full time, it is important to record the exact finishing time. If the finishing time is not exactly 3 minutes, record the exact finishing time in minutes and seconds on the Test Record.

Item Scoring. Score correctly marked pairs 1. If the examinee crosses out (X) a correctly identified pair, do not count it in the number correct. A scoring-guide overlay is provided for easy scoring. Do not include points for sample items or practice exercises when calculating the number correct.

≡ Rapid Reference 2.10 Test 4: Letter-Pattern Matching

Materials needed:

Standard Battery Test Book, Test Record, Response Booklet, pencil, stopwatch

Starting point:

Sample items and Practice Exercises for all examinees

Time limit:

3 minutes

Tips:

Do not allow examinee to study the items when presenting instructions.

Point to columns and turn pages in the Response Booklet as directed.

Make sure the examinee continues to top of each column after completing the previous column.

Examinees should cross out (X), not erase, any changes.

Correctly marked pairs that are crossed out are incorrect.

Do not cover extra lines.

Do not include sample items or practice exercises in the number correct.

Use the scoring-guide overlay.

Common Examiner Errors. Errors examiners commonly make include:

Failing to administer sample items and practice exercises correctly.

Not controlling the Response Booklet as directed in the Test Book.

Allowing examinee to erase errors rather than crossing them out.

Not recording the exact finishing time in minutes and seconds.

Not using the scoring-guide overlay to score the test.

Test 5: Phonological Processing

Phonological Processing (**Rapid Reference** 2.11) consists of three parts: Word Access, Word Fluency, and Substitution. You must administer all three parts to obtain derived scores for this test. The task in Word Access requires the examinee to provide a word that has a particular phonemic element in a specific location.

Word Fluency requires the examinee to name as many words as possible that begin with a stated sound within a 1-minute time span. Substitution requires the examinee to substitute part of a word to create a new word. Word Access and Substitution both require the use of the audio recording and audio equipment. Word Fluency does not require the use of the audio recording; rather, it requires the use of a stopwatch.

Administration. For all three parts, you may repeat any item if requested by the examinee. When you see letters printed within slashes, such as /p/, do not say the letter name; rather, say the phoneme (the most common sound of the letter).

Word Access. Word Access requires the use of the CD and good-quality audio equipment. Before beginning the test, locate the appropriate track on the audio recording based on the examinee's estimated ability (refer to the second "Suggested Starting Points" table for Word Access in the Test Book), and adjust the volume to a comfortable level on the examinee's headphones. Present Sample Items A through C and Items 1 through 3 orally. Because it is difficult to orally replicate correctly the isolated phonemes, present all remaining items using the audio recording. You may pause or stop the recording if the examinee needs more response time. If the examinee responds in a language other than English, say, "Tell me in English." If a person provides a response of two or more words, say, "Give me a one-word answer." When starting with Sample Item A, if the examinee does not respond correctly on Items 1 through 3 (has 0 correct), discontinue testing and record a score of 0 for the test.

Word Fluency. Word Fluency requires a stopwatch or a watch or clock with a second hand. Administer both items to all examinees. Each item has a 1-minute time limit. Do not count duplicate answers—for example, if the examinee says "diary" three times, mark only one correct response. If you cannot remember whether the examinee has duplicated a word, do not stop the examinee or ask if the response was already named. Instead, give the response credit and balance the scores if you are unsure of another response. If the examinee pauses for 10 seconds, say, "Go ahead. Say the words as quickly as you can." If the examinee responds in a language other than English, say, "Tell me in English."

Substitution. Substitution requires the use of the CD and good-quality audio equipment. Determine the starting item based on the number of points on Word Access. Before beginning the test, locate the track for Sample Item C on the audio recording, and adjust the volume to a comfortable level on the examinee's headphones. Present Sample Items A and B and Items 1 and 2 orally. Because it is difficult to orally replicate correctly the isolated phonemes, it is recommended that you present Sample Items C and D and all remaining test items using the audio recording; however, in rare cases, the items may be presented orally. In such cases, attempt to say each item in the same manner that it is presented on the audio recording. You may pause or stop the recording if the examinee needs more response time. When starting with Sample Item A, if the examinee does not respond correctly to Sample Item A and B even after the error correction procedures, discontinue testing and record a score of 0 for the test.

Item Scoring. Score correct responses 1 for all parts.

Word Access.   Score incorrect responses 0. Correct responses must be real English words. Count unadministered items below the basal as correct. Do not include sample items when calculating the number correct.

Word Fluency.   Use tally marks on the lines provided in the Test Record to record the number of correct responses for each item. Do not count duplicate answers or the words presented as the stimulus example (i.e., *milk, dog*) as correct. Any real words, including proper nouns, beginning with the specified sound are correct—even though the examples are nouns, any part of speech is acceptable.

Substitution.   Score incorrect responses 0. Count unadministered items below the basal as correct. Do not include sample items when calculating the number correct.

Common Examiner Errors.   Errors examiners commonly make include:

Failing to pause the recording if the examinee needs more response time.
Mispronouncing phonemes.
Failing to follow error correction procedures when specified.
Counting exact duplicate responses as correct in Word Fluency.
Failing to administer both items in Word Fluency for the full minute.

≡ *Rapid Reference 2.11 Test 5:*
Phonological Processing

Materials needed:

Standard Battery Test Book, Test Record, audio recording and audio equipment, stopwatch

Starting point:

WA: Sample item A or C for all examinees (refer to the "Suggested Starting Points" table in the Test Book)

WF: Item 1

S: determined by raw score on Word Access (refer to the "Suggested Starting Points" table in the Test Book)

Basal:

WA: 6 consecutive lowest-numbered items correct, or Item 1

WF: all examinees take both items

S: 6 consecutive lowest-numbered items correct, or Item 1

Ceiling:

WA: 6 consecutive highest-numbered items incorrect, or last item, except when beginning with Sample Item A. In that case, if the examinee has 0 correct on Items 1 through 3, discontinue testing.

WF: 1-minute time limit for each item.

S: 6 consecutive highest-numbered items incorrect, or last item, except when beginning with Sample Item A. In that case, if the examinee has 0 correct on the samples even after error correction, discontinue testing.

Tips:

Administer all three parts.

Do not penalize for mispronunciations resulting from articulation errors, dialect variations, or regional speech patterns.

WA: Use the audio recording.

WA: Pause the recording if the examinee needs more response time.

WA: Follow the error-correction procedure, which is located on the right side of the examiner's page.

WF: Use tally marks to record correct responses.

WF: Do not count duplicate responses.

WF: Do not ask examinee to repeat.

WF: Prompt the examinee after a 10-second pause.

S: Use the audio recording.

S: Follow the error-correction procedure, which is located on the right side of the examiner's page.

Test 6: Story Recall

Story Recall (**Rapid Reference** 2.12) requires the examinee to listen to a story and then recall as many details as possible about the story. The items become more difficult as the stories presented become more complex.

Administration. This test requires the use of the CD and good-quality audio equipment. Before beginning the test, locate the appropriate track on the audio recording based on the examinee's estimated ability (refer to the "Suggested Starting Points" table in the Test Book), and adjust the volume to a comfortable level on the examinee's headphones. Present all test items from the audio recording. Because examinee response time varies widely, the audio recording does not include additional time between stories; you must pause the audio recording after each story for the examinee to respond. If the person does not respond, say, "Tell me anything about the story you remember." Present this test using the audio recording because it is difficult to replicate the items orally in a consistent fashion. However, in rare cases, the stories may be presented orally. Attempt to say each story in the same manner that it is presented on the audio recording. Do not repeat any item during the test.

Continuation rules are presented after each set of two stories. These rules provide direction to the examiner regarding whether testing should continue or discontinue. Follow the continuation instructions to ensure the score is based on the best estimate of the examinee's recall ability.

Item Scoring. Score correct responses 1, incorrect responses 0. Slashes (/) separate the story elements on the Test Record. When scoring the test, place a check mark over each element recalled correctly. The examinee may recall the elements in any order. Each element includes a word or words in bold type, and the word(s) must be recalled exactly to receive credit. For example, if the word *park* is in bold, and the person says "playground," do not give credit for the element. Three exceptions apply to this scoring rule:

1. If the examinee responds with a synonym that preserves the meaning of the bold word, allow credit for the element (e.g., *speak* for *talk* or *kids* for *children*).
2. If the examinee responds with a derivation of or adds possessive case to a proper name, allow credit for the element (e.g., *Dougy* for *Doug* or *Rick's* for *Rick*).
3. If the examinee provides a response that varies in verb tense or number (singular/plural) from the bold word, allow credit for the element (e.g., *blew* for *blowing* or *star* for *stars*).

The words in the element that are not bold do not need to be recalled or the examinee can recall the general information or concept.

≡ *Rapid Reference 2.12 Test 6: Story Recall*

Materials needed:

Standard Battery Test Book, Test Record, audio recording audio equipment

Starting point:

Use the "Suggested Starting Points" table in the Test Book.

Basal:

Follow continuation instructions.

Ceiling:

Follow continuation instructions.

Tips:

Use the audio recording to administer the test.

Do not repeat or replay any stories.

Pause audio after each story.

Do not penalize for mispronunciations resulting from articulation errors, dialect variations, or regional speech patterns.

Words in bold type must be recalled exactly with a few exceptions (synonyms, derivation or adds possessive case to proper names, verb tense or number).

Elements may be recalled in any order.

Follow the continuation instructions.

Common Examiner Errors. Errors examiners commonly make include:

Not using the audio recording.

Not scoring the elements correctly.

Forgetting to pause the recording after each story.

Not following the continuation instructions.

Repeating a story if the examinee asks.

Test 7: Visualization

Visualization (**Rapid Reference** 2.13) consists of two subtests: Spatial Relations and Block Rotation. In the Spatial Relations subtest, the examinee is required to identify two or three pieces that form a complete target shape. As the items progress and become more difficult, the drawings of the pieces are rotated, and some distractor pieces become more similar in appearance to the target. In the Block Rotation subtest, the examinee must identify the two, rotated, three-dimensional block designs that match the target pattern. Items become more difficult as the number of blocks and the complexity of the pattern increase. You must administer both subtests to obtain derived scores for this test.

Administration. For both subtests, sample items follow the introductions to provide additional practice and to ensure the examinee understands the task. It is essential that you follow all pointing and scripting on the introductions and sample items and follow all scripted corrective feedback during the administration of the sample items. If the presence of the other items on the page confuses the examinee, use your hand or a piece of paper to uncover one item at a time. Test by complete pages.

Spatial Relations. When administering Spatial Relations, all examinees begin with the Introduction followed by sample items. Allow pointing responses, but, if the examinee knows letter names, encourage him or her to use letters for identifying the pieces. Through Item 15, if the examinee names only two pieces for which three puzzle pieces must be recalled, say, "And what else?" Do not prompt the examinee after Item 15 if he or she names only two pieces for which three pieces must be recalled.

Block Rotation. When administering Block Rotation, begin with either Introduction 1 or Introduction 3, depending on the individual's estimated ability or grade level, and then proceed to the sample items. It is important to note that, beginning at Item 6, examinees are directed not to touch the drawings and must find the two drawings that are the same as the target using only their eyes. Encourage examinees to say the letters to identify their choices rather than pointing. Each item has a 30-second time guideline. If the examinee has not responded after 30 seconds and does not appear to be trying to solve the problem, encourage a response and then move the examinee to the next item. However, if the examinee is still actively attempting to solve the problem, more time is allowed.

When beginning with Introduction 3, if the examinee does not respond correctly to either Item 6 or 7, go back to Introduction 1. Administer introductions, sample items, and Items 1 through 5 before continuing to Item 8.

Item Scoring. Score correct responses 1, incorrect responses 0. Do not include sample items when calculating the number correct.

Spatial Relations. For Spatial Relations, each puzzle piece must be identified correctly to receive a score of 1 (some puzzles require three pieces). The examinee may identify the puzzle pieces in any order.

Block Rotation. For Block Rotation, both drawings that match the stimulus drawing must be identified. If testing began with Introduction 3 and Items 1 through 5 were not administered, assume all five items are correct when calculating the number correct.

Common Examiner Errors. Errors examiners commonly make include:

Test 7A: Spatial Relations

Not administering sample items correctly.
Scoring first responses rather than last responses.
Failing to ask "And what else?" if the examinee identifies only two pieces (Items 11, 12, and15).
Asking "And what else?" if the examinee identifies only two pieces (Items 18, 20, and 22).

Test 7B: Block Rotation

Not providing all pointing and corrective feedback as indicated in the Test Book.
Allowing examinee to touch the items or point to them when trying to solve.
Using item timing guideline as a rule even though examinee is actively solving.

≡ *Rapid Reference 2.13 Test 7: Visualization*

....

Materials needed:

Standard Battery Test Book, Test Record, stopwatch

Starting point:

SR: Introduction and sample items for all examinees

BR: Introduction 1 or Introduction 3 and sample item(s) (refer to the "Suggested Starting Points" table in the Test Book) for all examinees

Basal:

Item 1

Ceiling (for each subtest):

5 consecutive highest-numbered items incorrect, or last test item

Tips:

Administer both subtests.

Encourage the examinee to use letters to identify responses in Spatial Relations.

Do not allow examinee to touch the drawings in Block Rotation (Item 6 and higher).

Follow the 30-second guideline in Block Rotation, but allow more time if the examinee is actively trying to solve.

Test by complete pages.

Do not include sample items in the number correct.

Test 8: General Information

General Information (**Rapid Reference** 2.14) contains two subtests: Where and What. In the former, the examinee is asked, "Where would you find [an object]?" In the latter, the examinee is asked, "What would you do with [an object]?" The initial items in each subtest draw from familiar everyday objects, and the items become increasingly difficult as the objects become more obscure or less familiar. You must administer both subtests to obtain derived scores for this test.

Administration. General Information is straightforward and easy to administer with no sample items, introductions, supplemental information, timing, or use of audio equipment. Be sure to review the exact pronunciation of the items before you begin testing. For some of the more difficult items, a pronunciation key is provided with the item in the Test Book; you also may consult any standard dictionary. If the examinee responds in a language other than English, say, "Tell me in English." If the examinee forgets the task requirement and responds to a "what" question with a "where" response, repeat the question using the complete sentence as presented on the item you started with (i.e., "What would people usually do with [an object]?"). Give this reminder only once during the administration of this subtest. Remember to complete, as needed, any query included in an item scoring key. Because this test has no visual stimuli for the examinee, testing may be discontinued when you reach the ceiling. There is no need to test by complete pages. Testing begins with an appropriate-level test item based on your estimate of the examinee's ability and proceeds until you obtain a ceiling.

Item Scoring. Score correct responses 1; score incorrect responses 0. Count unadministered items below the basal as correct.

Common Examiner Errors. Errors examiners commonly make include:

Failing to complete queries.
Mispronouncing the words when administering the items.
Providing the "what" prompt more than once.
Failing to include items below the basal when calculating the number correct.

≡ Rapid Reference 2.14 Test 8: General Information

Materials needed:

Standard Battery Test Book, Test Record

Starting point:

Use the "Suggested Starting Points" table in the Test Book

Basal (for each subtest):

4 consecutive lowest-numbered items correct, or Item 1

Ceiling (for each subtest):

4 consecutive highest-numbered items incorrect, or last item

Tips:

Administer both subtests.
Know the correct pronunciation of each item.

Provide only one reminder of the task on the What subtest if the examinee forgets the task requirement.

Do not penalize for mispronunciations resulting from articulation errors, dialect variations, or regional speech patterns.

Remember to complete any necessary additional item query.

Test 9: Concept Formation

Concept Formation (**Rapid Reference** 2.15) is a controlled learning task. Unlike some concept formation tasks that require an examinee to remember what has happened over a series of items, this test does not include a memory component. The Concept Formation task requires the individual to examine a stimulus set and then formulate a rule that applies to the item.

Administration. This test, like all controlled learning tests, requires strict adherence to the script and all pointing directions as well as attention to the type of corrective feedback required. The goal is to administer this test in exactly the same manner to each examinee so that the teaching and learning opportunities are identical. Administer this test without interruptions. Testing begins with either Introduction 1 or Introduction 2.

Pay close attention to the pointing instructions in Introductions 1 and 2, Sample Items A through E, and Items 1 through 5. Do not provide the examinee with any additional explanation. If the examinee makes an error, it is important to follow the script in the "Error or No Response" boxes on the right side of the examiner's page in the Test Book. If the presence of rows of geometric shapes on the page confuses the examinee, use your hand or a piece of paper to uncover one line at a time.

Sample Items A and B and Items 1 through 5 include scripted acknowledgment for correct responses in addition to scripted corrective feedback. On Sample Items C through I and Items 6 through Item 35, remember to provide the acknowledgment and give immediate, corrective feedback for incorrect responses. Vary the acknowledgment of correct responses. For example, give a nod of the head and/or provide comments such as "good," "right," or "that's correct." Do not allow signs of acknowledgment to become an automatic reaction to all responses, including incorrect ones; this confuses the examinee and disrupts the learning nature of the task. Because synonyms are acceptable, use the same word(s) that the examinee used when you give feedback or make corrections using the "Error or No Response" box. Do not acknowledge correct or incorrect responses on Items 36 through 40.

There is a 1-minute time limit per item for Items 27 through 40. If the examinee's time exceeds 1 minute, follow the directions in the "Error or Over 1 Minute" box on the right side of the examiner's page in the Test Book. Use a stopwatch to monitor the examinee's response time.

There are five cutoff rules at specified points in the Test Book; follow the instructions carefully. For example, if the examinee began with Introduction 1 and received a total score of 2, 1, or 0 on Items 1 through 5, discontinue testing. If the examinee started with Introduction 2 and received a total score of 1 or 0 on Sample Items C through E, administer Introduction 1, Sample Items A and B, and Items 1 through 5; and then discontinue testing. If the examinee began with Introduction 2 and received a total score of 1 or 0 on Items 6 through 11, present Introduction 1, Sample Items A and B, and Items 1 through 5; and then discontinue testing (base the examinee's score on Items 1 through 11).

Item Scoring. Score correct responses 1, incorrect responses 0. Score an item correct if the examinee provides a synonym or word that is similar in meaning to the word included in the scoring key (e.g., *large* for *big* or *small* for *little*). If beginning with Introduction 2 and Items 1 through 5 were not administered, include credit for Items 1 through 5 when calculating the number correct. Do not include sample items when calculating the number correct.

Common Examiner Errors. Errors examiners commonly make include:

Not following the corrective feedback instructions carefully.

Failing to use the synonym provided by the examinee when providing corrective feedback.

Not following all pointing directions.

Not acknowledging correct responses through Item 35.

Not adhering to a 1-minute time limit for Items 27 through 40

Incorrectly continuing to acknowledge correct responses for Items 36 through 40.

≣ Rapid Reference 2.15 Test 9: Concept Formation

Materials needed:

Standard Battery Test Book, Test Record, stopwatch

Starting point:

Use the "Suggested Starting Points" table in the Test Book

Basal:

Item 1 or Item 6

Ceiling:

Determined by cutoff rules

Tips:

Follow all pointing and corrective feedback directions carefully.

Complete queries as needed.

Acknowledge correct responses for sample items and Items 1 through 35.

Items 27 through 40 each have a 1-minute time limit.

Accept synonyms as correct.

Do not acknowledge correct or incorrect responses on Items 36 through 40.

Test 10: Numbers Reversed

Numbers Reversed (**Rapid Reference** 2.16) requires the examinee to listen to a group of numbers and then repeat the numbers back in reverse order. The items grow more difficult as the string of numbers becomes longer.

Administration. This test requires the use of the CD and good-quality audio equipment. Before beginning the test, locate the track for Sample Item D on the audio recording and adjust the volume to a comfortable level on the examinee's headphones. Present Sample Items A through C and Items 1 through 10 orally; present Sample Item D and the remaining test items from the audio recording.

Except for Sample Items A and D, do not repeat or replay any test items. Although the audio recording provides adequate time for most examinees to respond, examiners may pause or stop the recording if the examinee needs more response time. In rare cases, the items may be presented orally. In such cases, attempt to say each item in the same manner that it is presented on the audio recording—in an even voice at a rate of exactly 1 digit per second. Drop your voice slightly on the last digit in each series to signal to the examinee that the series has ended. Remind the examinee to say the numbers backward only when indicated in the Test Book. Because this test has no visual stimuli for the examinee, testing may be discontinued when you reach the ceiling. There is no need to test by complete pages.

Item Scoring. Score each correct response 1, each incorrect response 0. The examinee must say all numbers in the correct reversed order to receive a score of 1 on an item. Count all unadministered items below the basal as correct. Do not include sample items when calculating the number correct.

Common Examiner Errors. Errors examiners commonly make include:

Failing to administer sample items.
Failing to remind examinee to say the numbers backward.
Repeating items.
Failing to include credit for items below the basal when calculating the number correct.

≡ Rapid Reference 2.16 Test 10: Numbers Reversed

Materials needed:

Standard Battery Test Book, Test Record, audio recording and audio equipment

Starting point:

Sample Item A, B, or C for all examinees (refer to the "Suggested Starting Points" table in the Test Book)

Basal:

5 consecutive lowest-numbered items correct, or Item 1

Ceiling:

5 consecutive highest-numbered items incorrect, or the last item

Tips:

Administer Samples A, B, and C and Items 1 through 10 orally.
Administer Sample D and all remaining items from the audio recording.
Use the audio recording to administer the test.
Pause the recording if the examinee needs more response time.
Follow the error-correction procedure, which is located on the right side of the
    examiner's page, for the sample items.
Give reminders to say the numbers backward only as indicated in the Test Book.
Do not repeat or replay any items, other than Sample Items A and D.

Test 11: Number-Pattern Matching

Number-Pattern Matching (**Rapid Reference** 2.17) requires the examinee to find and mark two identical numbers in a row of six distractor numbers within a 3-minute period. The items become more difficult as they progress from single-digit numbers to triple-digit numbers.

Administration. This test requires the use of the Response Booklet, a pencil, and a stopwatch or watch with a second hand. All examinees begin with the sample items and complete the Practice Exercise to ensure that he or she understands the task before attempting the test items. When administering these training items, follow all directions carefully to ensure examinee comprehension. The supplemental information in shaded boxes on the right side of the examiner's page contains the additional administration instructions for corrective feedback. It is important to be familiar with this information and follow the directions. If the examinee scores 3 or fewer after the error-correction procedure on the Practice Exercise, discontinue testing and record a score of 0 for the test.

Do not allow the examinee to study the items while you are presenting the directions. If necessary during completion of the test, remind the examinee not to erase but to cross out (X) any incorrectly marked pair. Do not provide the examinee with a card or paper to block the items on this test. Remind the examinee to proceed row by row if he or she begins skipping around in the test.

Because examinees who do well and finish in less than the maximum allowable time will receive a higher ability score than individuals who work for the full time, it is important to record the exact finishing time. If finishing time is not exactly 3 minutes, record the exact finishing time in minutes and seconds on the Test Record.

Item Scoring. Score correctly marked pairs in the same row 1. If the examinee crosses out (X) a correctly identified pair, do not count it in the number correct. Do not count transposed numbers (e.g., 17 and 71 as correct. A scoring-guide overlay is provided for easy scoring. Do not include points for sample items or practice exercises when calculating the number correct.

Common Examiner Errors. Errors examiners commonly make include:

Failing to administer sample items and practice exercises correctly.
Not controlling the Response Booklet as directed in the Test Book.
Allowing the examinee to erase errors rather than crossing them out.
Not recording the exact finishing time in minutes and seconds.
Not counting transposed numbers as errors.
Not using the scoring-guide overlay to score the test.

≋ Rapid Reference 2.17 Test 11: Number-Pattern Matching

Materials needed:

Extended Battery Test Book, Test Record, Response Booklet, pencil, stopwatch

Starting point:

Sample items and Practice Exercises for all examinees

Time limit:

3 minutes

Tips:

Do not allow examinee to study the items when presenting instructions.
Point to columns and turn pages in the Response Booklet as directed.
Make sure the examinee continues to top of each column after completing the previous column.

Examinee should cross out (X), not erase, any changes.
Correctly marked pairs that are crossed out are incorrect.
Do not cover extra lines.
Do not include sample items or practice exercises in the number correct.
Use the scoring-guide overlay.

Test 12: Nonword Repetition

Nonword Repetition (**Rapid Reference** 2.18) requires that the examinee listen to a nonsense word from the audio recording and then repeat the word exactly. The items become more difficult as the number of syllables increases.

Administration. It is important to know the exact pronunciation of Items 1 through 7 before test administration because these items are administered orally. It is equally important to be very familiar with the pronunciation of the remaining nonwords to facilitate scoring. Each item in the Test Book includes a phonetic pronunciation key. Before administering this test for the first time, you should practice pronouncing Items 1 through 7 and listen to the audio recording while studying the pronunciation keys for Items 8 through 46 to ensure accurate scoring during test administration.

This test requires the use of the CD and good-quality audio equipment. Before beginning the test, locate the track for Item 8 on the audio recording and adjust the volume to a comfortable level on the examinee's headphones. Present Sample Items A and B and Items 1 through 7 orally, and present the remaining items from the audio recording. If the examinee needs additional response time, it is permissible to pause or stop the recording, but do not repeat or replay any items other than the sample items.

Because it is difficult to orally replicate the items, present this test using the audio recording; however, in rare cases, Items 8 through 22 may be presented orally. Attempt to say each item in the same manner that it is presented on the audio recording. Except for the sample items, do not repeat or replay any test items. The error correction procedure for the sample items allows for item repetition to ensure the examinee understands the task requirement.

If the examinee does not pronounce the nonword fluently but instead says it phoneme by phoneme or syllable by syllable, say, "Say the whole word smoothly." Give this reminder only once. For scoring purposes, use the examinee's last response. You may wish to record incorrect responses for later error analysis.

Because this test has no visual stimuli for the examinee, testing may be discontinued when you reach the ceiling. There is no need to test by complete pages.

Item Scoring. Score correct responses 1, incorrect responses 0. If the examinee places the accent on a syllable different from the one emphasized on the recording, do not penalize the examinee as long as he or she pronounces the nonword smoothly. You may find it helpful to watch the examinee's lips as he or she is responding. Count all unadministered items below the basal as correct. Do not include sample items when calculating the number correct.

Common Examiner Errors. Errors examiners commonly make include:

Not using the audio recording.
Forgetting to pause the recording if the examinee needs more response time.
Forgetting to provide the reminder to say the whole word.
Providing the reminder to say the whole word more than once.
Mispronouncing items when administering orally through Item 22.
Penalizing the examinee for emphasizing a syllable different from the one
     emphasized on the recording.
Failing to study the audio recording to ensure correct item scoring.

≡ Rapid Reference 2.18 Test 12: Nonword Repetition

Materials needed:

Extended Battery Test Book, Test Record, audio recording audio equipment

Starting point:

Administer sample items first as indicated in the Test Book, then use the "Suggested Starting Points" table in the Test Book

Basal:

6 consecutive lowest-numbered items correct, or Item 1

Ceiling:

6 consecutive highest-numbered items incorrect, or last item

Tips:

Use the audio recording.

Other than sample items, do not repeat or replay any test items.

Reminder to say the whole word smoothly can be given only once.

Pause the recording if the examinee needs more response time.

Phonetic pronunciations are provided in the Test Book to facilitate scoring.

Do not penalize for mispronunciations resulting from articulation errors, dialect variations, or regional speech patterns.

Do not penalize for emphasis on a syllable other than the one emphasized on the recording.

Watch the examinee's lips as he or she responds.

Test 13: Visual-Auditory Learning

Visual-Auditory Learning (**Rapid Reference** 2.19) is a controlled learning task. The examinee is asked to learn and recall a series of rebuses (pictographic representations of words) that, eventually, are combined into phrases and then sentences of increasing length and complexity.

Administration. Because Visual-Auditory Learning is a controlled learning task, it requires strict adherence to the script and all pointing directions as well as attention to the type of corrective feedback required. All examinees must have an identical opportunity to learn. Administer this test without interruptions.

There are seven introductions of symbols throughout the test. When new symbols are introduced, the examinee must verbalize the symbol name. Do not repeat the symbol name; the examinee should respond to a symbol only once each time it is presented. To ensure that the examinee does not have additional time to study the symbols on the introduction page, turn the page as soon as the examinee has named the last symbol. On the first story, point word by word until the examinee understands that he or she is supposed to read the symbols. If necessary, you may continue pointing throughout the test. If the presence of several lines on the page confuses the examinee, use your hand or a piece of paper to uncover one line at a time. It is recommended that you use a stopwatch or a watch or clock with a second hand to monitor response time.

Unlike Concept Formation, synonyms are not acceptable. The examinee must use the same word provided in the introductions. Give immediate, corrective feedback when an examinee makes an error but do not acknowledge correct responses. If an examinee makes an error or pauses for longer than 5 seconds, point to the symbol, say its name, and then point to the next symbol. During the test, it may be helpful if you keep your nondominant hand near the top or side of the Test Book easel to provide feedback quickly and easily. Do not discuss the symbols or help the examinee to form associations between the symbols and the words they represent.

On Introduction 7, two symbols are introduced that are suffixes, -ing and -s. The letter printed within slashes (i.e., /s/) indicates that you should say the sound of the letter (the phoneme), not the letter name. The arrows on the examiner's side of the Test Book indicate that you are to slide a finger from the new symbol (i.e., "-ing" and "-s") to the other two symbols (i.e., "riding" and "trees") and across them. This movement reinforces that two symbols (morphemes) will blend to form a whole word.

Item Scoring. Circle each word that the examinee misses or that you have to tell to the examinee after a 5-second pause. If the examinee gives a synonym for a word, such as *small* for *little*, count the response as an error and provide the required corrective feedback. For words with two symbols, such as "ride" and "ing," each symbol is a possible error. If the examinee responds incorrectly to the first symbol, correct the error without naming the second symbol. Count only the incorrect symbol as an error. For example, if the examinee says "rides" rather than "riding," immediately correct the second symbol and circle the suffix -ing on the Test Record. Or if the examinee says "driving" rather than "riding," immediately correct the first symbol and circle *ride* on the Test Record. If the examinee skips a word, point to the omitted word and say, "What is this?" If the examinee inserts a word, record the word on the Test Record, circle it, and count it as an error. Count the total number of errors to determine when to discontinue the test.

Common Examiner Errors. Errors examiners commonly make include:

Not requiring the examinee to repeat the name of the symbol during introductions.

Not providing immediate corrective feedback as directed in the Test Book.

Forgetting to apply a 5-second time limit to respond to symbols.

Saying more than the name of the symbol during corrective feedback.

Correcting both parts of words with two symbols (i.e., *riding, trees*) when only one part was an error.

Forgetting to count extra words, skipped words, and synonyms as errors.

Rapid Reference 2.19 Test 13: Visual-Auditory Learning

Materials needed:

Extended Battery Test Book, Test Record, stopwatch

Starting point:

Introduction 1

Basal:

Test Story 1

Ceiling:

Determined by cutoff rules

Tips:

Make sure the examinee repeats the name for each symbol during the introductions, but you should not repeat it.

Follow exact error-correction procedures: point to the symbol, say its name, and move immediately to the next symbol.

Count synonyms, skipped words, and extra inserted words as errors.

In words consisting of two symbols, score each symbol separately.

Use a stopwatch to monitor response time.

Circle all errors on the Test Record.

Test 14: Picture Recognition

Picture Recognition (**Rapid Reference** 2.20) requires that the examinee identify a subset of previously presented pictures within a field of distracting pictures. The stimuli and distracters for each item include varieties of the same type of object (e.g., several different leaves or several different lamps) to eliminate verbal mediation as a memory strategy. The difficulty of the items increases as the number of pictures in the stimulus set increases.

Administration. This test requires the administration of sample items to ensure that the examinee understands the task requirements. Therefore, it is important to follow all pointing directions and to provide the corrective feedback allowed during the administration of sample or training items. The supplemental information in shaded boxes on the right side of the examiner's page contains the additional administration instructions for corrective feedback. It is important to be familiar with this information and follow the directions.

Begin with Sample Item A or Sample Item C, depending on the examinee's estimated ability or grade level. Each item consists of two pages of pictures: a stimulus page and a response page. Show the stimulus page for only 5 seconds and then immediately turn to the response page. It is recommended that you leave your stopwatch running, rather than starting and stopping it, so that you can easily note the 5 seconds without drawing undue attention to the timing. Request that the examinee use letter names in his or her response; however, allow the examinee to point if necessary.

When starting with Sample Item A and the examinee responds correctly to no more than three items through Item 5, discontinue testing. However, if the examinee responds correctly to four or more items, continue to Sample Item C.

Item Scoring. Score correct responses 1, incorrect responses 0. All matching pictures must be identified to receive a score of 1, and the examinee may give the responses in any order. If the examinee gives more responses than required, score the last ones given (e.g., if four responses are given but only three are needed, base the score on the last three named). Count all unadministered items below the basal as correct. Do not include sample items when calculating the number correct.

Common Examiner Errors. Errors examiners commonly make include:

Giving the examinee more (or less) than 5 seconds to view the stimulus.
Not scoring last responses given if the examinee provides more responses than requested.

≡ *Rapid Reference 2.20 Test 14: Picture Recognition*

....

Materials needed:

Extended Battery Test Book, Test Record, stopwatch

Starting point:

Sample item A or C for all examinees (refer to the "Suggested Starting Points" table in the Test Book)

Basal:

6 consecutive lowest-numbered items correct, or Item 1

Ceiling:

6 consecutive highest-numbered items incorrect, or last item, except when beginning with Sample Item A. In that case, if the examinee responds correctly to three or fewer items on Items 1 through 5, discontinue testing.

Tips:

Show stimulus for only 5 seconds (leave stopwatch running).
Encourage the examinee to use letters to identify responses.
Score last responses given if the examinee gives more responses than requested.
Do not include sample items in the number correct.

Test 15: Analysis-Synthesis

Analysis-Synthesis (**Rapid Reference** 2.21) is a controlled learning task and is designed to measure the ability to reason and draw conclusions from given conditions. The examinee is given instructions on how to perform an increasingly complex procedure that requires him or her to examine and solve a series of puzzles.

Administration. Because Analysis-Synthesis is a controlled learning test, it requires exact administration and uninterrupted presentation. The goal is to administer this test in exactly the same manner to each examinee so that the teaching and learning opportunities are identical.

Begin the test with the Color Pretest for all individuals. If the examinee cannot be trained on the Color Pretest, check "Untrainable" on the Test Record and discontinue testing. For individuals who pass the Color Pretest, pay particular attention to the queries on the first few sample items. Also pay special attention to the pointing instructions for all items, including the three introductions. Do not provide the examinee with any additional explanation. If the presence of several puzzles on the page confuses the examinee, use your hand or a piece of paper to uncover one item at a time.

On Sample Item A through Item 28, acknowledge correct responses or give immediate, corrective feedback for incorrect responses following the "Error or No Response" box instructions in the Test Book. Vary the acknowledgment of correct responses; for example, give a nod of the head and/or provide comments such as "good," "right," or "that's correct." Do not allow signs of acknowledgment to become an automatic reaction to all responses, including incorrect ones; this will confuse the examinee and destroy the learning nature of the task. Do not acknowledge correct or incorrect responses on Items 29 through 35.

There is a 1-minute time limit per item for Items 26 through 35. If the examinee's time exceeds 1 minute, follow the directions in the "Error or Over 1 Minute" box on the right side of the examiner's page in the Test Book. Use a stopwatch to monitor the examinee's response time.

There are four cutoff rules at specified points in the Test Book; follow the instructions carefully to determine when to discontinue testing.

Item Scoring. Score correct responses 1, incorrect responses 0. Do not include sample items when calculating the number correct.

Common Examiner Errors. Errors examiners commonly make include:

Failing to administer the Color Pretest at all or doing so improperly.
Not following all pointing and corrective feedback instructions exactly.
Forgetting to acknowledge correct responses through Item 28.
Failing to read the paragraph that follows Sample Item E.
Forgetting to apply a 1-minute time limit to Items 26 through 35.
Incorrectly continuing to acknowledge correct responses for Items 29
    through 35.

≋ Rapid Reference 2.21 Test 15: Analysis-Synthesis

Materials needed:

Extended Battery Test Book, Test Record, stopwatch

Starting point:

Color Pretest followed by Introduction 1 for all examinees

Basal:

Item 1

Ceiling:

Determined by cutoff rules

Tips:

Adhere closely to all pointing and corrective feedback directions.

Complete queries as needed.

Acknowledge correct responses through Item 28.

Items 26 through 35 each have a 1-minute time limit.

Do not acknowledge correct or incorrect responses on Items 29 through 35.

The answers in the Test Book are correct even if you do not see how to solve the problem.

Test 16: Object-Number Sequencing

Object-Number Sequencing (**Rapid Reference** 2.22) requires the ability to hold information in immediate awareness, divide the information into two groups, and shift attentional resources to the two newly ordered sequences. This test requires the examinee to listen to a series that contains both digits and words, such as "dog, 2, ship, 8, 1, banana." The examinee must then attempt to reorder the information and repeat the objects in sequential order first, then the digits in sequential order.

Administration. This test requires the use of the CD and good-quality audio equipment. Before beginning the test, locate the appropriate track on the audio recording based on the examinee's estimated ability (refer to the "Suggested Starting Points" table in the Test Book), and adjust the volume to a comfortable level on the examinee's headphones. Present Sample Item A orally. Present all other sample items and test items from the audio recording. You may pause or stop the recording if an examinee needs more time. Except for the sample items, do not repeat or replay any test items. The error correction procedure for the sample items allows for item repetition to ensure the examinee understands the task requirement. In rare cases, the items may be presented orally. In such cases, attempt to say each item in the same manner that it is presented on the audio recording—in an even voice at a rate of exactly 1 word or digit per second. Your voice should drop slightly at the end of the series to signal to the examinee that the series has ended. Because this test has no visual stimuli for the examinee, testing may be discontinued when you reach the ceiling. There is no need to test by complete pages.

Item Scoring. Score correct responses 1, incorrect responses 0. Correct responses consist of objects named in the correct order followed by digits in the correct order. Any misplaced object or number, or if the response begins with the digits, is an incorrect response. Score responses for objects as correct if they sound very similar to (e.g., *cap* for *cat*) or if they rhyme with (e.g., *neat* for *meat*) a word in the stimulus series. Count all unadministered items below the basal as correct. Do not include sample items when calculating the number correct.

Common Examiner Errors. Errors examiners commonly make include:

Not scoring the items correctly (e.g., giving credit when an object or digit is misordered).
Not accepting similar-sounding or rhyming responses in the correct sequence as correct.
Failing to remind the examinee to say the things first and then the numbers.

≡ Rapid Reference 2.22 Test 16: Object-Number Sequencing

Materials needed:

Extended Battery Test Book, Test Record, audio recording and audio equipment

Starting point:

Sample Item A, then use the "Suggested Starting Points" table in the Test Book

Basal:

5 consecutive lowest-numbered items correct, or last item

Ceiling:

5 consecutive highest-numbered items incorrect, or last item

Tips:

Use the audio recording to administer the test.

Any time the examinee says digits first, score the item 0, and remind the examinee to say things first, then the numbers.

Accept similar-sounding or rhyming words as long as they are stated in the correct sequence.

Do not repeat or replay any test items—only sample items.

Pause the recording if the examinee needs more response time.

Do not penalize for mispronunciations resulting from articulation errors, dialect variations, or regional speech patterns.

Test 17: Pair Cancellation

Pair Cancellation (**Rapid Reference** 2.23) requires the examinee to find and circle a repeated pattern of objects throughout two pages full of objects and to do so as quickly as possible within a 3-minute time period.

Administration. This test requires the use of the Response Booklet, a pencil, and a stopwatch or watch with a second hand. All examinees begin with the sample items and complete the Practice Exercise to ensure that they understand the task before attempting the test items. When administering these training items, follow all directions carefully to ensure examinee comprehension. The supplemental information in shaded boxes on the right side of the examiner's page contains the additional administration instructions for corrective feedback. It is important to be familiar with this information and follow the directions. If the examinee scores 2 or fewer after the error-correction procedure on the Practice Exercise, discontinue testing and record a score of 0 for the test.

Do not allow the examinee to study the items while you are presenting the directions. If necessary during completion of the test, remind the examinee not to erase but to cross out (X) any incorrectly circled pair. Do not provide the examinee with a card or paper to block the items on this test. Remind the examinee to proceed row by row if he or she begins skipping around in the test.

Because examinees who do well and finish in less than the maximum allowable time will receive a higher ability score than individuals who work for the full time, it is important to record the exact finishing time. If finishing time is not exactly 3 minutes, record the exact finishing time in minutes and seconds on the Test Record.

Item Scoring. Score correctly circled pairs 1. The circled pair must contain a ball followed by a dog in the same row. Ignore responses in which an examinee circles a ball at the end of one row with a dog at the beginning of another row. Both parts of the pair must be at least partially circled to receive credit. The inclusion of part of a figure adjacent to a correctly circled pair is acceptable. However, inclusion of a complete figure adjacent to a correctly circled pair is not acceptable. Do not count the pair as correct in that case. A partially circled pair that does not include all of the dog or all of the ball is considered correct, as long as the intent is clear. A circle around a correctly chosen pair that overlaps with another circle is correct. If the examinee crosses out (X) a correctly identified pair, do not count it in the number correct. A scoring-guide overlay is provided for easy scoring. Do not include points for sample items or practice exercises when calculating the number correct.

Common Examiner Errors. Errors examiners commonly make include:

Failing to administer sample items and practice exercise correctly.
Not controlling the Response Booklet as directed in the Test Book.
Not presenting the Response Booklet opened to both pages when introducing the test items.
Allowing the examinee to erase errors rather than cross them out.
Misidentifying correct responses (includes crossed-out pairs, complete adjacent figure).
Not recording the exact finishing time in minutes and seconds.
Not using scoring-guide overlay to score the test.

≡ Rapid Reference 2.23 Test 17: Pair Cancellation

Materials needed:

Extended Battery Test Book, Test Record, Response Booklet, pencil, stopwatch

Starting point:

Sample items and Practice Exercises for all examinees

Time limit:

3 minutes

Tips:

Circled pair (ball followed by dog) must be in the same row.

Ignore responses in which an examinee circles a ball at the end of one row with a dog at the beginning of another row.

Inclusion of a complete figure adjacent to a correctly identified pair is scored incorrect.

A partially circled pair that does not include all of the dog or all of the ball is considered correct, as long as the intent is clear.

A circle around a correctly chosen pair that overlaps with another circle is correct.

Correctly marked pairs that are crossed out are incorrect.

Examinee should cross out, not erase, any changes.

Do not allow the examinee to study the items when presenting instructions.

Make sure the examinee continues to the second page after completing the first page.

Do not cover extra lines.

Test 18: Memory for Words

Memory for Words (**Rapid Reference** 2.24) requires the examinee to repeat lists of unrelated words in the correct sequence.

Administration. This test requires the use of the CD and good-quality audio equipment. Before beginning the test, locate the appropriate track on the audio recording based on the examinee's estimated ability (refer to the "Suggested Starting Points" table in the Test Book), and adjust the volume to a comfortable level on the examinee's headphones. Present Sample Item A orally. If the examinee does not understand the task, demonstrate further with additional pairs of words that are provided in the "Error or No Response" box on the right side of the examiner's page in the Test Book. Present Sample Item B and all test items from the audio recording. You may pause or stop the recording if the examinee needs more response time. Except for the sample items, do not repeat or replay any test items. In rare cases, the items may be presented orally. In such cases, attempt to say each item in the same manner that it is presented on the audio recording—in an even voice at a rate of exactly 1 word per second. Your voice should drop slightly on the last word in each series to signal to the examinee that the series has ended. Because this test has no visual stimuli for the examinee, testing may be discontinued when you reach the ceiling. There is no need to test by complete pages.

Item Scoring. Score correct responses 1, incorrect responses 0. The examinee must repeat the words in the exact order that they were presented to receive credit for an item. Responses are correct if they sound very similar to (e.g., *son* for *some*) or if they rhyme with (e.g., *bat* for *that*) a test word as long as they are in the correct sequence. Count unadministered items below the basal as correct. Do not include sample items when calculating the number correct.

Common Examiner Errors. Errors examiners commonly make include:

Not accepting similar-sounding or rhyming words in the correct sequence as correct.
Failing to pause the recording if the examinee needs more response time.
Repeating items when the examinee requests it.

≡ Rapid Reference 2.24 Test 18: Memory for Words

. . . .

Materials needed:

Extended Battery Test Book, Test Record, audio recording and audio equipment

Starting point:

Sample items, then use the "Suggested Starting Points" table in the Test Book

Basal:

4 consecutive lowest-numbered items correct, or Item I

Ceiling:

4 consecutive highest-numbered items incorrect, or last item

Tips:

Use the audio recording to administer the test.

Do not repeat or replay any test items—only sample items.

Pause the recording if the examinee needs more response time

Accept similar-sounding or rhyming words as long as they are in the correct sequence

Do not penalize for mispronunciations resulting from articulation errors, dialect variations, or regional speech patterns.

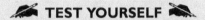

TEST YOURSELF

1. **Examiners must give all 18 tests in numeric sequence.**
   a. True
   b. False

2. **The first page after the tab in each test provides general information and instructions for that test.**
   a. True
   b. False

3. **When administering a test, always use the exact wording and instructions presented in the Test Book.**
   a. True
   b. False

4. **The best practice is to test by complete pages when stimulus material appears on the examinee's side of the Test Book.**
   a. True
   b. False

5. **The correct and incorrect keys in the Test Books include the only possible responses.**
   a. True
   b. False

6. **Which of the following apply to sample items or training items?**
   a. They are optional, and the examiner may administer them at his or her discretion.
   b. They are included in the calculation of the raw score.
   c. They are provided to ensure the examinee understands the task requirements.
   d. They do not contain a procedure to provide corrective feedback to the examinee.

7. Which of the following apply when administering an audio-recorded test?

    a. Look at the examinee while the item is being presented.

    b. Look at the examinee at the double beep to encourage a response.

    c. Look away from the examinee when the item is presented.

    d. Replay any items upon request of the examinee.

    e. a and b.

    f. b and c.

    g. c and d.

8. Which of the following apply when administering timed tests?

    a. Record the exact finishing time in minutes and seconds.

    b. Record the time limit even if the examinee finishes early.

    c. Allow the examinee to erase if he or she wants to change a response.

    d. Leave the Response Booklet in front of the examinee during all instructions.

9. Which of the following apply when using the Response Booklet?

    a. Examinees should erase their mistakes.

    b. Do not allow examinees to study the items when presenting instruction.

    c. Include Practice Exercises in the calculation of the raw score.

    d. Watch to ensure the examinee correctly continues to the next column and goes to the next page after completing a page.

    e. a and b.

    f. c and d.

    g. a and c.

    h. b and d.

10. All tests have the same basal and ceiling rules.

    a. True

    b. False

Answers: 1. b; 2. a; 3. a; 4. a; 5. b; 6. c; 7. f; 8. a; 9. h; 10. b

Three

HOW TO SCORE THE WJ IV COG

Melanie A. Bartels Graw

This chapter describes the steps involved in scoring the WJ IV COG. Item-level scoring occurs during test administration, and raw score calculation occurs after completion of each test. After those procedures are completed, data are entered into either the *Woodcock-Johnson Online Scoring and Reporting* (Schrank & Dailey, 2014) or the *WJ IV Interpretation and Instructional Interventions Program* (WIIIP; Schrank & Wendling, 2015a). These programs calculate all derived scores, variations among scores, and comparisons and discrepancies between scores.

Your job as an examiner is to interpret correctly, evaluate, and record the examinee's answers on the Test Record. You are required to calculate the raw score for each test and then enter the scores into the scoring program. Once you have entered the raw scores, the scoring programs allow you to choose from several scoring options.

The first part of this chapter includes information on item-level scoring; reminders for scoring each test are also included. The second part of this chapter describes the process for entering raw data into the online scoring and reporting program or WIIIP and creating a typical report—the Comprehensive Report created with the WIIIP. The available options for the Comprehensive Report are described.

ITEM SCORING

Two sets of scores are calculated when you administer the WJ IV COG. First, determine individual item scores for each item administered. Because basal and ceiling levels are determined by an examinee's pattern of correct and incorrect responses, individual items are scored during test administration. Second, calculate the total number correct, or raw score, following completion of the testing session. Generally, the raw score is determined by adding the number of correctly completed test items to the number of test items below the basal. However, some tests have special scoring considerations, such as Visual-Auditory Learning, where the raw score is determined by summing the number of errors.

The majority of items contained in the WJ IV COG tests are scored by recording 1 (correct) or 0 (incorrect) in the appropriate space on the Test Record. Spaces corresponding with items not administered are left blank. Items not administered generally include items either below the basal or above the ceiling or cutoff. **Rapid Reference** 3.1 lists helpful notations that you can use when recording item responses.

Item Scoring Keys

Most items in the Test Books contain scoring keys, which are intended as guides to determine how to score certain responses. The keys list the most frequent correct or incorrect responses provided by participants in the norming study. Because the keys were built on frequency of response, not all possible responses are included, and you may have to use your professional judgment in determining the score for an item. In cases where the examinee's response does not fall clearly in either the correct or incorrect category, you may wish to write the response on the Test Record and come back to it later.

≡ *Rapid Reference 3.1   Notations for Recording Responses*

....

 1 Correct response[*]
 0 Incorrect, or no response[*]
 Q Indicates a query
DK Indicates the response of "Don't Know"
NR Indicates "No Response"
SC Indicates a self-correction

[*]Except for Test 13, which is based on number of errors.

Sometimes more information is needed before scoring a response as either correct or incorrect. For certain responses, the query key provides a script designed to elicit another response from the examinee. Use professional judgment when querying responses that do not appear in these keys.

Do not use an unscored item in determining a basal or ceiling. If, after further consideration, it is still not clear how to score several items, balance the scores by scoring one item 1 and the other item 0. If you have several questionable responses, you should seek advice from a professional colleague who may be able to help you make a determination.

Scoring Multiple Responses

When an examinee provides multiple responses to an item requiring a single response, the general principle to follow is to score the last answer given. The last response, regardless of its correctness, is used to determine the final item score. Follow this procedure even if the examinee changes an earlier response much later in the testing session. In situations where the examinee provides two conflicting answers, query the response by asking the question "Which one?" or by directing the examinee to "Give just one answer."

Tests Requiring Special Scoring Procedures

Of the 18 WJ IV COG tests, two have special scoring procedures: Story Recall and Visual-Auditory Learning. The raw score for Story Recall is based on the number of correctly recalled elements in a group of administered stories. Although raw scores on most tests are computed by counting the number of correct responses, the raw score for Visual-Auditory Learning is determined by counting the total number of *errors*. The following section summarizes details for these tests. While studying this information, you should refer to a copy of the WJ IV COG Test Record for reference. For additional information, consult the WJ IV COG *Examiner's Manual* (Mather & Wendling, 2014).

Test 6: Story Recall. The score for Story Recall is based on the number of correctly recalled elements from a set of administered stories. When administering the test, place a check mark above each correctly recalled element on the Test Record. Count the number of check marks for each story and record the total in the box on the Test Record following each story. (Each check mark is the equivalent of 1 point.) Sum each set of two stories as indicated on the Test Record, and use that information to determine whether to continue or discontinue testing following the continuation instructions in the Test Book.

After completing the test, transfer the scores for each set of two stories (i.e., Stories 1–2, 3–4, 5–6, 7–8, and 9–10) to the "Score Entry" box located in the Test Record. If a group of stories was not administered, enter an X. Refer to this information when entering raw scores in the online scoring program(s).

To obtain an estimated age equivalent (AE) and grade equivalent (GE) from the "Scoring Table" in the Test Record, sum the scores for every two sets of stories administered (e.g., Stories 1 and 2 plus Stories 3 and 4) as indicated in the equation at the top of the "Scoring Table." If the starting point was misestimated and more than four stories were administered, use the scores corresponding to the last four stories administered following the continuation instructions to determine the correct column to use in the "Scoring Table."

Test 13: Visual-Auditory Learning. The score for Visual-Auditory Learning is based on the total number of errors. Score omitted words, inserted words, synonyms (e.g., *little* for *small*), and nonresponses as errors. A nonresponse occurs when the examinee fails to provide a response within 5 seconds. In such cases, the correct response is supplied by the examiner and the symbol is considered an error. For words with two symbols (e.g., *ride... ing*), each symbol is considered separately in scoring. Thus, if one part of a two-symbol word is incorrect and the other is correct, only one symbol is counted as an error. If both parts of a two-symbol word are incorrect (e.g., the examinee does not provide a response within 5 seconds), two errors are recorded.

Errors are counted throughout the entire administration and are periodically recorded in cumulative cutoff boxes that appear on the Test Record. Once all the errors are calculated, the total number of errors and the letter corresponding to the last set of Test Stories administered (i.e., A, B, C, D, or E) are recorded in the "Score Entry" box in the Test Record and entered in the online scoring program(s). When accessing the estimated AE and GE from the "Scoring Table" in the Test Record, refer to the column corresponding to the stories administered (e.g., 1, 1–2, 1–4, 1–6, or 1–7).

Scoring Guides

Letter-Pattern Matching, Number-Pattern Matching, and Pair Cancellation each includes a correct key in the Test Book. However, it is recommended that you use the scoring-guide overlays included in the test kit to prevent examiner error when calculating the raw score.

The overlays for Letter-Pattern Matching and Number-Pattern Matching are designed to lay to the left of the scoring column in the Response Booklet. With the page number and column number at the top of the overlay corresponding to the same page number and column in the Response Booklet, align the right edge of the scoring guide to the left of the scoring column in the Response Booklet. Turn the overlay upside down to score the next column on the same page. This layout allows you to scan quickly the page and mark the row correct (1) or incorrect (0). Sum the number of correct responses and enter the information on the Test Record.

The overlays for Pair Cancellation are designed with alignment markers to ensure proper alignment with the paired images. Align the stimulus image at the top of the scoring-guide overlay with the stimulus image at the top of the Response Booklet page. There is also a box at the bottom of the overlay that should surround the page number in the Response Booklet corresponding with the page number indicated on the overlay. This layout allows you to scan quickly the page and count the number of correctly identified pairs of items.

Obtaining Estimated Age and Grade Equivalent Scores (Optional)

You can manually obtain estimates of the age and grade equivalents for each test by using the scoring tables in the Test Record. This optional procedure is available if you need to obtain immediate developmental information. By utilizing the information provided in each test's scoring table, you can receive immediate feedback during the testing session regarding the examinee's estimated level of performance. Such feedback may serve to refine the selection of starting points in later tests, or suggest the need for further testing. The estimated scores obtained from these tables may differ slightly from the actual AE and GE scores reported by the online scoring and reporting program or WIIIP. Therefore, use the AE and GE generated by the scoring program for reporting purposes and the estimated AE and GE from the Test Record to inform immediate test administration.

Oral Vocabulary, Visualization, and General Information require summing the scores of the subtests to obtain a Total Number Correct to utilize the "Scoring Table" in the Test Record. The individual subtest scores must be entered in the online scoring program(s). Phonological Processing requires summing the scores for the subtests Word Access and Substitution and the item scores for Items 1 and 2 in the Word Fluency subtest.

Concept Formation and Analysis-Synthesis utilize cumulative cut-off scores. When accessing the estimated AE and GE from the "Scoring Table" in the Test Record, refer to the column corresponding to the items administered (e.g., 1–6, 1–11, 1–20, 1–29, or 1–40 for Concept Formation). The number correct and the corresponding letter indicating the cut-off point (e.g., A, B, C, D, or E for Concept Formation) must be entered in the online scoring program(s).

Following raw score calculation, refer to the appropriate scoring table in the Test Record and locate the number that matches the examinee's raw score in the number correct (raw score) column. Circle the entire row. The circled row provides the raw score (Number Correct, Total Number Correct, Number of Points, or Number of Errors), estimated AE, and estimated GE. Figure 3.1 illustrates the completion of this step for a girl who obtained a raw score of 20 on Verbal Attention and is in the fifth grade.

Test 3   Verbal Attention
Scoring Table
Encircle row for the Number Correct.

Number Correct	AE (Est)*	GE (Est)*
0	<3-6	<K.0
1	3-6	<K.0
2	4-4	<K.0
3	4-8	<K.0
4	5-0	<K.0
5	5-3	<K.0
6	5-6	K.1
7	5-9	K.3
8	6-0	K.6
9	6-3	K.9
10	6-7	1.1
11	6-10	1.4
12	7-2	1.8
13	7-7	2.1
14	8-0	2.6
15	8-7	3.2
16	9-3	3.8
17	10-0	4.6
18	10-10	5.4
19	11-9	6.4
20	13-0	7.6
21	14-7	9.1
22	16-10	11.4
>22	>30	>12.9

*AE and GE are estimates of the precise values provided by the scoring program.

Figure 3.1   Obtaining the estimated age and grade equivalents corresponding with 20 correct on Test 3: Verbal Attention

CAUTION

···

Common Errors in Obtaining Raw Scores and AE/GE from the Scoring Table on the Test Record

Forgetting to award credit for all items below the basal

Including sample or practice items in the computation of the raw score

Committing simple addition errors

Failing to use the scoring-guide overlays for the fluency tests

Not cumulatively totaling scores on tests with cutoffs (Test 9: Concept Formation, Test 13: Visual-Auditory Learning, and Test 15: Analysis Synthesis)

Not counting errors on Test 13: Visual-Auditory Learning

Transposing numbers

Neglecting to enter the raw scores for each subtest within a test (i.e., Test 1: Oral Vocabulary, Test 5: Phonological Processing, Test 7: Visualization, and Test 8: General Information), for each item (i.e., Test 5B: Phonological Processing–Word Fluency), or for each set of items (i.e., Test 6: Story Recall)

Neglecting to use the last four stories administered for Test 6: Story Recall to obtain estimated AE and GE from the "Scoring Table" on the Test Record

Neglecting to enter an X in the "Score Entry" box and subsequently in the scoring program for each set of stories not administered on Test 6: Story Recall

Entering the raw score incorrectly in the scoring program or using the wrong column to access the raw score in the scoring table

REMINDERS FOR SCORING EACH TEST

Before considering specific scoring reminders for each test, there are several general reminders to review. First, make it your practice to record incorrect responses on the Test Record. A subsequent analysis of these responses will be helpful in developing clinical inferences and recommendations. Second, remember that correct and incorrect answer keys are guides. They provide the most common correct or incorrect responses. On occasion, you may have to use judgment in determining the correctness of a response. Third, if an examinee changes a response, score the last response given. Finally, use your professional judgment in answering and asking questions of the examinee during testing. Following are specific scoring reminders for each test.

Test 1: Oral Vocabulary

Range:

Core test; raw score range A 0–31, B 0–32

Scoring Reminders:

- Both subtests must be administered to obtain derived scores.
- Score correct responses 1, incorrect responses 0.
- A response is scored correct (1) if it differs from the correct answer in verb tense or number; a response is scored incorrect (0) if it is a different part of speech from the correct answer.
- Mispronunciations resulting from articulation errors, dialect variations, or regional speech patterns are not considered errors.
- Accept 1-word responses only.
- For each subtest, enter the number of items answered correctly plus 1 point for each item below the basal in the "Number Correct" box.
- Do not include sample items in the number correct.
- Enter the number correct for each subtest in the online scoring program.

Test 2: Number Series

Range:

Core test; raw score range 0–42

Scoring Reminders:

- Score correct responses 1, incorrect responses 0.
- For items requiring two responses, both must be given correctly to receive 1 point.
- Record the total number of points (including all items below the basal) in the "Number Correct" box on the Test Record.
- Do not include sample items in the number correct.
- Enter the number correct in the online scoring program.

Test 3: Verbal Attention

Range:

Core test; raw score range 0–36

Scoring Reminders:

- Score correct responses 1, incorrect responses 0.
- Mispronunciations resulting from articulation errors, dialect variations, or regional speech patterns are not considered errors.
- For items requiring a specific response order, the response must be in the requested order to receive 1 point.
- Record the total number of points (including all items below the basal) in the "Number Correct" box on the Test Record.
- Do not include sample items in the number correct.
- Enter the number correct in the online scoring program.

Test 4: Letter-Pattern Matching

Range:

Core test; raw score range 0–84

Scoring Reminders:

- Score 1 for each correctly identified pair.
- To facilitate scoring, use the scoring-guide overlay provided in the test kit.
- Do not count practice exercises and sample items as points when calculating the total number correct.
- Record the completion time (in minutes and seconds) in the Time section on the Test Record. The time limit is 3 minutes. It is important to record the exact finishing time because the person's calculated scores are affected by finishing early.
- Record the total number of correctly identified pairs in the "Number Correct" box on the Test Record.
- Enter the number correct and the time in the online scoring program.

Test 5: Phonological Processing

Range:

Core test; raw score range A 0–21, B1 0–99, B2 0–99, C 0–15

Scoring Reminders:

- All three subtests must be administered to obtain derived scores.
- Mispronunciations resulting from articulation errors, dialect variations, or regional speech patterns are not considered errors.

Test 5A: Word Access and 5C: Substitution

- Score correct responses 1, incorrect responses 0.
- For each subtest, enter the number of items answered correctly plus 1 point for each item below the basal in the "Number Correct" box on the Test Record.
- Do not include sample items in the number correct.
- Enter the number correct for each subtest in the online scoring program.

Test 5B: Word Fluency

- Use tally marks to record each correct response on the Test Record.
- Duplicate responses do not receive credit.
- Variations of a response do receive credit (e.g., *do, doing, does*).
- Do not count words presented as stimulus examples (e.g., *milk, dog*)
- Record the total number of correct responses in the "Number Correct" box after each item on the Test Record.
- If the total score for an item exceeds 99, enter 99 as the number correct.
- Record the number correct for each *item* in the online scoring program.

Test 6: Story Recall

Range:

Core test; raw score range A 0–10, B 0–14, C 0–16, D 0–31, E 0–36

Scoring Reminders:

- Score correct responses 1, incorrect responses 0.
- Mispronunciations resulting from articulation errors, dialect variations, or regional speech patterns are not considered errors.
- Each story element is based on a keyword set in bold type that must be recalled exactly to receive a 1.
- Synonyms that preserve the meaning of the bold word are scored 1 (e.g., *speak* for *talk*)
- Derivations of or possessive case added to proper names are scored 1 (e.g., *Dougy* or *Doug* or *Rick's* for *Rick*).
- Responses that vary in verb tense or number (e.g., singular/plural) are scored 1 (e.g., *blew* for *blowing* or *star* for *stars*).
- Nonbold words do not need to be recalled or can be recalled as a general concept.

- To ensure accuracy when entering scores into the scoring program, record the total number correct for each set of stories administered or an *X* for unadministered sets in the "Score Entry" box on the Test Record.
- Enter the information from the "Score Entry" box on the Test Record in the online scoring program.

Test 7: Visualization

Range:

Core test; raw score range A 0–24, B 0–24

Scoring Reminders:

- Both subtests must be administered to obtain derived scores.
- Score correct responses 1, incorrect responses 0.
- For Block Rotation, include Items 1 through 5 in calculation of the number correct if testing began with Introduction 3 and Items 1 through 5 were not administered.
- For each subtest, enter the number of items answered correctly in the "Number Correct" box.
- Do not include sample items in the number correct.
- Enter the number correct for each subtest in the online scoring program.

Test 8: General Information

Range:

Standard Battery test; raw score range A 0–22, B 0–22

Scoring Reminders:

- Both subtests must be administered to obtain derived scores.
- Score correct responses 1, incorrect responses 0.
- Mispronunciations resulting from articulation errors, dialect variations, or regional speech patterns are not considered errors.
- For each subtest, enter the number of items answered correctly plus 1 point for each item below the basal in the "Number Correct" box.
- Enter the number correct for each subtest in the online scoring program.

Test 9: Concept Formation

Range:

Standard Battery test; raw score range A 0–5, B 0–11, C 0–20, D 0–29, E 0–40

Scoring Reminders:

- Score correct responses 1, incorrect responses 0.
- If an examinee provides a synonym for a word supplied in the scoring key (e.g., *small* for *little*), the item is considered correct and scored 1.
- If the first five items were not administered, consider all five items correct when calculating the score.
- Record the cumulative total number correct for the set of items in the corresponding cutoff box provided on the Test Record.
- To ensure accuracy when entering scores into the scoring program, record the total number correct and the letter corresponding to the block of items administered in the "Score Entry" box on the Test Record.
- Enter the information from the "Score Entry" box on the Test Record in the online scoring program.

Test 10: Numbers Reversed

Range:

Standard Battery test; raw score range 0–34

Scoring Reminders:

- Score correct responses 1, incorrect responses 0.
- All items below the basal are considered correct and are included in the total number correct.
- Do not include sample items in the number correct.
- Record the total number correct in the "Number Correct" box on the Test Record.
- Enter the number correct in the online scoring program.

Test 11: Number-Pattern Matching

Range:

Extended Battery test; raw score range 0–90

Scoring Reminders:

- Score 1 for each correctly identified pair.
- Transposed numbers (e.g., 17 and 71) are errors.
- To facilitate scoring, use the scoring-guide overlay provided in the test kit.
- Do not count practice exercises and sample items as points when calculating the total number correct.

- Record the completion time (in minutes and seconds) in the Time section on the Test Record. The time limit is 3 minutes. It is important to record the exact finishing time because the person's calculated scores are affected by finishing early.
- Record the total number of correctly identified pairs in the "Number Correct" box on the Test Record.
- Enter the number correct and the time in the online scoring program.

Test 12: Nonword Repetition

Range:

Extended Battery test; raw score range 0–46

Scoring Reminders:

- Score correct responses 1, incorrect responses 0.
- Mispronunciations resulting from articulation errors, dialect variations, or regional speech patterns are not considered errors.
- Emphasis placed on syllables differently from the audio recording are not errors.
- Words must be pronounced smoothly to be scored correct.
- Do not include sample items in the number correct
- Record the total number of points (including all items below the basal) in the "Number Correct" box on the Test Record.
- Enter the number correct in the online scoring program.

Test 13: Visual-Auditory Learning

Range:

Extended Battery test; raw score range A 0–6, B 0–12, C 0–40, D 0–81, E 0–109

Scoring Reminders:

- Score is based on the number of errors the examinee makes.
- Circle each word the examinee misses or is told after a 5-second pause.
- Synonyms are errors.
- Score omitted words, inserted words, and synonyms as errors.
- For words with two symbols (e.g., *ride … ing*), each symbol is considered separately in scoring. If one part of a two-symbol word is incorrect, score only the incorrect part as an error.

- Record the total number of errors at each cutoff point in the box provided on the Test Record.
- To ensure accuracy when entering scores into the scoring program, enter the number of errors and the letter corresponding to the set of Test Stories administered in the "Score Entry" box on the Test Record.
- Enter the information from the "Score Entry" box on the Test Record in the online scoring program.

Test 14: Picture Recognition

Range:

Extended Battery Test; raw score range 0–24

Scoring Reminders:

- Score correctly identified pictures 1.
- Pictures do not have to be identified in the same order as they appear on the stimulus page in the Test Book.
- If the examinee names more than the requested number of pictures, score only the last pictures identified (e.g., if three pictures must be identified and the examinee names four, score the last three responses given by the examinee).
- Do not include sample items in the number correct.
- Record the total number of points (including all items below the basal) in the "Number Correct" box on the Test Record.
- Enter the number correct in the online scoring program.

Test 15: Analysis-Synthesis

Range:

Extended Battery test; raw score range A 0–7, B 0–19, C 0–25, D 0–31, E 0–35

Scoring Reminders:

- Score correct responses 1, incorrect responses 0.
- Do not administer the test to an examinee who cannot be trained on the Color Pretest due to color discrimination or identification difficulties.
- Record the total number correct for the items administered in the corresponding cutoff box provided on the Test Record. Each cutoff is based on a cumulative total (i.e., 1–7, 1–19, 1–22, 1–31, or 1–35).
- Do not include points for pretest, introductory, or sample items when calculating the total number correct.

- To ensure accuracy when entering scores into the scoring program, enter the number correct and the letter corresponding to the items administered in the "Score Entry" box on the Test Record.
- Enter the information from the "Score Entry" box on the Test Record in the online scoring program.

Test 16: Object-Number Sequencing

Range:

Extended Battery test; raw score range 0–31

Scoring Reminders:

- Score correct responses 1, incorrect responses 0.
- Mispronunciations resulting from articulation errors, dialect variations, or regional speech patterns are not considered errors.
- Very similar-sounding responses (e.g., *cap* for *cat*) or rhyming responses (e.g., *pear* for *bear*) are considered correct.
- Do not include sample items in the number correct.
- Record the total number of points (including all items below the basal) in the "Number Correct" box on the Test Record.
- Enter the number correct in the online scoring program.

Test 17: Pair Cancellation

Range:

Extended Battery test; raw score range 0–133

Scoring Reminders:

- Score 1 for correctly identified pairs.
- Use the Pair Cancellation scoring-guide overlay to score this test.
- The circled pair must consist of a ball followed by a dog in the same row to receive credit.
- A correctly circled ball–dog pair that includes part of an adjacent figure is considered a correct response. However, if the other figure is included in its entirety, consider the response incorrect.
- A partially circled pair that does not include all of the dog or all of the ball is considered correct, as long as the intent is clear.
- A circle around a correctly chosen pair that overlaps with another circle is correct.
- Ignore responses in which an examinee circles a ball at the end of one row with a dog at the beginning of another row.

- If an examinee crosses out a correctly circled pair, consider the item incorrect.
- Do not include points for sample or practice items when calculating the total number correct.
- Record the total completion time, in minutes and seconds, in the Time section of the Test Record. There is a 3-minute time limit for this test. It is important to record the exact finishing time because the person's calculated scores are affected by finishing early.
- Record the total number of correctly circled pairs that were identified within the 3-minute time limit in the "Number Correct" box on the Test Record.
- Enter the number correct and the time in the online scoring program.

Test 18: Memory for Words

Range:

Extended Battery test; raw score range 0–26

Scoring Reminders:

- Score correct responses 1, incorrect responses 0.
- Examinees must repeat words in the exact order presented to receive credit.
- Very similar-sounding responses (e.g., *sheep* for *sleep*) or rhyming responses (e.g., *take* for *make*) are considered correct if stated in the correct sequence.
- Mispronunciations resulting from articulation errors, dialect variations, or regional speech patterns are not considered errors.
- Record the total number of points (including all items below the basal) in the "Number Correct" box on the Test Record.
- Enter the number correct in the online scoring program.

OBTAINING DERIVED SCORES

The remainder of the scoring procedure (obtaining derived scores) is completed using either the online scoring and reporting program or the WIIIP. Several options are available for creating these types of WJ IV COG reports:

- Score Report
- Comprehensive Report
- Profile Report
- Parent Report
- Examinee Data Record
- Roster Report

Score Report

The Score Report provides identifying examinee information, a list of the WJ IV tests administered and included in the report, the customizable Table of Scores, and Test Session Observations if included.

Comprehensive Report

The Comprehensive Report is available only with the WIIIP. This report includes identifying examinee information, a list of the WJ IV tests administered and included in the report, a narrative description of the Test Session Observations if included, an interpretive overview of the scores, instructional recommendations and interventions if included, and the Table of Scores.

Profile Report

There are two reports available with the Profile Report option: the Age/Grade Profile Report and the Standard Score/Percentile Rank Profile Report.

Age/Grade Profile Report. The Age/Grade Profile Report provides a graphic display of the individual's level of development by displaying the developmental zone (easy to difficult range) for each test and cluster administered. This profile may provide a meaningful interpretation of test performance in many situations, such as when discussing the educational significance of test results with parents.

Figure 3.2 includes a portion of a sample Age/Grade Profile Report. In this profile, each shaded area represents a zone along a grade developmental scale (if the report is scored by age, it is an age developmental scale). The lower point of the scale is the point at which the individual will find tasks easy (RPI = 96/90); the upper point of the scale represents the point at which the individual will find tasks difficult (RPI = 75/90).

Each shaded band is 20 *W* units wide—10 *W* points below and 10 *W* points above the obtained *W* score. However, the graphic display of the zones may vary in width. The variability is because a wide band reflects an ability that typically has a slow rate of change over time, and a narrow band reflects an ability that typically changes rapidly over time.

Standard Score/Percentile Rank Profile Report. The Standard Score/Percentile Rank Profile Report provides a graphic display of the individual's +/−1 standard error of measurement (SEM) confidence band surrounding each cluster and test standard score (SS) and percentile rank (PR). Figure 3.3 includes a portion of a sample Standard Score/Percentile Rank Profile Report. This profile

Profile Report

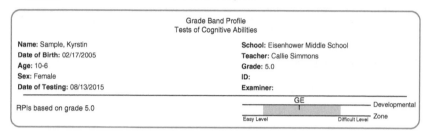

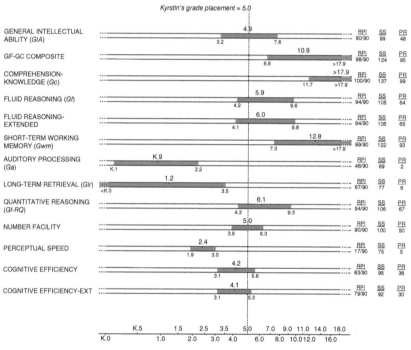

Figure 3.2 Portion of an Age/Grade Profile Report from the online scoring and reporting program

Profile Report

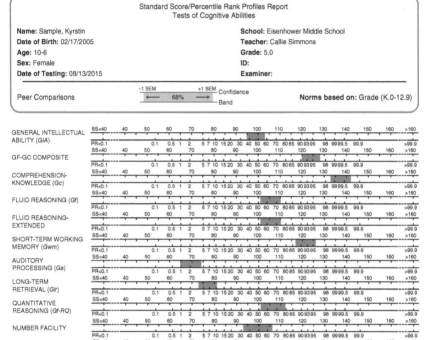

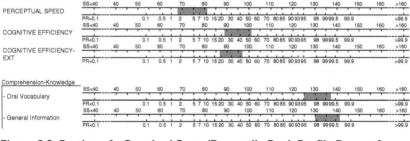

Figure 3.3 Portion of a Standard Score/Percentile Rank Profile Report from the online scoring and reporting program

allows you to visually examine bands of test scores to evaluate any differences among the tests or clusters included in the report. When comparing a single pair of tests or clusters, use the following guidelines for determining if any difference between the tests or clusters is significantly different:

1. If the confidence bands for the two tests or clusters overlap at all, assume that no difference exists between the two abilities.
2. If a separation exists between the ends of the two test or cluster bands that is less than the width of the wider of the two bands, assume that a possible difference exists between the two abilities.
3. If a separation exists between the ends of the two test or cluster bands that is greater than the width of the widest band, assume a difference does exist between the two abilities. However, note that if multiple comparisons are being made, the probability will increase that a difference of this size will be observed with greater frequency than if only a single pair of test scores are compared.

Parent Report

The Parent Report includes a brief description of the tests or clusters administered and a profile of the examinee's proficiency in the tests and clusters assessed based on group standing (percentile rank). This report is available in either English or Spanish.

Examinee Data Record

The Examinee Data Record report lists the raw scores and other information entered for the examinee. This report is useful to keep with the examinee's record.

Roster Report

The Roster Report is useful for reviewing a group of examinees (e.g., across a school district). You can view a customizable list of scores for a selected group of examinees and defined by demographic or subgroup.

CREATING A COMPREHENSIVE REPORT USING THE WIIIP

This section describes the steps involved in using the online WIIIP to create a Comprehensive Report with instructional interventions and interpretive overview. An example Comprehensive Report generated by the WIIIP is shown in Figure 3.31.

Step 1: Creating or Selecting a Caseload Folder

Each version of the scoring program uses caseload folders to organize and save cases (examinee records). After logging into the online scoring and reporting program or WIIIP, locate your caseload folder in the **Caseload Folders** section of the Dashboard or create a caseload folder (see Figure 3.4). To create a new caseload folder, select **Add Folder** at the top of the **Caseload Folders** section of the Dashboard. Type the name of the folder, and click *Save*. If you have already created a caseload folder, select the folder where the information will be saved by clicking the name of the folder. The folder will open, and the name of the folder will appear below the heading in the **My Recent Examinees** section of the Dashboard.

Step 2: Adding an Examinee

After selecting your caseload folder, to enter data for a new examinee click **Add Examinee** at the top of the **My Recent Examinees** section of the Dashboard to add a new person to the folder (see Figure 3.5).

The program automatically opens the **Add Examinee Information** page in the Administration tab (see Figure 3.6). Much of the information on this page is located on the first page of the Test Record, including the examinee's last name, first name, sex/gender, and date of birth. The other information on this page is located elsewhere in the examinee's student record. An asterisk denotes required fields (i.e., Last Name, First Name, Gender, Date of Birth, and Caseload Folder). Once you have entered all pertinent information, click *Save* or *Save and Add Another* at the bottom right of the screen. After saving the examinee, you can edit the examinee information, move the examinee to another caseload folder, share the examinee with another examiner or administrator, or add Test Records and Checklists information.

Step 3: Selecting Test Records for Data Entry

Once you have added an examinee, you are ready to select the data entry pages that correspond with the various WJ IV Test Records. To enter data, click the *Add* icon (see Figure 3.7) in the **Test Record/Checklist** column corresponding with the person's name in the **My Recent Examinees** section of the Dashboard. The program opens the **Select a Test Record/Checklist** list.

Alternatively, you can click the person's name in the **My Recent Examinees** section of the Dashboard or search for the examinee name using the Search/Edit function under **Manage Examinees** in the Administration tab. After locating the examinee and clicking his or her name, the examinee's identifying information

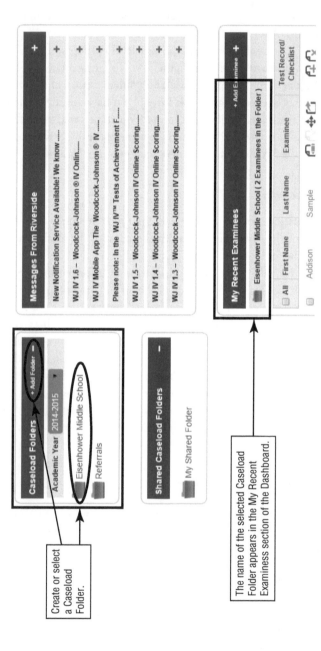

Figure 3.4 Caseload Folder section of Dashboard from the online scoring and reporting program

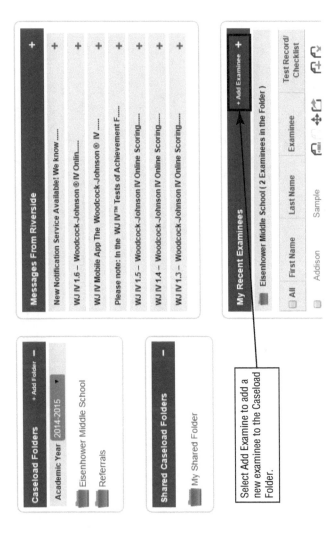

Figure 3.5 Add Examinee option at the top of My Recent Examinees section of the Dashboard from the online scoring and reporting program

From *Woodcock-Johnson IV™* (WJ IV™) Copyright © The Riverside Publishing Company. All rights reserved. Used by permission of the publisher. No part of this work may be reproduced or transmitted in any form or by any means, electronic or mechanical, including photocopying and recording or by any information storage or retrieval system without the proper written permission of The Riverside Publishing Company unless such copying is expressly permitted by federal copyright law. Address inquiries to: https://customercare.hmhco.com/contactus/Permissions.html

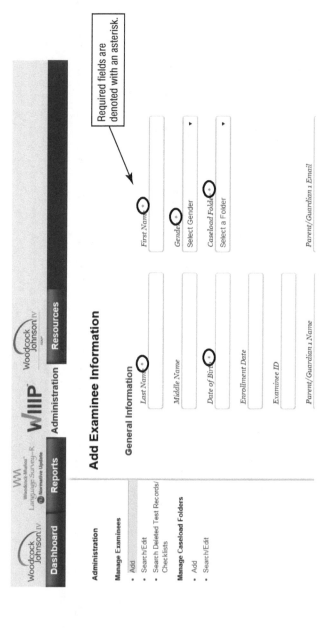

Figure 3.6 Add Examinee Information page from the online scoring and reporting program

From *Woodcock-Johnson IV*™ (WJ IV™) Copyright © The Riverside Publishing Company. All rights reserved. Used by permission of the publisher: No part of this work may be reproduced or transmitted in any form or by any means, electronic or mechanical, including photocopying and recording or by any information storage or retrieval system without the proper written permission of The Riverside Publishing Company unless such copying is expressly permitted by federal copyright law. Address inquiries to: https://customercare.hmhco.com/contactus/Permissions.html

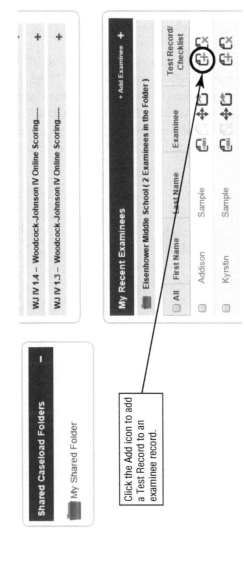

Figure 3.7 Click the *Add* icon to add a Test Record to an examinee record from the online scoring and reporting program

From Woodcock-Johnson IV™ (WJ IV™) Copyright © The Riverside Publishing Company. All rights reserved. Used by permission of the publisher:

105

appears at the top of the screen and the Test Records/Checklists for that person appear below that. To add Test Records and Checklists information, click *Add* located at the bottom right of the screen.

From the drop-down menu, select the appropriate Test Record(s) to add to the examinee record by clicking the box next to the test record name (see Figure 3.8); in this case, select WJ IV Tests of Cognitive Abilities. The data entry page opens for that test record (see Figure 3.9).

After opening a Test Record, the page corresponding to the selected Test Record opens and is made available for data entry. Note that some examinee-identifying information appears at the top of the screen based on the information entered when adding an examinee. Using the completed Test Record (paper copy) for your examinee, enter the remaining identifying information, including information about the examinee's school, teacher, and examiner.

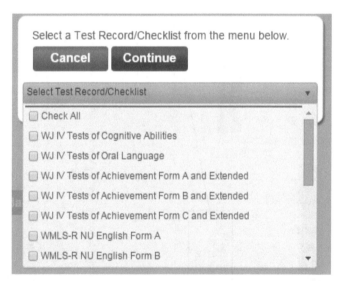

Figure 3.8 Selecting a Test Record menu from the online scoring and reporting program

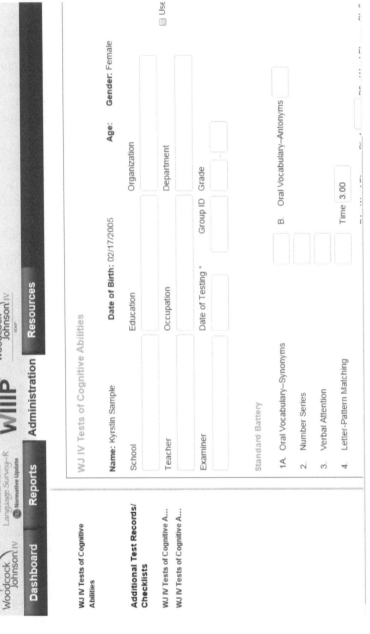

Figure 3.9 The WJ IV COG Test Record page from the online scoring and reporting program

At a minimum, you must enter the date of testing and at least one test score to generate a report. If you want to use grade norms to score the tests, you must also enter the person's grade.

From the paper Test Record, enter the raw score for each test administered. Notice when you click a cell to enter data, a status bar appears below the heading identifying the Standard Battery; this bar provides information about the valid raw score range for each test. Certain tests require additional information or a special data entry procedure. For example, you must enter the time for Letter-Pattern Matching, Number-Pattern Matching, and Pair Cancellation if it is anything other than 3 minutes and 0 seconds.

> For *Oral Vocabulary, Phonological Processing, Visualization, and General Information*, enter the raw score for each subtest or part of the test.
> For *Story Recall*, you must enter the number of points for each set of stories. If a set of stories was not administered, enter an *X*.
> For *Concept Formation, Visual-Auditory Learning, and Analysis-Syntheses*, you must also enter a letter designating the point at which testing ended based on the cutoff criteria.

Be sure to enter the information from the "Test Session Observations Checklist" and the two questions at the bottom of the front cover of each Test Record. Responses to the "Test Session Observations Checklist" and these questions provide important information when evaluating an individual's test scores.

DON'T FORGET

There are two questions on the front page of each Test Record that should be answered: "Do you have any reason to believe this testing session may not represent a fair sample of the examinee's abilities?" and "Were any modifications made to the standardized test procedures during this administration?"

If you have some reason for questioning the test results, click *Yes* to the first question and provide an explanation in the space provided. Possible reasons for questioning validity include (a) hearing or vision difficulties, (b) behavioral or attention difficulties that interfere with the examinee's ability to concentrate, and (c) certain background variables (e.g., English proficiency). Record any unusual test behaviors or answers observed during testing. Qualitative information of this nature can become significant during the analysis of test results.

If you did not follow the standardized test procedures exactly as prescribed in the examiner's manuals or in this book or if you did not use the exact wording provided on the examiner's page in the test book easel, you must click *Yes* in response to the second question and provide a description of the modifications that were made. Be sure to enter this information in the online scoring and reporting program. A response to either question may call into question the validity of the test results.

When finished entering all information from the Test Record, click *Save* on the bottom right of the screen to save the Test Record and review your entries. Before you are allowed to generate a report, you must first click *Commit Test Record* located below *Save* (see Figure 3.10). Subject data may be edited for up to 90 days after committing a test record (see Figure 3.11).

Step 4: Change or Review Report Options

Prior to generating a report, review the default report options to determine if you would like to make any changes before creating the report. To review the report options, click the **Reports** button at the top of the screen and select **Report Options** (see Figure 3.12). This selection opens the **Report Options** window.

The **Report Options** page contains scoring options, the option to use the examinee's ID instead of last name, and the option to include signatures in the report (see Figure 3.13). Changes made to these options affect all reports you create with the exception of the confidence band option, which does not affect the Standard Score/Percentile Rank Profile Report that is always based on the 68% confidence band.

Scoring Options. The scoring options allow you to select a cutoff to determine the significance of a variation or a discrepancy and determine the standard score (or percentile rank) confidence band that is displayed in the Table of Scores.

Discrepancy Cutoff. To determine if a target score that is included in the intra-cognitive variation procedures or the ability/achievement comparison procedures is significantly different from a criterion score, the significance level must be determined. You can either select the significance level from a drop-down list box or enter a specific standard deviation (*SD*) value.

The standard deviation selections in the WJ IV online scoring and reporting program and WIIIP utilize the standard error of the estimate (SEE). The SEE is the standard deviation of the discrepancy score distribution (Pedhazur, 1997) observed for subjects in the WJ IV norming sample. Discrepancy scores for norming subjects are the residuals from the linear-regression model that predict

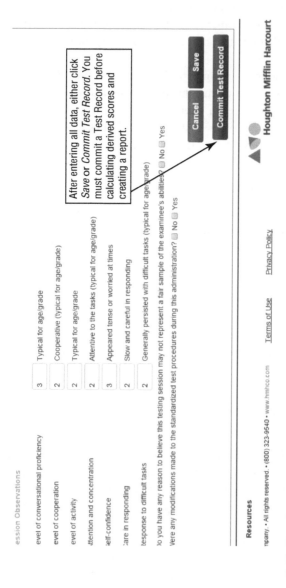

Session Observations

Level of conversational proficiency	3	Typical for age/grade
Level of cooperation	2	Cooperative (typical for age/grade)
Level of activity	2	Typical for age/grade
Attention and concentration	2	Attentive to the tasks (typical for age/grade)
Self-confidence	3	Appeared tense or worried at times
Care in responding	2	Slow and careful in responding
Response to difficult tasks	2	Generally persisted with difficult tasks (typical for age/grade)

Do you have any reason to believe this testing session may not represent a fair sample of the examinee's abilities? ☐ No ☐ Yes

Were any modifications made to the standardized test procedures during this administration? ☐ No ☐ Yes

After entering all data, either click *Save* or *Commit Test Record*. You must commit a Test Record before calculating derived scores and creating a report.

Cancel   **Save**

Commit Test Record

Houghton Mifflin Harcourt

Resources

Company. • All rights reserved. • (800) 323-9540 • www.hmhco.com   Terms of Use   Privacy Policy

Figure 3.10 The Commit Test Record button in the online scoring and reporting program

From *Woodcock-Johnson IV*™ (WJ IV™) Copyright © The Riverside Publishing Company. All rights reserved. Used by permission of the publisher. No part of this work may be reproduced or transmitted in any form or by any means, electronic or mechanical, including photocopying and recording or by any information storage or retrieval system without the proper written permission of The Riverside Publishing Company unless such copying is expressly permitted by federal copyright law. Address inquiries to: https://customercare.hmhco.com/contactus/Permissions.html

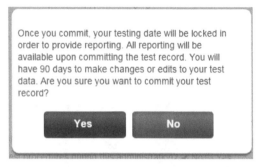

Figure 3.11 Onscreen message after committing a Test Record in the online scoring and reporting program indicating that you have 90 days to make changes or edit examinee data

From *Woodcock-Johnson IV*™ (WJ IV™) Copyright © The Riverside Publishing Company. All rights reserved. Used by permission of the publisher. No part of this work may be reproduced or transmitted in any form or by any means, electronic or mechanical, including photocopying and recording or by any information storage or retrieval system without the proper written permission of The Riverside Publishing Company unless such copying is expressly permitted by federal copyright law. Address inquiries to: https://customercare.hmhco.com/contactus/Permissions.html

a subject's standard score on a particular task (test or cluster) using the subject's age (or grade) and standard scores on one or more other tasks. The default for the program is set at 1.5 SEE. You can change the criterion for significance; the SEE ranges from 1.0 SEE to 2.3 SEE.

CAUTION

Discrepancy Cutoff Selection

If you select a smaller SEE cutoff for determining a significant discrepancy, you will identify a greater percentage of the population as having a significant discrepancy.

Conversely, if you select a larger SEE cutoff for determining a significant discrepancy, you will identify a smaller percentage of the population as having a significant discrepancy.

Selection of the SEE level for determining a significant discrepancy typically is made with reference to state or professional guidelines.

Confidence Band Selection.   Standard scores and percentile ranks are reported in the Table of Scores as a point score and an associated range of scores that reflects the range in which the examinee's true score probably falls.

Figure 3.12 Report button and Report Options submenu from the online scoring and reporting program

From *Woodcock-Johnson IV*™ (WJ IV™) Copyright © The Riverside Publishing Company. All rights reserved. Used by permission of the publisher. No part of this work may be reproduced or transmitted in any form or by any means, electronic or mechanical, including photocopying and recording or by any information storage or retrieval system without the proper written permission of The Riverside Publishing Company unless such copying is expressly permitted by federal copyright law. Address inquiries to: https://customercare.hmhco.com/contactus/Permissions.html

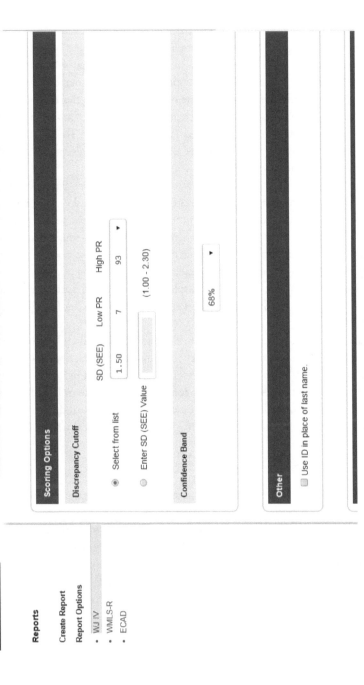

Figure 3.13 Report Options page from the online scoring and reporting program

The default for the program is set at the 68% confidence band. This band extends from a point representing 1 SEM below the examinee's obtained score to a point representing 1 SEM above the obtained score. At the 68% level of confidence, one out of three times the examinee's true score may fall outside of this band, although it is likely to be rather close. You may change this value to 90% or 95% by clicking the drop-down menu for **Confidence Band.**

For example, the 95% confidence band represents the range of scores in which an examinee's true score would be included 19 times out of 20. The 95% confidence band extends from 2 SEM below the examinee's obtained score to 2 SEM above the obtained score.

The selection of a more stringent (90% or 95%) confidence band will not increase the precision of measurement; the choice of the 90% or 95% confidence band increases the likelihood that the examinee's true score is represented within the range of scores. This may be important to consider in high-stakes decisions, such as when making a diagnosis of intellectual disability. Please note, however, that a selection of the 90% or 95% confidence band for reporting purposes in the Table of Scores will not affect the visual display of the standard score/percentile rank bands utilized in the Standard Score/Percentile Rank Profiles (SS/PR Profiles) Report.

The visual display provided on the SS/PR Profiles Report always is based on the 68% confidence band. The purpose of the visual displays on the SS/PR Profiles Report is to allow you to evaluate differences in an examinee's performance on the tests that were administered. If a wider confidence band were utilized for this purpose, few possible or real differences would be identified. (Real differences of a practical nature may be overlooked due to an artificial statistical stringency.)

Step 5: Selecting a Report Type

After you have committed a Test Record, you can elect to create a number of different reports, as described earlier in this chapter.

To create a report, move the cursor over the **Reports** button at the top of the screen and select **Create Report** from the submenu (see Figure 3.14). The Create Report page appears with a drop-down list of reports from which you can select. The report type you select determines the remaining report criteria selections. The remainder of this section describes the options available when selecting the Comprehensive Report.

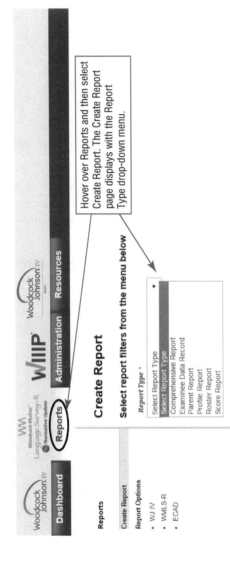

Figure 3.14 Create Report page displays after selecting the Reports button and Create Report from the submenu in the WIIIP

Step 6: Selecting Criteria to Create a Comprehensive Report

All fields with an asterisk are required to generate a Comprehensive Report. These fields include:

- Report Type
- Product
- Examinee Selection
- Test Record/Checklist
- Normative Basis
- Grouping Option
- Output Format

All other fields are optional, and if they are not changed the program will use the default settings.

Product. The product list includes whatever products are available to you. The Comprehensive Report is available only to users who have access to the WIIIP (see Figure 3.15). This is a required field, so you must make a selection to generate a report.

Examinee Selection. In this box, select the folder where you stored the examinee data for the report you are creating (see Figure 3.16). If the name does not

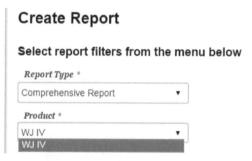

Figure 3.15 Product list scoring criteria option from the WIIIP

Figure 3.16 Examinee Selection scoring criteria option from the WIIIP

appear in the folder, you have not committed the Test Record. This is a required field, so you must make a selection to create a report. Once you have made your selection, click *Close* at the bottom of the box to save your selection.

Test Record/Checklist. All test record data that has been entered for the examinee will appear in the **Test Record/Checklist** box (see Figure 3.17). Select the test record(s) you want to include in the report. You can easily choose or clear the selection of any Test Record by clicking the circle next to the Test Record name. This is a required field, so you must make a selection to create a report. After verifying that you have selected the appropriate Test Records, click *Close* at the bottom of the box to save your choices.

Normative Basis. The next option presents the normative basis for calculating scores (see Figure 3.18). This is a required field, so you must make a selection to generate a report. There are four options:

Age norms. This option calculates all derived scores based on a comparison to other individuals of the same age.

Grade norms. This option calculates all derived scores based on a comparison to other individuals of the same grade (grade placement must have been entered in all selected Test Records for this option to appear).

Figure 3.17 Test Record/Checklist scoring criteria option from the WIIP

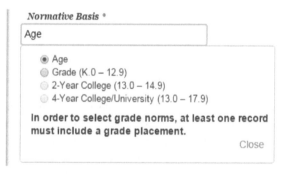

Figure 3.18 Normative Basis scoring criteria options from the WIIP

2-year college norms. This option is a variant of grade norms and is intended for use with students in 2-year community or technical colleges (a grade placement of 13.0–14.9 must be entered for all selected Test Records for this option to appear).

4-year college norms. This option is a variant of grade norms intended for use with students in 4-year colleges or universities, including graduate school (a grade placement of 13.0–17.9 must be entered for all selected Test Records for this option to appear).

Options. The Options section contains several optional clusters that you may elect to include. Figure 3.19 shows the default program selections. Select or deselect a cluster by clicking the box to add or remove the check mark, and then click *Close* to save your selection for that report.

Not all examiners use an overall or composite score, and some professionals do not believe that general intellectual ability (GIA) is a useful construct. Because the GIA may be included by default, uncheck the appropriate box if you choose not to include it.

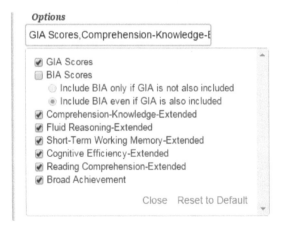

Figure 3.19 Optional cluster selection scoring criteria options from the WIIIP

From *Woodcock-Johnson IV* (WJ IV™) Copyright © The Riverside Publishing Company. All rights reserved. Used by permission of the publisher. No part of this work may be reproduced or transmitted in any form or by any means, electronic or mechanical, including photocopying and recording or by any information storage or retrieval system without the proper written permission of The Riverside Publishing Company unless such copying is expressly permitted by federal copyright law. Address inquiries to: https://customercare.hmhco.com/contactus/Permissions.html

If you make a selection in this section of criteria and the corresponding test data were not included, the section will not appear in the report. For example, Tests 1 through 7 must be administered to obtain a GIA score.

DON'T FORGET

Remember to deselect the GIA or BIA Scores in the Options section if you do not want them included in the Table of Scores and the WIIIP narrative overview.

Variations. The Variations section contains several optional intra-ability variation procedures that you may elect to include in the report (see Figure 3.20). The program automatically selects all options and includes the appropriate variations in the report based on the actual tests administered. Deselect a procedure by clicking the box to remove the check mark, and then click *Close* to save your selection for that report.

The WJ IV COG variation procedures are based on the practice of examining test performance to determine patterns of relative strengths and weaknesses.

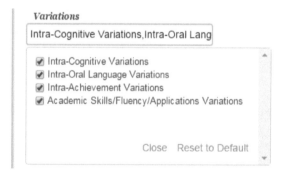

Figure 3.20 Variations scoring criteria options from the WIIIP

Because of the breadth of cognitive abilities covered, the WJ IV is well suited for this practice. This type of examination of test performance is recommended frequently, as suggested by the next quotation from the *Standards for Educational and Psychological Testing* (American Educational Research Association, American Psychological Association, & National Council on Measurement in Education, 2014):

> The interpretation of results from a cognitive ability test is guided by the theoretical constructs used to develop the tests. Some cognitive ability assessments are based on results from multidimensional test batteries that are designed to assess a broad range of skills and abilities. Test results are used to draw inferences about a person's overall level of intellectual functioning and about strengths and weaknesses in various cognitive abilities, and to diagnose cognitive disorders. (p. 156)

These variation procedures are bidirectional comparisons. This means that, when making these comparisons, there is equal interest in an individual's strengths and weaknesses. Each ability in the procedure is compared to the average of all of the other abilities in the comparison. The intra-cognitive procedure is based on WJ IV COG Tests 1 through 7. The examinee's average performance on six of the seven tests is used to predict the score for the other, remaining test. The predicted score is then compared to the obtained score to determine if there is a strength or weakness. If additional tests and clusters are administered, they also can be included in the procedure and will be compared to six of the first seven tests.

The intra-cognitive variation procedures can help an evaluator determine and document both strengths and weaknesses in cognitive abilities as well as define how these abilities are related to an individual's learning difficulties (Mather & Wendling, 2014). For example, a reading problem may be related to a cognitive weakness (such as poor phonological awareness or poor memory). The intra-cognitive variation procedure is most appropriate when the purposes of the evaluation are to determine why a student has an academic difficulty.

For additional information regarding intra-oral language, intra-achievement, and academic skills/fluency/applications variation procedures, see Mather and Wendling (2015).

Comparisons. The Comparisons section presents the comparison procedures that may be included in the report. Although most of these five comparison calculations involve analysis between batteries (WJ IV COG, WJ IV OL, and

WJ IV ACH), one of the discrepancy procedures—*Gf-Gc* Composite/Other Ability—can be utilized within the WJ IV COG battery alone. Figure 3.21 shows the various comparison procedures.

Comparison and discrepancy scores obtained from the WJ IV are actual discrepancies, not estimated discrepancies, because the WJ IV allows for direct comparisons of actual scores between measures. Using the WJ IV COG, WJ IV OL, and WJ IV ACH, ability/achievement comparison calculations can be made with greater accuracy and validity than would be possible by comparing scores from separately normed instruments. The WJ IV comparison and discrepancy procedures are psychometrically preferable to estimated discrepancies for at least two important reasons. First, the WJ IV comparisons and discrepancies do not contain the errors associated with estimated discrepancies (estimated discrepancy procedures do not control for unknown differences that exist when using two tests based on different norming samples). Second, the discrepancy procedures used by the online scoring and reporting program or WIIIP incorporate specific regression coefficients between all predictor and criterion variables at each age level to provide the best estimates of the population characteristics.

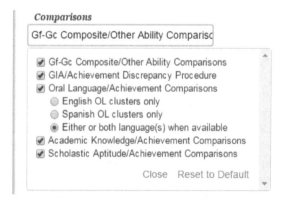

Figure 3.21 Comparisons scoring criteria options from the WIIIP

Gf-Gc Composite/Other Ability Comparisons. For some purposes, such as selective testing or determination of cognitive processing deficits, evaluators may wish to determine whether a discrepancy exists between an individual's *Gf-Gc* Composite score and one or a few WJ IV COG cluster scores. As with the other WJ IV comparison procedures, a correction for regression to the mean is implicit and the SEE is used to evaluate the statistical significance of any resulting *Gf-Gc* Composite/other ability comparison score.

The WJ IV COG clusters that can be evaluated against the *Gf-Gc* Composite score are: Short-Term Working Memory (*Gwm*), Short-Term Working Memory—Extended, Cognitive Processing Speed (*Gs*), Auditory Processing (*Ga*), Long-Term Retrieval (*Glr*), Visual Processing (*Gv*), Number Facility, Perceptual Speed, Cognitive Efficiency, and Cognitive Efficiency—Extended.

Comparison can also be made between *Gf-Gc* Composite and oral language abilities and achievement clusters when those tests are administered (see Schrank, McGrew, & Mather, 2015a, or the Appendix of this book for more information).

General Intellectual Ability/Achievement Comparisons. An intellectual ability/achievement comparison procedure is available using the GIA score (WJ IV COG tests 1 through 7) as the predictor across several WJ IV OL clusters and various achievement domains measured by the WJ IV ACH.

This procedure is intended to be used for certain diagnostic comparisons, such as documenting the presence and/or severity of a discrepancy between a full-scale intellectual ability score and any area of achievement or oral language, as part of the process for the determination of a specific learning disability. The procedure is more precise, however, than using a discrepancy score comparison table, such as is frequently suggested by many state departments of education.

Oral Language Ability/Achievement Comparisons. The oral language ability/achievement comparison procedure pertains to oral language and achievement scores obtained from the WJ IV OL and WJ IV ACH. It is an alternative ability/achievement discrepancy procedure often used in evaluation of a reading disability. Further details on this procedure can be obtained by consulting Mather and Wendling (2015).

Academic Knowledge/Achievement Comparisons. The academic knowledge/achievement comparison procedure is the only ability/achievement comparison available solely within the WJ IV ACH. It is another alternative ability/achievement discrepancy procedure. Because Academic Knowledge is a strong measure of acquired knowledge that does not require reading, writing, or math, it serves as a good ability measure to predict academic ability. Please consult Mather and Wendling (2015) for more information about this procedure.

Scholastic Aptitude/Achievement Comparisons. The scholastic aptitude/ achievement comparison procedure is used to compare a four-test scholastic aptitude composite score obtained from WJ IV COG to scores from a variety of academic clusters obtained from the WJ IV ACH. The purpose of the procedure is to compare a student's consistency of performance between levels of academic achievement and levels of associated cognitive abilities. In other words, the intent is to determine if the student is performing as well or as poorly as one would expect, given measured levels of associated cognitive abilities.

Students with specific learning disabilities may not exhibit a discrepancy but rather may exhibit consistency between the scholastic aptitude predictor compared to measures of achievement because a weak cognitive ability or abilities is reflected in a lower predicted achievement score. This occurs because the scholastic aptitude scores are highly related to the associated areas of academic achievement. The procedure is intended to determine if the examinee's achievement is consistent with his or her current abilities. In other words, a person with low math aptitude would be expected to have low math skills.

Report Style. The summary statements included in the Comprehensive Report can be based on standard score range descriptors or proficiency (*W* Diff) level descriptors. **Rapid Reference** 3.2 outlines the two alternate methods for constructing the summary narrative.

≡ Rapid Reference 3.2 Two Methods for Summarizing Performance on the WJ IV

Standard Scores

Standard Score Range	Description
131 and above	Very superior
121 to 130	Superior
111 to 120	High average
90 to 110	Average
80 to 89	Low average
70 to 79	Low
69 and below	Very low

Proficiency

W Diff	Description
+31 and above	Very advanced
+14 to +30	Advanced
+7 to +13	Average to advanced
−6 to +6	Average
−13 to −7	Limited to average
−30 to −14	Limited
−50 to −31	Very limited
−51 and below	Extremely limited

This is an important selection to make because your choice of method determines how an individual's performance is described. The two methods use similar or, in some cases, identical terms, but the derivation of the terms is different. For example, use of the term *average* as a descriptor of a standard score category does not necessarily mean the individual's proficiency was "average." It is necessary to understand how the *W* Diff and standard scores convey different levels of information to understand this apparent incongruence.

In the WJ IV, the underlying *W* scale is used for the derivation of the *W* Diff. The *W* scale is an equal-interval scale of measurement (Stevens, 1951)—a mathematical transformation of the Rasch (1960; Wright & Stone, 1979) model of data analysis, based on item response theory. The *W* scale has unique advantages for use in interpreting test results. The *W* Diff is a calculation describing the difference between an individual's test or cluster *W* score and the average *W* score obtained by people in the norm sample at his or her age (or grade). That is, the *W* Diff describes the distance between the individual's performance and the median performance of age or grade peers.

In **Rapid Reference** 3.2, the proficiency labels employ a *relative distance schema* to define proficiency. For example, individuals whose measured performance falls within 6 *W* points (higher or lower) of the median performance of age (or grade) peers are described as having "average" proficiency. Those whose measured performance falls 7 to 13 *W* points below the median performance of peers are described as having "limited to average" proficiency. Similarly, 14 to 30 *W* points above the median is described as "advanced" proficiency.

A standard score is a transformation of the percentile rank. Standard scores and percentile ranks describe relative rank, or ordinal position, in a group, not the relative distance from median performance. An individual's position in a group is based on the *SD* within the range of scores obtained by age or grade peers in the norm sample.

Why is the choice of using standard score ranges or *W* Diff categories so important when describing an individual's performance? The answer may not be immediately obvious, but a common illustration may be helpful. In this example, an individual whose performance falls at the 26th percentile is described as being within the "average" range when using standard score ranges. However, for illustrative purposes, the *W* Diff score for that individual may be 9 *W* points below the median score for age (or grade) peers; this individual's proficiency is described as "limited to average" when using the proficiency selection in the online scoring and reporting program or WIIIP. For many school or educational evaluations, it may be preferable to utilize the terms in the proficiency column. These terms describe low performance in terms of relative limitations.

When using the WJ IV COG, it is important to understand that *W* Diff categories always yield an accurate description of the individual's proficiency on a test or cluster whereas the standard score range categories may not. The purpose of the standard score is to describe relative position in a group only, not to describe proficiency. In test interpretation, interpreting the *W* Diff makes an important contribution to understanding an individual's proficiency with the measured tasks that cannot be obtained when using peer comparison scores (Jaffe, 2009).

In Figure 3.22, also note that you may elect to exclude from the report instructional recommendations and interventions as well as language of instruction statements, or you may include in the report an appendix with detailed interpretive information and brief descriptions of each test and cluster that was administered.

Interventions. When you click the Interventions field, a window opens with a list of all available formative and instructional interventions based on the examinee's test performance. You may preview each intervention and include it in the report by clicking the box next to the intervention database ID (see Figure 3.23). For more information about the formative interventions, which apply to the WJ IV ACH, please see Schrank and Wendling (2015b).

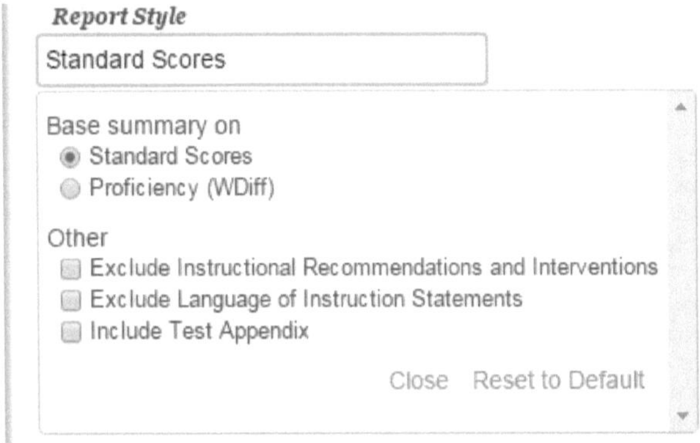

Report Style

Standard Scores

Base summary on
- ⦿ Standard Scores
- ○ Proficiency (WDiff)

Other
- ☐ Exclude Instructional Recommendations and Interventions
- ☐ Exclude Language of Instruction Statements
- ☐ Include Test Appendix

Close   Reset to Default

Figure 3.22 Report Style scoring criteria options from the WIIIP

The evidence-based instructional interventions provided with the WJ IV WIIIP are theoretically linked to broad and narrow CHC abilities and conceptually linked to the underlying cognitive process required for each test. Suggested interventions are generated based on the examinee's level of proficiency (limited, limited to average, or lower) on each test or cluster and are presented in summary form rather than presenting detailed implementation instructions. Generally, it is not appropriate to include every suggested intervention, so careful review of each intervention is recommended.

Score Selection Template. The Table of Scores included in the Score Report and the Comprehensive Report includes the *W* score for all clusters and tests by default. The following additional columns are included in the default settings

AE or GE: This column contains either the age-equivalent or grade-equivalent score for the test or cluster based on the normative basis selected. This score reflects the examinee's performance in terms of the age level or grade level in the norming sample at which the average raw score is the same as the examinee's raw score.

Intervention Selection

Database ID
- GSP-010-CompLim
- Gs04-010-ELSpellPatt
- Gs11-011-SpeedRep
- Ga12-010-IncExpNewW
- Ga12-030-VocalStrat
- Ga12-040-IncTimeRead
- Glr06-050-ActiveL
- Glr13-080-IncMeaning
- Gv07-030-Rehearsal
- Gv07-040-OverLearn
- Gv07-050-OrgStrat

Recommendations for Instruction:

Accommodations that may help compensate for Kyrstin's limitations in perceptual speed might include providing extended time, reducing the quantity of work required (breaking large assignments into two or more component assignments), eliminating or limiting copying activities, and increasing wait times after questions are asked as well as after responses are given.

| Clear Selection | Select All | Save | Cancel |

Figure 3.23 Intervention Selection page from the WIIIP

From *Woodcock-Johnson IV*™ (WJ IV™) Copyright © The Riverside Publishing Company. All rights reserved. Used by permission of the publisher. No part of this work may be reproduced or transmitted in any form or by any means, electronic or mechanical, including photocopying and recording or by any information storage or retrieval system without the proper written permission of The Riverside Publishing Company unless such copying is expressly permitted by federal copyright law. Address inquiries to: https://customercare.hmhco.com/contactus/Permissions.html

RPI: This column contains the Relative Proficiency Index (RPI), a score that provides a comparison of the examinee's performance to the average performance of age or grade peers. An RPI of 90/90 means that the examinee would be predicted to demonstrate 90% proficiency with similar tasks that average individuals in the comparison group (age or grade) would also perform with 90% proficiency. In Figure 3.24, the RPI of 75/90 for Story Recall is interpreted to mean that, when others at the examinee's age or grade show 90% success on similar tasks of constructing propositional

Sample, Kyrstin
August 13, 2015

Comprehensive Report

TABLE OF SCORES
Woodcock-Johnson IV Tests of Cognitive Abilities (Norms based on grade 5.0)

CLUSTER/Test	W	GE	RPI	SS (68% Band)
GEN INTELLECTUAL ABIL	500	4.9	90/90	99 (95-103)
Gf-Gc COMPOSITE	517	10.9	98/90	124 (120-128)
COMP-KNOWLEDGE (*Gc*)	529	>17.9	100/90	137 (133-142)
FLUID REASONING (*Gf*)	504	5.9	94/90	105 (101-110)
FLUID REASONING (Ext)	504	6.0	94/90	106 (101-110)
S-TERM WORK MEM (*Gwm*)	518	12.8	99/90	122 (117-126)
AUDITORY PROCESS (*Ga*)	479	K.9	46/90	69 (65-74)
L-TERM RETRIEVAL (*Glr*)	484	1.2	67/90	77 (73-81)
QUANTITATIVE REASONING	504	6.1	94/90	106 (101-112)
NUMBER FACILITY	498	5.0	90/90	100 (93-106)
PERCEPTUAL SPEED	470	2.4	17/90	75 (68-81)
COGNITIVE EFFICIENCY	499	4.2	83/90	95 (89-101)
COG EFFICIENCY (Ext)	494	4.1	79/90	92 (87-97)
Oral Vocabulary	522	13.0	99/90	131 (125-137)
Number Series	505	6.0	95/90	106 (101-112)
Verbal Attention	509	7.6	96/90	111 (104-117)
Letter-Pattern Matching	471	1.8	10/90	72 (63-80)
Phonological Processing	487	2.0	67/90	81 (75-87)
Story Recall	486	2.1	75/90	84 (77-90)
Visualization	504	9.4	95/90	110 (105-116)
General Information	537	>17.9	100/90	136 (130-141)
Concept Formation	503	5.8	93/90	103 (98-108)
Numbers Reversed	528	15.9	100/90	125 (120-130)
Number-Pattern Matching	469	3.0	27/90	83 (74-91)
Nonword Repetition	471	<K.0	26/90	69 (65-74)
Visual-Auditory Learning	482	K.5	58/90	78 (75-81)
Analysis-Synthesis	504	6.2	94/90	105 (98-111)

VARIATIONS	STANDARD SCORES			DISCREPANCY		Interpretation at
	Actual	Predicted	Difference	PR	SD	+ or - 1.50 SD (SEE)
Intra-Cognitive [Extended] Variations						
COMP-KNOWLEDGE (*Gc*)	137	95	42	>99.9	+3.44	Strength
FLUID REASONING (*Gf*)	105	98	7	74	+0.64	--
FLUID REASONING (Ext)	106	98	8	76	+0.70	--
S-TERM WORK MEM (*Gwm*)	122	98	24	98	+2.00	Strength
AUDITORY PROCESS (*Ga*)	69	102	−33	0.2	−2.85	Weakness
L-TERM RETRIEVAL (*Glr*)	77	101	−24	2	−1.98	Weakness
QUANTITATIVE REASONING	106	98	8	78	+0.76	--
PERCEPTUAL SPEED	75	103	−28	2	2.02-	Weakness
Oral Vocabulary	131	94	37	99.9	+3.09	Strength

Figure 3.24 A portion of the Table of Scores section of a WJ IV COG Comprehensive Report from the WIIIP

representations and recoding, this examinee is predicted to show only 75% success on these types of tasks.

SS (68% Band): This column contains the derived standard score for the cluster or test, based on a mean of 100 and a standard deviation of 15. This column also shows the 68% confidence band for each standard score. (If the confidence band was changed in the Report Options to 90% or 95%, the information reported here will reflect that selection.)

To change the list of scores included in the Table of Scores, select **New Score Selection Template** from the drop-down list in the Score Selection Template section and then select **Add Template** located at the top right of the drop-down list (see Figure 3.25). A new window will open with a list of several additional scores you may elect to include in your reports (see Figure 3.26). Select the scores by clicking the corresponding box (note: there is a limit to the amount of information that can be selected). When all selections are made, type a name for the score template and click *Save.* The new template that you created will appear in the drop-down list. Note that score templates are associated with the type of report, so if you always want to include a particular score regardless of the type of report, you will need to create a template for each report type.

Standard scores (standard score, normal curve equivalent, stanine, *T*, and *z* scores) and percentile ranks both convey information about relative position in a group. Examiners who prefer to display the percentile rank with the

Figure 3.25 New Score Selection Template option in the Score Selection Template scoring criteria option from the WIIIP

Name Your Template

Score Selection Template Name * *(50 character max)*

☐ Percentile Rank w/ Band	☐ Proficiency
☐ Percentile Rank	☐ NCE
☐ CALP	☐ Stanine Score
☑ Age Equivalent (AE)	☐ T Score
☐ Grade Equivalent (GE)	☐ z-score
☑ Relative Proficiency Index	☑ W Score
(RPI)	☐ W Difference
☑ Standard Score w/ Band	☐ Grade Equivalent Band
☐ Standard Score	

Cancel   **Save**

Figure 3.26 Additional scores that may be selected for inclusion in the Table of Scores from the WIIIP

corresponding confidence band, the percentile rank without the band, or one of the alternate standard scores can do so by changing the selection.

Including information about cognitive-academic language proficiency (CALP) levels is also an option. This information is reported in a separate section of the Table of Scores and helps describe the examinee's language proficiency. In the WJ IV COG, the CALP level is reported for the Comprehension-Knowledge (*Gc*) cluster. Additional clusters from the WJ IV OL and WJ IV ACH provide additional CALP-level information.

Selecting the Proficiency option adds a column to the Table of Scores that provides a verbal label corresponding to the individual's obtained *W* Diff score for the cluster or test. (See **Rapid Reference** 3.2 for a list of *W* Diff scores and corresponding labels.)

Selecting the *W* Difference adds a column to the Table of Scores that reports the difference between the person's test or cluster *W* score and the average test or cluster *W* score for the reference group in the norming sample.

Selecting the Age (or Grade) Equivalent Band adds a column labeled EASY to DIFF in the Table of Scores. It contains two age (or grade) scores representing a continuum, or developmental zone, from a lower age (grade) score to a higher age (grade) score. The zone represents a range along a developmental scale that encompasses an examinee's current level of functioning from easy (or independent level) to difficult (or frustration level) on the measured task or ability. At the lower end of the zone, the individual will perceive tasks as easy; at the higher end of the zone, the individual will perceive tasks as difficult.

Figure 3.24 displays a sample Table of Scores from the WIIIP. This sample utilizes the default options for display of certain types of information. (Note that the names of clusters always appear in all capital letters and test names appear in mixed case letters.)

Grouping Options. There are three choices for how the reported scores are grouped within the report (see Figure 3.27). You may list the clusters followed by the tests in numerical order, list the tests under the clusters with any tests not contributing to a cluster listed separately, or list the tests in numerical order under the cluster it applies to, as well as in an additional list of tests only. Grouping Option is a required field, so you must make a selection to generate a report.

Output Format. You may elect to create the report as a PDF file, a web page, or a Word document (see Figure 3.28). This is a required field, so you must make

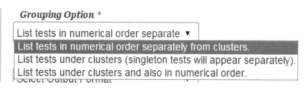

Figure 3.27 Grouping Options scoring criteria from the WIIIP

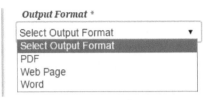

Figure 3.28 Output Format scoring criteria option from the WIIIP

a selection to generate a report. The Word option allows you to customize the report with any relevant additional text.

Step 7: Generating a Report

After you have made your report criteria selections, click either *Save to My Reports* or *Run Report* located at the bottom right of the screen. If you select Save My Report, a dialog box opens requesting a file name (see Figure 3.29).

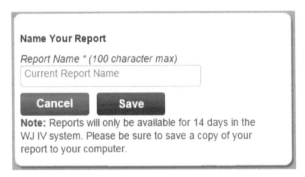

Figure 3.29 Name Your Report dialog box from the WIIIP

Reports are available in the WJ IV system for only 14 days. Within that time-frame you should save a copy of the report to your computer or review it and make changes before running it again. Your saved reports appear in the **My Saved Reports** section of the Dashboard (see Figure 3.30).

If you select Run Report, the report is output as you selected (PDF file, web page, or Word document). After reviewing your report, you may edit the subject information, edit the report if output to Word, and save it to your computer. An example Comprehensive Report generated by the WIIIP is shown in Figure 3.31.

Figure 3.30 My Saved Reports section of the Dashboard from the WIIIP

Comprehensive Report

Name: Sample, Kyrstin
Date of Birth: 02/17/2005
Age: 10 years, 6 months
Sex: Female
Date of Testing: 08/13/2015

School: Eisenhower Middle School
Teacher: Callie Simmons
Grade: 5.0
ID:
Examiners:

TESTS ADMINISTERED

Woodcock-Johnson IV Tests of Cognitive Abilities

TEST SESSION OBSERVATIONS

Observations of Kyrstin's behavior were made during the *Tests of Cognitive Abilities*. Her conversational proficiency seemed typical for her grade level. She was cooperative throughout the examination; her activity level seemed typical for her grade. During the examination, she seemed attentive to the tasks, but at times she appeared tense or worried. She responded slowly and carefully to test questions, generally persisting with difficult tasks.

INTERPRETIVE OVERVIEW OF SCORES

The scores derived from this administration can be interpreted at different levels. Interpretation of Kyrstin's performance can be based upon single tests and/or upon logical-empirical combinations of tests called clusters. Variations within a group of scores are evaluated to determine if any relative strengths and weaknesses exist.

Kyrstin's overall intellectual ability, as measured by the WJ IV General Intellectual Ability cluster, is average when compared to others in her grade. By comparison, a composite index of Kyrstin's fluid reasoning and comprehension-knowledge intellectual abilities is in the advanced range. However, the scores on two of the component tests are significantly different, making it problematic to interpret Kyrstin's Gf-Gc Composite score as a single measure of intellectual level.

Among the WJ IV cognitive measures, Kyrstin's proficiency level is within the very advanced range for one test (General Information); within the advanced range for two clusters (Comprehension-Knowledge and Short-Term Working Memory) and two tests (Oral Vocabulary and Numbers Reversed); and within the average to advanced range for two tests (Verbal Attention and Visualization). Her proficiency is within the average range for five clusters (Fluid Reasoning, Fluid Reasoning 3, Quantitative Reasoning, Number Facility, and Cognitive Efficiency) and three tests (Number Series, Concept Formation, and Analysis-Synthesis). Her proficiency is within the limited to average range for one cluster (Cognitive Efficiency-Extended) and two tests (Phonological Processing and Story Recall); within the limited range for two clusters (Auditory Processing and Long-Term Retrieval) and three tests (Number-Pattern Matching, Nonword Repetition, and Visual-Auditory Learning); and within the very limited range for one cluster (Perceptual Speed) and one test (Letter-Pattern Matching).

An analysis of variations among Kyrstin's cognitive scores suggests that Oral Vocabulary, General Information, Comprehension-Knowledge, Numbers Reversed, and Short-Term Working Memory are relative strengths for her. She demonstrated relative weaknesses in Letter-Pattern Matching, Phonological Processing, Perceptual Speed, Nonword Repetition, Auditory Processing, Visual-Auditory Learning, and Long-Term Retrieval.

Figure 3.31 Sample Comprehensive Report from the WIIIP

From *Woodcock-Johnson IV™* (WJ IV™) Copyright © The Riverside Publishing Company. All rights reserved. Used by permission of the publisher. No part of this work may be reproduced or transmitted in any form or by any means, electronic or mechanical, including photocopying and recording or by any information storage or retrieval system without the proper written permission of The Riverside Publishing Company unless such copying is expressly permitted by federal copyright law. Address inquiries to: https://customercare.hmhco.com/contactus/Permissions.html

Sample, Kyrstin
August 13, 2015   Comprehensive Report

When compared to a measure of intellectual ability comprised solely of fluid reasoning and comprehension-knowledge abilities, Auditory Processing, Long-Term Retrieval, Perceptual Speed, and Cognitive Efficiency-Extended were relative weaknesses (significantly lower than predicted) for Kyrstin.

INSTRUCTIONAL RECOMMENDATIONS AND INTERVENTIONS

Based on noted limitations in Kyrstin's cognitive performance:

Accommodations that may help compensate for Kyrstin's limitations in perceptual speed might include providing extended time, reducing the quantity of work required (breaking large assignments into two or more component assignments), eliminating or limiting copying activities, and increasing wait times after questions are asked as well as after responses are given.

Repetition is an important factor in building speed. Repeated and extensive practice may enable Kyrstin to perform some tasks in a more automatic fashion to increase performance speed. Activities can be teacher directed or student directed. Related computer programs or games can provide opportunities to practice responding quickly. Select computer programs or games that provide Kyrstin with immediate feedback and maintain a record of her performance over time.

Increased time spent reading can increase familiarity with the phonological representations that make up words. During silent reading, subvocal rehearsal of words is an effective strategy that may need to be explicitly taught to Kyrstin.

Active learning (or attending to and thinking about the material) is important for Kyrstin to acquire new knowledge or to benefit from any memory strategies. She may have better recall when she is actively involved in the learning process.

Overlearning—continual reexposure to information or continual repracticing of a skill even after initial proficiency has been achieved—frequently improves storage and recall of information. Review and rehearsal of previously acquired information, even just one additional review, promotes overlearning.

Figure 3.31 (continued)

Sample, Kyrstin
August 13, 2015   Comprehensive Report

TABLE OF SCORES
Woodcock-Johnson IV Tests of Cognitive Abilities (Norms based on grade 5.0)

CLUSTER/Test	W	GE	RPI	SS (68% Band)
GEN INTELLECTUAL ABIL	500	4.9	90/90	99 (95–103)
Gf-Gc COMPOSITE	517	10.9	98/90	124 (120–128)
COMP-KNOWLEDGE (*Gc*)	529	>17.9	100/90	137 (133–142)
FLUID REASONING (*Gf*)	504	5.9	94/90	105 (101–110)
FLUID REASONING (Ext)	504	6.0	94/90	106 (101–110)
S-TERM WORK MEM (*Gwm*)	518	12.8	99/90	122 (117–126)
AUDITORY PROCESS (*Ga*)	479	K.9	46/90	69 (65–74)
L-TERM RETRIEVAL (*Glr*)	484	12	67/90	77 (73–81)
QUANTITATIVE REASONING	504	6.1	94/90	106 (101–112)
NUMBER FACILITY	498	5.0	90/90	100 (93–106)
PERCEPTUAL SPEED	470	2.4	17/90	75 (68–81)
COGNITIVE EFFICIENCY	499	4.2	83/90	95 (89–101)
COG EFFICIENCY (Ext)	494	4.1	79/90	92 (87–97)
Oral Vocabulary	522	13.0	99/90	131 (125–137)
Number Series	505	6.0	95/90	106 (101–112)
Verbal Attention	509	7.6	96/90	111 (104–117)
Letter-Pattern Matching	471	1.8	10/90	72 (63–80)
Phonological Processing	487	2.0	67/90	81 (75–87)
Story Recall	486	2.1	75/90	84 (77–90)
Visualization	504	9.4	95/90	110 (105–116)
General Information	537	>17.9	100/90	136 (130–141)
Concept Formation	503	5.8	93/90	103 (98–108)
Numbers Reversed	528	15.9	100/90	125 (120–130)
Number-Pattern Matching	469	3.0	27/90	83 (74–91)
Nonword Repetition	471	<K.0	26/90	69 (65–74)
Visual-Auditory Learning	482	K.5	58/90	78 (75–81)
Analysis-Synthesis	504	6.2	94/90	105 (98–111)

Figure 3.31 (*continued*)

Sample, Kyrstin
August 13, 2015   Comprehensive Report

	STANDARD SCORES		DISCREPANCY		Interpretation at
VARIATIONS	Actual	Predicted	Difference	PR	SD	+ or – 1.50 SD (SEE)

Intra-Cognitive [Extended] Variations

VARIATIONS	Actual	Predicted	Difference	PR	SD	Interpretation
COMP-KNOWLEDGE (Gc)	137	95	42	>99.9	+3.44	Strength
FLUID REASONING (Gf)	105	98	7	74	+0.64	—
FLUID REASONING (Ext)	106	98	8	76	+0.70	—
S-TERM WORK MEM (Gwm)	122	98	24	98	+2.00	Strength
AUDITORY PROCESS (Ga)	69	102	−33	0.2	−2.85	Weakness
L-TERM RETRIEVAL (Glr)	77	101	−24	2	−1.98	Weakness
QUANTITATIVE REASONING	106	98	8	78	+0.76	—
PERCEPTUAL SPEED	75	103	−28	2	−2.02	Weakness
Oral Vocabulary	131	94	37	99.9	+3.09	Strength
Number Series	106	98	8	75	+0.67	—
Verbal Attention	111	98	13	83	+0.96	—
Letter-Pattern Matching	72	102	−30	2	−2.11	Weakness
Phonological Processing	81	102	−21	4	−1.74	Weakness
Story Recall	84	101	−17	9	−1.32	—
Visualization	110	98	12	81	+0.86	—
General Information	136	96	40	99.9	+2.97	Strength
Concept Formation	103	98	5	63	+0.33	—
Numbers Reversed	125	98	27	99	+2.21	Strength
Number-Pattern Matching	83	102	−19	8	−1.42	—
Nonword Repetition	69	102	−33	1	−2.43	Weakness
Visual-Auditory Learning	78	101	−23	5	−1.65	Weakness
Analysis-Synthesis	105	98	7	69	+0.50	—

	STANDARD SCORES		DISCREPANCY		Interpretation at
COMPARISONS	Actual	Predicted	Difference	PR	SD	+ or – 1.50 SD (SEE)

Gf-Gc Composite/Other Ability Comparisons

COMPARISONS	Actual	Predicted	Difference	PR	SD	Interpretation
S-TERM WORK MEM (Gwm)	122	114	8	73	+0.62	—
PERCEPTUAL SPEED	75	111	−36	1	−2.49	Weakness
AUDITORY PROCESS (Ga)	69	114	−45	<0.1	−3.64	Weakness
L-TERM RETRIEVAL (Glr)	77	112	−35	0.3	−2.71	Weakness
NUMBER FACILITY	100	112	−12	17	−0.95	—
COGNITIVE EFFICIENCY	95	112	−17	10	−1.30	—
COG EFFICIENCY (Ext)	92	114	−22	5	−1.68	Weakness

Figure 3.31 (continued)

Sample, Kyrstin
August 13, 2015

Comprehensive Report

Appendix A: Detailed Interpretation of Clusters and Tests

This appendix provides information about each ability measure, including a description of Kyrstin's developmental level, a comparison to age peers using a standard score range classification, and a description of her proficiency level.

WJ IV Tests of Cognitive Abilities

Intellectual Ability

General Intellectual Ability represents a measure of Kyrstin's overall intelligence. Kyrstin's performance on General Intellectual Ability is comparable to that of the average student in grade 4.9. Her general intellectual ability standard score is in the average range (percentile rank of 48; standard score of 99). Her overall intellectual ability is average (RPI of 90/90).

The *Gf-Gc* Composite is a combined measure of Kyrstin's lexical (word) knowledge; general cultural knowledge; and quantitative, deductive, and inductive reasoning. Although Kyrstin's composite standard score is within the superior range, her performance varied on two different types of tasks requiring fluid and crystallized cognitive abilities. Kyrstin's performance is very advanced on general knowledge tasks. Her performance is average on inductive reasoning tasks.

Cognitive Clusters

Comprehension-Knowledge (*Gc*) is a language-based measure of Kyrstin's declarative knowledge. It includes semantic memory and the ability to communicate her knowledge and understanding verbally. Kyrstin's verbal knowledge and comprehension are above those of the average student in grade 17.9. Her comprehension-knowledge standard score is in the very superior range (percentile rank of 99; standard score of 137). Her verbal ability is advanced (RPI of 100/90); she will probably find it very easy to succeed on grade-level verbal knowledge and comprehension tasks.

Fluid Reasoning (*Gf*) is a measure of Kyrstin's ability to use inductive, deductive, and quantitative reasoning to form concepts and solve problems. Kyrstin's fluid reasoning ability is comparable to that of the average student in grade 5.9. Her fluid reasoning standard score is in the average range (percentile rank of 64; standard score of 105).

Fluid Reasoning—Extended is a broad measure of inductive, deductive, and quantitative reasoning. Kyrstin's fluid reasoning ability is comparable to that of the average student in grade 6.0. Her fluid reasoning standard score is in the average range (percentile rank of 65; standard score of 106).

Short-Term Working Memory (*Gwm*) measured Kyrstin's ability to attend to, hold, and manipulate information in working memory. Kyrstin's working memory capacity is comparable to that of the average student in grade 12.8. Her short-term working memory standard score is in the superior range (percentile rank of 93; standard score of 122). Her short-term working memory capacity is advanced (RPI of 99/90); she will probably find it very easy to succeed on grade-level tasks such as attending to and manipulating information in working memory.

Auditory Processing (*Ga*) includes the ability to encode, synthesize, and discriminate auditory stimuli, including the ability to employ phonological processes in task performance. Kyrstin's auditory processing ability is comparable to that of the average student in grade K.9. Her auditory processing standard score is in the very low range (percentile rank of 2; standard score of 69). Her ability to effectively employ phonological processes is limited (RPI of 46/90); she will probably find it very difficult to succeed on grade-level tasks requiring auditory processing.

Figure 3.31 (continued)

Sample, Kyrstin
August 13, 2015   Comprehensive Report

Long-Term Retrieval (*Glr*) is the ability to encode and retrieve (reconstruct) information. Kyrstin's long-term storage and retrieval abilities are comparable to those of the average student in grade 1.2. Her long-term retrieval standard score is in the low range (percentile rank of 6; standard score of 77). Her ability to store and fluently retrieve information is limited (RPI of 67/90); she will probably find it very difficult to succeed on grade-level tasks involving storage and retrieval of information.

Quantitative Reasoning is the ability to reason deductively and inductively with numbers, mathematical relations, and operations. Kyrstin's quantitative reasoning is comparable to that of the average student in grade 6.1. Her quantitative reasoning standard score is in the average range (percentile rank of 67; standard score of 106).

Number Facility represents fluency with numbers, including number-pattern comparisons and the ability to manipulate numbers in working memory. Although Kyrstin's number facility standard score is within the average range, her performance varied on two different types of number facility tasks. Kyrstin's performance is advanced on working memory capacity tasks. Her performance is limited on numeric pattern recognition tasks.

Perceptual Speed measured Kyrstin's ability to recognize and match orthographic and numeric patterns quickly and accurately under time constraints. Kyrstin's perceptual speed is comparable to that of the average student in grade 2.4. Her perceptual speed standard score is in the low range (percentile rank of 5; standard score of 75). Her ability to rapidly compare visual patterns that use alpha or numeric symbols is very limited (RPI of 17/90); she will probably find it extremely difficult to succeed on grade-level tasks requiring visual perceptual speed.

Cognitive Efficiency is a combined index of Kyrstin's ability to perform visual-perceptual matching tasks rapidly and accurately and her level of working memory capacity, both of which are foundational for complex cognitive functioning. Although Kyrstin's cognitive efficiency standard score is within the average range, her performance varied on two different types of cognitive efficiency tasks. Kyrstin's performance is advanced on working memory capacity tasks. Her performance is very limited on orthographic pattern recognition tasks.

Cognitive Efficiency—Extended is a broad, combined index of Kyrstin's ability to perform visual-perceptual matching tasks rapidly and accurately and her level of working memory capacity, both of which are foundational for complex cognitive functioning. Although Kyrstin's cognitive efficiency standard score is within the average range, her performance varied on two different types of cognitive efficiency tasks. Kyrstin's performance is advanced on working memory capacity tasks. Her performance is very limited on orthographic pattern recognition tasks.

<u>Cognitive Tests</u>

Oral Vocabulary is a measure of Kyrstin's comprehension of words. This test had two parts, requiring her to listen to a word and provide an accurate antonym and then listen to a word and provide an accurate synonym. Kyrstin's oral vocabulary ability is comparable to that of the average student in grade 13.0. Her Oral Vocabulary standard score is in the very superior range (percentile rank of 98; standard score of 131). Her knowledge of words and their meanings is advanced (RPI of 99/90); she will probably find it very easy to succeed on grade-level oral vocabulary tasks.

Number Series is a test of quantitative, deductive, and inductive reasoning. This test required Kyrstin to supply the missing number from a sequence of numbers following a mathematical pattern. Kyrstin's performance on Number Series is comparable to that of the average student in grade 6.0. Her Number Series standard score is in the average range (percentile rank of 66; standard score of 106).

Figure 3.31 (*continued*)

Sample, Kyrstin
August 13, 2015   **Comprehensive Report**

Verbal Attention is a test of short-term working memory that required Kyrstin to listen to a list of animals and numbers and then answer a question based on the sequence of information. Kyrstin's verbal working memory is comparable to that of the average student in grade 7.6. Her Verbal Attention standard score is in the high-average range (percentile rank of 76; standard score of 111). Her ability to retain information in working memory and then answer questions based on the information is average to advanced (RPI of 96/90); she will probably find it easy to succeed on grade-level verbal working memory tasks.

Letter-Pattern Matching measured the speed at which Kyrstin was able to make visual symbol discriminations among a series of letter patterns. Kyrstin's orthographic processing speed is comparable to that of the average student in grade 1.8. Her Letter-Pattern Matching standard score is in the low range (percentile rank of 3; standard score of 72). Her speed of orthographic processing is very limited (RPI of 10/90); she will probably find it extremely difficult to succeed on grade-level tasks requiring rapid discrimination among letter patterns.

Phonological Processing assessed Kyrstin's word retrieval abilities using phonological cues. Kyrstin's ability to access words based on phonology is comparable to that of the average student in grade 2.0. Her Phonological Processing standard score is in the low-average range (percentile rank of 10; standard score of 81). Her ability to access words based on phonology is limited to average (RPI of 67/90); she will probably find it difficult to succeed on grade-level phonologically-mediated word access tasks.

Story Recall measured Kyrstin's listening ability and reconstructive memory. The task required her to recall details of increasingly complex stories. Kyrstin's performance on Story Recall is comparable to that of the average student in grade 2.1. Her Story Recall standard score is in the low average range (percentile rank of 14; standard score of 84). Her ability to recall details of complex stories is limited to average (RPI of 75/90); she will probably find it difficult to succeed on grade-level story listening and retelling tasks.

Visualization measured two aspects of visual-spatial processing involving visual feature detection and mental rotation of objects. One part of the test required Kyrstin to identify the two or three pieces that form a completed target shape. The other part required her to identify rotated block configurations that correspond to a target configuration. Kyrstin's ability to visualize is comparable to that of the average student in grade 9.4. Her Visualization standard score is near the higher end of the average range (percentile rank of 75; standard score of 110). Her ability to employ visual-spatial manipulation in working memory is average to advanced (RPI of 95/90); she will probably find it easy to succeed on grade-level visual-spatial tasks.

General Information measured Kyrstin's general verbal knowledge. This test required Kyrstin to tell where specific objects might be found, and to tell what might be the purpose of other specific objects. Kyrstin's performance on General Information is above that of the average student in grade 17.9. Her General Information standard score is in the very superior range (percentile rank of 99; standard score of 136). Her general verbal knowledge is very advanced (RPI of 100/90); she will probably find it extremely easy to succeed on grade-level tasks requiring verbal expression of general knowledge.

Concept Formation is a test of fluid reasoning. This test required Kyrstin to use inductive reasoning in categorical thinking. Kyrstin's performance on Concept Formation is comparable to that of the average student in grade 5.8. Her Concept Formation standard score is in the average range (percentile rank of 58; standard score of 103).

Numbers Reversed is a test of working memory capacity. This test required Kyrstin to hold a sequence of numbers in immediate awareness and then reverse the sequence. Kyrstin's performance on Numbers Reversed is comparable to that of the average student in grade 15.9. Her Numbers Reversed standard score is in the superior range (percentile rank of 95; standard score of 125). Her span of apprehension and recoding in working memory is advanced (RPI of 100/90); she will probably find it very easy to succeed on grade-level working memory capacity tasks.

Figure 3.31 (continued)

Sample, Kyrstin
August 13, 2015   **Comprehensive Report**

Number-Pattern Matching is a test of perceptual speed. This test measured the speed at which Kyrstin was able to make visual discriminations among groups of numbers. Kyrstin's performance on Number-Pattern Matching is comparable to that of the average student in grade 3.0. Her Number-Pattern Matching standard score is in the low-average range (percentile rank of 12; standard score of 83). Her perceptual speed with number patterns is limited (RPI of 27/90); she will probably find it very difficult to succeed on similar grade-level tasks requiring speeded discrimination among number patterns.

Nonword Repetition measured Kyrstin's phonological short-term memory. Kyrstin's performance on Nonword Repetition is below that of the average student in grade K.0. Her Nonword Repetition standard score is in the very low range (percentile rank of 2; standard score of 69). Her ability to remember and repeat increasingly complex nonwords is limited (RPI of 26/90); she will probably find it very difficult to succeed on similar grade-level phonological short-term storage tasks.

Visual-Auditory Learning is a measure of the ability to learn, store, and retrieve a series of visual-auditory associations. In this test, Kyrstin was required to learn and recall the names of rebuses (pictographic representations of words). Kyrstin's performance on Visual-Auditory Learning is comparable to that of the average student in grade K.5. Her Visual-Auditory Learning standard score is in the low range (percentile rank of 7; standard score of 78). Her visual-auditory learning and retrieval ability are limited (RPI of 58/90); she will probably find it very difficult to succeed on grade-level tasks requiring paired-associate learning, storage, and retrieval.

Analysis-Synthesis is a test of general sequential (deductive) reasoning. This test required Kyrstin to analyze the components of an incomplete logic puzzle in order to name the missing parts. Kyrstin's performance on Analysis-Synthesis is comparable to that of the average student in grade 6.2. Her Analysis-Synthesis standard score is in the average range (percentile rank of 62; standard score of 105).

Figure 3.31 *(continued)*

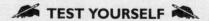

🖋 TEST YOURSELF 🖋

1. **When querying responses, you should score the last response given.**
   a. True
   b. False

2. **If an examinee provides an incorrect response to the first part of a two-symbol word on Test 13: Visual-Auditory Learning, you should:**
   a. Score both symbols as incorrect.
   b. Score both symbols as correct if the second part is identified correctly.
   c. Score each symbol separately.
   d. Query the examinee and ask him or her to attempt the word again.

3. **For which of the following test(s) are synonyms considered an acceptable response?**
   a. Visual-Auditory Learning
   b. Concept Formation
   c. Both a and b.
   d. None of the above. If an examinee provides a synonym in response to an item (e.g., says *little* for *small*), the response is considered an error.

4. **If an examiner inadvertently exceeds the time limit for any of the timed tests, that test must not be scored and should be declared invalid.**
   a. True
   b. False

5. **The raw score for which of the following test(s) is based on the total number of errors committed?**
   a. Test 9: Concept Formation
   b. Test 15: Analysis-Synthesis
   c. Test 13: Visual-Auditory Learning
   d. All of the above

6. **On Test 12: Nonword Repetition, the examinee must emphasize the same syllables as those emphasized on the audio recording.**
   a. True
   b. False

7. **Examiners should ensure that all sample items are not included in the calculation of raw scores.**
   a. True
   b. False

8. **On Item 6 in Test 6: Story Recall, how many points does the following response receive? Dougy had a mask that he used in the water. He saw fishes and turtles that were different colors and shapes. It was like magic!**
   a. 3
   b. 4
   c. 5
   d. 6

9. **Examiners have the option of calculating all cluster scores either by hand or by using the WJ IV online scoring and reporting program.**
   a. True
   b. False

10. **What scores best illustrate a person's proficiency in a particular ability?**
   a. Standard score and age equivalent
   b. Grade equivalent and percentile rank
   c. Normal curve equivalent and CALP
   d. Age or grade equivalent and relative proficiency index

Answers: 1. a; 2. c; 3. b; 4. b; 5. c; 6. b; 7. a; 8. d; 9. b; 10. d

Four

HOW TO INTERPRET THE WJ IV COG

Fredrick A. Schrank

T he WJ IV COG measures the psychological constructs of intellectual
ability and broad and narrow cognitive abilities as articulated by contemporary Cattell-Horn-Carroll (CHC) theory. Contemporary CHC theory
is a combined interpretive model that is derived from the research traditions
of Cattell (1987), Horn (1968, 1991), Horn and Stankov (1982), and Carroll
(1993, 1998, 2003). However, contemporary CHC theory has moved beyond
its initial specifications in the WJ III (Woodcock, McGrew, & Mather, 2001a);
it has evolved primarily through the efforts of McGrew (2005, 2009), Schneider
and McGrew (2012), and McGrew, LaForte, and Schrank (2014). Interpretation
of the WJ IV COG requires knowledge of these constructs.

This chapter integrates and moves beyond the information provided in the
WJ IV *Technical Manual* (McGrew et al., 2014) and the WJ IV COG *Examiner's
Manual* (Mather & Wendling, 2014) by summarizing a trove of related research
(much of it from outside the WJ IV literature) that provides support to interpretation of the constructs that the WJ IV COG measures. The research reviewed for
the development of this chapter resulted in the formulation of a set of operational
definitions that objectively describe what each test and cluster measures. Operational definitions are required in any objective science (McFall, 1991, 2000).
In addition, this chapter provides another perspective on the validity of the WJ
IV COG that may allow assessment professionals to independently evaluate the
fidelity with which the WJ IV authors have translated the relatively abstract CHC
theoretical constructs into specific operations for measurement.

Although CHC theory helps us describe the nature of human cognitive abilities, it is important to recognize from the outset that the abilities defined by CHC

theory are not static properties but rather abstractions that describe dynamic processes or capacities that people possess differentially. Horn (1991) stated this most eloquently and imaginatively:

> Ability, cognitive capability, and cognitive processes are not segments of behavior but abstractions that we have applied to indivisible flow of behavior. One cannot distinguish between reasoning, retrieval, perception, and detection. The behavior one sees indicates all of these, as well as motivation, emotion, drive, apprehension, feeling, and more. Specifying different features of cognition is like slicing smoke——dividing a continuous, homogeneous, irregular mass of gray into ... what? Abstractions. (p. 199)

The cognitive abilities, processes, or capacities that the WJ IV COG measures are not entities of physical science but abstractions based on psychological theory. In the WJ IV, the CHC terminology is a way to organize objective test results into meaningful expressions about relatively abstract cognitive characteristics. Figure 4.1 displays a stepladder to help illustrate how three levels of abstraction can be applied to understanding the WJ IV COG test and cluster scores. The abstraction stepladder analogy is based on the general semantic principles developed by Korzybski (1933/2000), who sought to advance scientific thinking. Some

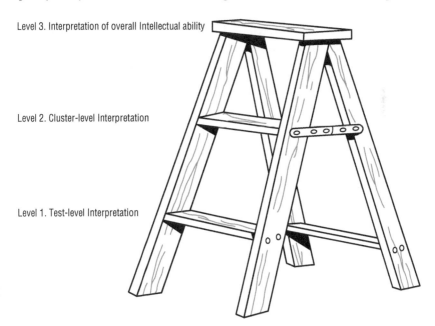

Level 3. Interpretation of overall Intellectual ability

Level 2. Cluster-level Interpretation

Level 1. Test-level Interpretation

Figure 4.1 Stepladder of Abstraction applied to WJ IV COG interpretation

of Korzybski's principles for formulation of scientific thought were subsequently popularized in a Book of the Month Club selection by Hayakawa (1939/1978), which readers could use to evaluate meaning in everyday language (the stepladder of abstraction analogy first appeared in Hayakawa's book).

Although the concept of intelligence is impossible to describe in concrete terms, the process of abstracting helps us describe and understand its nature. In the WJ IV COG, the nature of human intelligence that is described by contemporary CHC theory finds expression at three levels of abstraction, as described next.

The Lowest Level of Abstraction: The WJ IV COG Tests. The lowest step on the stepladder represents test-level interpretation of the WJ IV COG. This chapter provides operational definitions of the cognitive levels or processes that each WJ IV COG test measures. As operational definitions, each test explains (to the examinee) "what to do" and defines (for the examiner) "what to observe" to obtain a measure of its effects. The WJ IV COG tests are direct scales of measurement, and, being at the lowest level of abstraction, provide the most concrete ("extensional" is the term used by Hayakawa) descriptions of cognitive functioning within the WJ IV COG. Test-level interpretation—because it is the most concrete and least abstract— often can yield the most objective and meaningful insights into cognitive performance.

The Middle Level of Abstraction: The WJ IV COG Clusters. To infer that an individual has a defined level of a specified type of ability, particularly a broad cognitive ability, we must leap across a huge chasm. That is, we must infer the existence of a relatively static concept from a small set of measures that are linked both empirically and theoretically. To help bridge that chasm, the WJ IV COG clusters are defined to combine two or more operational definitions into an interpretive generalization. The commonality observed between the two narrow dynamic processes frequently helps define an individual's level of ability at a higher level of abstraction—as a broad cognitive ability. Consequently, the WJ IV COG clusters representing the broad CHC abilities—Comprehension-Knowledge (*Gc*), Fluid Reasoning (*Gf*), Short-Term Working Memory ((*Gwm*), Cognitive Processing Speed (*Gs*), Long-Term Storage and Retrieval (*Glr*), Auditory Processing (*Ga*) and Visual Processing (*Gv*)—are really only semantic abstractions derived from two or more measured samples of a defined broad cognitive construct. (Several narrow cognitive ability clusters also are available that combine two tests that are similar in some way or have a defined diagnostic purpose, such as Perceptual Speed [P], Number Facility [N], Quantitative Reasoning [RQ], or Cognitive Efficiency.)

Moving up a step on a stepladder has a purpose and a benefit. It allows us to extend our reach to grasp or do something we otherwise could not. It allows us to describe an aspect of an individual's cognitive functioning in terms of a broad or narrow class of abilities or processes. As a benefit, we often can make generalizations about a broad or narrow, although still circumscribed, category of cognition.

The Top Level of Abstraction: Conceptualizations of Intelligence. At the top of the abstraction stepladder, the General Intellectual Ability (GIA) score is a first-principal-component measure of intelligence. GIA, a calculation of g, represents a very high level of abstraction, because its nature cannot be described in terms of unique information content or cognitive processes. Like the construct of g, the WJ IV COG GIA score can be described only in terms of its constituent cognitive abilities and processes. Alternatively, because intelligence can be conceptualized as primarily Gf and Gc (Schrank, McGrew, & Mather, 2014), the WJ IV COG includes a special-purpose measure of intellectual level based on four tests that represent the two highest-order (g-loaded or g-saturated) factors included in CHC theory (McGrew, 2005, 2009; McGrew et al., 2014; Schneider & McGrew, 2012). Finally, intellectual ability can be estimated from a small subset of tests measuring Gf, Gc, and Gwm with the Brief Intellectual Ability (BIA) score.

The three levels of WJ IV COG scores allow professionals to move up and down the stepladder of abstraction to describe the level and nature of an individual's cognitive abilities and intelligence. The terms used to describe cognitive functioning will vary based on the level of abstraction or generalization required by the purpose of the evaluation. Moving up the stepladder, higher-level abstractions can be properly and uniformly made from starting points in operational definitions of narrow cognitive abilities from the component tests. From the top level, intellectual ability can be described in terms of its component abilities and processes. Moving down the stepladder, abilities at any level can be described as members of a broad class of abilities or construct defined by the next higher level. Interpretation of WJ IV COG scores can focus on any of the three levels, depending on the purpose of an evaluation.

LEVEL 1: TESTS MEASURING ONE OR MORE NARROW COGNITIVE ABILITIES

The 18 WJ IV COG tests provide the scales of measurement upon which the entire interpretive system is based. Each test in the WJ IV COG measures one or more of the narrow cognitive abilities defined by CHC theory. Because the individual tests represent the lowest level on the stepladder of abstraction, in most cases, the individual WJ IV COG test results can be defined in terms of narrow operational definitions. In this section, operational definitions derived from CHC theory are supported by related research that helps define the underlying neurocognitive precepts being measured by the tests.

The WJ IV COG is designed to foster interpretation at the test as well as at the cluster level. For example, the intra-cognitive variation procedure is based on test-level variations. This procedure is useful for determining if any within-individual strengths and weaknesses exist among the abilities or processes measured by the tests. In addition, individual test results are particularly useful for aligning measured limitations in specific cognitive abilities, processes, or mechanisms of learning with theoretically consistent instructional interventions, suggestions for learning, or accommodations. Links between WJ IV COG test performance and instructional interventions have been suggested by Mather and Jaffe (2015) and Schrank and Wendling (2015a). Consequently, when one of the purposes of an evaluation includes linking cognitive assessment results to instructional interventions, test-level interpretation—Level 1 on the stepladder of abstraction—provides the most direct linkage for targeting interventions to any measured limitations in cognitive abilities and processing.

Test 1: Oral Vocabulary

Test 1: Oral Vocabulary measures a lexical-semantic process that begins with the identification of a word from orthographic, phonological, or morphological codes and moves to the activation of, and access to, associated meanings from the individual's lexicon (semantic memories of stored words) (Verhoeven & Perfetti, 2008). In CHC theory, this test primarily measures a narrow aspect of Comprehension-Knowledge (*Gc*) referred to as lexical knowledge (VL; vocabulary knowledge), or knowledge of words and word meanings.

An analysis of the task and cognitive processing requirements for Test 1: Oral Vocabulary suggests that an auditory or visual form of a stimulus word is connected to a conceptual understanding in semantic memory, which then activates or primes its meaning in the lexicon and consequently activates closely associated words (Caplan, 1992; Gazzaniga, Ivry, & Mangun, 1998). Synonym and antonym associations from known stimulus words are matched more or less directly and automatically in the neural semantic memory networks of individuals with large vocabularies (Martin, 1998). A response to unknown or unfamiliar words can be attempted by parsing or segmenting the printed stimulus word into any recognizable phonological, orthographic, or morphological units (Van Orden & Goldinger, 1994, 1996) to glean clues that can be used to support the information search function within working memory.

CAUTION: MIND THE GAP

One problem in relating cognitive neuroscience research to CHC theory is that differences in terminology must be bridged. For example, tests of Comprehension-Knowledge (Gc) also can be described as measures of semantic memory, long-term memory, secondary memory, or verbal ability. *Semantic memory* refers to a type of long-term memory where words, facts, or ideas are stored.

Vocabulary learning follows a developmental trajectory (Biemiller, 2001), expands and deepens across the life span, but there are large individual differences in word knowledge among children and adults (Vermeer, 2001). Depth of word knowledge is a critical component of the *lexical quality hypothesis* (Perfetti & Hart, 2001). Low lexical quality, defined as less accessible knowledge of word meanings, can result in problems understanding oral and written language (Perfetti, 2007; Perfetti & Hart, 2001) or a semantic deficit (Nation & Snowling, 1998). In contrast, individuals with high lexical quality are more efficient in semantic processing. For example, an individual with high lexical quality will take less time to determine that printed words such as *gait* and *fence* are not related in meaning (Perfetti & Hart, 2001).

Deficits in word knowledge and automaticity are important targets for intervention. When words are recognized easily and automatically, mental resources in oral and reading comprehension are freed up to facilitate the acquisition of new information and knowledge (National Reading Panel, 2000; Perfetti, 1998; Samuels & Flor, 1997; Spear-Swerling & Sternberg, 1994).

Test 1: Oral Vocabulary is a particularly important test because knowledge of words is critically important to school success (R. C. Anderson & Nagy, 2001; Baker, Simmons, & Kame'enui, 1998) and no area of cognition is more responsive to intervention than vocabulary knowledge. Cognitive neuroscience provides several learning principles for increasing knowledge of words. For example, vocabulary will be more readily acquired when the words are contextualized with real-world examples (Medina, 2008). Re-exposure of previously presented vocabulary words in a variety of contexts strengthens the encoding and retrieval process (Medina, 2008; Stahl, 2005).

To be maximally effective, interventions for vocabulary development must be multifaceted and appropriate to the person's age and ability level (National

Reading Panel, 2000). For young children, interventions for the development of word knowledge should include creating a language-rich environment (Beck, McKeown, & Kucan, 2002; Gunn, Simmons, & Kame'enui, 1995; Hart & Risley, 2003; Nisbett, 2009), frequent exposures and practice with words in context (Gunn et al., 1995; Hart & Risley, 2003), reading aloud to the child (M. J. Adams, 1990), and text talks (Beck & McKeown, 2001).

For older children and adolescents, an effective program of interventions often includes provisions for: increased time spent reading (Cunningham & Stanovich, 1991; Herman, Anderson, Pearson, & Nagy, 1987); reading for different purposes (R. C. Anderson, 1996; National Reading Panel, 2000; Stahl, 1999); intentional explicit word instruction (Beck et al., 2002; Nagy, 2005; National Reading Panel, 2000); direct instruction in morphology (Anglin, 1993; Baumann, Edwards, Boland, Olejnik, & Kame'enui, 2003; Baumann, Kame'enui, & Ash, 2003; Blachowicz & Fisher, 2000; Carlisle, 2004; Graves, 2000; National Reading Panel, 2000); development of word consciousness (R. C. Anderson & Nagy, 1992; Graves & Watts-Taffe, 2002; Nagy & Scott, 2000); independent word-learning strategies (Anglin, 1993; Bauman, Edwards, et al., 2003; Bauman, Kame'enui, et al., 2003; Blachowicz & Fisher, 2000; Carlisle, 2004; Graves, 2000; National Reading Panel, 2000); and use of computerized word-learning programs (Davidson, Elcock, & Noyes, 1996; National Reading Panel, 2000). Teaching new words as part of a group of closely related words, or synonyms, is more effective that learning words from a list of unrelated words (Templeton, Bear, Invernizzi, Johnston, Flanigan, Townsend, Helman, & Hayes, 2015). Vocabulary knowledge can be enhanced by application of word analysis principles, such as semantic feature analysis (Anders & Bos, 1986; Pittelman, Heimlich, Berglund, & French, 1991), and intervention strategies, such as semantic mapping (Sinatra, Berg, & Dunn, 1985) and keeping a vocabulary journal (Templeton et al., 2015). See **Rapid Reference 4.1**.

≡ Rapid Reference 4.1 Interpretation of Test 1—Oral Vocabulary

Operational Definition: Measures knowledge of words and word meanings
Primary Broad CHC Factor: Comprehension-Knowledge (Gc)
Narrow CHC Abilities: Lexical Knowledge (VL); Language Development (LD)
Median g loading: .72
Stimuli: Visual (text); auditory (words)

Task Requirements: Listening to a word and providing a synonym; listening to a word and providing an antonym

Inferred Cognitive Processes: Semantic activation and access; word stimuli segmenting or parsing

Response Modality: Oral (words)

Related Educational Interventions or Accommodations: Creating a vocabulary-rich environment, particularly reading aloud to a young child and discussing new words; text talks; directed vocabulary thinking activities; explicit teaching of specific words; direct instruction in morphology; teaching new vocabulary words with other words closely associated in meaning; semantic feature analysis; semantic maps; use of computer technology to develop word knowledge; association of key words to prior knowledge; reexposure of words; reading for a variety of purposes; independent word-learning strategies, such as keeping a vocabulary journal.

Test 2: Number Series

Test 2: Number Series is a test of fluid reasoning (*Gf*) that measures the ability to identify and apply an analog or rule to complete a numerical sequence. From the perspective of CHC theory, the test is cognitively complex (Holzman, Pellegrino, & Glaser, 1983) and requires the application of several narrow abilities and executive functions. Quantitative reasoning (RQ) is involved because the test is a measure of reasoning with numbers; general sequential reasoning (deduction) (RG) is required to determine the analog or rule that solves the task; and induction (I) is required to determine the value that completes the numeric analogy. The executive function of placekeeping (Hambrick & Altmann, 2015) supports the systematic exploration of hypotheses that effect problem solution. To deduce a pattern in an item sequence, an individual must be able to count and, depending on the difficulty level of the item, carry out foundational arithmetic operations, including addition, subtraction, multiplication, and division; so the task also requires the application of mathematics knowledge (KM).

Low performance on Number Series may be difficult to explain without a comprehensive evaluation of other abilities. To perform successfully, an individual must have a foundation in math facts (Geary, 1990; Geary & Brown, 1991). The level and integrities of related broad and narrow CHC abilities can play supporting or inhibiting roles in performance of this task, including retrieval of counting sequences and/or math facts from semantic memory (Temple, 1991), cognitive processing speed (*Gs*), Working Memory Capacity (WM), and Attentional Control (AC). In Number Series, all of these abilities work conjointly and may help explain why this test is one of the most predictive cognitive tests in the WJ IV for almost all domains of achievement (McGrew et al., 2014).

The lowest-numbered items on Number Series require retrieval of counting sequences from semantic memory. Higher-numbered items require execution of a strategy to induce a solution to the problem and an analog relationship among existing numbers in the series must be deduced. To effect an analog, the relationship between a pair of successive numbers in the sequence must be active in working memory to apply (or modify and then apply) the deduced relationship to other pairs of successive numbers in the sequence (Geary et al., 1991). The systematic evaluation of serial hypotheses requires placekeeping ability (Hambrick & Altmann, 2015). If a hypothesis turns out to be incorrect, the placekeeping system selects the next most plausible hypothesis without returning to those already rejected and without skipping any that might turn out to be correct. Working Memory Capacity (WM) deficits can affect rate of placekeeping decay, the ability to allocate attention to the task, and level of activation associated with problem solving (Bertling, 2012; Cowan, 1988; Woltz, 1988). How much information can be processed also can be affected by Cognitive Processing Speed (*Gs*) (Kail, 1992). When speed of numeric information processing is inhibited, the inferred relationships between pairs of numbers in a series can decay in working memory before an answer is induced (Baddeley, 1986; Stigler, Lee, & Stevenson, 1986).

An inability to solve the lowest-numbered Number Series items may suggest a need for the development of foundational knowledge in mathematics. This can be developed with manipulatives and board games that require counting and which help develop a sense of numeric quantity, patterns, core mathematical concepts, and the relationships among numbers (Gersten et al., 2008; National Council of Teachers of Mathematics, 2000; Ramani & Seigler, 2005). A key ability to be learned is the concept of "counting on" (Gersten et al., 2009; National Council of Teachers of Mathematics, 2000). Additional interventions include the development of seriation, pattern recognition, and geometric sequencing skills (National Council of Teachers of Mathematics, 2000) and "math talk" intervention that requires the teacher to listen and provide corrective feedback as the student explains his or her reasoning, step by step, to obtain solutions to problems (High/Scope Educational Research Foundation, 2003; Kroesbergen & Van Luit, 2003). See **Rapid Reference 4.2.**

≡ Rapid Reference 4.2 Interpretation of Test 2—Number Series

Operational Definition: Measures quantitative reasoning
Primary Broad CHC Factor: Fluid Reasoning (*Gf*)
Narrow CHC Abilities: Quantitative Reasoning (RQ); General Sequential Reasoning (deduction) (RG); Induction (I); Math Knowledge (KM)
Median g loading: .62
Stimuli: Visual (numeric)
Task Requirements: Determining a numerical sequence
Inferred Cognitive Processes: Representation and manipulation of points on a mental number line; identifying (deducing) and applying an underlying rule/principle to complete a numerical sequence (inducing)
Response Modality: Oral (number name)
Related Educational Interventions or Accommodations: Develop a sense of numeric quantity; teach number patterns and core math concepts; counting by increments; use of manipulatives; math talk

Test 3: Verbal Attention

Test 3: Verbal Attention measures working memory capacity, attentional control, and executive search and updating processes required for answering questions based on verbally presented strings of unrelated object names and numbers in primary memory. The task involves listening to a series of intermingled numbers and animal names, holding the sequence in primary memory, and then listening to and answering a specific question regarding one piece of the information from the sequence. Verbal Attention measures the size of a person's attentional focus in primary memory (Cowen et al., 2005; Unsworth & Engle, 2007b). In CHC theory, Verbal Attention measures both Working Memory Capacity (WM) and Attentional Control (AC), both aspects of Short-Term Working Memory (*Gwm*). Verbal Attention is a cued recall task. The task represents the Unsworth and Engle (2007b) dual-component model of working memory capacity in which information is maintained in primary memory through the controlled allocation of attention and a focus of attention is retrieved through a cue-dependent search process.

CAUTION: MIND THE GAP

In the cognitive neurosciences, different words can have the same or a similar meaning. *Working memory* is sometimes referred to as primary memory, immediate awareness, or attentional focus.

Performance on this test is aided by maintaining focus of attention and/or the ability to retrieve information that has been displaced from attention (Shipstead, Lindsey, Marshall, & Engle, 2014). A response can be driven by either of two separate mechanisms: a fast-acting, fairly automatic process for information that is actively maintained or a slower, more controlled recollection process for information that must be reconstructed and returned to focal attention (Yonelinas, 2002). Examiners may want to carefully observe an individual's response to the more difficult items to ascertain if the individual simply gives up in response to difficult tasks or appears to attempt to reconstruct all or part of the stimulus string in an effort to derive an answer.

Verbal Attention is an important task because it represents the individual's baseline capacity to focus on critical information and resist attentional capture by distraction (Shipstead et al., 2014), apart from the influence of interruption. Thus, it is suggested that Verbal Attention measures the integrity of attention that provides multi-item maintenance in primary memory (Cowan, 2001). Verbal Attention results may be both reflective and predictive of situations where information needs to be actively maintained for cued searches to retrieve relevant information.

Unsworth and Engle (2007a) suggested that a key to understanding the relationship of working memory to fluid reasoning is the link between active maintenance of information and controlled, cue-dependent search processes that can be used to update or refresh memory traces. The cued recall tasks in Verbal Attention may tap the real-time updating function of working memory suggested by Bunting, Cowan, and Saults (2006); Dahlin, Stigdotter Neely, Larsson, Bäckman, and Nyberg (2008); and Miyake, Friedman, Emerson, Witzki, Howerter, and Wager (2000). Kosslyn, Alpert, and Thompson (1995) suggested that the "information-lookup" process plays a critical role in working memory. The real-time updating and information-lookup functions may explain why Verbal Attention is so predictive of achievement (McGrew et al., 2014), particularly reading comprehension ability, as comprehension of lengthy passages requires constant updating of the contents of running working memory.

Low performance on Verbal Attention suggests limitations in the ability to actively maintain and/or retrieve information from working memory (Unsworth & Engle, 2007b). For young children, active learning environments promote attention to task demands (Marzano, Pickering, & Pollack, 2011). For some individuals, compensatory strategies may be required, including frequent repetition of key information, reduction of abstractions, or simplifying complex instructions (Alloway, 2011; Gathercole & Alloway, 2008). Use of maintenance rehearsal for information in primary memory may be specifically taught (Medina, 2008). Use of mnemonics can be helpful for focusing attention when learning rules, patterns, and word lists (Wolfe, 2001). See **Rapid Reference 4.3**.

≡ Rapid Reference 4.3 Interpretation of Test 3—Verbal Attention

Operational Definition: Measures temporary storage of verbal information and the cue-dependent search function of primary memory
Primary Broad CHC Factor: Short-Term Working Memory (*Gwm*)
Narrow CHC Abilities: Working Memory Capacity (WM); Attentional Control (AC)
Median *g* loading: .64
Stimuli: Auditory (words, numbers)
Task Requirements: Listening to a series of numbers and animals intermingled, holding the sequence in working memory, and then answering a specific question regarding the sequence
Inferred Cognitive Processes: Controlled executive function; working memory capacity; maintenance of verbalized stimuli in primary memory; real-time updating and information look-up; attentional control
Response Modality: Oral (number names or words)
Related Educational Interventions or Accommodations: Rehearsal; active learning environments; complex computer games; reduce distractions; reduction in amount of material to be remembered at any one time; simplifying linguistic structures of verbal material; restructuring complex tasks into separate and independent steps; Repeating important information

Test 4: Letter-Pattern Matching

In CHC theory, Test 4: Letter-Pattern Matching is a measure of broad Cognitive Processing Speed (*Gs*) and the narrow ability of Perceptual Speed (P). The task requires the examinee to make rapid visual discriminations by locating and circling two identical letter patterns in a row of six possible options. Two-letter patterns match exactly; the other four letter patterns are foils that are often slight variants of the target letter pattern.

Beyond the initial 30 items that include only single-letter matches, there is an important distinction between the correct and incorrect letter-pattern combinations. Mather and Wendling (2014) stated: "The letter patterns that match are always a possible English spelling pattern (e.g., *oa* or *sh*), whereas the other patterns are impossible or less frequent letter strings (e.g., *ao* or *hs*)" (p. 15). Consequently, performance on this test can be aided by orthographic awareness or orthographic knowledge. *Orthographic awareness* refers to individuals' implicit or explicit attention to orthographic knowledge—stored mental representations of specific words or word parts (Apel, 2010, 2011; Conrad, 2008; Holmes, Malone, & Redenbach, 2008; A. C. Jones, Folk, & Rapp, 2009; Moll & Landerl, 2009; Richards, Berninger, & Fayol, 2009; Wolter & Apel, 2010).

Performance on Test 4: Letter-Pattern Matching is facilitated by well-developed sublexical orthographic recognition efficiency. Individuals who are sensitive to orthographic regularities in English spelling will possess an advantage. Individuals who are able to quickly recognize a letter sequence that can be held in working memory as a single orthographic unit can more quickly scan other letter sequences for the target pattern without having to hold a span of unrelated letters in working memory while searching for a match. Sublexical orthographic recognition efficiency allows the individual to treat the recognized pattern as a single unit for comparison purposes to other letter strings rather than holding a string of unrelated letters in memory span while searching for a matching letter string.

Limited proficiency on Letter-Pattern Matching may be related to reading and spelling problems. Learning to process orthographic information quickly and efficiently is thought to play a critical role in the development of automatic word recognition skill that supports reading fluency (Apel, 2009) and is related to reading speed (O'Brien, Wolf, Miller, Lovett, & Morris, 2011). Individuals with dyslexia often show deficits on tasks that require rapid detection of letter position (Cornelissen & Hansen, 1998; Cornelissen, Hansen, Hutton, Evangelinou, & Stein, 1998; Katz, 1977; Pammer, Lavis, Hansen, & Cornelissen, 2004). Limitations in perceptual letter pattern recognition may interfere with orthographic memory formation, resulting in spelling problems (Gerber, 1984), such as an overreliance on phonology rather than orthographic knowledge when spelling (Cornelissen, Bradley, Fowler, & Stein, 1994).

Examiners should determine if low performance on Letter-Pattern Matching is related to lack of knowledge of orthography. WJ IV ACH Test 16: Spelling of Sounds will provide useful information on the individual's knowledge of common English spelling rules. Individuals with weaknesses in orthography may benefit from one or more targeted interventions that focus on learning and recognition of specific English-language spelling patterns (Blevins, 2001; Moats, 2004, 2009). If the nature of the problem is primarily cognitive processing speed, then repetitive practice, speed drills, and use of computer games that require an individual to make decisions quickly can be helpful (Tallal et al., 1996). Accommodations, such as extended time, may be required for limitations in perceptual speed if the limitation impairs the individual's ability to demonstrate knowledge under time constraints. See **Rapid Reference 4.4**.

≡ Rapid Reference 4.4 Interpretation of Test 4—Letter-Pattern Matching

Operational Definition: Measures orthographic visual perceptual discrimination ability under timed conditions
Primary Broad CHC Factor: Processing Speed (Gs)
Narrow CHC Abilities: Perceptual Speed (P), more specifically orthographic perceptual speed
Median g loading: .54
Stimuli: Visual
Task Requirements: Rapidly locating and marking two identical letters or letter patterns among a defined set
Inferred Cognitive Processes: Speeded visual perception and matching; visual discrimination; access to orthographic memory representations; orthographic processing
Response Modality: Motoric (drawing lines through)
Related Educational Interventions or Accommodations: Focus on learning and recognition of specific English-language orthographic patterns; emphasize speediness; build perceptual speed via repetition; extended time; reducing quantity of work; eliminating or limiting copying activities

Test 5: Phonological Processing

Test 5: Phonological Processing is based on a growing body of evidence that suggests phonological codes are a route to lexical access (Leinenger, 2014). Phonological coding in working memory can be described as a sensation of "hearing" word sounds or words in our heads. Lukatela and Turvey (1994b) called phonological coding "the initial and primary code by which a word accesses its representation in the internal lexicon" (p. 333). Because phonological codes create the most stable and retrievable short-term memory coding system, they also can be used to activate, integrate, restructure, and/or sustain information in working memory (Baddeley, 1979; Baddeley, Eldridge, & Lewis, 1981; Klatt, 1979; Levy, 1978; McCusker, Hillinger, & Bias, 1981; Slowiaczek & Clifton, 1980). Perhaps this helps explain why Test 5: Phonological Processing is so highly related to general intelligence(g) and is so predictive of academic achievement, particularly in reading and writing (McGrew et al., 2014).

In CHC theory, Phonological Processing is primarily a measure of Auditory Processing (*Ga*) and the narrow ability of Phonetic Coding (PC). However, the factor structure is complex and includes aspects of Comprehension-Knowledge

(*Gc*), such as semantic memory and other narrow ability variance, specifically Language Development (LD), Speed of Lexical Access (LA), and Word Fluency (FW). This test is also cognitively complex because it invokes multiple cognitive operations and parameters of cognitive efficiency in phonological processing. Part A Word Access measures the depth of word access from phonemic cues; this part of the test requires an examinee to provide a word that has a specific phonemic element in a specific location. Part B Word Fluency measures the breadth and fluency of word activation from phonemic cues; this part requires an examinee to name as many words as possible (in 1 minute) that begin with a specified sound. Part C Substitution measures lexical substitution from phonemic cues in working memory; this part requires an examinee to delete a part of a word (typically a phoneme) and substitute a different phoneme to produce a new target word. Together, the three parts measure the depth, breadth, and phonological working memory required for lexical activation, access, and restructuring via phonological codes. Thus, it can be suggested that Test 5: Phonological Processing involves the reasoning and memory functions required to tap long-term phonological knowledge—an important link between primary (working) memory and long-term memory (G. Jones, Gobet, & Pine, 2007).

The effective use of phonological codes to access words is related to success in reading (Daneman & Newson, 1992; Leinenger, 2014). The relationship is explained by the phonological mediation hypothesis (Van Orden, 1987; Van Orden & Goldinger, 1996), which suggests that phonology can convey or transmit phonological information to facilitate word identification. Efficiency of phonological coding is applicable to all stages of the reading process, from word identification to passage comprehension (Leinenger, 2014). For example, when reading silently, the process of phonological coding often produces the sensation of the inner voice that occurs when orthographic information is recoded into phonological information. The recoded phonological information can then activate—by making a connection to—candidate words in the individual's lexicon. Van Orden and Goldinger (1996) suggested, "We read in order to 'hear,' in order to understand" (p. 206).

Some researchers have argued that phonological codes are the primary means by which readers achieve lexical access (Lukatela & Turvey, 1994a, 1994b; Van Orden, 1987). This view is supported by eye tracking and electroencephalographic and magnetic field images of the brain showing that readers begin to generate phonological codes prior to actually fixating on the target word (Ashby, 2010; Ashby, Sanders, & Kingston, 2009; Cornelissen et al., 2009; Miellet & Sparrow, 2004; Pollatsek, Lesch, Morris, & Rayer, 1992; Slattery, Pollatsek, & Rayner, 2006; Wheat, Cornelissen, Frost, & Hansen., 2010).

Consequently, it seems likely that phonological coding is important in understanding how words can be activated (Lukatela, Lukatela, & Turvey, 1993). Phonological coding is especially important for beginning readers, but it is also important for mature readers when approaching difficult, infrequent, or unfamiliar words (Jared, Levy, & Rayner, 1999; McCusker et al., 1981). Chace, Rayner, and Well (2005) found evidence that less skilled readers do not use phonological codes effectively and that even normal readers can find their reading disrupted without efficient application of phonological codes. Evaluation of the efficacy of phonological coding may be particularly important for poor readers but also can provide information on the integrity of phonological coding for readers of all levels.

Interventions for young children with limited proficiency on Test 5: Phonological Processing include playing games that focus on sounds of words (M. J. Adams, 1990; Bridge, Winograd, & Haley, 1983; Glazer, 1989; LINKS, 2002; Lundberg, Frost, & Peterson, 1988; National Reading Panel, 2000; Rauth & Stuart, 2008; Strickland, 1991), including games that increase production of words beginning with the same sound (German, 2002b), or rhyming and alliteration games (Bradley & Bryant, 1983).

For beginning readers with identified limitations in phonological processing, explicit, systematic, synthetic phonics programs are recommended (National Reading Panel, 2000; Snow, Burns, & Griffin, 1998; Stanovich, 1994; Torgesen, 1997; Torgesen et al., 1999). For older children, adolescents, and young adults, oral practice with common onset-rime patterns of spoken words (Bentin & Leshem, 1993; Hatcher, Hulme, & Ellis, 1994; Lundberg et al., 1988; Melby-Lervag, Lyster, & Hulme, 2012; National Institute for Literacy, 2008; National Institute of Child Health and Human Development, 2000; Troia, 1999) as well as targeted small-group instruction in syllable dividing and rehearsal (German, 2002a; Muter, Hulme, Snowling, & Taylor, 1997) can be effective.

Some individuals with limitations in phonological processing may benefit from explicit modeling of the pronunciation of new words (LINKS, 2002; National Reading Panel, 2000; Rauth & Stuart, 2008) with intensive focus on syllable-by-syllable word pronunciation in the learning phase (Altmann, 1999). For individuals with severe limitations, semantic cues may need to be provided (Hicklin, Best, Herbert, Howard, & Osborne, 2002; Kennison, Fernandez, & Bowers, 2014). See **Rapid Reference 4.5**.

≡ Rapid Reference 4.5 Interpretation of Test 5—Phonological Processing

Operational Definition: Measures word activation, fluency of word access, and word restructuring via phonological codes

Primary Broad CHC Factor: Auditory Processing (*Ga*)

Conjoint Broad CHC Factors: Comprehension-Knowledge (*Gc*)

Narrow CHC Abilities: Phonetic coding (PC); Language Development (LD); Word Fluency (FW); Speed of Lexical Access (LA)

Median g loading: .71

Stimuli: Auditory (phonemes; words)

Task Requirements: Providing a word with a specific speech sound; naming as many words as possible that begin with a specified sound; substituting part of a word to make a new word

Inferred Cognitive Processes: Phonological activation and access to stored lexical entries; speeded lexical network activation; phonological working memory

Related Educational Interventions or Accommodations: Activities that focus on the sounds in words; games to increase production of words with the same sound; rhyming and alliteration games; pictures to stimulate fluent production of object names; oral practice with onset-rime patterns of spoken words; explicit modeling of word pronunciations; intensive practice on word pronunciation in the learning phase; explicit, systematic, synthetic phonics instruction; targeted small-group instruction in syllable dividing and rehearsal; use of semantics in word instruction

Test 6: Story Recall

Test 6: Story Recall, a test of Long-Term Storage and Retrieval (*Glr*), requires listening to and retelling the principal components of an orally presented story. The name of the test is somewhat of a misnomer, however, as "recall" is an oversimplification—albeit a popularly used description—for the integration of a number of cognitive abilities and execution of processes involved in performance of this task (Kintsch, 1988, 1990; van den Broeck, 1997). Listening (LS) ability is a fundamental skill that enables the individual to focus on the relevant aspects of the story (Oakhill, Hartt, & Samols, 2005). As more elements are added to the story, they are also added to a mental representation that is held in working memory via the process of *mapping*, a central feature of cognition (Ashcraft, 2002; Zhou & Black, 2000). An individual's general (background) knowledge (K0) supports the construction of a coherent meaning-based mental representation of the story (Kintsch, 1988). In the listening phase, executive functions are required to continually update the mental representations, within working memory, along different dimensions of meaning such as time or space elements, causation, or even inferences of intentionality (Zwann, Langston, & Graesser, 1995; Zwann & Radvansky, 1998).

The story recall task is one of the oldest experimental formats in the history of cognitive psychology, as reported in the book *Remembering* by Bartlett (1932/1967) (see Figure 4.2). Bartlett is noted for his recall experiment using a story called the "War of the Ghosts." Bartlett asked his British study participants to remember details of a story that originated from Canadian First Nation's folklore. In the recall phase, Bartlett observed that background knowledge affected long-term retrieval of facts. Aspects of the story that were not part of Edwardian English culture were sometimes not remembered at all, or those particular story details were changed to reflect the listener's prior knowledge. For example, story details about a "canoe" were often recalled as a "boat." The important insight from Bartlett's study is that story details are not simply "recalled" but rather "reconstructed" from the listener's background knowledge (K0 in CHC theory).

In Story Recall, the encoding process relies on an individual's background knowledge to support the construction of a meaningful mental representation in the listening phase, which, when subsequently successfully reconstructed in the retelling phase, is called a Meaningful Memory (MM) in CHC theory. Consequently, the story "recall" misnomer referred to at the beginning of this section suggests that task performance is more accurately described as *story reconstruction*. The listening phase is the mental-model construction phase; the retelling phase is the reconstructive phase. Additionally, by going "beyond CHC theory" to incorporate story-relevant research from the broad neuroscience literature, it can be inferred that the story construction-reconstruction phases both occur within working memory (and are limited by its capacity). In short, Story Recall requires listening ability; background knowledge for the words, objects, or situations that are described in the storytelling phase; and attention to details; and it is constrained by working memory capacity.

This interpretation of the cognitive processes involved in Test 6: Story Recall has implications for intervention when Listening (LS)ability, background Knowledge (K0), and/or Meaningful Memory (MM) are limited. Also, examiners should consider whether the ability to retain the story elements might be influenced by the individual's Working Memory Capacity (WM), which places limits on the volume of information that can be reconstructed into a coherent

Figure 4.2 F. C. Bartlett's *Remembering*
Cambridge University Press

and connected representation of the objects, events, or situations in the story retelling phase (van den Broeck, 1989).

For young children, the development of listening ability is supported with opportunities to hear and practice language (Hart & Risley, 1995; Moats, 2001). Active learning (Marzano et al., 2001), which involves attending to and thinking about the material, is particularly useful for acquisition of new knowledge and benefits the encoding and retrieval processes. For individuals in school, memory for meaningful information is an important aspect of academic competence. Oral elaboration of material to be learned is especially useful for associating the new information with prior knowledge (Clark & Paivio, 1991; Medina, 2008; Paivio, 2006). Use of visual representation (De Koning & van der Schoot, 2013; Greenleaf & Wells-Papanek, 2005) helps the learner construct mental representations of the material to be learned, thereby improving the encoding and retrieval process. Direct instruction in semantics, syntax, and pragmatics (National Reading Panel, 2000; Tomeson & Aarnoutse, 1998) is helpful for understanding and using oral language. Mnemonics can be especially helpful in learning rules, patterns, and word lists (Wolfe, 2001). See **Rapid Reference 4.6**.

≡ *Rapid Reference 4.6 Interpretation of Test 6—Story Recall*

Operational Definition: Measures listening ability with attention to orally-imparted details; formation of mental representations in the stimulus phase; story reconstruction in the response phase

Primary Broad CHC Factor: Long-Term Storage and Retrieval (*Glr*)

Conjoint Broad CHC Factor: Comprehension-Knowledge (*Gc*)

Narrow CHC Abilities: Meaningful Memory (MM); Listening Ability (LS); General Information (K0)

Median *g* loading: .58

Stimuli: Auditory (orally presented stories)

Task Requirements: Listening to and reconstructing story details

Inferred Cognitive Processes: Construction of propositional representations and recoding

Response Modality: Oral (words, phrases, or sentences)

Related Educational Interventions or Accommodations: Opportunities to hear and practice language; active learning; direct instruction in semantics; elaborative rehearsal; use of visual representations; use of mnemonics

Test 7: Visualization

Test 7: Visualization measures the ability to internally image spatial forms or shapes, often by rotating or manipulating them in the imagination. The test includes two parts. Part A Spatial Relations requires analyzing and drawing inferences about whole-to-part relationships from two-dimensional puzzlelike drawings. This part of the test relies heavily on size and shape perception, although some items require mental rotation ability. Part B Block Rotation is primarily a three-dimensional imaging task that requires deciding which two options, among several, are rotated images of the stimulus shape. In CHC theory, Test 7: Visualization is a measure of Visual Processing (*Gv*) and the narrow ability of Visualization (Vz)— the mental processes used in analyzing, imagining transformations, and drawing inferences from visual images.

Visualization ability is cognitively significant because it requires an individual to mentally transform images in a prospective fashion (Frick, Möhring, & Newcombe, 2014). Representing and transforming visual-spatial relationships occurs in working memory, sometimes called visuospatial working memory (Coluccia & Louse, 2004). Some researchers suggest that visualization supports working memory (Tommasi & Laeng, 2012), particularly the construct of the visuospatial sketchpad (Baddeley, 1986).

Good visualization skills are associated with successful performance in a wide variety of outcomes ranging from managing everyday tasks, such as navigating the environment, using tools, solving practical problems, comprehending assembly instructions, to successful performance in science, technology, engineering, and mathematics (Shea, Lubinski, & Benbow, 2001; Uttal et al., 2013; Wai, Lubinski, & Benbow, 2009). Visualization ability may be related to the ability to construct mental representations. This ability is a common mechanism of fundamental importance in many cognitive domains and for the development of academic skills, including number sense (Gunderson, Ramirez, Beilock, & Levine, 2012) and reading comprehension (De Koning & van der Schoot, 2013).

Individuals who are unable to create a mental representation of an object cannot hold and manipulate the image in working memory (Hegarty & Waller, 2005). A variety of informal and formal methods can help develop or improve visualization skills (Uttal, Miller, & Newcombe, 2013). For young children, use of gestures, block play, puzzle play, and use of spatial language by parents and teachers help develop visualization skills (Newcombe, 2010). Computerized video games (Feng, Spence, & Pratt, 2007; Green & Bavelier, 2003) can make spatial tasks familiar and enjoyable (Uttal, Miller, et al., 2013). Playing video games can improve attention and other foundational skills. Attention to spatial details can improve with relevant training (Castel, Pratt, & Drummond, 2005; Feng et al., 2007; Green & Bavelier, 2007). Green and Bevalier (2003, 2007) showed that subitizing (i.e., recognizing a number without using other mathematical processes, such as counting) capacity improved with video training; video game players could hold a greater number of visual elements in working memory and act upon them. They also showed that video game players have a shorter attentional blink, increasing their ability to take in and use rapidly changing visual information.

Mental rotation skills can be taught specifically (Baenninger & Newcombe, 1989; Feng et al., 2007; Tzuriel & Egozi, 2010), such as using quick drawings for planning and communication of understanding (Wheatley, 1996) or even a semester-long course in spatial training (Sorby, 2009). Training can target better encoding of visual stimuli (Sims & Mayer, 2002), more efficient transformational processes (Kail & Park, 1992), or strategy usage (Stieff, 2007). Strategy training is effective for development of mental rotation skills, such as using a global-holistic or gestalt-like strategy instead of a part-by-part approach (Stieff, 2007; Stieff, Dixon, Ryu, Kumi, & Hegarty, 2014; Tzuriel & Egozi, 2010). Just and Carpenter (1985) found that study participants could learn to home in on and then compare selected key aspects of a figure to determine whether the specific elements match the stimulus figure rather than attempting to mentally rotate an entire complex visual stimulus. Integrating spatially challenging activities into the curriculum is an easy-to-implement suggestion for improving visualization skills (Federation of American Scientists, 2006; Foreman et al., 2004; Gee, 2003; McAuliffe, 2003; Newcombe, Utall, & Sauter, 2013). Part of the training for mental rotation is for learners to become faster at mental object rotation (Kail & Park, 1992). See **Rapid Reference 4.7.**

≡ Rapid Reference 4.7 Interpretation of Test 7—Visualization

Operational Definition: Measures size and shape perception, part-to-whole analysis, and mentally transforming two- and three-dimensional images
Primary Broad CHC Factor: Visual Processing (Gv)
Narrow CHC Abilities: Visualization (Vz)
Median g loading: .61
Stimuli: Visual (shapes, design patterns)

Task Requirements: Identifying the subset of two-dimensional pieces needed to form a complete shape; identifying two three-dimensional rotated block patterns that match a target
Inferred Cognitive Processes: Visual feature detection; mental manipulation of visual images; matching
Response Modality: Oral (letters) or motoric (pointing)
Related Educational Interventions or Accommodations: Activities designed to develop ability to discriminate visual features, mentally manipulate visual images, and match visual information; increased exposure to graphs, charts, maps; video games; three-dimensional sketching exercises

Test 8: General Information

Test 8: General Information measures an individual's level of general (verbal) information, as aspect of Comprehension-Knowledge (*Gc*). The test uses two types of questions to assess level of general object knowledge: where objects typically are found and what a typical function of the object is. Hintzman (1978) called this type of object knowledge *generic memory*, or general object knowledge.

Martin's (2009) neurocognitive research suggested that the type of object knowledge that is assessed in this test is based on cognitive representations of core object properties, or *semantic primitives*. Cognitive neuroscience defines semantic primitives as mental representations of objects that are stored via the visual processing system for perceiving object form or motion. These primitives are assumed to underpin object meaning in perception—regardless of stimulus modality (visual, auditory, tactile) or format (pictures, words) —and in thought and imagination. In other words, an examinee is not able to answer the question "Where would you usually find _____?" or "What do people usually do with _____?" without a *mental representation* of the object (a semantic primitive that represents the object construct).

Cattell (1987) posited that, in addition to verbal ability, the broad construct of *Gc* represents individual differences in prior knowledge. Test 8: General Information is useful as a measure of an individual's prior knowledge—the level of general knowledge an individual brings to the learning situation. Integration of prior knowledge with new information underlies performance on many complex cognitive tasks. In fact, a common denominator in many complex tasks is the requirement to access relevant long-term memories and integrate prior knowledge with new problem information to construct new cognitive representations (Hannon & Daneman, 2014; Oberauer, Süß, Wilhelm, & Wittman, 2008).

Cognitive neuroscience has provided an important cue to learning that is particularly relevant to the development of background knowledge; this cue is suggested by the use of the term *embodied cognition* to imply that object concepts are grounded in perception and action systems and use of all sensory modalities (Barsalou, 2008; Wilson, 2002; Zwaan & Taylor, 2006). As stated by Patterson, Nestor, and Rogers (2007), "Essentially all current theoretical positions about semantic memory share the view that much of the content of our semantic memory relates to perception and action, and is represented in brain regions that are responsible for perceiving and acting" (p. 1033). Martin (2009) stated that "the information about salient object properties—such as how they look, move, and are used, along with our affective associations to them—is stored in the neural systems that support perceiving, acting, and feeling" (p. 1041). Consequently, some ways to build background knowledge through the principle of embodied cognition include introducing new topics with demonstrations or field experiences that involve multiple sensory modalities to influence the learner's perceptions, actions, and feelings.

Limited proficiency on Test 8: General Information may be due to lack of background knowledge. One of the primary intervention principles for limitations in General Information involves connecting current instruction to prior knowledge or building background knowledge. For example, an important instructional intervention for an individual with limited background knowledge involves developing a connection between the topic of instruction and what the learner already knows. This is sometimes referred to as activating prior knowledge. Activating what a student already knows from personal experience, prior schooling, or family history will assist the student in understanding of current instructional tasks. When students are encouraged to relate their background knowledge to the material being studied, they are more engaged in learning (Moje et al., 2004). Teachers can help a student activate prior knowledge by asking such questions as "What do you remember or know about _____?"

Some ways to help build background knowledge (when little or none exists) include introducing new topics with short video clips, demonstrations, or field experiences. Reading to children that is accompanied by text talks (Beck & McKeown, 2001) helps provide a fund of general information. Reading for different purposes and at different levels of difficulty will expose an individual to new names of things that may never be encountered in oral language alone (National Reading Panel, 2000; Stahl, 1999). Cooperative learning environments—students working together in small groups—are especially useful for developing background knowledge because they provide the opportunity for peers to elaborate and discuss information (Nisbett, 2009). See **Rapid Reference 4.8**.

☰ Rapid Reference 4.8 Interpretation of Test 8—General Information

Operational Definition: Measures general object knowledge
Primary Broad CHC Factor: Comprehension-Knowledge (Gc)
Narrow CHC Abilities: General (verbal) Information (KO)
Median g loading: .59
Stimuli: Auditory (questions)
Task Requirements: Identify where objects are found and what people typically do with an object
Inferred Cognitive Processes: Semantic activation and access to mental representations of objects (semantic primitives)
Response Modality: Oral (phrases or sentences)
Related Educational Interventions or Accommodations: Text talks; reading for different purposes; use of relevant, real-world examples for learning; cooperative learning environments

Test 9: Concept Formation

Test 9: Concept Formation measures the ability to categorize and compare (Andrewes, 2001), a basis for abstracting universal or rational concepts (Wang, 1987). In CHC theory, Concept Formation is a test of Fluid Reasoning (*Gf*) that measures the narrow ability of induction (I), or inference. This test uses a visual format to assess higher-level conceptual understanding. The test evaluates how well an individual can conceptualize with language constructs. Eysenck (1999) referred to this process as the *eduction* of relations.

In contrast to the Number Series test, Concept Formation measures verbal, language-based inductive reasoning. The first five items measure categorical perception (Goldstone & Hendrickson, 2010) that requires understanding of the word *different* and the more abstract concept of "most different." These items measure the ability to recognize and identify the essential rather than any secondary, characteristic of target objects. This is the first stage in the development of an object concept.

The ability to form and use language concepts provides the basis for higher-level cognition. Item 6 and beyond require familiarity with, and understanding of, a number of terms including *red, yellow, big, little, round, square, one,* and *two.*

Test 9: Concept Formation measures an important aspect of cognition because human beings organize their world into language concepts that, in turn, affect their understanding of the world around them (Andrewes, 2001). A number of interventions may be useful in developing inductive reasoning abilities. For young children, repeated opportunities to sort and classify objects are important in developing categorical reasoning skills (Klauer, Willmes, & Phye, 2002). Hands-on problem-solving tasks provide children with opportunities to be actively engaged in learning. A teacher can demonstrate reasoning skills using a think-aloud procedure to model the steps involved in solving a problem. For individuals of any age, interventions that are designed to develop skills in categorization and drawing conclusions, that involve connecting new concepts to prior knowledge, that use teacher demonstrations and guided practice, and that provide feedback on performance may positively influence the development of conceptual reasoning abilities (Klauer et al., 2002; Nisbett, 2009). Explicit inductive reasoning training has been shown to be effective (Klauer & Phye, 2008; Phye, 1989; 1997; Tomic & Klauer, 1996). Some commercially available board and computer games have been shown to be beneficial for developing reasoning abilities (Mackey, Hill, Stone, & Bunge, 2010). Cooperative learning groups and reciprocal teaching (Palincsar & Brown, 1984) are also effective ways to actively engage a student in learning and developing reasoning skills.

Teaching a student to slow down in response to difficult tasks can allow for adequate time to process all parts of a complex problem (Medina, 2008). Making meaningful associations is a primary means of learning and evaluating information. Use of graphic organizers, such as Venn diagrams, T-charts or concept maps, can help students think conceptually and can assist in learning by linking new information to prior knowledge (Marzano et al. 2001). See **Rapid Reference 4.9**.

Test 10: Numbers Reversed

Test 10: Numbers Reversed measures the ability to temporarily store and recode orally presented information—a complex span task (Daneman & Carpenter, 1980). This test requires the individual to remember a series of serially presented numbers and then perform a complex processing task—reversing the sequence of numbers. Typically, performing a complex span task requires intense allocation of resources that displaces information in running memory (Unsworth & Engle, 2006) so the information must be maintained by active engagement of controlled attention (Kane, Brown, et al., 2007; Kane, Conway, Hambrick, & Engle, 2007). Performance on complex span tasks, such as Numbers Reversed, is strongly predictive of an individual's attentional control in the service of complex cognitive processing (Hutchison, 2007; Unsworth & Spillers, 2010) and provides a strong reflection of the executive attention aspects of working memory (Engle, 2002; Kane, Brown, et al., 2007; Kane, Conway, et al., 2007). In terms of CHC

≣ Rapid Reference 4.9 Interpretation of Test 9—Concept Formation

Operational Definition: Measures verbal (language-based) inductive reasoning
Primary Broad CHC Factor: Fluid Reasoning (*Gf*)
Narrow CHC Abilities: Induction (I)
Median *g* loading: .59
Stimuli: Visual (drawings)
Task Requirements: Identifying, categorizing, and determining rules
Inferred Cognitive Processes: Rule-based categorization; rule-switching; induction/inference
Response Modality: Oral (words)
Related Educational Interventions or Accommodations: Categorize using real objects; develop skills in drawing conclusions; perform hands-on problem-solving tasks; make meaningful associations; inductive reasoning training; provide concrete examples of grouping objects; commercially available reasoning games; think-aloud procedures; cooperative learning groups; reciprocal teaching; graphic organizers; slowing down in response to difficult reasoning tasks

theory, Numbers Reversed measures Working Memory Capacity (WM) and Attentional Control (AC).

Two concepts from Baddeley and Hitch's (1974) working memory model often are used to describe two cognitive processing functions that may be called up when performing Numbers Reversed—the phonological loop and the visual-spatial sketchpad. The phonological loop refers to a temporary store of verbal information, such as storage of the oral stimulus string input. Many individuals report solving this task by maintaining or updating awareness of the verbal string of information through strategic auditory rehearsal prior to oral recitation of the reversed sequence. Also, some individuals report constructing a mental image of the number sequence and then reversing the sequence orally as if reading the numbers from right to left rather than left to right. This mental image strategy is similar to the Baddeley-Hitch concept of the visual-spatial sketchpad.

Working memory capacity is determined by the efficacy with which chunks of information are created and dissolved as the context of the situation changes. It is typically believed that three to five chunks of information can be actively maintained in primary memory (Shipstead et al., 2014). Use of chunking strategies may be helpful in making more efficient use of available short-term memory by recoding the information (Hardiman, 2003). Rehearsal (repeated and extensive

☰ Rapid Reference 4.10 Interpretation of Test 10—Numbers Reversed

Operational Definition: Measures temporary storage and recoding of numeric information in primary memory

Primary Broad CHC Factor: Short-Term Working Memory (*Gwm*)

Median g loading: .65

Narrow CHC Abilities: Working Memory Capacity (WM); Attentional Control (AC)

Stimuli: Auditory

Task Requirements: Listening to and holding a span of numbers in immediate awareness and then reversing the sequence

Inferred Cognitive Processes: Attention to verbal stimuli and then reversing the sequence in working memory

Response Modality: Oral (numbers)

Related Educational Interventions or Accommodations: Chunking strategies; rehearsal; provide visual cues; complex computer games; reduce distractions; reduce working memory loads (reduction in amount of material to be remembered at any one time); simplifying linguistic structures of verbal material; restructuring complex tasks into separate and independent steps); repeating important information

practice) provides a way for a student to perform a task in a more automatic fashion and thereby lessen the demands on working memory (Mahncke, Bronstone, & Merzenich, 2006; Tallal et al., 1996). Individuals with very limited working memory capacity may require accommodations, such as keeping oral directions short and simple, paraphrasing length instructions, or providing visual cues; reducing the overall amount of material to be remembered; restructuring complex tasks into separate independent steps; and monitoring classroom performance to make sure students remember what they are supposed to be doing (Gathercole & Alloway, 2008). See **Rapid Reference 4.10.**

Test 11: Number-Pattern Matching

Test 11: Number-Pattern Matching measures the narrow ability of Perceptual Speed (P), or visual-perceptual ability under timed conditions in which a perceived configuration is compared to a an array that includes the target configuration and a number of slight variants of the pattern to determine a match. Perceptual Speed (P) is a narrow ability of the broad Cognitive Processing Speed (*Gs*) factor.

Although the first 30 items use single-digit numbers for target and comparison purposes in the broad focus of attention (Cowen, 2001), performance on the remainder of the test may be facilitated by well-developed number chunking mechanisms in the narrow focus of attention. Individuals who are able to mentally represent a string of numbers as a 1-item chunk will possess a processing advantage over individuals who perceive each string of numbers as an unassociated series of numerals. For example, perceiving the number "935" as a unit, perhaps represented subvocally as "nine hundred thirty five" or "nine thirty five," represents cognitive transformation of the string into a single chunk with established place values. In contrast, subvocalizing "nine," "three," and "five" uses three chunks of information in working memory whose relative order can be more readily confused during a rapid visual search. Perception of a target 2- or 3-digit number string as a single chunk provides a narrow focus of attention (Oberauer, 2002) that can be compared to each of the other number strings on the line. Chunking is an important aspect of cognitive processing efficiency (Oberauer & Hein, 2012). Because individuals can maintain only about four chunks of information in the broad focus of working memory (Cowan, 2001), and individuals can narrow their focus of attention to a single chunk at any given time (Oberauer, 2002), the cognitive mechanism of number chunking allows people to perceive and process multidigit numbers more rapidly and efficiently.

Perceptual speediness sometimes can be improved by repetitive practice, speed drills, and use of computer games that require an individual to make decisions quickly (Klingberg, 2009; Mahncke et al., 2006; Tallal et al., 1996). For example, repetition is an important factor in building speed. Repeated and extensive practice may enable an individual to perform the same tasks in a more automatic fashion to increase speeded performance. Speed drills focus performance on completing a task quickly. However, perceptual speed limitations may have implications for the provision of educational accommodations (Ofiesh, 2000; Shaywitz, 2003). Accommodations that compensate for limitations in perceptual speed include providing extended time, reducing the quantity of work required (breaking large assignments into two or more component assignments), and eliminating or limiting copying activities. See **Rapid Reference 4.11**.

Test 12: Nonword Repetition

In Test 12: Nonword Repetition, the examinee listens to a made-up stimulus word that is modeled after a typical phonemic word pattern in English. To repeat a novel phonological nonword form successfully, the examinee needs to maintain an acoustic representation in working memory long enough to support a subsequent articulation of the nonword. Similar nonword repetition

≣ Rapid Reference 4.11 Interpretation of Test 11—Number-Pattern Matching

Operational Definition: Measures numeric visual perceptual discrimination ability under timed conditions
Primary Broad CHC Factor: Cognitive Processing Speed (Gs)
Narrow CHC Abilities: Perceptual Speed (P)
Median g loading: .54
Stimuli: Visual
Task Requirements: Rapidly locating and marking identical numbers from a defined set
Inferred Cognitive Processes: Speeded visual perception and matching; visual discrimination
Response Modality: Motoric (marking)
Related Educational Interventions or Accommodations: Focus on learning and expression of place value in mathematics; speed drills; build speed via repetition; computer matching games; extended time; reducing quantity of work; eliminating or limiting copying activities

tests have gained wide acceptance because the task demands closely match the phonological processes involved in learning new words (Coady & Evans, 2008; Gathercole, 2006; Gathercole, Hitch, Service, & Martin, 1997) and because many individuals who perform poorly on nonword repetition tasks often have difficulties learning the phonological form of language (Archibald & Gathercole, 2007). Many researchers have suggested that use of a brief nonword repetition test is a relatively time-efficient and reliable way to identify individuals with or at risk for language impairments (Bishop, North, & Donlan, 1996; Coady & Evans, 2008; Conti-Ramsden, 2003; Conti-Ramsden, Botting, & Farragher, 2001; Conti-Ramsden & Hesketh, 2003; Dollaghan & Campbell, 1998; Ellis Weismer et al., 2000, Gray, 2003; Horohov & Oetting, 2004; Taylor, Lean, & Schwartz, 1989).

Nonword Repetition is a complex task requiring a number of perceptual, phonological, cognitive, and motor processes, including speech perception (an acoustic representation), phonological encoding (segmenting the nonword into smaller speech units that can be stored in working memory), phonological short-term memory capacity (temporary storage for the novel phonological string), phonological assembly (formulating a motor plan that assembles the speech unit segments), and oral production (articulation). In addition, repetition accuracy may be influenced by lexical knowledge. Individuals with larger oral vocabularies will have access to, and articulatory experience with, a greater number of lexical entries that may pose similarities, in part or phonotactic structure, to the target nonword (Beckman & Edwards, 2000; Bishop et al., 1996; Coady & Aslin, 2004; Coady & Evans, 2008, Dollaghan, Biber, & Campbell, 1995; Edwards, Beckman, & Munson, 2004; Gathercole, 1995, 2006; Gathercole & Baddeley, 1989, 1990; Metsala, 1999; Munson, 2001; Munson, Kurtz, & Windson, 2005). Because Nonword Repetition taps so many underlying skills and is so interrelated with vocabulary development, interpretation of the precise nature of any limitations often cannot be made without additional evaluation.

The complex nature of nonword repetition tests is reflected in historical differences of opinion about the precise nature of what is measured by this type of task. Seminal research by Gathercole and others (A. M. Adams & Gathercole, 1995, 1996, 2000; Gathercole, 1995; Gathercole & Adams, 1993, 1994; Gathercole & Baddeley, 1989; Gathercole, Willis, & Baddeley, 1991a, b; Gathercole, Willis, Emslie, & Baddeley, 1991, 1992; Gathercole et al., 1997; Gathercole, Service, Hitch, Adams, & Martin, 1999) suggests that nonword repetition tasks measure phonological short-term working memory capacity, sometimes referred to as the phonological loop. Not all researchers agree. Metsala (1999) suggested that nonword repetition tests primarily measures phonological sensitivity and not working memory per se. Others have argued that the constructs of phonological working memory and phonological sensitivity are both manifestations of phonological processing ability (Bowey, 1996, 1997, 2001; MacDonald & Christiansen, 2002). Subsequent research by Archibald and Gathercole (2007) suggested that performance on nonword repetition tasks is best explained by a combination of two factors—short-term working memory and "a further ability that is specific to the repetition of novel multisyllabic phonological forms" (p. 923). Although primarily auditory and phonological in nature, nonword repetition ability is constrained by phonological storage capacity (Baddeley, Gathercole, & Papagno, 1998; Gathercole, 2006). Analysis of the WJ IV COG Nonword Repetition test within the context of the WJ IV standardization sample and contemporary CHC theory supports this latter explanation. That is, Test 12: Nonword Repetition measures both span in Short-Term Working Memory (*Gwm*) and phonological sensitivity in Auditory Processing (*Ga*) (McGrew et al., 2014). The CHC narrow abilities include Phonetic Coding (PC), Memory for Sound Patterns (UM), and Auditory Memory Span (MS).

Interventions for limited proficiency on Nonword Repetition focus on phonologically based language-development activities. Increased exposure to new words will simultaneously increase exposure to the variations in sound segments that

≡ Rapid Reference 4.12   Interpretation of Test 12—Nonword Repetition

Operational Definition: Measures phonological short-term working memory, sensitivity, and capacity

Primary Broad CHC Factor: Auditory Processing (*Ga*)

Conjoint Broad CHC Factor: Short-Term Working Memory (*Gwm*)

Narrow CHC Abilities: Phonetic Coding (PC); Memory for Sound Patterns (UM); Auditory Memory Span (MS)

Median *g* loading: .52

Stimuli: Auditory

Task Requirements: Listening to a novel phonological word form and repeating it exactly

Inferred Cognitive Processes: Acoustic representation, phonological encoding, temporary storage of the novel phonological string, phonological assembly

Response Modality: Oral (words)

Related Educational Interventions or Accommodations: Increased exposure to new words; repeating (uttering) new words when they are learned; activities that require repetition and construction of nonwords; vocalization strategy for new words; increased time spent reading

make up words (Bentin & Leshem, 1993; Hatcher et al., 1994; Lundberg et al., 1988; Melby-Lervag et al., 2012; Muter et al., 1997; National Institute for Literacy, 2008; National Institute of Child Health and Human Development, 2000; Troia, 1999). Teaching an individual to repeat (utter) the new word after it is heard is an effective strategy for vocalizing the sound segments that make up words (Archibald & Gathercole, 2006; Gathercole, Tiffany, Briscoe, Thorn, & the ALSPAC Team, 2005; Metsala, 1999; Metsala & Walley, 1998). Activities that specifically require repetition and construction of nonwords may be both effective and enjoyable (Metsala, 1999; Metsala & Walley, 1998; Michas & Henry, 1994). Increased time spent reading also will provide exposure to more words and their component sounds (Majerus, Van Der Linde, Mulder, Meulemans, & Peters, 2004). See **Rapid Reference 4.12**.

Test 13: Visual-Auditory Learning

Test 13: Visual-Auditory Learning measures the narrow ability of Associative Memory (MA), or paired-associate learning, an aspect of Long-Term Storage and

Retrieval (*Glr*). Kosslyn and Thompson (2000) defined Associative Memory as a subprocess of memory that combines information from two types of properties in the learning phase and in the retrieval phase compares the stimulus information with stored representations. For example, in Visual-Auditory Learning, the initial task requires associating the visual rebus symbol with a verbal label.

The controlled-learning format of this test employs a directed spotlight attention procedure (Brefczynski & DeYoe, 1999; Gazzaniga et al., 1998; Klingberg, 2009; Sengpiel & Hubener, 1999) that prepares the individual to encode the stimulus. The retrieval phase requires the examinee to match a rebus presentation with its stored semantic representation; this process is called *identification*. When the rebus is identified, the examinee has access to the name associated with the stored representation. If the stimulus is not automatically matched to a stored verbal representation in the object-properties-encoding subsystem, the individual may suggest a hypothesis based on the closest lexical match by means of an "information lookup" subprocess. The information lookup has been shown to play a critical role in working memory (Kosslyn et al., 1995). The feedback procedure used in Visual-Auditory Learning provides a correction to any faulty hypothesis.

The directed-spotlight attention procedure employed in Visual-Auditory Learning provides a cue to the intervention known as *active learning* (Marzano et al., 2001). Active learning is required for the creation of meaning-based codes that are used subsequently to relate new information or task requirements to previously acquired knowledge. Varying the learning tasks, incorporating emotions and novelty, and fostering creativity are ways to promote active learning.

Other interventions for limitations in encoding, storing, or retrieving information include rehearsal and overlearning (Squire & Schacter, 2003), mnemonics (Wolfe, 2001), and use of visual representations or illustrations (Greenleaf & Wells-Papanek, 2005). For example, rehearsal is a critical factor in learning. Because memories consolidate across time, some individuals may benefit from shorter sessions at repeated intervals rather than one long session. For some students with limitations, dividing learning into three, 50-minute sessions with 10-minute breaks in between sessions may be preferable to a single, 3-hour study period. Recitation is one method of rehearsal in which the individual reviews his or her notes on the information, covers the notes, and then recites aloud the material to be learned. This oral recitation technique incorporates more senses than just thinking about the notes and leads to better recall. Overlearning improves storage and recall. This occurs when the individual continues to review and rehearse information he or she already knows. Even one additional review can significantly increase recall. See **Rapid Reference 4.13**.

≡ Rapid Reference 4.13 Interpretation of Test 13—Visual-Auditory Learning

Operational Definition: Measures visual-auditory paired associate encoding in the learning phase; identification and word retrieval in the response phase

Primary Broad CHC Factor: Long-Term Storage and Retrieval (*Glr*)

Narrow CHC Abilities: Associative Memory (MA)

Stimuli: Visual (rebuses) and auditory (words) in the learning condition; visual (rebuses) in the recognition condition

Task Requirements: Learning and recalling words associated with pictographic representations

Inferred Cognitive Processes: Paired-associative encoding via directed spotlight attention; storage and retrieval

Response Modality: Oral (phrases or sentences)

Related Educational Interventions or Accommodations: Active, successful learning experiences; rehearsal; overlearning; mnemonics; illustrate or visualize content

Test 14: Picture Recognition

Test 14: Picture Recognition requires the examinee to form and remember—in a few seconds—mental images (representations of visual stimuli) that cannot easily be encoded verbally. Verbal mediation is reduced because all images presented for each item belong to the same semantic category. In CHC theory, Picture Recognition measures Visual Memory (MV), a narrow ability of Visual Processing (*Gv*). Visual Memory is a durable, limited-capacity system for short-term retention of visual information (Zhang & Luck, 2009).

Visual memory is related to, but different from, iconic memory. Iconic memory is experienced as the phenomenon of still "seeing" a visual trace of the stimulus image in the mind's eye after the stimulus is removed. Iconic memories fade rapidly (Averbach & Coriell, 1961; Sperling, 1960), usually within 80 to 100 milliseconds after removal of the stimulus (Di Lollo, 1980), although quickly associating some prior knowledge about the physical properties of the stimulus can support the retention of the sensory image for up to 300 to 500 milliseconds (Irwin & Yeomans, 1986). Iconic memories have little influence on Visual Memory (MV), which is more durable. The passive storage of visual images is called the visual cache (Baddeley & Hitch, 1994), part of the working memory system. Although images in the visual cache are more durable than iconic memories, the visual cache is of limited capacity, typically three to four items

≡ Rapid Reference 4.14 Interpretation of Test 14—Picture Recognition

Operational Definition: Measures formation (passive storage) of images in the visual cache and recognition of previously presented visual stimuli
Primary Broad CHC Factor: Visual-Spatial Thinking (Gv)
Narrow CHC Abilities: Visual Memory (MV)
Median g loading: .45
Stimuli: Visual (pictures)
Task Requirements: Identifying a subset of previously presented pictures within a field of distracting pictures
Inferred Cognitive Processes: Formation of visual memories and matching of visual stimuli to stored representations
Response Modality: Oral (letters) or motoric (pointing)
Related Educational Interventions or Accommodations: Activities designed to discriminate/match visual features and recall visual information

(Luck & Vogel, 1997). Images can be retained in the visual cache for several seconds (Vogel, Woodman, & Luck, 2001).

Individuals with limited performance on Picture Recognition may benefit from interventions designed to develop skills in attending to and discriminating visual features, matching, and recalling visual information. Visual memory can be improved through extensive practice (Zhang & Luck, 2009). As accommodations, it may be helpful to provide repeated exposures to printed visuals, isolate visual information that is presented (e.g., exposing only a limited amount of visual information on a page), or use auditory modalities to compensate for limitations in visual memory (Greenleaf & Wells-Papanek, 2005). See **Rapid Reference 4.14**.

Test 15: Analysis-Synthesis

From the perspective of CHC theory, Test 15: Analysis-Synthesis is a measure of Fluid Reasoning (*Gf*) that primarily measures the narrow ability of general sequential, or deductive, reasoning (RG; defined as the ability to draw correct conclusions from stated conditions or premises, often from a series of sequential steps). Because of its use of specific solution keys that, if followed correctly, furnish the correct answer to each test item, Analysis-Synthesis also can be described as a measure of algorithmic reasoning (Gazzaniga et al., 1998). Algorithmic reasoning can be specifically taught.

⩦ Rapid Reference 4.15 Interpretation of Test 15—Analysis-Synthesis

Operational Definition: Measures algorithmic, deductive reasoning
Primary Broad CHC Factor: Fluid Reasoning (*Gf*)
Narrow CHC Abilities: General Sequential Reasoning (RG)
Median g loading: .64
Stimuli: Visual (drawings)
Task Requirements: Analyzing puzzles (using symbolic formulations) to determine missing components
Inferred Cognitive Processes: Algorithmic reasoning; deduction
Response Modality: Oral (words)
Related Educational Interventions or Accommodations: Deductive reasoning using concrete objects; hands-on problem-solving tasks; metacognitive strategies; think-aloud procedures

Young children can be taught to use deductive reasoning using concrete objects and hands-on problem-solving tasks, although repetition and review often will be required. Asking a young child to verbalize what he or she has learned is an effective intervention. Using riddles is a fun way to develop deductive reasoning skills. For example, play, "I'm thinking of something _____," wherein an object is described in terms of some concept or attribute; the child must identify the object based on questions he or she asks.

For older children and adolescents, teaching metacognitive strategies and then providing opportunities to practice the strategies are important in developing higher-level reasoning skills. These metacognitive strategies will help the individual be aware of, monitor, and control his or her learning (Manning & Payne, 1996; Pressley, 1990). The individual would be taught to think about the task, set goals, use self-talk, monitor progress, and then to reward him- or herself once the task was accomplished. Some specific strategies that might be incorporated include teaching the individual to compare new concepts to previously learned concepts or to use analogies, metaphors, or similes when approaching a task (Greenleaf & Wells-Papanek, 2005). See **Rapid Reference 4.15**.

Test 16: Object-Number Sequencing

Test 16: Object-Number Sequencing is the most cognitively complex of the WJ IV Working Memory Capacity (WM) tests. Of all the WJ IV COG tests,

Object-Number Sequencing is the most highly correlated with the construct of general intelligence, or *g* (McGrew et al., 2014). In addition, Object-Number Sequencing is likely the best example of controlled attention as proposed by Engle and Kane (2004)—the controlled, sustained attention required for maintaining and/or recovering access to stimuli in working memory.

The model of working memory developed by Cowan (1995) and the extension of Cowan's model by Oberauer (2002, 2009) and Oberauer and Hein (2012) have particular relevance for understanding the cognitive processes that are required and used in Object Number Sequencing. In addition to any activated long-term memories that are retrieved into working memory, Oberauer and Hein (2012) distinguished between a region of direct access and a focus of attention. The region of direct access provides a broad focus and has a limited capacity, about four chunks of information (Cowan, 2001; Oberauer & Kliegel, 2006). The primary function of the broad focus is to bind or chunk multiple representations or units together for information processing, such as assembling new structures out of the selected representations. Oberauer and Hein (2012) described this as a cognitive "blackboard." The narrow focus then selects the information that is needed from the blackboard for a cognitive operation or task performance. What is important about this model is that it explicitly states that there can be only one narrow focus of attention at a time.

As applied to Object-Number Sequencing, the objects and numbers presented for each item must be retained in sequential order in the broad focus blackboard of working memory. Then a list of objects must be created, requiring a single narrow focus of attention. After the sequentially ordered object list is created, the individual must return to the broad focus blackboard and create a new narrow focus of attention by creating a sequential list of numbers from the broad focus. Although memory traces in the broad focus of attention suffer from temporal decay, they can be refreshed by bringing them back into attentional focus (Barrouillet & Camos, 2012).

Complex? Yes! An individual must maintain a broad focus of attention in order to create a narrow focus of attention for the first task requirement and then return to, and thereby refresh, the broad focus blackboard to create a second narrow focus. What makes Object-Number Sequencing so complex is that it requires temporary maintenance of the stimulus string while creating the list of objects. When an individual is successful at creating the list of objects in order but then fails at creating the list of numbers, the broad focus of attention has suffered from temporal decay as a consequence of processing demands required to create a narrow focus of attention. It is difficult to maintain to-be-remembered items while alternately performing a processing task (Shipstead et al., 2014). This is

≡ Rapid Reference 4.16 Interpretation of Test 16—Object-Number Sequencing

Operational Definition: Measures assembly of new cognitive structures out of information maintained in working memory
   Primary Broad CHC Factor: Short-Term Working Memory (*Gwm*)
   Narrow CHC Abilities: Working Memory Capacity (WM)
   Median *g* loading: .74
   Stimuli: Auditory
   Task Requirements: Listening to a series of numbers and words intermingled and then recalling in two reordered sequences
   Inferred Cognitive Processes: Attention to a sequence of acoustic, verbalized stimuli and then dividing the sequence in working memory
   Response Modality: Oral (words, numbers)
   Related Educational Interventions or Accommodations: Focus attention on one thing at a time; avoid multitasking

because "processing and storage compete for attention, which constitutes a limited resource" (Barrouillet & Camos, 2012, p. 413).

Low performance on Object-Number Sequencing suggests difficulties in maintaining serially ordered representations in primary memory in the course of complex task performance (Unsworth & Engle, 2007b). Individuals with very limited proficiency on Object-Number Sequencing may benefit by learning to avoid multitasking and by focusing attention on one thing at a time (Alloway, 2011; Gathercole & Alloway, 2007). See **Rapid Reference 4.16**.

Test 17: Pair Cancellation

Test 17: Pair Cancellation measures *speeded visual perceptual attention*. Perceptual attention is an aspect of attention that is responsible for preferential concentration on stimuli of relative importance (Andrewes, 2001). The test requires an individual to work as rapidly as possible while maintaining a controlled, sustained focal attention on a cue and visual target (LaBerge, 2000) or "attentional template" (Desimone & Duncan, 1995). In terms of CHC theory, Pair Cancellation measures Perceptual Speed (P) and Attention and Concentration (AC), both narrow abilities subsumed under Cognitive Processing Speed (Gs). However, Pair Cancellation is a cognitive complex task also requiring the individual to scan a visual array (Spatial Scanning; SS), which may explain its partial relationship to tests of Visual Processing (*Gv*).

Attention is the mental process of concentration on a stimulus or other mental event—an important aspect of all focused cognitive activity (Ashcraft, 2002). The ability to sustain one's attention is an important cognitive trait (Unsworth, 2015). Sustained attention, also called vigilance, is an aspect of *cognitive control* (Bunge et al., 2009; Posner & DiGirolamo, 2000). The term *cognitive control* is used in cognitive neuroscience to refer to a set of processes that guide thought and action to achieve a current goal (Race, Kuhl, Badre, & Wagner, 2009). Cognitive control is necessary for higher cognitive functions, particularly for maintaining goal attainment in the face of distractions. Cognitive control is particularly important in tasks where acquired knowledge provides an insufficient resource to satisfy task demands. Good cognitive control supports working memory, selective attention, long-term retrieval, response inhibition, and response selection (Cohen, Dunbar, & McClelland, 1990; Desimone & Duncan, 1995; Miller & Cohen, 2001; Race et al., 2009).

Careful analysis of test performance is necessary to determine appropriate interventions and/or accommodations related to limitations on Test 17: Pair Cancellation. If limited performance is due primarily to lack of perceptual speed, then educational interventions and/or accommodations may be similar to those noted for Letter-Pattern Matching and Number-Pattern Matching. However, if many errors of commission occur during test performance (such as frequently circling an incorrect set) that resulted in poor performance, the individual may benefit from interventions to increase cognitive control, such as slowing down on speeded tasks to increase response accuracy. See **Rapid Reference 4.17**.

Test 18: Memory for Words

Test 18: Memory for Words is a simple running memory span or serial recall task that measures primary memory in a more direct relationship than any of the other WJ IV Short-Term Working Memory (*Gwm*) tests. In Memory for Words, the examinee is presented with an oral sequence of unrelated words and is asked to recall the sequence in its presented order. Because there is no cued recall or intervening complex task to perform, Memory for Words provides a direct measure of moment-to-moment storage capacity of focal attention (Bunting et al., 2006). Running memory tasks, such as Memory for Words, are useful because they likely provide a more direct measure of absolute Working Memory Capacity (WM) when complex processing is not required (Broadway & Engle, 2010; Bunting et al., 2006).

The task involved in Memory for Words has been widely used in basic scientific research, and many models have been developed to explain performance

≡ Rapid Reference 4.17 Interpretation of Test 17—Pair Cancellation

Operational Definition: Measures symbolic visual perceptual discrimination ability requiring cognitive control under timed conditions
Primary Broad CHC Factor: Processing Speed (Gs)
Narrow CHC Abilities: Attention and Concentration (AC); Perceptual Speed (P); Spatial Scanning (SS)
Median g loading: .51
Stimuli: Visual (pictures)
Task Requirements: Rapidly identifying and circling instances of repeated pattern
Inferred Cognitive Processes: Cognitive control; focal attention; task vigilance
Response Modality: Motoric (circling)
Related Educational Interventions or Accommodations: Emphasize speediness; slow down if errors are caused by working too quickly; increase perceptual speed with computer games

on this type of task and why errors are made (J. R. Anderson & Mattessa, 1997; Brown & Hulme, 1995; Burgess & Hitch, 1996). There are some general principles. First, longer lists of words are more difficult to remember than shorter lists. Additionally, the words recalled from the first portion of each item are more accurately recalled than words in the later portion of the item (this is called the *primacy effect*). However, the last word in each item has a higher probability of being recalled than the word immediately preceding it (this is called the *recency effect*).

Mueller (2002) suggested that many individuals who perform well on this type of task use a strategy to encode and/or recall the words. For example, some individuals use chunking strategies to encode the unrelated words into distinct blocks (or ordered subsets) of words (or create compound nonwords), and some individuals use rehearsal as a strategy to maintain or refresh the string of words in immediate awareness (Logie, Della Sala, Laiacona, & Chalmers, 1996). Upon recall, some individuals are error adverse, meaning they might attempt to avoid making an overt error by simply recalling only the words they are certain of and stop when unsure of what word comes next in the sequence. Other individuals attempt to reconstruct the sequence of words by filling in, or guessing, one or more unrecalled words in a sequence.

Young children with limited performance on Memory for Words may benefit from listening and repeating games, where the length of the verbal span of items is increased gradually (Alloway, 2012; Alloway & Alloway, 2013;

≣ Rapid Reference 4.18 Interpretation of Test 18—Memory for Words

Operational Definition: Measures storage capacity for unrelated words in primary memory

Primary Broad CHC Factor: Short-Term Working Memory (*Gwm*)

Narrow CHC Abilities: Auditory Memory Span (MS)

Median g loading: .61

Stimuli: Auditory

Task Requirements: Listening to and repeating a list of unrelated words in correct

Inferred Cognitive Processes: Retention of lexical entries in primary memory and span of verbal storage

Response Modality: Oral (words)

Related Educational Interventions or Accommodations: Listening and repeating games; mnemonics; chunking strategies

---

Alloway & Archibald, 2008; Alloway, Gathercole, Adams, & Willis, 2005; Dehn, 2008). For older children and adults, chunking strategies (grouping related items into units, making the information more manageable to understand, store, and recall) (Hardiman, 2003) can be taught explicitly. Mnemonics also may be useful for learning rules, patterns, and word lists (Wolfe, 2001). See **Rapid Reference 4.18**.

LEVEL 2: CLUSTERS MEASURING BROAD AND NARROW COGNITIVE ABILITIES AND COGNITIVE EFFICIENCY

The WJ IV COG tests are organized into clusters for interpretive purposes. Interpretation at the cluster level yields certain advantages for professionals. For example, the clusters are composed of two or more tests that are aspects of a broad CHC construct. To add greater clarity to interpretation of the WJ IV COG at the cluster level, **Rapid Reference 4.19** provides a definition of what each cluster measures. Each cluster definition is derived from the operational definitions of the component tests that were presented earlier in this chapter. For example, the WJ IV Comprehension-Knowledge (*Gc*) cluster measures comprehension of words and general knowledge. This is a more specific and precise definition of what the WJ IV COG Comprehension-Knowledge (*Gc*) cluster actually measures when compared to the global CHC Theory description of Comprehension-Knowledge (*Gc*) as "the breadth and depth of knowledge and

≡ Rapid Reference 4.19 What the WJ IV COG Clusters Measure

Cluster	Measures
Comprehension-Knowledge	Comprehension of words and general object knowledge
Comprehension-Knowledge—Extended	Comprehension of words and general object knowledge, including knowledge of object names
Fluid Reasoning	Quantitative and verbal reasoning
Fluid Reasoning—Extended	Quantitative, algorithmic, and verbal reasoning
Short-Term Working Memory	Cue-dependent search and recoding functions from temporary stores of verbal and numeric information in primary memory
Short-Term Working Memory—Extended	Cue-dependent search, recoding, and assembly functions from temporary stores of verbal and numeric information in primary memory
Cognitive Processing Speed	Orthographic and symbolic visual perceptual discrimination ability and attentional control under timed conditions
Auditory Processing	Word activation, access, restructuring via phonological codes and phonological sensitivity capacity in working memory
Long-Term Storage and Retrieval	Consolidation (encoding) of semantic (meaning-based) representations into secondary memory
Visual Processing	Visual-spatial analysis, formation of internal visual images, mental transformation of images in working memory, passive storage, and recognition of images
Cognitive Efficiency	Efficiencies of orthographic visual perceptual discrimination ability under timed conditions and temporary storage and recoding of numeric information in primary memory
Cognitive Efficiency—Extended	A combination of orthographic visual perceptual discrimination ability under timed conditions and cue-dependent search and recoding functions from temporary stores of verbal and numeric information
Perceptual Speed	Orthographic visual perceptual discrimination ability under timed conditions
Quantitative Reasoning	Quantitative and nonnumeric algorithmic reasoning
Auditory Memory Span	Storage capacity for unrelated words and connected discourse in primary memory
Number Facility	Efficiencies of visual perceptual discrimination, temporary storage, and processing of numeric information in working memory
Vocabulary	Knowledge of object names and words and their meanings

skills that are valued by one's culture" (Schneider & McGrew, 2012, p. 122). Schneider and McGrew (2012) were referring to a broad category of cognition; the definitions provided in this chapter are both operational and specific to the WJ IV.

Because the clusters contain more than one test, the reliabilities are higher than for individual tests. Consequently, any generalizations that are made from a cluster are based on two or more samples of ability, which reduces the possibility of making overgeneralizations from a narrow sampling of ability. This fact makes clusters the recommended level of interpretation for decision making.

Each test reflects a different perspective on the broad CHC ability. CHC factor loadings reveal how each test represents the broad ability, a unique ability, or a combination of abilities. These factor loadings are summarized in Table 4.1, which will be referenced in this section of the chapter.

There will be occasions when the tests that compose a cluster yield significant differences in derived scores. The Standard Score/Percentile Rank Profile report is a helpful tool for determining if any two tests that comprise a cluster are significantly different. The procedures for determining if two tests are significantly different are presented in Chapter 3 of this book. In addition, the WIIIP (Schrank & Wendling, 2015a) produces a detailed description of test and cluster performance. This description produces a cautionary note when the tests that comprise a cluster are significantly different.

When the tests that are included in a cluster are significantly different from one another, the derived scores that the cluster yields may not be generalizable and should be supplemented (and perhaps supplanted) by the component test information. That is where the stepladder of abstraction helps—professionals can move down the stepladder of abstraction and describe performance on the component tests. When the tests that compose a cluster differ significantly from one another, test-level information may be more helpful than cluster-level information for understanding the individual's cognitive profile.

Comprehension-Knowledge (Gc)

Keith and Reynolds (2010) aptly observed that CHC assessment professionals sometimes describe Comprehension-Knowledge (Gc) in at least two very different ways but may assume that the same construct is being discussed. Professionals sometimes refer to Gc as a type of broad cognitive capacity (such as crystallized intelligence) or more narrowly as a type of acquired knowledge (such as verbal ability). The lack of clarity as to the precise nature of Gc is deeply rooted in the history of CHC theory. Although Cattell (1941, 1943, 1963) suggested that

Table 4.1 Median Broad CHC Factor Loadings for Primary WJ IV COG Clusters

Battery & Test #	Test Name	Comprehension-Knowledge (Gc)	Fluid Reasoning (Gf)	Short-Term Working Memory (Gwm)	Cognitive Processing Speed (Gs)	Auditory Processing (Ga)	Long-Term Retrieval (Glr)	Visual Processing (Gv)	Quantitative Knowledge (Gq)
									Other CHC Factors
COG-01	Oral Vocabulary	**0.87**							
COG-02	Number Series		**0.79**						
COG-03	Verbal Attention			**0.77**					
COG-04	Letter-Pattern Matching				**0.74**				
COG-05	Phonological Processing	0.27				**0.62**			
COG-06	Story Recall						**0.57**		
COG-07	Visualization							**0.74**	
COG-08	General Information	**0.78**							
COG-09	Concept Formation		**0.69**						
COG-10	Numbers Reversed			**0.48**					0.25
COG-11	Number-Pattern Matching				**0.79**				
COG-12	Nonword Repetition				0.59	**0.18**			
COG-13	Visual-Auditory Learning						**0.51**		
COG-14	Picture Recognition							**0.49**	
COG-15	Analysis-Synthesis		*0.63*						
COG-16	Object-Number Sequencing			*0.75*					
COG-17	Pair Cancellation				**0.58**				0.22
COG-18	Memory for Words								
OL-01	Picture Vocabulary	***0.82***							
OL-05	Sentence Repetition	0.26		0.49					

Standard Battery — COG-01 through COG-10
Extended Battery — COG-11 through COG-18
Other Tests — OL-01, OL-05

From *Woodcock-Johnson IV™* (WJ IV™) Copyright © The Riverside Publishing Company. All rights reserved. Used by permission of the publisher. No part of this work may be reproduced or transmitted in any form or by any means, electronic or mechanical, including photocopying and recording or by any information storage or retrieval system without the proper written permission of The Riverside Publishing Company unless such copying is expressly permitted by federal copyright law. Address inquiries to: https://customercare.hmhco.com/contactus/Permissions.html.

verbal ability and crystallized intelligence were not synonymous, Carroll (1993) argued that is purely a matter of individual preference whether *Gc* is interpreted as crystallized intelligence or verbal ability.

The WJ IV COG Comprehension-Knowledge (*Gc*) cluster is derived from two tests, Test 1: Oral Vocabulary and Test 8: General Information. Table 4.1 provides the median test loadings for each of these two tests on the broad *Gc* factor. Both tests are strong yet distinctively different measures of the factor (.87 and .78, respectively). CHC theory, an analysis of the task requirements of each of the component tests, and a review of related research combine to suggest that the WJ IV Comprehension-Knowledge (*Gc*) cluster is broadly based, measuring comprehension of words (an aspect of verbal ability) and general knowledge (an aspect of crystallized intelligence).

The Comprehension-Knowledge (*Gc*) cluster provides important information for psychological and educational evaluations. Niileksela, Reynolds, Keith, and McGrew (2016) found that the WJ IV COG *Gc* cluster is related to the development of the WJ IV *Tests of Achievement* (WJ IV ACH; Schrank, Mather, & McGrew, 2014a) Basic Reading Skills, Reading Comprehension, Reading Rate, Math Calculation Skills, Mathematics Problem Solving, and Basic Writing Skills clusters. The *Gc* cluster was found to be both particularly and strongly related to the Passage Comprehension and Reading Vocabulary tests. The strong relationship to these two different measures of reading can be understood as reflecting both the *comprehension* and *knowledge* aspects of *Gc*. The Passage Comprehension test is a measure of the ability to construct a mental representation of what is being read while reading. As such, it more accurately reflects the influence of the comprehension aspect of *Gc*. The Reading Vocabulary test is a measure of knowledge of words and their meanings derived from printed text; it reflects the influence of the knowledge aspect of *Gc*. In a related study of the relationship of the WJ IV CHC factors to reading achievement, Cormier, McGrew, Bulut, and Funamoto (2015) also found that the WJ IV COG *Gc* cluster is related to several aspects of reading as measured by the WJ IV ACH, including the Basic Reading Skills, Reading Comprehension, Reading Fluency, and Reading Rate clusters. By implication, carefully tailored and implemented interventions that address any limitations found in one or more of the component *Gc* tests may support the development of foundational knowledge for skill development in an associated area of academic achievement, such as reading. This relationship has important implications for cognitive intervention because no broad factor of cognition may be more amenable to improvement through intervention than *Gc*.

The WJ IV COG Comprehension-Knowledge (Gc) cluster is also strongly related to the development of writing and mathematics abilities. Cormier, Bulut,

McGrew, and Frison (2015) found that Comprehension-Knowledge (*Gc*) is the strongest CHC cluster for predicting of Basic Writing Skills for children and adolescents from age 8 through 19 and that the importance of *Gc* on Basic Writing Skills increases with age. Cormier, Bulut, McGrew, and Frison (2015) speculated that vocabulary knowledge, in particular, may influence the ability to spell and edit text. Cormier, McGrew, Bulut, and Singh (2015) determined that Comprehension-Knowledge (*Gc*) is moderately related to Math Calculation Skills and Mathematics Problem Solving for individuals from age 10 to 19.

The WJ IV COG provides an option for increasing the breadth of *Gc* measurement. The Comprehension-Knowledge-Extended cluster can be obtained when the Picture Vocabulary test from the WJ IV *Tests of Oral Language* (WJ IV OL; Schrank, Mather, & McGrew, 2014b) is also administered. The Picture Vocabulary test measures knowledge of object names from picture stimuli rather than word stimuli. The three-test Comprehension-Knowledge—Extended cluster measures comprehension of words and general knowledge, including knowledge of object names. Administration of this cluster may be desirable as an overall index of Comprehension-Knowledge in some instances. For example, a relatively better performance on Picture Vocabulary (which measures knowledge of object names using pictured objects) may offset some of the effects of a lesser performance on Oral Vocabulary (which measures knowledge of synonyms and antonyms for vocabulary words). Note that when the Picture Vocabulary test is administered in conjunction with Test 1: Oral Vocabulary, a narrow Vocabulary (VL/LD) cluster also is obtained. The Vocabulary cluster measures knowledge of object names and words and their meanings.

DON'T FORGET

The Comprehension-Knowledge (*Gc*) cluster measures comprehension of words and general object knowledge. The Comprehension-Knowledge—Extended cluster measures comprehension of words and general knowledge, including knowledge of object names. The Vocabulary (VL/LD) cluster measures knowledge of object names and words and their meanings.

Fluid Reasoning (*Gf*)

The WJ IV COG Fluid Reasoning (*Gf*) cluster is derived from two tests, Test 2: Number Series and Test 9: Concept Formation. Table 4.1 indicates that both tests are strong measures of fluid reasoning (.79 and .69, respectively), although each test measures a different aspect of fluid reasoning. Number Series primarily measures deductive and inductive quantitative reasoning; Concept Formation measures verbal, language-based inductive reasoning. CHC theory, an analysis of the task requirements of each of the component tests, and a review of related research combine to suggest that the WJ IV Fluid Reasoning (*Gf*) cluster measures both quantitative and verbal reasoning.

The *Gf* cluster also provides important information for psychoeducational evaluations. For example, a deficit in Fluid Reasoning may provide insights into observed difficulties in learning or may suggest that reasoning skills in academic content areas might need to be specifically modelled and taught. Specifically, Cormier, McGrew, Bulut, and Funamoto (2015) found that the WJ IV COG Fluid Reasoning (*Gf*) cluster is related to all areas of reading as measured by the WJ IV ACH, including Basic Reading Skills, Reading Comprehension, Reading Rluency, and Reading Rate. Niileksela et al. (2016) found that *Gf* is related to Reading Comprehension. Because reading comprehension requires inferential mapping of words and the relationships among words onto continually updated mental representations as a passage or story is being read, concept formation and verbal reasoning ability are likely involved. In fact, Cormier, McGrew, Bulut, and Funamoto (2015) found that Fluid Reasoning is related to all aspects of reading.

Cormier, McGrew, Bulut, and Singh (2015) determined that Fluid Reasoning (*Gf*) has a strong relationship to Math Calculation Skills and Mathematics Problem Solving for individuals from age 10 to 19 and contributes unique information toward explain an individual's academic achievement in mathematics, that is, beyond the information provided by *g*. Niileksela et al. also noted the particular influence of Fluid Reasoning on mathematics applications for individuals beyond age 8; the connection makes practical sense because applied mathematics requires manipulation of number relationships, an aspect of quantitative reasoning. Also, as Niileksela and colleagues pointed out, both fluid reasoning and applied mathematics require the allocation of significant cognitive resources and complex relational integration.

Cormier, Bulut, McGrew, and Frison (2015) found that Fluid Reasoning (*Gf*) is a strong predictor of Written Expression. Cormier, Bulut, McGrew, and Frison speculated that limitations in *Gf* can result in cognitive overload in expressive writing tasks.

The Fluid Reasoning—Extended cluster can be obtained by also administering Test 15: Analysis-Synthesis. Analysis-Synthesis is a measure of algorithmic, deductive reasoning. Consequently, the Fluid Reasoning—Extended cluster measures a combination of quantitative, algorithmic, and verbal reasoning, using both deductive and inductive cognitive processes. Note that when

Test 15: Analysis-Synthesis is administered in conjunction with Test 2: Number Series, the narrow ability Quantitative Reasoning (RQ) also is obtained. This cluster measures quantitative and nonnumeric, algorithmic reasoning.

DON'T FORGET

The Fluid Reasoning (*Gf*) cluster measures quantitative and verbal reasoning. The Fluid Reasoning—Extended cluster measures quantitative, algorithmic, and verbal reasoning. The Quantitative Reasoning (RQ) cluster measures quantitative and nonnumeric algorithmic reasoning.

Short-Term Working Memory (*Gwm*)

The WJ IV COG construct of Short-Term Working Memory (*Gwm*) evolved from the earlier concept of Short-Term Memory (*Gsm*), although the two terms sometimes are used interchangeably. In the WJ IV COG, the broad *Gwm* cluster combines tests that measure running memory storage, cued recall, and complex processing in primary memory. Primary memory represents the allocation of attention that serves to maintain a distinct number of separate representations active for ongoing processing (Unsworth & Engle, 2007b).

The change in cluster terminology to include the word *working* reflects contemporary nomenclature wherein *working memory* refers to a dynamic, temporary storage system that allows information—either sensory inputs or prior knowledge—to be held in immediate awareness and manipulated. "Working memory is the cognitive system that allows people to retain access to a limited amount of information, in the service of complex cognition" (Shipstead et al., 2014, p. 116). Within this conceptualization, other CHC abilities, such as Fluid Reasoning (*Gf*), Auditory Processing (*Ga*), Visual Processing (*Gv*) and Long-Term Storage and Retrieval (*Glr*), operate within working memory. It may be of interest to note that this grouping of broad CHC abilities was referred to as the "thinking abilities" in Woodcock's (1993) cognitive performance model.

All of the WJ IV COG Short-Term Working Memory (*Gwm*) tests are capacity measures of working memory, a diagnostically important and quantifiable aspect of the more broadly encompassing working memory construct. In the contemporary neurosciences, working memory capacity is recognized as playing a major role in performance of a wide range of cognitive tasks that require holding information that is needed for cognition in the present moment (Oberauer & Hein, 2012).

CAUTION: MIND THE GAP
···

Working memory is a broad neuroscientific construct that refers to a dynamic system for temporary storage and manipulation of information in human cognition. In the WJ IV COG, all of the Short-Term Working Memory (*Gwm*) tests are measures of *Working Memory Capacity* (WM), a diagnostically important, but circumscribed, aspect of the broad construct of working memory.

The Short-Term Working Memory (*Gwm*) cluster is derived from two tests, Test 3: Verbal Attention and Test 10: Numbers Reversed. Table 4.1 indicates that, as a single test, Verbal Attention best represents the WJ IV broad *Gwm* construct (.77 factor loading). Numbers Reversed has a moderate loading (.48) on the *Gwm* factor, perhaps due to a partial loading (.25) on Quantitative Knowledge (*Gq*). Each test measures working memory capacity quite differently. Verbal Attention measures temporary storage of verbal information and includes the cue-dependent search function in primary memory. Numbers Reversed measures temporary storage and recoding of numeric information in primary memory.

The WJ IV COG *Gwm* cluster, then, can be defined operationally as measuring cue-dependent search and recoding functions from temporary stores of verbal and numeric information in primary memory. A combination of qualitatively different working memory capacity tasks creates a cluster that is more broadly predictive of outcomes on a wide variety of cognitive tasks (Oberauer, Süß, Schulze, Wilhelm, & Wittman, 2000; Unsworth & Engle, 2006).

For example, Cormier, McGrew, Bulut, and Funamoto (2015) found that the *Gwm* cluster is related to the development of Basic Reading Skills and Niileksela et al. (2016) noted the particular influence of Short-Term Working Memory on Basic Writing Skills. Cormier, Bulut, McGrew, and Frison (2015) also found that Short-Term Working Memory (*Gwm*) was a moderate predictor of Basic Writing Skills for school-age children and adolescents and a strong predictor of Written Expression after age 17. Cormier, Bulut, McGrew, and Frison, citing the works of Berninger, Whitaker, Feng, Swanson, and Abbott (1996), suggest that working memory efficiency influences compositional fluency and accuracy of writing; they also cited Beard, Myhill, Riley, and Nystrand (2009) to support the suggestion that working memory is required for the application of punctuation, planning, and revising in the writing process.

Cormier, McGrew, Bulut, and Singh (2015) suggested that the *Gwm* cluster may be moderately associated with the development of Math Calculation Skills and Mathematics Problem Solving for individuals from age 10 to 19. Analyses of the WJ IV data for the creation of the Scholastic Aptitude clusters suggested the predictive power of Numbers Reversed for mathematics problem solving (McGrew et al., 2014).

The three-test Short-Term Working Memory—Extended cluster can be obtained when Test 16: Object-Number Sequencing also is administered. The extended cluster is especially useful for obtaining a cluster score that includes a greater mix of working memory tasks. Object-Number Sequencing adds important information about the ability to assemble new cognitive structures out of the information maintained in primary memory. (Also, recall that Object-Number Sequencing loads very highly on g.) Consequently, the Short-Term Working Memory—Extended cluster measures the cue-dependent search, recoding, and assembly functions in primary memory from temporary stores of verbal and numeric information.

Working Memory Capacity (WM) can be measured through a variety of tasks that make different types of demands on cognition. Consequently, an additional Short-Term Working Memory (*Gwm*) test, Test 18: Memory for Words, also is available. Memory for Words measures storage capacity for unrelated words in primary memory, a running memory span task. Although the four different *Gwm* tests reflect different applications of working memory and different levels of cognitive complexity, independent research suggests that less complex running memory span tasks reflect the same fundamental functions as complex span tasks (Shipstead et al., 2014) but "provide slightly different perspectives on the cognitive processes that define this construct" (p. 117). When Memory for Words is administered in conjunction with the Sentence Repetition test from the WJ IV OL, a narrow Auditory Memory Span (MS) cluster is made available. This cluster measures an individual's storage capacity for unrelated words and connected discourse in primary memory.

DON'T FORGET

The Short-Term Working Memory (*Gwm*) cluster measures cue-dependent search and recoding functions from temporary stores of verbal and numeric information in primary memory. The Short-Term Working Memory—Extended cluster measures cue-dependent search, recoding, and assembly functions from temporary stores of verbal and numeric information in primary memory. The Auditory Memory Span (MS) cluster measures storage capacity for unrelated words and connected discourse in primary memory.

Perceptual Speed (P) and Cognitive Processing Speed (Gs)

A review of research suggests that Perceptual Speed (P) is defined by the ability to quickly and accurately compare letters, numbers, objects, pictures, or patterns, often called "simple, fast inspection tasks" (Cornoldi & Giofré, 2014, p. 261). In the WJ IV COG, the Perceptual Speed (P) cluster was designed to measure rapid processing with two educationally relevant types of stimuli that represent critical visual inspection efficiencies that are related to reading, writing, and mathematics fluency. The Perceptual Speed (P) cluster measures orthographic visual perceptual discrimination ability under timed conditions.

Although both component tests are timed perceptual discrimination tasks, they differ in form of stimuli. Test 4: Letter-Pattern Matching measures letter pattern visual perceptual discrimination ability and Test 11: Number-Pattern Matching measures numeric visual perceptual discrimination ability. However, as Kail and Ferrer (2007) suggested, perceptual speed tests are not only tests of speed but are also tests of cognitive and motor processing. Control of attentional resources may be a factor in interpretation (Cornoldi & Giofré, 2014; Coyle, 2003). An individual's levels of acquired knowledge and mechanisms of cognitive efficiency also should be considered when interpreting this narrow ability. For example, beyond the age of 6 or 7, an individual's performance may be facilitated by acquired number or letter pattern knowledge and the development of the cognitive mechanism of chunking, wherein a pattern of numerals can be perceived as a single number or some combinations of letters can be recognized and perceived as a common English spelling pattern. From the chunking perspective, significant differences between tests that comprise this cluster may suggest either stronger letter or number chunking facility. Alternatively, an error analysis may suggest a tendency to misperceive (e.g., transpose) the relative order of specific letters or numbers.

Visual perceptual inspection time tasks correlate only moderately with overall intellectual ability (Grudnik & Kranzler, 2001; Hunt, 1980, 2011), and some highly gifted individuals do not have particularly advanced processing speed abilities (Reams, Chamrad, & Robinson, 1990) or may expend more time in the service of correctness (Gridley, Nelson, Rizza, & Decker, 2003). However, limitations in visual perceptual speed and accuracy can have practical implications for academic tasks that require processing visual information quickly and accurately, particularly during periods of time pressure. Nelson (2009) suggested that slow processing of simple information (such as is measured by the WJ IV COG Perceptual Speed cluster) "may impede learning of novel information by making it more time-consuming to process the information and/or by leaving less time and mental energy for the complex task of understanding the information" (p. 25). Niileksela et al. (2016) suggested that the ability to perform simple visual perceptual tasks quickly and efficiently has implications for performance on tasks that require reading under time pressure. Consequently, if determined to be relevant by the results of a comprehensive cognitive and academic evaluation, a limitation in the WJ IV Perceptual Speed cluster may suggest that the ability to demonstrate acquired knowledge can be compromised by timed conditions.

In CHC theory, Perceptual Speed (P) is a narrow aspect of Cognitive Processing Speed (Gs). However, both tests of Perceptual Speed have very strong loadings on the broad Cognitive Processing Speed (Gs) cluster. The loading for Letter-Pattern Matching is .74, and the loading for Number-Pattern Matching is .77. In contrast, the WJ IV Cognitive Processing Speed (Gs) cluster is composed of Test 4: Letter-Pattern Matching and Test 17: Pair Cancellation. Pair Cancellation has a mixed loading of .58 on Gs and .22 on Visual Processing (Gv). Consequently, Pair Cancellation can provide greater breadth to the evaluation of processing speed. Pair Cancellation measures picture-symbol visual perceptual discrimination ability requiring cognitive control under timed conditions. Consequently, the Cognitive Processing Speed (Gs) cluster measures orthographic and symbol visual perceptual discrimination ability and attentional control under timed conditions.

Cognitive Processing Speed and Perceptual Speed are strongly related to performance in all academic areas (Niileksela et al., 2016), perhaps because cognitive processing speed is so closely related to academic task fluency. Cormier, McGrew, Bulut, and Singh (2015) determined that Cognitive Processing Speed (Gs) has a strong relationship to Math Calculation Skills for individuals from age 10 to 19 and contributes unique information toward explaining an individual's academic achievement in mathematics. Consequently, an individual's performance on either of these clusters can be very informative and may suggest the need for extended time accommodations when visual perceptual or processing speed limitations restrict the ability to demonstrate knowledge under timed conditions.

Finally, the WJ IV COG includes a two-test Number Facility (N) cluster that is partly a function of numeric processing speed but partly a function of something more fundamental. The cluster is based on two tests, Test 10: Numbers Reversed and Test 11: Number-Pattern Matching. The ability to chunk single numerals into larger, multinumeral chunks in working memory facilitates performance on both tasks and may be the source of common variance between the two component tests. Together, the Number Facility cluster measures the combined efficiencies of visual perceptual discrimination, temporary storage, and processing of numeric information in working memory.

DON'T FORGET

The Perceptual Speed (P) cluster measures orthographic visual perceptual discrimination ability under timed conditions. The Cognitive Processing Speed (Gs) cluster measures orthographic and picture-symbol visual perceptual discrimination ability and attentional control under timed conditions. The Number Facility (N) cluster measures the efficiencies of visual perceptual discrimination, temporary storage, and processing of numeric information in working memory.

Auditory Processing (Ga)

As a factor of intelligence, Auditory Processing (Ga) has received much less attention than the parallel construct of cognition, Visual Processing (Gv). This is a historical anomaly, considering how important auditory abilities are to academic performance, particularly orthographic skill development. The emergence of auditory processing as an important cognitive construct is linked to the seminal works of Stankov and Horn (1980) and Horn and Stankov (1982). Auditory Processing (Ga) became more firmly established as a factor of intellectual ability by Carroll (1993).

Conzelmann and Süß (2015) acknowledged the contributions of Seidel (2007) when they defined auditory intelligence as "the ability to discriminate, remember, reason, and work creatively on auditory stimuli, which may consist of tones, environmental sounds, and speech units" (p. 2). With the publication of the WJ IV, the operational definition of Auditory Processing (Ga) has been reconceptualized and distinguished from measures of phonological awareness by an increased emphasis on tasks that involve memory and reasoning processes with auditory stimuli (Conzelmann & Süß, 2015). Of all the broad ability clusters in the WJ IV, the Auditory Processing (Ga) cluster most closely reflects a confluence of several WJ IV design goals—increasing cognitive task complexity (requiring a mix of cognitive functions and parameters of cognitive efficiency), ecological relevance, and diagnostic importance. Performance on each test requires a combination of narrow abilities that span one or more broad abilities (factor complexity). The two component Ga tests are Test 5: Phonological Processing and Test 12: Nonword Repetition.

Test 5: Phonological Processing measures three aspects of speech sound processing that lead to the construction of lexical representations from phonological codes. Also referred to as phonological reasoning or phonological sensitivity, these types of tasks are closely associated with word learning (de Jong, Seveke, & van Veen, 2000). Phonological processing is considered important when learning to read because phonology is mapped onto orthography when sounding out words (Liberman, Shankweiler, & Liberman, 1989; Wagner, Torgesen, Laughon, Simmons, & Rashotte, 1993; Wagner, Torgesen, & Rashotte, 1994). Although composed of three parts, the overall test score reflects a combination of reasoning with auditory stimuli in primary memory and word retrieval from secondary memory. Phonological Processing loads primarily on Auditory Processing (*Ga*; .62) as well as Comprehension-Knowledge (*Gc*; .27). Test 5: Phonological Processing is one of the highest *g*-loading tests in the WJ IV COG (.71) and is a component test in all of the reading and writing Scholastic Aptitude clusters.

CAUTION: MIND THE GAP

Long-term memory sometimes is referred to as secondary memory; both terms also can refer to aspects of Comprehension-Knowledge (*Gc*).

Test 12: Nonword Repetition is a cognitively complex test that primarily measures phonological short-term storage capacity and requires phonemic sensitivity, encoding, assembly, and oral production of the assembled sequence. In terms of the representative CHC factors, Nonword Repetition loads on Short-Term Working Memory (*Gwm*; .59) and Auditory Processing (*Ga*; .18). Although the primary loading is on working memory, this combination of processes is interpreted as the narrow ability of Memory for Sound Patterns (UM) in CHC theory (McGrew et al., 2014). Tests of nonword repetition yield marked individual differences between individuals (Gathercole & Baddely, 1989; Gathercole, Willis, Emslie, & Baddeley, 1992, 1994). Research with nonword repetition tasks has suggested links between nonword repetition and new word learning (Gathercole, 2006; Michas & Henry, 1994) and vocabulary development (Edwards et al., 2004).

DON'T FORGET

The Auditory Processing (*Ga*) cluster measures word activation, access, restructuring via phonological codes, and phonological sensitivity-capacity in working memory.

The WJ IV COG Auditory Processing (*Ga*) cluster can provide important information for a psychoeducational evaluation, particularly for an evaluation where reading and writing difficulties are of concern. Cormier, McGrew, Bulut, and Funamoto (2015) found that the WJ IV COG Auditory Processing (*Ga*) cluster is related to the development of Basic Reading Skills and is a particularly strong predictor of Word Attack skills in the WJ IV ACH. Niileksela et al. (2016) determined that Auditory Processing (*Ga*) is related to both Basic Reading Skills and Reading Comprehension. Cormier, Bulut, McGrew, and Frison (2015) found that the WJ IV COG Auditory Processing (*Ga*) cluster is a moderate predictor of Basic Writing Skills for school-age children and adolescents and a moderate predictor of Written Expression until age 10.

When additional information on phonological abilities is required, evaluators can administer the WJ IV OL Segmentation and Sound Blending tests to determine an individual's levels of proficiency on two foundational phonological skills. Although there are many practical implications for intervention based on performance on each of the WJ IV Auditory Processing (*Ga*) tests, limited auditory processing abilities can suggest the need for a more comprehensive evaluation of measured auditory processing difficulties.

Long-Term Storage and Retrieval (*Glr*)

The WJ IV COG Long-Term Storage and Retrieval (*Glr*) cluster is derived from two tests, Test 6: Story Recall and Test 13: Visual-Auditory Learning. In contrast to tests that are purely measures of retrieval abilities, these two tests primarily measure the memory consolidation processes that are necessary for subsequent retrieval. Story Recall measures listening ability and attention to orally imparted details that facilitate the formation of meaning-based (semantic) mental representations that are encoded in memory. The recall phase measures the ability to reconstruct story details. In cognitive psychology, this is sometimes is referred to as reconstructive memory; in CHC theory, it is called the narrow ability of Meaningful Memory (MM). Test 13: Visual-Auditory Learning measures paired-associate encoding in the learning phase. The subsequent rebus-identification phase assesses the consolidation of learning via the directed, spotlight-attention paired-associate encoding technique. In CHC theory, this test measures the narrow ability of Associative Memory (MA). When combined, the *Glr* cluster measures consolidation (encoding) of semantic (meaning-based) representations in long-term memory.

DON'T FORGET

The Long-Term Storage and Retrieval (*Glr*) cluster measures consolidation (encoding) of semantic (meaning-based) representations into secondary memory.

Within the WJ IV, an important distinction must be made between the *Glr* cluster and its component tests that measure storage *and* retrieval functions versus the other clusters and tests that measure the retrieval function only. A Speed of Lexical Access (LA) cluster exists in the WJ IV OL whose component tests are Rapid Picture Naming and Retrieval Fluency. Also, Part B Word Fluency of Test 5: Phonological Processing measures a retrieval-only function. Rapid Picture Naming, Retrieval Fluency, and Word Fluency all measure retrieval of names and words from previously stored knowledge; these tests do not assess the memory consolidation function that is the primary distinguishing characteristic of the *Glr* cluster.

Readers must move "beyond CHC theory" to the cognitive neurosciences to more adequately understand the nature of the *Glr* cluster. From that perspective, both tests in the *Glr* cluster measure the processes by which semantic memories (Tulvig, 1972, 1985) are created. Whether it is through the development and consolidation of mental representations from orally imparted discourse in Test 6: Story Recall or through the association of words with rebus representations in Test 13: Visual-Auditory Learning, each test is a standardized experiment for assessment of semantic memory consolidation. Consequently, Long-Term Storage and Retrieval (*Glr*) represents an important link between working memory and long-term memory. This link is critically important for education; it is the gateway between information to be learned and learned information. In summary, the storage aspect of the *Glr* tests and clusters represents the consolidation of semantic memories, which is critically important to learning.

Visual Processing (Gv)

The WJ IV COG Visual Processing (*Gv*) cluster is derived from two tests, Test 7: Visualization and Test 14: Picture Recognition. Table 4.1 indicates that the Visualization test is a strong measure of visual processing (.74). Although both tests involve visual perception (the process of extracting features from visual stimuli), the Visualization test requires more active cognitive processing. Test 7: Visualization has two parts. Part A Spatial Relations measures the ability to apprehend spatial forms or shapes, often by rotating or manipulating them in the imagination. Through the process of visual feature detection (Biederman, 1987, 1990), puzzle pieces are matched to components of the target shape. Part B Block Rotation requires visual-spatial manipulation, a component of working memory (Posner, 1978). In contrast, Test 14: Picture Recognition requires the examinee to form and remember—in a few seconds—iconic representations of the visual stimuli (Averbach & Sperling, 1961; Neisser, 1967) that cannot easily be encoded verbally. Recognition occurs when a visual input matches a stored visual memory (Kosslyn & Thompson, 2000). When combined as a single construct, the WJ IV

COG Visual Processing (*Gv*) cluster measures visual-spatial analysis, formation of internal visual images, mental transformation of images in working memory, passive storage, and recognition of images stored in memory.

DON'T FORGET

The Visual Processing (*Gv*) cluster measures visual-spatial analysis, formation of internal visual images, mental transformation of images in working memory, passive storage and recognition of images.

Niileksela et al. (2016) determined that the Visual Processing (*Gv*) cluster is related to mathematics applications from the preschool level throughout the school years. This relationship appears to be consistent with the work of Lubinski (2010), who suggested that visual-spatial abilities are important in academic areas where reasoning with figures, patterns, and shapes is essential. De Cruz (2012) explained that a variety of spatial representations are utilized in the performance of mathematics operations and that—even across cultures—human beings make associations between numbers and space.

Cognitive Efficiency

The Cognitive Efficiency cluster is a summary of the speed and efficiency with which an individual processes basic orthographic and verbal information. Test 4: Letter-Pattern Matching and Test 10: Numbers Reversed compose the Cognitive Efficiency cluster. The Cognitive Efficiency—Extended cluster includes those two tests plus Test 3: Verbal Attention and Test 11: Number-Pattern Matching. The Cognitive Efficiency—Extended cluster measures orthographic visual perceptual discrimination ability under timed conditions and the executive cue-dependent search and recoding functions from temporary stores of verbal and numeric information. These two clusters may also tap the efficiency of binding or chunking letter or number sequences into manageable units for information processing.

DON'T FORGET

The Cognitive Efficiency cluster measures the speed and efficiency with which an individual processes basic orthographic and verbal information. The Cognitive Efficiency—Extended cluster measures a combination of orthographic visual perceptual discrimination ability under timed conditions and cue-dependent search and recoding functions from temporary stores of verbal and numeric information.

Although processing speed and short-term working memory tasks have their own relationships to general intelligence and academic achievement, there may be an increased value to the combined Cognitive Efficiency scores, as defined earlier. Processing speed has the function of a valve that helps to control the flow of information required for reasoning and divergent thinking (Deary, 2000; Neubauer, 1997; Vock, Preckel, & Holling, 2011). Increased speed of processing is related to the ability to efficiently process information during problem solving because information can be represented, interpreted, and integrated before relevant traces fade away from immediate awareness (Hale & Fry, 2000; Kail, 1991, 2000). Increases in processing speed are related to increases in working memory capacity, which, in turn, is related to higher levels of intelligence and academic achievement (Demetriou, Christou, Spanoudis, & Platsidou, 2002; Halford, Wilson, & Phillips, 1998; Walczyk et al., 2007). The executive processes employed in working memory may represent the bridge between processing speed and intelligence (Conway, Cowan, Bunting, Therriault, & Minkoff, 2002; Conway, Kane, & Engle, 2003; Engle, 2002). For example, individuals often need to remain cognizant of hypotheses about potential or intermediary solutions (such as what information can be eliminated from consideration) in complex problem solving.

Limitations in Cognitive Efficiency may result in greater consequences than limitations in either the Perceptual Speed (P) or Short-Term Working Memory (*Gwm*) clusters alone. Conjoint limitations in both of the constituent cognitive speed and short-term working memory functions can exert an indirect influence on academic achievement by negatively affecting reasoning and divergent (creative) thinking (Vock et al., 2011). Although a weakness in the Cognitive Efficiency cluster may not, by itself, be a diagnostic marker for any specific learning disability or clinical disorder, it is often noticed in a variety of clinical conditions where the effects of limited or impaired cognitive efficiency can constrain more complex cognitive and academic performance (Mather & Wendling, 2014).

LEVEL 3: CLUSTERS MEASURING INTELLECTUAL ABILITY AND SCHOLASTIC APTITUDES

The WJ IV COG includes three distinct options for determining the intellectual level of an individual: The Brief Intellectual Ability (BIA) score; the General Intellectual Ability (GIA) score; and the *Gf-Gc* Composite. Each cluster includes a different combination of tests for determining intellectual ability. The BIA includes the first three tests in the standard battery; the GIA includes the first seven tests; and the *Gf-Gc* Composite is derived from a selection of four tests from the standard battery. In addition, differential Scholastic Aptitude clusters can be derived from selected combinations of WJ IV COG tests. See **Rapid Reference 4.20**.

≡ Rapid Reference 4.20 Intellectual Ability and Scholastic Aptitude Clusters in the WJ IV COG

Brief Intellectual Ability (BIA): Tests 1–3
General Intellectual Ability (GIA): Tests 1–7
Gf-Gc Composite: Tests 1, 2, 8, and 9
Scholastic Aptitude Clusters (tests vary depending on academic cluster to be predicted)

The GIA, Gf-Gc Composite, and BIA score are highly reliable measures of intellectual level that meet or exceed commonly accepted professional criteria for use in making important decisions. The Scholastic Aptitude cluster reliabilities are slightly lower than the reliabilities for the three WJ IV COG intellectual ability clusters.

≡ Rapid Reference 4.21 Median Reliability Coefficients

Median Reliability Coefficients for Three Intellectual Ability Scales in the WJ IV COG

Cluster	Median r_{cc}
Brief Intellectual Ability (BIA)	0.94
General Intellectual Ability (GIA)	0.97
Gf-Gc Composite	0.96
Reading Aptitude A	0.89
Reading Aptitude B	0.90
Math Aptitude A	0.89
Math Aptitude B	0.89
Writing Aptitude A	0.89
Writing Aptitude B	0.90

Brief Intellectual Ability (BIA)

The Brief Intellectual Ability (BIA) score is a short but highly reliable measure of intellectual ability (median reliability .94). The BIA is derived from the first three tests in the cognitive battery. The three tests are equally weighted in the BIA score. The cluster composition includes Test 1: Oral Vocabulary, Test 2: Number Series, and Test 3: Verbal Attention. These tests represent markers for three important CHC abilities for estimating general intellectual ability, or g. The BIA represents a combination of verbal Comprehension-Knowledge (Gc), quantitative Fluid Reasoning (Gf), and the executive information-lookup and storage capacity functions in Short-Term Working Memory (Gwm). Although Gf and Gc often are considered the two most important cognitive abilities (Hunt, 2000, 2011), Barrouillet and colleagues have suggested that high working memory capacity (Gwm) is related to increased potential for knowledgeable, reasoned solutions to problems (Barrouillet, Gauffroy, & Lecas, 2008; Barrouillet, Grosset, & Lecas, 2000; Barrouillet, Portrat, & Camos, 2011; Markovits & Barrouillet, 2002).

DON'T FORGET

The BIA score is a highly reliable, short measure of intellectual ability that is derived from three tests that measure knowledge of words and their meanings, quantitative reasoning, and temporary storage of verbal information, including the cue-dependent search function of primary memory. The BIA score is suitable for many screening, selection, and reevaluation purposes, particularly when a comprehensive evaluation of cognitive abilities or a complete diagnostic profile of abilities are not required.

General Intellectual Ability (GIA)

The GIA score is derived from the first seven tests in the cognitive standard battery. Each of the seven tests was selected, from other alternatives, for inclusion in the GIA score because it is a highly representative, single measure of one of the seven primary broad CHC abilities; has high loadings on general intelligence (g); is high in cognitive complexity; and is a strong predictor of achievement in the WJ IV ACH (McGrew et al., 2014).

The GIA score is a measure of psychometric g, one of psychology's oldest and most solidly established constructs—and the first authentic latent variable in the history of psychology. The existence of g was originally hypothesized by Galton (1869/1978) and was later established empirically by Spearman (1904). Because the best measure of *g* is based on the broadest spectrum of important cognitive abilities (Jensen, 1998), the WJ IV COG GIA score is derived from seven tests, each representing the best single measure of one of seven broad CHC abilities. Consequently, the WJ IV COG GIA score provides professionals with the best singular predictor—*across individuals*—of overall school achievement and other life outcomes that have some relationship to general intelligence.

It may be important to understand that *g* (and, by inference, the WJ IV GIA score) does not represent an ability per se; rather, it is a distillation of abilities. Unlike the WJ IV tests and clusters, *g* simply cannot be described in terms of information content. That is, there is no singular defining characteristic of *g* that can be stated in psychological terms. Much like the construct of *g*, the WJ IV COG GIA score cannot be defined as a distinct cognitive ability because it is an amalgam of several important cognitive abilities, functions, or processes into a single-score index.

The WJ IV COG GIA score represents a distillate of several cognitive abilities and the primary source of variance that is common to all of the tests included in its calculation. The Appendix D of the WJ IV *Technical Manual* (McGrew et al., 2014) contains the smoothed *g* weights for each of the seven tests included in the GIA score by technical age groups. A review of these weights suggests that at any age, the component *Gf* and *Gc* tests combined contribute approximately 35% to the GIA score. The remaining 65% of the obtained score is based on the individual's performance on other tests that Schneider and McGrew (2012) categorized as either sensory-domain abilities or indices of cognitive efficiency.

DON'T FORGET

The WJ IV COG GIA score is a highly reliable and valid measure of psychometric *g* that is distilled from seven tests that assess a broad spectrum of important cognitive abilities and functions, including: knowledge of words and their meanings; quantitative reasoning; temporary storage of verbal information, including the cue-dependent search function of primary memory; orthographic visual perceptual discrimination ability under timed conditions; word activation, fluency of word access, and word restructuring via phonological codes; listening and attention to orally imparted details that facilitate formation and reconstruction of mental representations; and size and shape perception, part-to-whole analysis, and mentally transforming two- and three-dimensional images. Because thescore is a first-principle component score based on a broad spectrum of important cognitive abilities, it is the best estimate of *g* available in the WJ IV.

Psychometric g and the GIA score represent psychological constructs at the highest level of abstraction. Some scholars of intelligence, notably Horn (1991), maintained that g is merely a statistical artifact that should not overshadow an evaluation of more constitutional abilities, such as Gf and Gc. Others, such as Jensen (1998), referred to g as a property of cognitive processing. For example, Jensen said that g "reflects individual differences in information processing as manifested in functions such as attending, selecting, searching, internalizing, deciding, discriminating, generalizing, learning, remembering, and using incoming and past-acquired information to solve problems and cope with the exigencies of the environment" (p. 117).

Gf-Gc Composite

The Gf-Gc Composite is a special-purpose measure of intellectual level based on four academically predictive tests that represent the two highest-order (g-loaded or g-saturated) factors included in the CHC theory of cognitive abilities (McGrew, 2005, 2009; McGrew et al., 2014; Schneider & McGrew, 2012). Fifty percent of the Gf-Gc Composite is derived from two Gc tests (Test 1: Oral Vocabulary and Test 8: General Information), and the other 50% is derived from two Gf tests (Test 2: Number Series and Test 9: Concept Formation). When combined, Gf and Gc represent 100% of the contribution to the measurement of an individual's intellectual ability level that is defined by the Gf-Gc Composite. Although composed of only four tests, the Gf-Gc Composite yields highly stable scores, with reliability values comparable to the GIA score. The median Gf-Gc Composite reliability is .96 compared to the median reliability for the GIA score of .97, as reported in the Appendix C of the *Technical Manual* (McGrew et al., 2014) and in the **Appendix** of this book.

CAUTION: MIND THE GAP

Assessment professionals sometimes want to know if an observed difference between the WJ IV GIA and Gf-Gc Composite scores is unusual in the population. K. S. McGrew (personal communication, Dec. 21, 2015) suggested that 8 standard score points is a practical approximation of 1 standard deviation of the difference score distribution (SEE) for base rate analysis of GIA/Gf-Gc cluster score differences. A difference between the GIA and the Gf-Gc Composite of 12 standard score points (1.5 SEE) is likely to be found in 13% of the population; a difference of 13 standard score points (1.65 SEE) is likely to be found in 10% of the population.

The *Gf-Gc* Composite was developed to be an alternative measure of intellectual level or intellectual development that is more representative of the Horn and Cattell theoretical tradition than the GIA score, which is more aligned with the Carroll three stratum model. However, the *Gf-Gc* Composite is not merely a theoretical exercise; the score can have great practical importance. For some individuals with specific learning disabilities, the WJ IV GIA or any full scale intelligence score may not provide the best description of attained intellectual level. This is particularly true when a significant limitation is present in one of the basic cognitive processes, storage and processing functions, or mechanisms of cognitive efficiency that are included in calculation of the GIA or overall intelligence score. Although these abilities contribute to the GIA score, they also can be identified as possible contributors to the disability. In such cases, the *Gf-Gc* Composite may be the preferred measure of intellectual development because it does not include the psychological processing limitations that are presumed to underlie a specific learning disability (SLD). The removal of processing mechanisms from the *Gf-Gc* measure of intellectual development can help professionals isolate any specific cognitive limitations that may be related to difficulties in learning and may be important to identifying the nature of the specific disability itself.

DON'T FORGET

The *Gf-Gc* Composite can be used as an alternate measure of intellectual level or development. Although highly correlated with the GIA score, the *Gf-Gc* Composite is less influenced by cognitive processing and cognitive efficiency abilities or disabilities.

Schrank and colleagues (2015a; see also the **Appendix** of this book) proposed a number of reasons why the *Gf-Gc* Composite can be particularly useful in SLD identification. First, the relative influence of any functional limitations in one or more of the basic cognitive processes, storage and processing functions, or cognitive efficiency mechanisms often is minimized in the *Gf-Gc* Composite. The *Gf-Gc* Composite is particularly useful when an individual has benefited from the investment of effort and experience in spite of limitations in *Gwm*, *Ga*, *Gv*, *Glr*, *Gs*, or any of their associated narrow abilities, such as perceptual speed, working memory capacity, or phonological processing. Second, within the WJ IV assessment system, the *Gf-Gc* Composite can be compared to levels of academic achievement as well as to measures of basic cognitive processes, storage and retrieval functions, mechanisms of cognitive efficiency, and/or critical cognitive-linguistic competencies. The WJ IV *Gf-Gc* Composite/Other Ability comparison procedure yields a profile of cognitive, linguistic, and achievement abilities that may reveal a pattern of strengths and weaknesses relative to the *Gf-Gc* Composite. **Rapid Reference 4.22** lists the WJ IV COG, OL, and ACH clusters that can be compared to the *Gf-Gc* Composite.

≡ Rapid Reference 4.22 WJ IV COG, OL, and ACH Clusters that Can Be Compared to the Gf-Gc Composite

WJ IV COG Clusters

Short-Term Working Memory (*Gwm*)
Short-Term Working Memory—Extended
Cognitive Processing Speed (*Gs*)
Auditory Processing (*Ga*)
Long-Term Storage and Retrieval (*Glr*)
Visual Processing (*Gv*)
Auditory Memory Span (MS)
Number Facility (N)
Perceptual Speed (P)
Cognitive Efficiency
Cognitive Efficiency—Extended

WJ IV OL Clusters

Phonetic Coding (PC)
Speed of Lexical Access (LA)

WJ IV ACH Clusters

Brief Achievement
Broad Achievement
Reading
Broad Reading
Basic Reading Skills
Reading Comprehension

Reading Comprehension—Extended
Reading Fluency
Reading Rate
Mathematics
Broad Mathematics
Math Calculation Skills
Math Problem Solving
Written Language
Broad Written Language
Basic Writing Skills
Written Expression
Academic Skills
Academic Fluency
Academic Applications
Phoneme-Grapheme Knowledge

An understanding of the nature and purpose of the *Gf-Gc* Composite, particularly in comparison to the GIA score, is critically important to competent interpretation of the WJ IV COG. The **Appendix** of this book provides more information on the *Gf-Gc* Composite and its use in the identification of an SLD.

DON'T FORGET

When a cognitive limitation is identified in one or more of WJ IV COG Tests 3 through 7, consider using the *Gf-Gc* Composite as a measure of intellectual development. The **Appendix** of this book provides support for use of this composite in the identification of an SLD.

Scholastic Aptitude Clusters

The WJ IV COG differential Scholastic Aptitude clusters may be one of the most difficult concepts to understand and/or explain to others, primarily because they are largely atheoretical. Each Scholastic Aptitude cluster may best be interpreted as small set of WJ IV cognitive tests that is statistically associated with performance on different WJ IV achievement clusters. The purpose of these clusters is solely to determine if an individual's current academic performance level in any particular domain is consistent with, or discrepant from, his or her performance on the related Scholastic Aptitude cluster. The required set of tests to obtain a Scholastic Aptitude cluster differs by academic domain (and, in some cases, by subdomain). The selective testing table for the Scholastic Aptitude clusters is found in Chapter 2.

Although the Scholastic Aptitude clusters are useful for comparing an individual's current academic performance levels to his or her levels of domain-associated cognitive abilities, the term *aptitude* may suggest that these clusters predict something that they do not. These clusters do not estimate an individual's potential for future scholastic success. In addition, these clusters are not intended for use in determining the presence of an SLD. In fact, use of the Scholastic Aptitude clusters as ability measures in an ability-achievement discrepancy comparison is "counter to the inherent meaning of an ability-achievement discrepancy found in most federal and state definitions of (and criteria for identifying) learning disabilities" (Flanagan, McGrew, & Ortiz, 2000, p. 383). Students with an SLD may not exhibit a Scholastic Aptitude/Achievement discrepancy because a closely related weak cognitive ability or abilities often are reflected in a lower predicted achievement score.

CAUTION
....

The WJ IV COG Scholastic Aptitude scores are not intended to be used as intellectual ability measures in an ability-achievement discrepancy model for determination of a specific learning disability; nor are these clusters intended to predict an individual's potential for long-term academic success.

So what, then, is the purpose of the Scholastic Aptitude clusters? Perhaps the best use of these clusters is for short, selective, referral-focused assessments (McGrew, 2012; McGrew & Wendling, 2010) where the aptitude-achievement comparison is used descriptively, not diagnostically. The description can yield information about whether an individual currently is performing academically as well as would be expected based on a small set of closely associated cognitive abilities. Alternatively, as part of a comprehensive evaluation, the Scholastic Aptitude/Achievement comparison may provide additional descriptive information about concordance or discrepancy between selected measures of cognition and expected academic performance.

STEP-BY-STEP INTERPRETATION OF THE WJ IV COG

One of the design objectives for the WJ IV COG was to place the tests in an order that facilitates interpretation. By following one of the recommended administration protocols, key interpretive procedures are automated by the Online Scoring and Reporting Program or WJ IV Interpretation and Instructional Interventions Program. In terms of administration, the general principle is to begin at the beginning and discontinue testing at a defined point that provides the level of interpretive information that is desired or required. Although this is not the only approach to administering the WJ IV COG, it is the approach developed by the senior author of the WJ IV COG (and this book), and it represents a time-efficient method that provides a defined starting point with several options that provide increasingly greater levels of interpretive depth.

Interpretation of the WJ IV COG requires a higher level of competence than simply administering and scoring the tests. Two variation and comparison procedures help examiners define profiles of intra-individual strengths and weaknesses, but even when a strength or weakness is identified, more information is required to interpret the test or cluster results. To be competent in interpreting the WJ IV COG, examiners must know how to use developmental-level information (such as age or grade equivalents), proficiency-level information (such as Relative Proficiency Indexes [RPIs] and proficiency terms), as well as measures of relative standing in a group (such as standard scores or percentile ranks) appropriately. Determination of the practical and educational implications of test results is an important part of the interpretive process.

Step 1

As a general rule, administer WJ IV COG Tests 1 to 7 to facilitate an evaluation of any intra-individual differences among component scores. For a number of reasons, these are called the core tests in the WJ IV COG. Administering Tests 1 to 7 often yields the most essential cognitive information in the least amount of testing time. Each of the first seven tests was selected by the author team as the best single measure of the broad ability for purposes of a cognitive evaluation. As described earlier in this chapter, interpretation of the abilities that are measured by each of the first seven tests is supported by CHC factor loadings as well as external research with the same or similar tasks.

Remember the stepladder of abstraction discussed at the beginning of this chapter? The WJ IV COG tests represent abilities and cognitive processes that are at the lowest level of abstraction—that is, they are the closest to important, extensional (real-life) representations of a broad class of CHC abilities as practicable. In addition, each of the seven tests is highly related to academic achievement and can be conceptually linked to related instructional interventions or accommodations. Unless there is a specific purpose for obtaining a cluster score, it may not be necessary or desirable to administer more than one test from each of the seven CHC broad abilities.

WJ IV COG Tests 1 to 7 yield the GIA score as well as test-level information for seven distinct cognitive tests, each representing a different broad cognitive ability. Based on prior hypotheses or information obtained during testing, additional tests can also be administered on a selective testing basis, but administering tests 1 to 7 provides the foundation for an evaluation of relative strengths and weaknesses in an individual's cognitive profile.

There are at least two practical reasons to alter the administration guidance provided in this step. The first example is if only a brief (15–20 minute) measure of intellectual ability is desired. When one purpose of a cognitive evaluation is to obtain a brief intelligence measure to rule out an intellectual disability or to provide a short but high-quality measure of general intellectual functioning, consider administering only Tests 1 to 3 to obtain the Brief Intellectual Ability (BIA) score. The BIA is a measure of high psychometric quality. It is highly correlated with the GIA score (~.93) and, for some purposes (such as an evaluation for placement in a program for the cognitively gifted),may be a preferred intellectual ability score because it is based on three important broad CHC abilities and does not include a test of processing speed. The second example is if information on only selected cognitive abilities is desired, such as in a highly tailored assessment for evaluation of specific broad or narrow cognitive abilities or measurement of Scholastic Aptitude clusters for reading, math, or writing. For those purposes, simply consult the selective testing tables and administer the designated cognitive tests that meet the specific objectives of the evaluation. (However, note that you will not obtain the analysis of intra-cognitive variations without administering each of the first seven tests.)

DON'T FORGET

Tests 1 through 7 must be administered to obtain the Intra-Cognitive Variations (strengths and weaknesses) analysis.

Step 2

If cluster scores are desired, administer selected additional tests to evaluate strengths and weaknesses of the cluster scores. The WJ IV COG selective testing table (see Chapter 2, Rapid Reference 2.1) provides a guide for selective administration of tests to obtain the WJ IV cognitive composites, broad CHC factors, and several narrow ability or other clinical clusters. After administering each of Tests 1 to 7, examiners can consult the Scoring Table in the Test Record to derive age- and grade-equivalent scores. Considering this information in conjunction with test session observations and other information can lead an examiner to administer one or more related tests to obtain a cluster score for a broad ability. For example, if an examinee appears to be struggling with the requirements of Test 4: Letter-Pattern Matching and the resulting age- and grade-equivalent score seemed low for the individual's actual age or grade, an evaluator may want to administer another speeded test, such as Test 11: Number-Pattern Matching to obtain a Perceptual Speed (P) cluster. In this instance, adding an additional test that will yield a cluster score may help substantiate a limitation in Perceptual Speed (P) that could result in an implication for an accommodation, such as the provision of extended time. As another example, an observed difficulty in performance on Test 5: Phonological Processing may suggest administration of Test 12: Nonword Repetition to determine if a more general limitation exists in Auditory Processing (*Ga*).

For several good reasons, many examiners routinely administer all 10 tests in the standard cognitive battery (Tests 1–10). By administering tests 1 to 10, examiners obtain several key clusters: Comprehension-Knowledge (*Gc*), Fluid Reasoning (*Gf*), Short-Term Working Memory (*Gwm*), Cognitive Efficiency, and the *Gf-Gc* Composite. In addition to the strengths and weaknesses evaluation of all 10 tests in the standard battery, the *Gc*, *Gf*, and *Gwm* clusters are also included in the intracognitive variation procedure. Additionally, when administering Tests 1 to 10, a new interpretive comparison is available: The *Gwm* and Cognitive Efficiency clusters are compared to the *Gf-Gc* Composite to determine if either of these clusters is a strength or weakness relative to the composite of fluid reasoning and comprehension-knowledge intellectual abilities. Because so much potentially valuable information is obtained from Tests 1 to 10, administration of this set of tests is considered a *standard WJ IV COG administration protocol.* A valuable benefit of administering Tests 1 to 10 as a standard protocol is that any of the non-*Gf* and non-*Gc* clusters from the WJ IV COG, WJ IV OL, or WJ IV ACH are also compared to the *Gf-Gc* Composite to determine if other strengths or weaknesses exist relative to the *Gf-Gc* Composite.

DON'T FORGET

Tests 1 through 10 yield a standard WJ IV COG administration protocol that includes an analysis of relative strengths and weaknesses among the component tests and selected CHC clusters (*Gc*, *Gf*, *Gwm*); yields the BIA, GIA, and *Gf-Gc* Composite scores; and provides a comparison of the Short-Term Working Memory (*Gwm*) and Cognitive Efficiency clusters to the *Gf-Gc* Composite.

However, the important point of this step is that evaluators may selectively administer any of WJ IV COG Tests 8 to 18 (in addition to Tests 1–7) to obtain cluster scores for inclusion in the intracognitive variations procedure. Cluster scores for seven broad abilities are available: Comprehension-Knowledge (*Gc*), Fluid Reasoning (*Gf*), Short-Term Working Memory (*Gwm*) Cognitive Processing Speed (*Gs*), Auditory Processing (*Ga*), Visual Processing (*Gv*), and Long-Term Storage and Retrieval (*Glr*). Extended clusters are available for some abilities: Fluid Reasoning—Extended, and Short-Term Working Memory—Extended clusters can be obtained by administering the three component tests. A Cognitive Efficiency—Extended cluster may be obtained by administering the four component tests. Important narrow ability clusters also can be obtained and included in the variations analysis, including some potentially important abilities such as Perceptual Speed (P) and Quantitative Reasoning (RQ). In addition, when selected tests from the WJ IV OL are included, the Phonetic Coding (PC), Speed of Lexical Access (LA), Auditory Memory Span (MS), Vocabulary (VL/LD), and Comprehension-Knowledge-Extended clusters also can be included in the analysis of relative cognitive strengths and weaknesses.

The WJ IV COG intra-cognitive variation and *Gf-Gc* Composite/Other Ability comparison procedures are based on the practice of examining test performance to derive a profile of relative strengths and weaknesses. Often referred to as a pattern of strengths and weaknesses (PSW) model, this form of interpretation is consistent with Brackett and McPherson's (1996) suggestion that "[a] major value of detecting severe discrepancies within and between areas of cognition is the focus on cognitive processing components of learning disabilities" (p. 79). Because these procedures make it possible to identify a relative cognitive processing delay as early as first grade, they may be particularly useful for identification of a specific learning disability. However, the presence of a strength or weakness is relative to the individual alone; other scores and procedures must be considered to determine the practical significance of an individual's WJ IV COG performance.

Step 3

Evaluate the practical implications of cluster and test performance by reviewing the RPI and/or proficiency levels. Although the IntraCognitive Variation and *Gf-Gc* Composite/Other Ability comparison procedures can inform an evaluator if any uneven pattern of cognitive abilities exists, those procedures do not provide information about the practical implications of the individual's cognitive ability levels. Proficiency-level information provides the most useful information about an individual's cognitive performance. Always include either the proficiency-level labels or RPI scores in a score report to review the practical implications of an individual's WJ IV COG performance. The proficiency labels are the most useful because often they are more easily understood than RPI scores. Does the individual have any limitations in cognitive performance as measured by the WJ IV COG? If so, the proficiency-level terms will draw attention to these limitations.

In the WJ IV Online Scoring and Reporting Program and the WIIIP, the *W* Diff is used to create the RPI and the proficiency-level terms (see Rapid Reference 3.2 in Chapter 3 for details). In some cases, the RPI and proficiency levels can yield critical information that other types of scores cannot.

CAUTION: STANDARD SCORES YIELD INFORMATION ABOUT RELATIVE STANDING, NOT PROFICIENCY

Some assessment professionals believe that standard scores or standard score classifications describe an individual's proficiency, but they do not. Standard scores and percentile ranks reflect relative group standing. Attributions of ability level from standard score classifications are inferences that can, in some instances, lead to incorrect interpretations. To be competent in WJ IV COG interpretation, examiners need to know how to use proficiency-level information. Sole reliance on standard scores is an *error of omission*, particularly because RPI and proficiency labels are a fundamental component of the WJ IV interpretive model, are readily available for selection on the score report and, in some instances, may be critical to interpretation.

Step 4

Determine the educational implications of cognitive performance. One of the most salient reasons that professional examiners use the WJ IV COG is because it offers a strong theoretical, conceptual, and research-based foundation for linking assessment results to instruction. A WJ IV COG assessment is often the most valuable when it results in suggestions for intervention. The 18 tests included in the WJ

IV COG provide measures of seven broad abilities and several narrow abilities as defined by CHC theory. As described earlier in this chapter, performance on each test requires a different application of cognitive processing. Individual tests and clusters may be related differentially to the development of language, reasoning, reading, math, and writing abilities. Consequently, when using the WJ IV COG, evaluators can apply knowledge of a student's differentiated cognitive proficiencies to structure, augment, and individualize instructional interventions and/or suggest accommodations to an educational plan.

DON'T FORGET

One of the primary reasons assessment professionals use the WJ IV COG is because it offers a strong theoretical, conceptual, and research-based foundation for linking assessment results to intervention.

Information contained in this chapter provides several suggested linkages between limitations in test performance and evidence-based, individualized educational interventions or accommodations. CHC theory and an analysis of the cognitive processing requirements of each test provides the basis for an alignment of test results with interventions that, if implemented with fidelity, may increase vocabulary knowledge, increase reasoning strategies, or trigger more efficient cognitive processing. Although many individuals develop cognitive abilities through incidental learning, for some students, specific types of knowledge, reasoning, or and even processing skills may need to be explicitly modeled, taught, and practiced in an educational setting. As suggested by Wong, Harris, Butler, and Graham (2003), "An implication, borne out in research, is that student performance should improve when teachers structure instruction and academic work to cue effective processing" (p. 392). Linking the results of cognitive assessment to instructional strategies, learning objectives, and intervention plans makes cognitive assessment relevant. The *WJ IV Interpretation and Instructional Interventions Program* (WIIIP; Schrank & Wendling, 2015a) is an optional online resource for linking test results to instructional interventions that was developed from a fundamental belief that a quality WJ IV evaluation should make a difference in the educational program of a student. In the WIIIP, individually targeted suggestions for interventions are generated automatically, based on the individual's *W* Diff score for each WJ IV test or cluster. From the auto-generated list, an assessment professional or evaluation team can review and determine if any aligned intervention is appropriate for the individual and elect it for inclusion in an intervention plan.

Step 5

Integrate all of the information the WJ IV COG provides to help address the referral question. Remember that an evaluation is a psychological case study, and the focus of the case study is an individual, not the WJ IV or CHC theory. CHC theory is a psychometric theory of intelligence that provides a professional grammar to aid in understanding different cognitive abilities, it is not a cookbook for conducting an evaluation; and although the WJ IV is likely the most comprehensive system for evaluation of contemporary cognitive abilities, oral language, and academic achievement, it is useful only for the value of the information that it provides about an individual. The WJ IV provides information about the cognitive abilities of an individual from multiple perspectives. Each test and cluster provides a full range of derived scores that each provide a unique perspective on the individual's performance. Although both age and grade norms are available in the WJ IV, frequently age norms are preferred for cognitive ability assessment. Here are some of the most useful scores and procedures

- An individual's raw scores are transformed into Age-Equivalent (AE) scores that express the individual's performance in terms of the age equivalent in the standardization sample that is associated with the raw score. As such, these scores provide information about an individual's developmental age.
- Proficiency levels describe the individual's ability with the measured tasks relative to individuals of the same age (or grade, if grade norms are selected). These terms have objective meaning because they are tied directly to task proficiency as measured by the W Diff. The associated RPI scores express the W Diff as a ratio scale that compares the individual's relative task proficiency when compared to the typical, or median, individual of the same age (or grade).

DON'T FORGET

The RPI and proficiency levels provide criterion-referenced interpretation to an individual's performance on the WJ IV COG. The RPI scores use a ratio scale to describe how proficient the individual is with cognitive tasks when compared to a same-aged individual at the median ability level. The proficiency levels describe the individual's ability on each test or cluster using descriptive terms that many parents, teachers, and other professionals usually can understand.

- Standard Scores and Percentile Ranks provide information about the individual's relative position among peers. Standard Scores are often required and can be useful for some comparative purposes. Because Standard Scores lack objective meaning, however, the corresponding percentile ranks are recommended because they yield descriptive information on how common or rare the individual's ability level is within the general population. Additionally, Percentile Rank information is more commonly understood by both professional and nonprofessional consumers of report information. Standard scores, in contrast, often are misinterpreted.

- The Intra-Cognitive Variations and *Gf-Gc* Composite/Other Ability comparison procedure are both useful for describing an individual's abilities in terms of a profile of relative strengths and weaknesses; parents, teachers, and other professionals can easily understand that, as individuals, everyone has relative strengths and weaknesses.

- The Intra-Cognitive Variations procedure evaluates each test and cluster to a predicted score based on the individual's performance on tests of six distinctively different cognitive performance indicators. This procedure helps isolate any individual-specific strengths or weaknesses that can be used in understanding an overall cognitive profile of an individual.

- The *Gf-Gc* Composite/Other Ability Comparison procedure often can provide the most insightful comparisons of intellectual level (as defined by the *Gf-Gc* Composite) to other cognitive clusters that measure lower-order cognitive processing, storage and processing functions, or mechanisms of cognitive efficiency. This procedure is particularly useful when an individual's *Gf* and *Gc* abilities are relatively intact when compared to other cognitive abilities that may be a source of a cognitive or learning disability. In addition, the *Gf-Gc* Composite can be compared to other WJ IV oral language and achievement clusters that are not primarily *Gf* or *Gc* to create a comprehensive assessment of an individual's strengths and weaknesses relative to the *Gf-Gc* Composite. This procedure may be particularly relevant for the identification of an SLD (Schrank et al., 2015a).

DON'T FORGET

....

Recommended Scores, Descriptors, and Comparisons for an Integrative Review

Age-Equivalent Scores
Proficiency-Level Terms
Percentile Ranks (Based on Age Norms)
Intracognitive Variations Procedure
Gf-Gc Composite/Other Ability Comparison Procedure

In summary, the final step is an integrative review of the information the WJ IV provides, particularly the recommended scores and descriptive labels. Understand how each score is interpreted. Review the results of the variation and comparison procedures to help develop a profile of the individual's performance on the WJ IV, and use the WJ IV COG information in conjunction with other relevant information to address the referral question or reason for the evaluation. The WJ IV COG provides well-supported (valid) measures of distinct cognitive abilities, includes procedures for determining relative strengths and weaknesses among those abilities, and utilizes an objective measurement methodology for determining the presence and severity of any cognitive limitations. When properly interpreted, results from the WJ IV COG can inform an evaluator when a relative cognitive weakness is also a limitation. Limitations in cognitive abilities can be identified and addressed through associated interventions and/or accommodations. Throughout the process, maintain your focus on the individual, his or her needs, and the referral question.

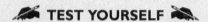

TEST YOURSELF

1. **The abilities measured by the WJ IV COG are not entities of physical science, they are semantic abstractions based on contemporary CHC theory.**
   a. True
   b. False

2. **Who is credited with initially developing the stepladder of abstraction?**
   a. Alfred Korzybski
   b. S. I. Hayakawa
   c. John Horn
   d. John Garruto

3. **Test 1: Oral Vocabulary measures long-term semantic memory?**
   a. True
   b. False

4. **When one of the purposes of an evaluation includes linking cognitive assessment results to instructional interventions, cluster-level interpretation provides the most direct linkage for targeting interventions to any measured limitations in cognitive abilities and processing.**
   a. True
   b. False

5. **Which Short-Term Working Memory (*Gwm*) test measures the executive search and updating processes required for answering questions based on verbally presented strings of unrelated object names and numbers in primary memory?**
   a. Verbal Attention
   b. Numbers Reversed
   c. Object-Number Sequencing
   d. None of the above

6. **Which test measures orthographic visual perceptual discrimination ability under timed conditions?**
   a. Pair Cancellation
   b. Phonological Processing
   c. Letter-Pattern Matching
   d. Coding

7. **From the perspective of cognitive psychology, Test 6: Story Recall might more accurately be called:**
   a. Story Remembering
   b. Story Reconstruction
   c. Story Retelling
   d. Bedtime Stories

8. **Test 7: Visualization has two parts. What are the two parts?**
   a. Symbol Search and Block Rotation
   b. Pair Cancellation and Visual Matching
   c. Spatial Relations and Block Rotation
   d. Spatial Relations and Pair Cancellation

9. **Test 11: Number-Pattern Matching measures what narrow CHC ability?**
   a. Numerosity (N)
   b. Perceptual Speed (P)
   c. Quantitative Reasoning (RQ)
   d. Visualization (Vz)

10. **Test 12: Nonword Repetition measures both span in Short-Term Working Memory (*Gwm*) and phonological sensitivity in Auditory Processing (*Ga*).**
    a. True
    b. False

11. **Which of the WJ IV COG tests has the highest median loading on general intellectual ability (*g*)?**
    a. Oral Vocabulary
    b. Number Series
    c. Phonological Processing
    d. Object-Number Sequencing

12. **Which cluster measures consolidation (encoding) of semantic (meaning-based) representations into secondary memory?**
    a. Short-Term Working Memory (*Gwm*)
    b. Cognitive Efficiency
    c. Long-Term Storage and Retrieval (*Glr*)
    d. *Gf-Gc* Composite

13. **Which single test best represents the broad construct of Short-Term Working Memory (*Gwm*)?**
    a. Verbal Attention
    b. Numbers Reversed
    c. Object-Number Sequencing
    d. Memory for Words

14. **Which cluster measures word activation, access, restructuring via phonological codes and phonological sensitivity capacity in working memory?**
    a. Short-Term Working Memory (*Gwm*)
    b. Cognitive Efficiency
    c. Auditory Processing (*Ga*)
    d. Comprehension-Knowledge (*Gc*)

15. **Which cluster is the best measure of psychometric g?**
    a. *Gf-Gc* Composite
    b. Brief Intellectual Ability (BIA)
    c. General Intellectual Ability (GIA)
    d. Scholastic Aptitudes

16. **Which measure of intellectual ability do the WJ IV authors recommend for use in identification of a specific learning disability when a deficit exists in one or more areas of cognitive processing?**
    a. General Intellectual Ability (GIA)
    b. Brief Intellectual Ability (BIA)
    c. Scholastic Aptitudes
    d. *Gf-Gc* Composite

17. **What is the recommended use for the Scholastic Aptitude clusters?**
    a. Short, selective, referral-focused assessments
    b. Determining aptitude for learning in a specific content area
    c. Estimating long-term potential for academic success
    d. Determining the presence of a specific learning disability

18. **Which tests must be administered to obtain the basis for the Intra-Cognitive Variations Procedure?**
    a. Tests 1–3
    b. Tests 1–7
    c. Tests 1–10
    d. Tests 1–14

19. Which of the following is an example of proficiency-level information on the WJ IV COG?

a. Standard Scores

b. Percentile Ranks

c. Relative Proficiency Indexes

d. Age-Equivalent Scores

20. What should be the primary focus for a case study or evaluation using the WJ IV COG?

a. Contemporary CHC theory

b. Putting standard scores into the cross-battery software

c. Calculation of an ability-achievement discrepancy

d. The individual being evaluated

Answers: 1. a; 2. b; 3. a; 4. b; 5. a; 6. c; 7. b; 8. c; 9. b; 10. a; 11. d; 12. c; 13. a; 14. c; 15. c; 16. d; 17. a; 18. b; 19. c; 20. d

Five

STRENGTHS AND WEAKNESSES
OF THE WJ IV COG

Robert Walrath, John O. Willis, and Ron Dumont

W ith the publication of the WJ IV *Tests of Cognitive Abilities* (WJ IV COG) (Schrank, McGrew, & Mather, 2014b), *Tests of Achievement* (WJ IV ACH) (Schrank, Mather, & McGrew, 2014a), and *Tests of Oral Language* (WJ IV OL) (Schrank, Mather, & McGrew 2014b), clinicians now have the ultimate toolbox for psychoeducational assessment, assessing changes over time, and research. Although this chapter focuses on the strengths and weaknesses of the WJ IV COG, its integration with the WJ IV ACH and WJ IV OL batteries requires some specific mention of these tests as well.

DEVELOPMENT AND STRUCTURE

The *Woodcock Johnson III Normative Update* (Woodcock, McGrew, Schrank, & Mather, 2001, 2007) has been extensively revised to create the *Woodcock-Johnson IV* (Schrank, McGrew, & Mather, 2014a) with tests added, deleted, renamed, and relocated among the WJ IV COG, ACH, and OL batteries. The WJ IV COG now consists of 18 tests (10 in the Standard Battery and 8 in the Extended Battery), including 6 new or modified tests as reported in the WJ IV COG *Examiner's Manual* (Mather & Wendling, 2014). Oral Vocabulary (formerly Verbal Comprehension), Verbal Attention, Letter-Pattern Matching, Phonological Processing, Visualization (which includes Spatial Relations and Block Rotation tests), and Nonword Repetition have been either added or modified.

In addition, several tests from the WJ III COG have been moved to other batteries: Rapid Picture Naming, Retrieval Fluency, Sound Blending, and Sentence Repetition (formerly Memory for Sentences) have been moved to the WJ IV OL battery; Number Matrices has been moved from the WJ III COG to the WJ IV ACH; and Story Recall has been moved from the WJ III ACH to the WJ IV COG battery. With the discontinuation of the WJ III *Diagnostic Supplement* (Woodcock, McGrew, Mather, & Schrank, 2003), the revision of the WJ IV ACH, and the development of the WJ IV OL battery, 50 tests are now available across all three batteries, allowing broad coverage of discrete skills and abilities.

WJ IV COG Composites and Clusters

The WJ IV COG core tests (Tests 1–7) are used for calculating the General Intellectual Index (GIA) and for determining relative strengths and weaknesses among seven tests measuring distinct aspects of cognitive functioning. Additional tests may be added from the WJ IV COG, ACH, or OL as determined by the examiner. The *Gf-Gc* Composite is new to the WJ IV COG and consists of four tests (Oral Vocabulary, Number Series, General Information, and Concept Formation) that are designed to create an estimate of intellectual ability based on the two highest or most complex g abilities (*Gc*, Comprehension-Knowledge, and *Gf*, Fluid Reasoning). The Brief Intellectual Ability (BIA) score is available with the administration of the first three tests (Oral Vocabulary, Number Series and Verbal Attention).

Also new to the WJ IV COG, although similar in concept to Woodcock-Johnson (Woodcock & Johnson, 1977) and Woodcock-Johnson Revised (Woodcock & Johnson, 1989a) veterans, are the Scholastic Aptitude clusters, each of which is based on four tests that are highly related to a selected achievement area. There are two aptitude clusters available in the area of Reading (Reading Aptitude A for the Reading, Broad Reading, Reading Comprehension, Reading Fluency, and Reading Rateclusters; Reading Aptitude B for the Basic Reading Skillscluster), two in the area of Mathematics (Mathematics Aptitude A for Mathematics, Broad Mathematics, and Math Calculation Skills; Math Aptitude B for MathProblem Solving), and two in the area of Writing (Written Language Aptitude A for Written Language, Broad Written Language, and Written Expression; Written Language Aptitude B for Basic Writing Skills). These scores are especially useful in understanding whether an individual's difficulties in an academic area are expected or unexpected, based on his or her performance on closely related cognitive tests. According to Mather and Wendling (2014):

> because they compare the predicted scores with obtained scores for examinees in the WJ IV norm sample, the resulting aptitude-achievement discrepancy scores are actual discrepancy norms. The Scholastic Aptitude scores the most precise predictors of specific curricular performance in the near term. (p. 20)

If an examiner's goal is assessment of one particular area of achievement, the one or two relevant Scholastic Aptitude Clusters will be more efficient and may be more useful than the entire GIA or *Gf-Gc* Composite.

Similar to the WJ III COG, the seven primary Cattell-Horn-Carroll (CHC) broad ability clusters can each be derived from two WJ IV COG tests: Comprehension Knowledge (*Gc*), Fluid Reasoning (*Gf*), and Short-Term Working Memory (*Gwm*) from the Standard Battery; and Long-Term Storage and Retrieval (*Glr*), Auditory Processing (*Ga*), Cognitive Processing Speed (*Gs*), and Visual Processing (*Gv*) from the Standard and Extended Batteries. Extended versions of *Gf* and *Gwm* can be created by adding an additional Extended Battery test and an extended version of *Gc* by adding Picture Vocabulary from the OL battery. Short-Term Working Memory (*Gwm*) was formerly called Short-Term Memory (*Gsm*) and summarizes performance from the Verbal Attention and Numbers Reversed tests. "Cognitive" was added to the Processing Speed cluster to better identify this cluster as an aspect of *cognitive* efficiency (Reynolds & Niileksla, 2015).

The WJ IV COG also has been revised to better reflect CHC narrow ability clusters. Perceptual Speed (P), Quantitative Reasoning (RQ), Number Facility (N), and Cognitive Efficiency (*Gs+Gwm*) are all available from the administration of WJ IV COG Standard and Extended Battery tests. Two additional narrow ability clusters, Auditory Memory Span (MS) and Vocabulary (VL), require a combination of tests from the WJ IV COG and WJ IV OL. **Rapid Reference 5.1** presents additional information about the test development and structure.

Test Scores and Scoring

With two exceptions, scoring for most of the tests is very straightforward. Test 13, Visual-Auditory Learning, is scored by counting the number of errors. Test 6, Story Recall, does not use typical basal and ceiling rules, and examiners should closely follow the scoring directions on page 62 of the *Examiner's Manual*. As noted, the *Examiner's Manual* provides detailed guidance. Scoring for several WJ IV COG tests has been simplified from the WJ III versions. For example, on the WJ III COG Spatial Relations, a multiple-choice test with one to three correct choices for each item, scoring was based on four possible sets of items with progression to the next set determined by a cutoff score for each set, which was a challenging clerical task for the examiner. Raw scores for the 33 items could range from 0 to 81.

On the WJ IV COG, Test 7A Spatial Relations (now a subtest of the Visualization test), items are scored pass-fail, testing is halted after incorrect responses

≡ Rapid Reference 5.1 Primary Strengths and Weaknesses of the WI IV COG

Test Development and Structure

Primary Strengths	Primary Weaknesses
Addition of a separate Oral Language Battery provides three conormed batteries: COG, ACH, and OL.	Examiners must purchase three batteries to make full use of the WJ IV.
The COG battery has 18 tests (and examiners can select additional COG and OL tests) covering a very broad array of information.	The extraordinary breadth of the WJ IV batteries requires that each test be relatively brief.
Six Scholastic Aptitude clusters are available to aid in prediction of reading, math, and writing achievement.	
The new *Gc-Gf* Composite is designed to provide an estimate of intellectual ability based on the two highest g abilities.	
Narrow CHC abilities of Perceptual Speed, Quantitative Reasoning, Number Facility, Cognitive Efficiency, Auditory Memory Span, and Vocabulary are now available.	The *Examiner's* and *Technical Manuals* offer little guidance on when to use the *Gf-Gc* instead of other scores.
The WJ IV COG can be administered with only the Test Books, Test Records, and Response Booklet, but there is also a very helpful examiner's manual that is needed for scoring some tests.	Auditory Memory Span and Vocabulary require tests from the WJIV OL battery
Test materials are user friendly and durable.	
The Selective Testing Tables on pp. v and vii of the easel are extremely useful.	

to the five highest items administered (no items sets), and the range of possible scores for the 24 items is simply 0 to 24. Test 7B Block Rotation (also a subtest on the Visualization test) has been similarly simplified from the WJ III COG Diagnostic Supplement (Woodcock, McGrew, Mather, & Schrank (2003).

One of the greatest strengths of the WJ IV COG is the power of the *Woodcock-Johnson Online Scoring and Reporting* program (Schrank & Dailey, 2014), which: saves time; permits scoring by 1-month rather than 3-, 6-, or

12-month intervals of age or grade; allows a multiplicity of different clusters for various purposes; and precludes errors in looking up, calculating, and recording scores (but not clerical errors in entering raw scores). A few examiners suggest that this capability is also a weakness: There is no way to score the test without a computer or computerized device, and examiners must have faith in the reliability and security of the online data storage. Off-line scoring through the Woodcock-Johnson® IV Mobile Scoring and Reporting App is available. This app is a convenient way for examiners to add and access important examinee information on the go. Just like the web-based scoring program, this mobile app gives you the ability to add and modify caseload folders and examinees and generate PDF score reports. As with any new technology, examiners must take the time to learn the new system. Just as with the WJ III Compuscore, the new online scoring provides many options the end user will find extremely valuable. These include, to name just a few, the ability to customize scoring templates based on an individual user's preferences; the choice of a vast array of scores to report (e.g., Standard Scores [SS], Normal Curve Equivalents (NCE), stanines, *W* scores, PR, PR ranges, and variation and comparison scores); and a new "Roster" report that collects all the scores from various examinees into one report.

As anyone who hand-scored the WJ-R (Woodcock & Johnson, 1989a) knows, there simply is no possible way to provide printed tables of norms at 1-month age and grade intervals for the 18 tests and 23 CHC broad and narrow clusters, for the many scores, for differences between them, and for myriad comparisons between tests and clusters when using all three WJ IV batteries. Having scores based on single months of age or grade rather than spans of several months or even years prevents the sometimes dramatic overnight changes in derived scores on other tests as a student switches, for example, from Fall to Spring norms (Willis & Dumont, 2002, pp. 115–116). In our opinion, that virtue and the wide variety of clusters and interpretive reports that will become available justify the necessary exclusive reliance on computerized scoring. Additionally, the use of computer algorithms to accurately pinpoint a person's abilities (whether cognitive, oral language, or academic achievement) makes the WJ IV one of the most technically sophisticated batteries available. Those who already use optional computer scoring for other tests will be especially happy. Most of us who tend to eschew computer scoring probably will be nervous but pleased with the results.

The *Examiner's Manual* (Mather & Wendling, 2014, p. 36) warns examiners that "not all possible correct and incorrect answers are listed in the keys. Judgment is required when scoring some responses" and elaborates on this important issue. When given responses that are not listed and are not clearly correct or incorrect, examiners may need to consult dictionaries, thesauruses, and other references to ensure correct scoring. Examiners must not simply assume that their knowledge is always correct and exhaustive and that the examinee's unfamiliar response is wrong. It is possible that an examinee may come up with a response that is mathematically or logically correct but is not listed in the keys. Examiners would need to determine (perhaps in consultation with a colleague) if they will accept such responses as correct. For example, during this review, these authors discovered that one item (#41) on the Number Series test may have an additional correct answer that is not listed on the easel pages. The item requires the examinee to fill in the missing number or numbers to an incomplete series of numbers. Although all items can be answered correctly using whole numbers, there is no prohibition in the test's directions that fractions are not allowed. Therefore, for this one item, the two missing numbers not listed as correct answers are $74\,2/3$ and $79\,1/3$. This solution comes by adding $4\,2/3$ to each number in the sequence. It appears that since this test is considered a test of fluid reasoning (novel problem solving), this correct solution, although not listed in the key and unlikely to be encountered very often, demonstrates the actual process being tapped.

Otherwise correct responses in languages other than English are no longer accepted on the WJ IV COG (the WJ IV OL includes three Spanish-language tests). This prudent change should serve to reduce interexaminer variability since, for example, many examiners might know that *caballo* means "horse" but fewer might recognize *cheval* or *Pferd* as synonyms. **Rapid Reference 5.2** provides additional information about strengths and weaknesses of WJ IV scoring.

Test Interpretation

Mather and Wendling, in the WJ IV COG *Examiner's Manual*, described four cumulative levels of interpretation that are seen as necessary to completely describe a person's performance. Level 1 information is qualitative observations of the examinee throughout testing and error analysis of individual test items. The authors suggested (and we agree) that the "Test Sessions Observations Checklist" in the test protocol will aid in obtaining this type of information. This information may be helpful in describing examinee behavior, considering the influence of that behavior on test results, and making recommendations for instruction. Level 2 or Level of Development information is obtained by looking at sums of item scores and the age or grade level that corresponds in the normative sample. This norm-referenced information may be expressed in Rasch Ability scores (test or cluster *W* scores) as well as age or grade equivalents. This information may aid in describing developmental levels and may help in placement decisions or recommendations for instructional levels. Level 3 or

≣ Rapid Reference 5.2 Primary Strengths and Weaknesses of the WJ IV COG

Test Scoring

Primary Strengths	Primary Weaknesses
Computer scoring permits calculation of many scores and comparisons that would be impossible with hand-scoring.	Scoring exclusively by computer precludes checking by hand-scoring and delays preliminary scoring until a computer is available.
Computer scoring eliminates errors in arithmetic and in looking up scores in printed tables.	Computer scoring does not prevent typographic errors in entering scores and may make it more difficult to catch those errors.
Off-line score entry through mobile apps is available.	Initially, only online scoring will be available, which may be difficult for itinerant evaluators.
	Some examiners will be tempted to enter the scores, print the Score Report and Parent Report, and just sign and distribute the printouts.
Computer scoring permits norms to be based on 1-month intervals of age or grade, preventing large overnight changes in scores between, for example, Fall and Spring norms or norms for age 9:0—9:6 and 9:7—9:11.	Given the tremendous technical precision of and broad choices available from the online scoring, examiners must understand any and all scores chosen for interpretation. Simply letting the software produce scores or identify differences between scores could lead to misinterpretations of the results.
Score Reports (scores and calculations of variations and comparisons) are available. The *Woodcock Interpretation and Instructional Interventions™ Program* (WIIIP; Schrank & Wendling, 2015a) (comprehensive report and optional interventions) is available for purchase at http://www .riversidepublishing.com/products/wj-iv/ wiiip.html Scoring of most tests is straightforward. The *Examiner's Manual* provides detailed guidance for scoring the other tests.	

Proficiency information is obtained by looking at Rasch scale score differences from a grade or age reference point. This criterion-referenced information (Relative Proficiency Index, CALP level, or Test or Cluster W DIFF) helps determine level of difficulty of tasks related to developmental level and may help with placement decisions based on proficiency. Although written for the WJ III, Jaffe's (2009) paper on W scores and Relative Proficiency Index (RPI) scores is still applicable to the WJ IV and may help examiners make more and better use of the RPI for explaining test performance. Finally, Level 4 or Relative Group Standing information is obtained through norm-referenced comparisons using standard scores and percentile ranks to establish an examinee's position relative to peers.

There are now four comparisons available for intra-ability: intra-cognitive, intra-achievement, intra-oral language, and academic skills/fluency/applications. Intra-cognitive variations are calculated using the first seven tests to develop predicted scores based on the average performance of six tests to be compared to the score on the seventh. Additional WJ IV COG tests and subtests from other batteries can be included in this analysis. The *Examiner's Manual* provides detailed explanations on how these comparisons are formulated. The examiner should be grateful that online scoring makes possible so many potentially useful scores and comparisons but also should be selective in choosing what data to include in the report. The reader should not be overwhelmed by myriad statistics, and the examiner should not fall into the mindless habit of relying on the same statistics for every case. Different levels of interpretation and different scores serve different purposes. **Rapid Reference 5.3** summarizes the primary strengths and weaknesses related to interpretation of the WJ IV COG.

Standardization, Reliability, and Validity

The WJ IV COG was normed on an extremely large, carefully selected sample including 664 preschoolers, 3,891 students in grades K–12, 775 college and graduate students, and 2,086 other adults drawn from 46 states and the District of Columbia. There were six to eight sampling variables for various age levels, all of which closely matched the 2010 US Census projections, and partial subject weighting was used to make the matches even more accurate. Not all examinees took all tests, but a sophisticated planned incomplete data collection, multiple matrix sampling design was employed, which actually may yield more accurate norms. This procedure is thoroughly explained in the WJ IV *Technical Manual* (McGrew, LaForte, & Schrank, 2014), which also provides extensive cluster summary and reliability statistics for all tests and clusters in Appendices B and C of that manual. Special Group Studies are reported for nine clinical groups,

Rapid Reference 5.3   Primary Strengths and Weaknesses of the WJ IV COG

Test Interpretation

Primary Strengths	Primary Weaknesses
Application of the most recent reformulations of CHC theory to WJ IV COG, ACH, and OL batteries provides a common interpretive framework within the WJ IV and with other tests using CHC theory.	
The General Intellectual Index (GIA) is derived from the first seven core tests, and the Brief Intellectual Ability (BIA) score is derived from the first three tests.	Examiners need to select and report the clusters that provide useful information about the examinee.
Many new cluster and test comparisons and improved comparison procedures have been added.	Examiners need to refrain from running and reporting all possible comparisons.
Administration of the seven core tests permits calculation of predicted score for each test based on the other six scores. Other tests and clusters also can be compared to the appropriate predicted achievement score.	
Cognitive Academic Language Proficiency (CALP) (Cummins, 2003) scores are provided for the Comprehension-Knowledge (Gc) cluster	

although not for persons with hearing impairments. However, the WJ IV COG *Examiner's Manual* provides valuable information about testing persons with hearing impairments.

The *Technical Manual* provides specific test and cluster reliabilities at each age, not just for entire tests. Those reliabilities are generally very strong with median scores across all ages ranging from .74 to .97 for individual tests and .86 to .97 for clusters. Test-retest reliabilities (stability coefficients) are provided only for the speeded tests.

The *Technical Manual* also includes a great deal of information on the latest developments in contemporary CHC theory and extensive factor analytic data supporting the internal structure of the WJ IV. Concurrent validity studies show moderate to strong correlations between WJ IV COG and the *Wechsler Intelligence Scale for Children–4th Edition* (WISC-IV; Wechsler, 2003); *Wechsler Adult Intelligence Scale–4th Edition* (WAIS-IV; Wechsler, 2008); *Wechsler Preschool and Primary Scale of Intelligence, 3rd Edition* (WPPSI; Wechsler, 2002); and the *Kaufman Assessment Battery for Children–2nd Edition* (KABC-II; Kaufman & Kaufman, 2004).

Correlations with the *Stanford Binet Intelligence Scales, 5th Edition* (SB5; Roid, 2003) are less robust and likely related to a lack of strong evidence of CHC factors in the SB-5 (Canivez, 2008). **Rapid Reference 5.4** provides additional information about the standardization, reliability, and validity of the WJ IV COG.

STRENGTHS OF THE WJ IV COG

Manuals

Clearly one strength of the WJ IV is the amount of information available to examiners to aid in understanding the test, its development, use, and interpretive approaches. Information is provided in different resources, including the 360+-page *Technical Manual*, the *Examiner's Manual*, the test easels, the *Examiner Training Workbook* (Wendling, 2014), and the multiple WJ IV assessment service bulletins and author newsletters available from the Riverside WJ IV website. Although too much information should never be thought of as a problem, we must hope that examiners using the WJ IV will take advantage of the materials and not be overwhelmed by them. Reading through the *Technical Manual* may seem to some like a tedious chore, but doing so provides much-needed information for understanding the results that are obtained. A careful, thoughtful reading of all materials will help the examiner understand the vast amount of information the WJ IV can provide. Understanding standard scores, percentile ranks, RPIs, Variation scores, and Comparison scores (to name just a few types of scores available) is surely necessary to competent interpretation. Also, understanding several statistical nuances (e.g., why the same standard score may give three different percentile ranks; why two low test scores might combine to form an even lower cluster score; or why Standard Scores and Relative Proficiency Indexes may give very different pictures of an examinee's abilities) is important when explaining results to laypeople.

Three Conormed Batteries

Although we are reviewing only the WJ IV COG, we must note the tremendous power of using genuinely conormed tests of cognitive abilities, oral language, and

≡ *Rapid Reference 5.4 Primary Strengths and Weaknesses of the WI IV ACH*

Standardization, Reliability, and Validity

Primary Strengths	Primary Weaknesses
Extremely large norming samples (664 preschoolers, 3,891 students in grades K–12, 775 college and graduate students, and 2,086 adults.	Not all examinees took all tests, but a sophisticated planned incomplete data collection, multiple matrix sampling design was employed, which actually may yield more accurate norms.
Examinees were drawn from 46 states and the District of Columbia.	
There were six sampling variables for preschool, seven for school, five for college, and eight for adults.	
The norming sample closely matched the 2010 US Census projections on these variables, and partial subject weighting was used to refine the matches.	
Cluster summary and reliability statistics for all tests and clusters can be found in Appendices B and C of the *Technical Manual*.	
Special Group Studies are reported for 9 clinical groups.	Persons with hearing impairments were not included in the clinical groups.
Item Response Theory statistics provide specific test reliabilities at each age or grade.	
Reliabilities are generally very strong.	
The *Technical Manual* includes a great deal of information on the latest developments in CHC theory and extensive factor analytic data supporting the internal structure.	
Concurrent validity studies show moderate to strong correlations between the WISC–IV, KABC–II, and WPPSI–III, and WAIS–IV.	The *Technical Manual* does not include test-retest stability coefficients for nonspeeded tests.

academic achievement. Three WJ IV OL tests are used to complete or extended WJ IV COG clusters: Comprehension-Knowledge (*Gc*), Auditory Memory Span (*Gwm*-MS), and Vocabulary (*Gc*-VL/LD). It is invaluable to be able to compare, for example, cognitive and achievement scores and be certain that differences are attributable to the examinee's abilities, not to differences between norming samples. As discussed, WJ IV COG Scholastic Aptitude clusters can be compared with precision to WJ IV ACH clusters.

Variety of Tests

The 18 COG tests and 50 tests of the three WJ IV batteries cover an extraordinary range of discrete abilities. If examiners take the time and make the effort to mindfully plan an assessment, the WJ IV offers tremendous opportunities to tailor an assessment precisely to referral questions and concerns.

Statistical Strengths

The WJ COG, as discussed, is characterized by an outstanding norming sample and generally very strong evidence of reliability and validity. Since examiners, not publishers, are responsible for evaluating the technical adequacy of their instruments, these statistical strengths and the extensive, detailed information in the *Technical Manual* are very important.

Norms are provided at 1-month intervals for both age and grade for the WJ IV COG as well as for the WJ IV ACH and OL. These dual norms are unusual (if not unique) among individually administered intelligence tests and allow examiners always to compare age-based scores with age-based scores from another test battery or grade-based scores with other grade-based scores. It is never necessary to compare, for example, an age-based intellectual ability score with a grade-based achievement score.

User Friendliness

The test easels are easy to use (and all of the WJ IV COG tests can be placed in a single easel for ease of transportation and storage) and have so far proven durable. On pages v and vii of the easel is a "Selective Testing Table" clearly showing which tests are needed for each cognitive composite, CHC Factor, and each narrow ability and other clinical cluster and each possible Scholastic Aptitude/Achievement comparison. Those tables are extremely useful in planning and guiding an assessment and are worth photocopying for those purposes for each evaluation. (The WJ IV ACH and OL batteries include similar tables.) The Test Record form and Response Booklet are attractive, easy to use, and sturdy.

WEAKNESSES OF THE WJ IV COG

In general, weaknesses associated with the WJ IV COG are relatively few and might be classified more as quibbles than actual weaknesses.

GIA versus *Gf-Gc*

The authors of the WJ IV have introduced a new measure of Fluid Reasoning (*Gf*) and Comprehension-Knowledge (*Gc*). This new, *Gf-Gc* Composite, may prove to be extremely useful for evaluators when there are differences between it and the GIA. The GIA includes all seven of the most important CHC broad cognitive (not academic achievement) abilities, both "higher-level" cognitive abilities, such as *Gf*, and "lower-level" processing, such as *Gs*, measuring overall psychometric *g*, the third stratum in Carroll's (1993) hierarchy. This model is similar to the total scores on several intelligence tests but is unique in including seven broad abilities. The *Gf-Gc* composite, includes only *Gf* and *Gc* abilities, omitting "lower-level" processing abilities, more in the early tradition of Cattell (1941; 1943; 1963, 1987) and Horn (1994; Cattell & Horn, 1978) (F. A. Schrank, personal communication, August 17, 2015). Some critics (e.g., Willis & Dumont, 1994) have complained that total scores mixing higher- and lower-level cognitive abilities in a proxy for *g* are likely to obscure the true intellectual potential of persons with specific learning disabilities (SLDs) and other processing disorders. The addition of the *Gf-Gc* Composite is a welcome approach to this concern. However, some examiners are concerned about the lack of specific, concrete rules to guide the selection of the *Gf-Gc* or the GIA. Although the WJ IV Assessment Service Bulletin 3 (Schrank, McGrew, & Mather, 2015a; see also Appendix of this book) is extremely useful in understanding the differences between the *Gf-Gc* composite and the GIA, the decision of which composites to report and interpret is left to the examiner's clinical judgment. School districts that insist on rigid statistical formulas for identifying SLDs may struggle with this need for clinical judgment (McGrew, 1994). The bulletin does an excellent job of presenting the rationale for considering the *Gf-Gc* as an "alternative index of intellectual level" (p. 5). It describes how the *Gf-Gc* may be useful in the determination of SLD, noting that "it makes sense to compare the often intact *Gf-Gc* Composite with the individual's other, less efficient, abilities, both in cognitive processing and academic achievement" (p. 10).

Table 5.1 Anthony's WJ IV COG Scores

CLUSTER/Test	W	RPI	SS	(68% Band)
GENERAL INTELLECTUAL ABILITY	483	74/90	84	(80–87)
Oral Vocabulary	486	78/90	89	(83–95)
Number Series	466	46/90	84	(79–89)
Verbal Attention	480	69/90	87	(81–93)
Letter-Pattern Matching	485	65/90	88	(79–98)
Phonological Processing	487	74/90	86	(81–92)
Story Recall	488	86/90	94	(90–99)
Visualization	495	91/90	102	(97–108)
Gf-Gc COMPOSITE	488	85/90	94	(90–98)
Oral Vocabulary	486	78/90	89	(83–95)
Number Series	466	46/90	84	(79–89)
General Information	502	96/90	108	(103–113)
Concept Formation	498	93/90	104	(100–108)

For example, take the case of Anthony, a 9-year, 8-month-old administered the WJ IV COG (Table 5.1). His overall GIA standard score of 84 is 10 points lower than his *Gf-Gc* standard score of 94. It seems as if the GIA may be underestimating his reasoning and acquired knowledge abilities. In this particular case, the examiner, after considering all information about Anthony, might focus interpretation of intellectual ability on the *Gf-Gc* rather than the GIA and evaluate the other tests to determine the influence of processing weaknesses on Anthony's academic performance. Many authorities observe that broad-spectrum measures of *g* (of which the WJ IV COG GIA is the broadest as well as being firmly based in CHC theory) accurately predict academic and vocational performance. Processing weaknesses diminish both total test scores and achievement, so the predictive power is not surprising. However, a goal of special education and related services is to help a student achieve at levels closer to the student's intellectual potential in spite of disabilities. The WJ IV COG *Gf-Gc* Composite is very helpful in pursuing this goal. We understand the problems faced by evaluators working in environments that demand a single, numerical measure of "ability" to compare with numerical measures of "achievement," but evaluators need to apply sound clinical judgment in selecting and interpreting the most helpful measures of ability and abilities for each student (McGrew, 1994).

Online Score Report

Raw scores are entered into the WJ IV online scoring program, but the typical score report does not show those scores. Although it is not listed in the Score

Selection Template, the online score report does provide an option to print out raw scores—the actual scores the program uses to calculate all results—but only by choosing Examinee Data Record, under "Report Type." The typical score report used by examiners does not allow for the reporting of the raw scores. Examiners should not blindly accept that the printout results are accurate. The accuracy of the score report is entirely dependent on the data inputted into it—human error when entering the raw data will result in inaccuracies. Without the raw scores on the printout, there is no easy way to check that the raw scores entered match the record form. Raw scores should not be included in final evaluation reports (readers will attempt to interpret them!), but we always must compare the record form to the actual data-input page of the online program. A student should not be denied services or a defendant sentenced to death because of an examiner's typo.

Note that there currently is no way to obtain the standard score category descriptors (e.g., "Average") from the online scoring program. Standard score category descriptors are available in the narrative but not the tables in the Comprehensive Report option of the *WJ IV Interpretation and Instructional Interventions Program* (WIIIP; Schrank & Wendling, 2015a), which is sold separately from the WJ IV test batteries. Other category description choices (e.g., RPI proficiency levels, CALP descriptions) are readily available from the WJ IV score template choices. This may cause some confusion and interpretation issues. We have already seen some examiners give standard scores labels associated with the RPI proficiency descriptions. Given the technology and the speed with which programs can be created or modified, we hope that this addition to the scoring software will be made in an update.

Comparisons between Scores

The combination of cognitive abilities, achievement, and oral language batteries in the WJ IV permits a variety of comparisons between scores. Along with the options for reporting different types of scores, the scoring program provides the examiner information regarding two types of *difference score* information: *variations* and *comparisons*. *Variation* scores describe a person's results in terms of a pattern of relative strengths and weaknesses; *comparison* scores typically examine whether the examinee's performance is outside the range of predicted scores. Examiners must exercise judgment and self-restraint in selecting those options that are best suited to answer the referral questions, respond to the referral requests, and make sense to the various readers of the report. Different purposes require different scores. A dozen pages of myriad scores and analyses is overwhelming to most readers. Some examiners have fallen into the pernicious habit of simply adding an uninterpreted page or two of text to the computer printout from the WJ III or other instruments, a habit that should not be perpetuated with the WJ IV or any test. For the use of future evaluators, we may want to append the WJ IV printout to our report, but, if we report scores at all, we need to select the most useful and appropriate ones and insert them in the report.

Given the sheer number of comparisons that are possible, examiners should, on any test or battery allowing multiple comparisons, be cautious in selecting a limited number of planned comparisons. Unless there is a statistical correction made for the multiple comparisons on any test battery, the chances of obtaining a significant difference by pure chance increase above the probability level set for each single comparison. As with many test batteries, it appears that no statistical correction is made on the WJ IV.

These authors were unable to find analyses of between-test comparisons in the variation/discrepancy analysis available from the score report. For example, in the case of Anthony (Table 5.1), the two *Gc* measures (Oral Vocabulary and General Information) differ by 19 points, while the two *Gf* measures (Number Series and Concept Formation) differ by 20 points, yet there is no information provided in the score report to reflect whether these score differences are statistically significant. An option to have paired comparisons in the WJ IV score report (at least for all two-test clusters) would be useful. These comparisons are available in the *WJ IV Interpretation and Instructional Interventions Program* (WIIIP) (Shrank & Wendling, 2015a), which is sold separately from the WJ IV test batteries.

The examiner does have the opportunity to run a different, separate Standard Score Profile Report that provides a graphic display of all scores banded as range of scores based upon the 68% confidence level. Using these bands, one can estimate whether the bands overlap—if they do overlap, there is no real difference between the obtained scores; if the score bands do not overlap, if separation between bands is less than the width of the wider band, assume a possible significant difference exists. Additionally, if separation between bands is greater than the width of the wider band, assume a significant difference exists.

Record Form

Several tests present multiple items to the examinee on a single easel page. For example, Oral Vocabulary-Synonyms presents four items on each page until the final page, which contains three items. The administration rules provided in the easel are quite clear. For example, with regard to a basal rule, the directions state: "Test by complete page until the 6 *lowest-numbered items administered are correct,* or until you have administered the page with item 1" (italics in original). Although the easel provides this useful and important rule, the record form does not, simply stating "Basal: 6 lowest correct." This shorthand has created problems for both new and experienced evaluators who are used to discontinuing a test after a certain number of consecutive passes or failures. We wish that the record form for the tests utilizing this "page rule" were more explicit.

Concluding Comment

Clearly, the WJ IV COG is an extremely valuable addition to the field of intellectual testing and offers a strongly theory-based, statistically sound, extremely well documented, and flexible tool for cognitive assessment. It retains the best aspects of the WJ III and includes many refinements and improvements. The capacity of the WJ IV COG to be used in conjunction with the conormed WJ IV ACH and OL batteries adds to its considerable utility.

As discussed at length in this chapter, the strengths of the WJ IV COG outweigh the weaknesses that we were able to discover, and, in fairness, some of those "weaknesses" are opportunities for examiner error rather than flaws in the battery itself. The authors of this chapter will be using the WJ IV COG in our practices and our psychology training programs.

🖋 TEST YOURSELF 🖋

1. **The WJ IV COG, ACH, and OL batteries provide 50 tests from which any combination can be administered.**
   a. True
   b. False
2. **Which of the following is a new cluster in the WJ IV COG?**
   a. General Intellectual Index (GIA)
   b. Brief Intellectual Ability (BIA)
   c. *Gf-Gc* Composite
   d. Comprehension-Knowledge (*Gc*)
3. **The Scholastic Aptitude Clusters can predict performance in the achievement areas of Reading, Math, and Writing.**
   a. True
   b. False
4. **Level 2 interpretation of the WJ IV COG:**
   a. Helps predict examinee classroom behavior.
   b. Contains norm referenced information.

    c. Describes developmental strengths and weaknesses.

    d. Both b and c.

5. When considering overall cognitive ability, examiners should:

    a. Always use the GIA.

    b. Always use the *Gf-Gc* composite.

    c. Use clinical judgment in selecting the most appropriate score.

    d. Avoid reporting any overall score to maintain objectivity.

6. A strength of the WJ IV COG is:

    a. Different scores are used for individual tests and for clusters.

    b. The *Technical Manual* is available in CD format.

    c. It must be given with the WJ IV ACH battery.

    d. None of the above.

7. The word "Cognitive" was added to the name of the Processing Speed Cluster to better identify it as a measure of *cognitive* efficiency.

    a. True

    b. False

8. A strength of the WJ IV COG is:

    a. The amount of information available through test manuals.

    b. That it is conormed with the WJ IV ACH and WJ IV OL batteries.

    c. The new Scholastic Aptitude clusters.

    d. All of the above.

9. Level 4 interpretation of the WJ IV COG includes:

    a. Observation of test behaviors.

    b. Age or grade equivalents.

    c. Relative Proficiency Index (RPI) scores.

    d. Standard scores and percentile ranks.

10. Norms based on 1-month intervals:

    a. Are a strength because they avoid dramatic score changes overnight.

    b. Are a weakness because they do not group examinees with all peers of the same age or grade.

    c. Are a strength because age norms and grade norms are interchangeable.

    d. Are a weakness because they are not familiar to examiners.

11. A strength of the WJ IV COG is that:

    a. It is a practical test without a theoretical bias.

    b. It is based on and provides extensive coverage of Cattell-Horn-Carroll (CHC) theory factors.

    c. It is designed to be interpreted by the Planning, Attention-Arousal, Simultaneous and Successive (PASS) theory of intelligence or the Triarchic Theory of Intelligence at the examiner's discretion.

    d. It does not require any interpretation.

12. **A weakness of the WJ IV COG is that:**

   a. It has a small norming sample.
   b. The manuals are brief and unclear in many instances.
   c. Examiners relying on the record form alone without studying the manuals or easels might misapply basal and ceiling rules.
   d. Scores must be laboriously hand-calculated and looked up in the *Norms Manual*.

13. **Scores on the WJ IV:**

   a. Are based on both age and grade for the COG, ACH, and OL.
   b. Are based on age for the COG but on both age and grade for the ACH and OL.
   c. Are based on age for the COG and OL but on both age and grade for the ACH.
   d. Must be reported by age norms for the COG and grade norms for the ACH.

Answers: 1. a; 2. c; 3. a; 4. d; 5. c; 6. b; 7. a; 8. d; 9. d; 10. a; 11. b; 12. c; 13. a

Six

ILLUSTRATIVE CASE STUDIES

Scott L. Decker

This chapter provides score results from children who were administered the WJ IV *Tests of Cognitive Abilities* (WJ IV COG; Schrank, McGrew, & Mather, 2014b). The review of scores from each case study is guided by the interpretive guidelines described in previous chapters. The case studies presented in this chapter are not meant to provide definitive or cookbook steps for diagnostic evaluations. Rather, case studies are presented to demonstrate the general principles in the application of increasingly in-depth cognitive testing in an applied context. As such, many of the details for each case have been simplified to place the primary focus on the interpretive value of WJ IV COG scores and intra-cognitive variations.

The WJ IV COG can be used flexibly with a variety of approaches in clinical applications, various interpretive methods, theoretical approaches, and comprehensive models. Although validity and reliability of interpretation requires adherence to specific directions in test administration, interpretation of the WJ IV COG in clinical applications is based on a variety of factors, including the experience and theoretical orientation of the clinician and the setting and purposes for which the evaluation is being conducted. Consequently, no single model describes the totality of the WJ IV COG use. As demonstrated in the case studies, the WJ IV COG measures are useful for identifying and characterizing performance limitations across a wide variety of cognitive tasks.

This chapter is organized to illustrate the general guidelines presented in Chapter 4 of this book for interpreting performance on the WJ IV COG:

1. As a general rule, administer WJ IV COG Tests 1 to 7 to facilitate an evaluation of any intra-individual differences among component scores.

2. If cluster scores are desired, administer selected additional tests to evaluate strengths and weaknesses of the cluster scores.
3. Evaluate the practical implications of cluster and test performance by reviewing the Relative Proficiency Index (RPI) and/or proficiency levels.
4. Determine the educational implications of cognitive performance.

The case studies in this chapter are presented in a sequential order to approximate these general guidelines of test administration and interpretation. As demonstrated in the case studies, the order of tests on the WJ IV COG provides a sequence of tests that may help structure an evaluation. The Brief Intellectual Ability (BIA) scores can be obtained by administering Tests 1 through 3. Adding Tests 4 through 7 provide the General Intellectual Ability (GIA) score. An overall GIA composite is derived from Tests 1 through 7 to provide a general measure of cognitive ability, or *g*. Prior to using the GIA in decision making, it is important to evaluate the component test scores to ensure that the overall composite is a valid indicator of intellectual level. Additionally, the intra-cognitive variations procedure provides information on relative strengths and weaknesses among the component tests; however, a single measure is insufficient for determining strengths and weaknesses in a broad domain of cognition. Each subsequent test that is administered following administration of the core tests provides additional information that can be combined to form broad clusters not available when only the core tests are administered.

The Standard Battery (Tests 1–10) provides a small set of tests that can yield samples of behavior in a variety of cognitive domains in a fairly short amount of time. It is the minimum battery recommended for standard diagnostic evaluations as it yields a variety of information including: GIA, three Cattell-Horn-Carroll (CHC) broad factors (*Gc*, *Gf*, *Gwm*), and Intra-Cognitive Variations at the test (1–10) and factor (*Gc*, *Gf*, and *Gwm*) level. Other clusters are also derived from the Standard Battery, including the *Gf-Gc* Composite and the Cognitive Efficiency cluster. When all 10 tests in the Standard Battery are administered, the *Gwm* and Cognitive Efficiency clusters are automatically compared to the *Gf-Gc* Composite to determine if either cluster is a strength or weakness relative to the *Gf-Gc* Composite.

Other broad CHC factors and narrow ability clusters are available with administration of additional tests that help provide information that is useful in evaluating cognitive functioning. Oral language and academic achievement measures can provide additional information that can be integrated in various ways. Additionally, the WJ IV provides a variety of score metrics that may serve different purposes. (See Chapter 2 for details on scores.)

Just as test performance can be interpreted at different levels of abstraction, diagnostic decision making also can be characterized by different levels of abstraction. A score from a single test provides only limited information. Scores from multiple tests and relationships between tests add additional value. Ultimately, as suggested in step 4 of the interpretive guidelines, test results are integrated within a contextual framework to support or refute different hypotheses and answer specific questions.

The case studies reviewed here are simplified for demonstration purposes. Additionally, the scores and discrepancy information presented in the case studies are only a selected subset of information that can be found using the WJ IV online scoring and reporting program. Exploration of additional scoring features is encouraged.

CASE 1. JON—GENERAL COGNITIVE ABILITY AND INTRA-COGNITIVE VARIATIONS

Jon is a 6-year-old male who was noted by teachers as having learning problems in multiple areas. Additionally, some motor delays were evident. According to teachers, Jon had difficulty learning across different situations and seemed developmentally behind most other children in his classroom. As part of an initial evaluation, Jon was administered the WJ IV COG core tests (Tests 1–7). Jon's scores and a description of his performance on each of the WJ IV COG tests and the GIA cluster can be found in Table 6.1.

Tests 1 to 7 provide a representative measure from each CHC broad factor. (See Chapter 4 for specific details about what each test measures.) Additionally, a GIA composite is derived, which provides a global index of cognitive performance

Table 6.1 Selection of a Score Report for Jon Following Administration of Core Tests 1 through 7

CLUSTER/Test	RPI	SS (68% Band)	PR (68% Band)	PR	Proficiency
GEN INTELLECTUAL ABIL	11/90	64 (60–69)	<1 (<1–2)	1	Very Limited
Oral Vocabulary	39/90	75 (69–82)	5 (2–12)	5	Limited
Number Series	1/90	60 (53–68)	<1 (<1–2)	0.4	Extremely Limited
Verbal Attention	39/90	79 (73–86)	8 (3–17)	8	Limited
Letter-Pattern Matching	1/90	70 (57–82)	2 (<1–12)	2	Extremely Limited
Phonological Processing	22/90	70 (63–77)	2 (<1–6)	2	Very Limited
Story Recall	37/90	69 (63–74)	2 (<1–4)	2	Limited
Visualization	36/90	73 (67–79)	3 (1–8)	3	Limited

that is weighted by each measure loading on a general factor. That is, tests with a higher g loading are given greater weight or influence in the GIA.

Jon's standard score (SS) for the GIA was very low, and his overall cognitive performance can be described as very limited when compared to others of his age. However, the GIA should never be interpreted without a prior review of test- and composite-level discrepancies. The degree of variance or spread in specific test scores provides an indication as to whether the GIA provides a valid representation of cognitive abilities. In some cases, a low GIA can be obtained from very low scores on specific measures (especially measures with high g loadings), while other scores are in the average range. In such cases, it may be inaccurate to determine that a general intellectual problem exists when in fact the low GIA is due to specific cognitive delays.

CAUTION

The GIA, like all global composite scores, may conceal more than it reveals. Significant scatter among scores can provide initial evidence of a processing problem. Awareness of how test score scatter may impact the overall composite is especially important for schools using Ability–Achievement Discrepancy models. As a caution, always examine test and composite score discrepancies prior to using the GIA as the basis of important decisions.

A brief review of Jon's standard scores indicates a general uniform distribution. However, a closer examination of the Relative Proficiency Indexes (RPIs) and proficiency descriptions (which are based on the W Diff) reveals that Jon has some areas of cognition that are more limited than others. His performance on the Number Series and Letter-Pattern Matching tests was extremely limited. His performance on Phonological Processing was very limited. These represent Jon's lowest areas of proficiency and may provide insights into his greatest needs for intervention—a greater focus on the development of number sense, orthographic awareness, and phonological awareness (see Chapter 4).

The WJ IV COG Intra-Cognitive Variations procedure (see Table 6.2) reveals no relative cognitive strengths or weaknesses among the component tests for Jon.

To briefly summarize Jon's case, the overall score pattern provides clear evidence of a general intellectual delay. His standard scores are generally very low without large differences on specific measures of different cognitive constructs. The RPI and proficiency-level descriptions provide more detailed information on Jon's cognitive limitations that can be used to relate test results to educational

Table 6.2 Intra-Cognitive Variations for Jon Following Administration of Core Tests 1 to 7

Variations	STANDARD SCORES			DISCREPANCY		Interpretation at +/− 1.5 SD (SEE)
	Actual	Predicted	Difference	PR	SD	
Oral Vocabulary	75	69	6	71	+0.55	—
Number Series	60	71	−11	18	−0.93	—
Verbal Attention	79	75	4	62	+0.31	—
Letter-Pattern Matching	70	77	−7	28	−0.58	—
Phonological Processing	70	71	−1	45	−0.13	—
Story Recall	69	79	−10	20	−0.84	—
Visualization	73	78	−5	35	−0.39	—

planning. At this point, no further cognitive measures were administered. Likely all additional measures would be consistent with the existing test scores, which are sufficient to answer the referral question. Based on Jon's scores, it could be predicted that his measured academic performance would be consistent with his GIA score. Additionally, measures of adaptive behavior and qualitative background information should be evaluated in light of the GIA score to confirm the hypothesis of a general cognitive delay and to rule out language, cultural, or other potential influences on his cognitive performance.

CASE 2. JOSé—ADDING CLUSTER INFORMATION TO THE CORE TESTS

José is an 8-year-old male referred for academic learning problems. His teachers noted that José has difficulty in following directions when compared to other children in his class. Additionally, his ability to comprehend classroom instructions seems developmentally delayed. Test and cluster results from the WJ IV COG standard battery for José can be found in Table 6.3.

José's GIA is in the average range of standard scores (SS = 91), with standard scores generally falling in the low-average to average range for most tests; however, a visual review of all of the test standard scores suggests a discrepancy between his Oral Vocabulary score (SS = 72) from his scores on other cognitive measures. A review of the RPI scores and proficiency levels shows that José's Oral Vocabulary proficiency is very limited; all of his other test scores reveal average to advanced cognitive proficiencies. As discussed in Chapter 4, Oral Vocabulary

Table 6.3 Selection of a Score Report for José Following Administration of Core Tests I to 7

CLUSTER/Test	RPI	SS (68% Band)	PR (68% Band)	PR	Proficiency
GEN INTELLECTUAL ABIL	89/90	99 (96–103)	48 (39–57)	48	Average
Oral Vocabulary	22/90	62 (58–68)	<1 (<1–2)	0.5	Very Limited
Number Series	97/90	110 (105–116)	76 (63–85)	76	Average to Advanced
Verbal Attention	86/90	97 (91–103)	42 (28–58)	42	Average
Letter-Pattern Matching	99/90	113 (104–122)	81 (61–93)	81	Advanced
Phonological Processing	92/90	103 (97–108)	57 (43–70)	57	Average
Story Recall	91/90	101 (97–105)	53 (42–63)	53	Average
Visualization	95/90	109 (104–115)	73 (60–84)	73	Average

measures knowledge words and the lexical-semantic process that begins with the identification of a word and proceeds to accessing associated words and word opposites from the individual's lexicon. A review of the intra-cognitive variations procedure for Tests 1 to 7 (see Table 6.4) also suggests a relative weakness in José's oral vocabulary ability.

DON'T FORGET
....

It is important to integrate a variety of information to confirm and disconfirm a hypothesis of cognitive weaknesses and strengths as revealed by specific cognitive measures.

By itself, a low score on a single test is insufficient for inferring a specific cognitive weakness to a broad category of cognition. When only a single test is administered from a broad CHC category, it may be difficult to broadly interpret the significance of extremely low scores. Low scores at the test level may be the result of a specific cognitive weakness or the result of normal variation in the distribution of scores. Interpretive uncertainty can be reduced by providing additional cluster-level information to confirm or disconfirm a hypothesis of a cognitive deficit derived from a single test.

Because Test 1: Oral Vocabulary is a measure of the broad CHC category of Comprehension-Knowledge (Gc), testing was continued by administering Test 8: General Information to yield a Gc composite score, based on two different samples

Table 6.4 Intra-Cognitive Variations for José Following Administration of Core Tests I to 7

| Variations | STANDARD SCORES | | | DISCREPANCY | | Interpretation at |
	Actual	Predicted	Difference	PR	SD	+/− 1.5 SD (SEE)
Intra-Cognitive [Extended] Variations						
Oral Vocabulary	62	105	−43	<0.1	−3.78	Weakness
Number Series	110	98	12	86	+1.08	—
Verbal Attention	97	100	−3	41	−0.22	—
Letter-Pattern Matching	113	98	15	87	+1.14	—
Phonological Processing	103	99	4	63	+0.33	—
Story Recall	101	99	2	55	+0.14	—
Visualization	109	98	11	80	+0.84	—

Table 6.5 Intra-Cognitive Variations for José Following Administration of Tests I to 8

Variations	Actual	Predicted	Difference	PR	SD	+/− 1.5 SD (SEE)
Intra-Cognitive [Extended] Variations						
COMP-KNOWLEDGE (Gc)	63	105	−42	<0.1	−344	Weakness
Oral Vocabulary	62	105	−43	<0.1	−3.78	Weakness
Number Series	110	98	12	86	+1.08	—
Verbal Attention	97	100	−3	41	−0.22	—
Letter-Pattern Matching	113	98	15	87	+1.14	—
Phonological Processing	103	99	4	63	+0.33	—
Story Recall	101	99	2	55	+0.14	—
Visualization	109	98	11	80	+0.84	—
General Information	69	104	−35	1	−2.51	Weakness

of a broad area of cognition. Comparative information then can be evaluated for both the derived composite as well as the individual measures (see Table 6.5).

José's performance on Test 8: General Information (SS = 69) was consistent with his score on Test 1: Oral Vocabulary (SS = 69), which was also a specific weakness. Furthermore, the *Gc* composite (Comprehension-Knowledge; SS = 63) was also indicated to be an intra-individual weakness. José's performance on General Information confirmed a problem related to comprehension of words and general vocabulary background knowledge. Subsequent testing with other language measures, academic tests, and cross-referencing with parent and teacher reports provided additional support for José's need for intensive language development services.

This case study demonstrates the unique structure of the WJ IV COG for flexibly adding additional measures into the core cognitive tests to help draw broader generalizations from an initial suggestion of a cognitive limitation and relative weaknesses.

CAUTION
....

Low scores on language-related cognitive measures can be difficult to interpret as they may stem from a variety of issues, many of which require additional assessment. For the purposes of this example, however, José's case demonstrates his need for intensive English-language development activities as part of his educational program.

CASE 3. TANYA—EVALUATING THE PRACTICAL IMPLICATIONS OF A HEAD INJURY

Tanya is a 16-year-old female who sustained a head injury during a soccer match when her head collided with another player. Although she did not lose consciousness after the accident, she subsequently reported occasional headaches that began to interfere with her ability to pay attention during class. Her teachers did not notice any major changes in her behavior before and after the accident other than an increase in the incidence of late or incomplete assignments. This was unusual because prior to the accident, Tanya was described as being very attentive to due dates and was rarely late on assignments. Additionally, other attention-related academic problems were noted by her teachers.

Concerned, her parents requested a comprehensive evaluation. The WJ IV COG was administered along with a comprehensive neuropsychological battery of tests as part of a 6-month follow-up on her progress. Although Tanya was never formally assessed with academic measures, both parent and teacher reports suggested her academic performance to be typical for her age.

A review of the test scores from the core battery (see Table 6.6) indicated Tanya's GIA is in the average range of standard scores (SS = 93) and her overall cognitive proficiency is also within the average range (RPI = 84/90). However, there are large variations across individual test scores that may attenuate the GIA as an estimate of her overall cognitive ability.

Table 6.6 Selection of a Score Report for Tanya Following Administration of Core Tests 1 to 7

CLUSTER/Test	RPI	SS (95% Band)	PR (95% Band)	PR	Proficiency
GEN INTELLECTUAL ABIL	84/90	93 (86–100)	32 (18–49)	32	Average
Oral Vocabulary	95/90	108 (97–119)	70 (42–89)	70	Average
Number Series	96/90	109 (99–119)	72 (47–89)	72	Average to Advanced
Verbal Attention	90/90	100 (89–112)	51 (22–79)	51	Average
Letter-Pattern Matching	1/90	63 (49–77)	<1 (<1–6)	1	Extremely Limited
Phonological Processing	59/90	78 (67–88)	7 (1–22)	7	Limited
Story Recall	79/90	87 (76–97)	19 (6–43)	19	Limited to Average
Visualization	99/90	126 (111–142)	96 (77–> 99)	96	Advanced

DON'T FORGET

The GIA is a g-weighted composite that provides greater weight to the constructs of Gf and Gc. However, any cognitive processing limitations observed in Tests 3 through 7 may attenuate the GIA as an overall estimate of cognitive ability.

An interpretation of Tanya's test scores is challenging due to very low scores from different CHC domains. Specifically, her standard score from Letter-Pattern Matching (a measure of Gs) is in the very low range; Phonological Processing (a measure of Ga) is in the low range; and Story Recall (a measure of Glr) was in the low-average range of standard scores. Proficiency-level information reveals that Tanya's orthographic visual perceptual discrimination ability under timed conditions (Letter-Pattern Matching) was extremely limited (RPI = 1/90); her word activation, word access, and word restructuring via phonological codes (Phonological Processing) is limited (RPI = 59/90); and her listening ability and ability to form and recall mental representations (Story Recall) is limited to average (RPI = 79/90).

By administration of additional tests from the WJ IV COG, cluster-level information was obtained to help with the interpretation and generalization of test results. Two tests were administered to obtain scores for each cluster. Scores from the second cluster measure not only provide confirming or disconfirming

Table 6.7 Selection of a Score Report for Tanya Following Administration of Tests to Yield Selected Cluster Scores

Variations	STANDARD SCORES			DISCREPANCY		Interpretation at +/- 1.5 SD (SEE)
	Actual	Predicted	Difference	PR	SD	
Intra-Cognitive [Extended] Variations						
COMP-KNOWLEDGE (Gc)	107	94	13	85	+1.02	—
FLUID REASONING (Gf)	124	93	31	99.7	+2.76	Strength
S-TERM WORK MEM (Gwm)	96	95	1	51	+0.03	—
COG PROCESS SPEED (Gs)	64	101	-37	0.4	-2.67	Weakness
L-TERM RETRIEVAL (Glr)	102	98	4	63	+0.33	—
Oral Vocabulary	108	84	14	89	+1.20	—
Number Series	109	94	15	88	+1.18	—
Verbal Attention	100	96	4	63	+0.34	—
Letter-Pattern Matching	63	101	-38	0.2	-2.81	Weakness
Phonological Processing	78	99	-21	5	-1.65	Weakness
Story Recall	87	98	-11	20	+0.84	—
Visualization	126	93	33	99	+2.43	Strength
General Information	105	95	10	77	+0.75	—
Concept Formation	130	95	35	99.8	+2.88	Strength
Numbers Reversed	93	96	-3	40	-0.25	—
Visual-Auditory Learning	113	98	15	84	+0.98	—
Pair Cancellation	75	101	-26	3	-1.90	Weakness

evidence of relative cognitive strengths and weaknesses but also yield broad composite scores. Tanya's cluster and component test scores can be found in Table 6.7.

Research studies have supported a link between processing speed deficits and attention as a result of head and brain injuries (Cicerone, 1996; Mathias & Wheaton, 2007; Rutter, 1981). Because there is documentation of a head injury, there is likely a causal relationship between the head injury event and the low and very low processing speed scores. A cursory review of Tanya's test scores shows that the range of standard scores is wide (from a low of 63 to a high of 130), and the RPI scores and proficiency levels also reveal a widely dispersed profile

Table 6.8 Selected Intra-Cognitive Variations for Tanya

Variations	STANDARD SCORES			DISCREPANCY		Interpretation at +/− 1.5 SD (SEE)
	Actual	Predicted	Difference	PR	SD	
Intra-Cognitive [Extended] Variations						
COMP-KNOWLEDGE (Gc)	107	94	13	85	+1.02	—
FLUID REASONING (Gf)	124	93	31	99.7	+2.76	Strength
S-TERM WORK MEM (Gwm)	96	95	1	51	+0.03	—
COG PROCESS SPEED (Gs)	64	101	−37	0.4	−2.67	Weakness
L-TERM RETRIEVAL (Glr)	102	98	4	63	+0.33	—

of cognitive performance ranging from extremely limited on Letter-Pattern Matching to very advanced on Concept Formation. Intra-cognitive variations among Tanya's cluster scores (see Table 6.8) help provide evidence for a pattern of strengths and weaknesses in broad cognitive abilities.

To verify the impact of a cognitive limitation in processing speed on academic achievement in Tanya's case, academic achievement data was collected. Prior to interpretation of academic data, it is often useful to propose hypotheses of academic strengths and weaknesses based on the cognitive profile. Given Tanya's educational history, average to high-average academic performance would be expected. Tanya's strength in Gf may likely contribute to success in mathematics problem-solving. Deficits in processing speed are linked most concretely to limitations in performance on academic fluency measures because both involve performance under timed conditions (see Table 6.9).

Tanya's broad academic performance is generally in the average range of standard scores. However, her Broad Reading standard score (SS = 83) does not reveal her limited (RPI = 41/90) broad reading proficiency. A review of her component reading test-level scores suggests that reading fluency is both discrepantly low (Sentence Reading Fluency SS = 68) and extremely limited (1/90). Her mathematics test and cluster scores range from low average (Math Facts Fluency SS = 80 but limited RPI = 26/90) to average to advanced (Applied Problems SS = 108 and RPI = 96/90).

Table 6.9 Selected Reading and Mathematics Test and Cluster Scores for Tanya

CLUSTER/Test	RPI	SS (95% Band)	PR (95% Band)	PR	Proficiency
BROAD READING	41/90	83 (76–90)	13 (5–25)	13	Limited
BROAD MATHEMATICS	77/90	92 (86–98)	30 (18–45)	30	Limited to Average
Letter-Word Identification	81/90	95 (88–102)	37 (20–56	30	Limited to Average
Applied Problems	96/90	108 (99–117)	71 (48–88)	71	Average to Advanced
Passage Comprehension	93/90	103 (93–112)	57 (33–79)	57	Average
Calculation	79/90	94 (86–102)	35 (18–55)	35	Limited to Average
Sentence Reading Fluency	1/90	67 (56–80)	2 (<1–9)	2	Extremely Limited
Math Facts Fluency	26/90	80 (71–90)	10 (3–25)	10	Limited

Test scores and discrepancy analyses can provide objective evidence of cognitive and academic limitations and the statistical rarity of a score or pattern of scores. However, linking the referral concerns to test scores and test scores to intervention action plans requires competency in integrating diverse sources of information. From the available evidence, the data presented in this case appears to be a clear clinical interpretation. Tanya had a head injury. Serious head injuries are known to result in deficits in mental processing speed. Processing speed deficits were evident from the cognitive assessments, but Tanya had average to high average scores on other measures of cognition and achievement. The hypothesis of cognitive processing speed deficits causing performance deficits in academic achievement was supported by limitations in reading and math fluency measures. The descriptive profile of Tanya's unique cognitive strengths weaknesses provides a fairly plausible explanation for not only the measured academic deficits, but also provides support for the teacher and parent's perceptions of her behavior in class.

As discussed in Chapter 4, Cognitive Processing Speed (*Gs*) can affect performance in all academic areas, perhaps because it is so closely related to academic task fluency. Tanya's performance on this cluster suggests the need for extended time accommodations when processing speed limitations restrict her ability to demonstrate knowledge, particularly when she must demonstrate her knowledge under timed conditions.

DON'T FORGET

···

The WJ IV COG tests are useful for measuring cognitive performance, but only well-trained and knowledgeable assessment professionals can use test data to suggest clinical hypotheses, interpret proficiency, and develop related intervention plans.

CASE 4. JACK—DETERMINING THE EDUCATIONAL IMPLICATIONS OF A TRAUMATIC BRAIN INJURY

Jack is a 13-year-old male who sustained a traumatic brain injury during a car accident. Prior to the accident, Jack had an exceptional academic record and was in gifted and accelerated classes. No cognitive, learning, or behavioral problems were noted prior to the injury; however, significant concerns emerged shortly after his injury. Concerns were noted by teachers and parents related to attention and completing assignments. A cognitive evaluation was requested by the parents but was refused by the school since there was no documentation of a history of academic problems. Consequently, an independent educational evaluation that included tests from the WJ IV was completed at a private clinic. Results from the core cognitive tests can be found in Table 6.10.

Jack's overall GIA is in the average range of standard scores (SS = 110); however, a cursory glance over the component tests suggests significant differences among test scores. Based on the initial review of core test scores, cluster-level

Table 6.10 Selection of a Score Report for Jack following Administration of Core Tests I to 7

CLUSTER/Test	RPI	SS (95% Band)	PR (95% Band)	PR	Proficiency
GEN INTELLECTUAL ABIL	94/90	110 (101–118)	74 (54–89)	74	Average
Oral Vocabulary	95/90	110 (99–121)	75 (48–92)	75	Average to Advanced
Number Series	100/90	134 (122–147)	99 (93– >99)	30	Very Advanced
Verbal Attention	98/90	118 (105–130)	88 (64–98)	88	Advanced
Letter-Pattern Matching	29/90	82 (66–98)	12 (1–46)	12	Limited
Phonological Processing	52/90	73 (62–84)	3 (<1–14)	3	Limited
Story Recall	94/90	110 (102–118)	75 (54–89)	75	Average
Visualization	97/90	117 (105–128)	87 (64–97)	87	Average to Advanced

information was deemed to be important to yield an analysis of cognitive strengths and weaknesses at the broad ability level. Administration of additional tests provided the CHC cluster scores, the Cognitive Efficiency cluster, the *Gf-Gc* Composite as well as *Gf-Gc*/Other Ability Comparison procedure. CHC composite and subtest scores can be found in Table 6.11.

As noted in Case 3, a brain injury can result in limitations in cognitive processing speed. In Jack's case, Letter-Pattern Matching, which is a measure of

Table 6.11 Selected Test and Cluster Scores for Jack

CLUSTER/Test	RPI	SS (95% Band)	PR (95% Band)	PR	Proficiency
GEN INTELLECTUAL ABIL	94/90	110 (101–118)	74 (54–89)	74	Average
Gf-Gc COMPOSITE	99/90	125 (118–133)	95 (88–99)	95	Advanced
COMP-KNOWLEDGE (*Gc*)	97/90	116 (107–124)	85 (69–94)	85	Average to Advanced
FLUID REASONING (*Gf*)	99/90	128 (118–137)	97 (89– >99)	97	Advanced
S-TERM WORK MEM (*Gwm*)	75/90	89 (79–99)	23 (8–47)	23	Limited to Average
COG PROCESS SPEED (*Gs*)	48/90	86 (74–97)	17 (4–42)	17	Limited
L-TERM RETRIEVAL (*Glr*)	92/90	103 (96–110)	58 (40–75)	58	Average
COGNITIVE EFFICIENCY	20/90	72 (59–85)	3 (<1–15)	3	Very Limited
Oral Vocabulary	95/90	110 (99–121)	75 (48–92)	75	Average to Advanced
Number Series	100/90	134 (122–147)	99 (93– > 99)	30	Very Advanced
Verbal Attention	98/90	118 (105–130)	88 (64–98)	88	Advanced
Letter-Pattern Matching	29/90	82 (66–98)	12 (1–46)	12	Limited
Phonological Processing	52/90	73 (62–84)	3 (<1–14)	3	Limited
Story Recall	94/90	110 (102–118)	75 (54–89)	75	Average
Visualization	97/90	117 (105–128)	87 (64–97)	87	Average to Advanced
General Information	98/90	118 (107–129)	88 (68–97)	88	Advanced
Concept Formation	97/90	111 (101–121)	78 (54–92)	78	Average to Advanced
Numbers Reversed	14/90	68 (56–81)	2 (<1–10)	2	Very Limited
Visual-Auditory Learning	88/90	97 (89–105)	42 (22–63)	42	Average
Pair Cancellation	68/90	92 (80–104)	30 (10–61)	30	Limited to Average

processing speed, is in the low-average range of standard scores (SS = 82). However, his proficiency on Letter-Pattern Matching is limited (RPI = 29/90). Jack's Phonological Processing is in the low range of standard scores (SS = 73); his phonological processing proficiency is also limited (RPI = 52/90). This test consists of three parts (Word Access, Word Fluency, and Substitution). Because the Word Fluency segment involves timed performance, there is a possibility that any limitations in processing speed also may impact his overall Phonological Processing score. Indeed, a qualitative review of his raw scores on each of these subtests suggests that low raw scores on the Word Fluency subtest are a primary contributor to his overall low standard score on Phonological Processing.

A review of some of the other WJ IV COG tests provides additional insights into differences across cognitive abilities (see Table 6.11). The pattern of scores is unexpected for a child with an exceptional academic record.

Short-Term Working Memory (*Gwm*) and Cognitive Processing Speed (*Gs*) are both in the low-average range of standard scores. However, there is mixed support for a broad *Gwm* deficit, as scores in this composite reveal significant differences in performance. For example, Jack's performance on Numbers Reversed was in the very low range of standard scores (SS = 68), but his Verbal Attention was in the high average range (SS = 118). In such situations, it is often helpful to first review the detailed cognitive processing elements involved with each measure (see Chapter 4) to determine if some unique cognitive process would account for such a discrepant pattern of performance. Verification can be obtained by follow-up testing using measures specific to hypothesized cognitive processes. Jack's proficiency with tasks requiring active maintenance of information in working memory and utilization of cue-dependent searches through the contents of working memory is advanced (RPI = 98/90). These types of tasks are similar to the types of working memory requirements required in typical classroom performance, where a student is required to maintain information in working memory and answer a question about it. In contrast, Jack's proficiency with tasks that require both temporary storage and transforming or recoding information in working memory is very limited (RPI = 14/90). Processing information in the context of storage is extremely difficult for Jack. In contrast, his Cognitive Processing Speed (*Gs*) test scores were in the low-average to average range of standard scores; seemingly similar. His proficiency with tasks requiring orthographic visual perceptual discrimination speed (Letter-Pattern Matching) is limited (RPI = 29/90), but his proficiency with tasks requiring nonorthographic, symbolic visual perceptual discrimination speed (Pair Cancellation) is limited to average (RPI = 68/90).

A closer examination of Jack's other derived clusters can be useful. For example, the Cognitive Efficiency cluster may yield insights into a better description of Jack's cognitive limitations because it consists of two measures that were lowest from each of the *Gwm* and *Gs* clusters (Numbers Reversed and Letter-Pattern Matching). Jack's performance on the Cognitive Efficiency cluster yielded a low standard score (SS = 72) and very limited proficiency (RPI = 20/90). As described in Chapter 4, this cluster measures the efficiencies of orthographic visual perceptual discrimination ability under timed conditions and temporary storage and recoding of numeric information in primary memory. The purpose of this cluster is to create a type of executive summary of the speed and efficiency with which an individual processes basic orthographic and verbal information. Limitations identified by this cluster can be a red flag for greater consequences than limitations in either the Cognitive Processing Speed or Working Memory Capacity clusters alone.

Similar to Tanya's case (Case 3), deficits in cognitive processing speed may most closely be related to academic fluency measures, since both involve timed performance. Results from an evaluation of Jack's academic performance on the WJ IV ACH can be found in Table 6.12.

Clearly, Jack's reading and reading fluency is not impaired. Although speculative, the child's well-developed Comprehension-Knowledge (*Gc* SS = 116) likely supports and influences his high levels of reading ability. However, Jack is limited (RPI = 53/90) in Math Facts Fluency (SS = 88), which may appear surprisingly low in comparison to his other math scores (Applied Problems SS =130; Calculation SS = 124) but is not surprising in relation to his performance on the Cognitive Efficiency cluster. Tasks involving rapid retrieval of mathematics facts will likely be very difficult for Jack; a provision for extended time on timed, high-stakes mathematics calculations tests may be necessary for Jack to demonstrate his level of mathematics knowledge.

Table 6.12 Selected WJ IV ACH Test and Cluster Scores for Jack

CLUSTER/Test	RPI	SS (95% Band)	PR (95% Band)	PR	Proficiency
BROAD READING	99/90	118 (110–125)	88 (75–95)	88	Advanced
BROAD MATHEMATICS	98/90	114 (107–120)	82 (68–91)	82	Advanced
Letter-Word Identification	96/90	107 (98–115)	67 (45–84)	67	Average to Advanced
Applied Problems	100/90	130 (120–117)	98 (91– > 99)	98	Very Advanced
Passage Comprehension	99/90	120 (109–131)	91 (73–98)	91	Advanced
Calculation	99/90	124 (115–134)	95 (84–99)	95	Advanced
Sentence Reading Fluency	100/90	115 (105–126)	85 (64–96)	85	Advanced
Math Facts Fluency	53/90	88 (79–97)	20 (8–41)	20	Limited

Table 6.13 *Gf-Gc* Composite/Other Ability Comparisons for Jack

| COMPARISONS | STANDARD SCORES | | | DISCREPANCY | | Interpretation at +/− 1.5 SD (SEE) |
	Actual	Predicted	Difference	PR	SD	
Gf-Gc Composite/Other Ability Comparisons						
S-TERM WORK MEM (*Gwm*)	89	114	−25	2	−2.07	Weakness
COG PROCESS SPEED (*Gs*)	86	109	−23	4	−1.76	Weakness
L-TERM RETRIEVAL (*Glr*)	103	113	−10	21	−0.79	—
COGNITIVE EFFICIENCY	72	113	−41	<0.01	−3.21	Weakness
READING	114	119	−5	34	−0.41	—
BROAD READING	118	117	1	51	+0.01	—
MATHEMATICS	128	119	9	83	+0.95	—
BROAD MATHEMATICS	114	118	−4	33	−0.45	—
MATH CALCULATION SKILLS	104	116	−12	15	−1.02	—

The best estimate of Jack's intellectual level is provided by the *Gf-Gc* Composite (SS = 125), a measure of intellectual ability that is derived only from tests of verbal comprehension and fluid intelligence. Unlike Jack's GIA score (SS = 110), the *Gf-Gc* Composite does not include any tests of cognitive processing, speed, or efficiency that are identified weaknesses for Jack. The evaluation of Jack's cognitive processing, cognitive efficiency, and academic achievement scores in comparison to his *Gf-Gc* Composite (see Table 6.13) resulted in a profile of strengths and weaknesses that supported the determination of a disorder in a basic cognitive processes.

A review of Jack's *Gf-Gc* Composites/Other Ability Comparisons suggests that, in relation to his knowledge and reasoning abilities, Jack has weaknesses in Short-Term Working Memory (*Gwm*) and Cognitive Processing Speed (*Gs*). Together, these weaknesses also are reflected in a cognitive efficiency weakness that may have greater educational implications than a weakness in either *Gwm* or *Gs* alone. As described in Chapter 4, limitations in cognitive efficiency can exert an indirect influence on academic achievement by negatively affecting reasoning and divergent (creative) thinking. A weakness in the Cognitive Efficiency cluster often is associated with a variety of clinical conditions where the effects of limited or impaired cognitive efficiency can constrain more complex cognitive and academic performance.

The pattern of scores found with Jack is highly unusual for a child with an exceptional academic history, but the pattern is typical for a child with a brain injury. As demonstrated by this case, often additional test and cluster information is needed to derive definitive conclusions. For Jack, the WJ IV COG profile is informative for verifying that the brain injury has resulted in limitations in cognitive performance. Additionally, the results point to the specific cognitive domains that are affected and provide a verification of the behavioral and academic problems noted by Jack's teacher. When all of the background information and test data are considered, the results of this comprehensive evaluation support Jack's need for related academic interventions and/or accommodations at school.

CHAPTER SUMMARY

Four case studies were reviewed to highlight how the WJ IV COG can be used flexibly for different evaluation purposes. Although all four cases were obtained from a private clinic, the cases and procedures described are models for school-based practice as well. In the hands of a highly trained and knowledgeable assessment professional, the WJ IV COG is a useful battery of tests that provides information on intellectual ability, a wide variety of important factors of cognition and information processing, a profile of relative strengths and weaknesses, documentation of any functional limitations in specific cognitive abilities, and a link to educational and rehabilitative planning, interventions, or any needed accommodations.

Seven

ILLUSTRATIVE CASE STUDIES

John M. Garruto

T his chapter provides illustrative case studies, where you will get the chance to review the various scores and the results of the different variation and comparison procedures. Although the primary focus of this book is the WJ IV COG, tests and clusters from the WJ IV ACH and the WJ IV OL may be included to help with interpretation. The focus of this chapter is to apply the skills that you have acquired with administration.

As you go through each case study, you will be encouraged to look at the score profile and think about it. Think about what the General Intellectual Ability (GIA) score tells you. Think about what the *Gf-Gc* Composite tells you and how it is different from the GIA. Think about what the various Cattell-Horn-Carroll (CHC) cluster scores tell you. Think about what the other narrow abilities tell you. Finally, look at the various tests that comprise the clusters and see if there is overlap between the confidence bands of the standard scores; if not, consider some reasons for the lack of overlap. You may want to have the Selective Testing Table out to remember which tests are components of each cluster. After that, take a look at some of the background information and revisit and perhaps revise your hypotheses. Do the same thing within the context of the observations. From there, you should be able to look at the cases with a clinical eye. Let's begin with an easier, more straightforward case, a child by the name of Jacob.

CASE 1. JACOB—ANALYSIS OF THE GIA, *GF-GC*, CHC, AND SCHOLASTIC APTITUDE CLUSTERS AND TESTS

Jacob is a 9-year-old student in elementary school. To begin, review Table 7.1 and start thinking about what may be going on with Jacob. Do not forget to

Table 7.1 Cluster and Test Scores with Intra-Cognitive Variations for Jacob

CLUSTER/Test	W	RPI	SS (90% Band)	PR (90% Band)	Proficiency
GEN INTELLECTUAL ABIL	491	78/90	86 (80–92)	18 (9–31)	Limited to Average
Gf-Gc COMPOSITE	490	77/90	89 (84–94)	24 (14–35)	Limited to Average
COMP-KNOWLEDGE (Gc)	497	87/90	97 (89–104)	41 (24–60)	Average
COMP-KNOWLEDGE (Ext)	497	88/90	97 (91–104)	43 (28–59)	Average
FLUID REASONING (Gf)	483	64/90	86 (80–92)	17 (9–29)	Limited
FLUID REASONING (Ext)	484	65/90	85 (80–90)	16 (9–26)	Limited
S-TERM WORK MEM (Gwm)	477	46/90	77 (67–86)	6 (1–18)	Limited
COG PROCESS SPEED (Gs)	478	30/90	81 (73–90)	11 (3–25)	Limited
AUDITORY PROCESS (Ga)	483	57/90	75 (68–83)	5 (2–13)	Limited
L-TERM RETRIEVAL (Glr)	493	86/90	93 (87–99)	33 (20–48)	Average
VISUAL PROCESSING (Gv)	495	86/90	95 (86–103)	36 (18–57)	Average
QUANTITATIVE REASONING	489	79/90	92 (86–98)	30 (18–45)	Limited to Average
NUMBER FACILITY	467	25/90	75 (64–86)	5 (<1–18)	Limited
PERCEPTUAL SPEED	478	37/90	84 (74–93)	14 (4–33)	Limited
VOCABULARY	494	83/90	93 (86–101)	33 (17–52)	Average
COGNITIVE EFFICIENCY	472	22/90	73 (63–83)	3 (<1–13)	Very Limited
COG EFFICIENCY (Ext)	477	41/90	78 (70–86)	7 (2–18)	Limited
Oral Vocabulary	490	76/90	88 (79–97)	21 (8–43)	Limited to Average
Number Series	494	87/90	98 (90–105)	44 (26–63)	Average
Verbal Attention	493	83/90	95 (85–105)	36 (15–62)	Average
Letter-Pattern Matching	483	33/90	83 (72–95)	13 (3–38)	Limited
Phonological Processing	484	60/90	77 (67–88)	7 (1–20)	Limited
Story Recall	492	86/90	95 (86–103)	36 (18–58)	Average
Visualization	499	92/90	104 (95–113)	60 (36–80)	Average
General Information	503	93/90	104 (95–113)	61 (38–81)	Average
Concept Formation	473	32/90	75 (68–82)	5 (2–12)	Limited
Numbers Reversed	462	13/90	67 (55–80)	1 (<1–9)	Very Limited
Number-Pattern Matching	472	41/90	87 (75–100)	19 (4–49)	Limited
Nonword Repetition	482	55/90	82 (74–89)	11 (4–24)	Limited
Visual-Auditory Learning	494	85/90	94 (88–100)	35 (22–50)	Average
Picture Recognition	490	75/90	89 (78–99)	23 (8–48)	Limited to Average
Analysis-Synthesis	485	68/90	89 (82–96)	23 (11–38)	Limited to Average
Pair Cancellation	473	28/90	83 (73–93)	13 (4–32)	Limited

VARIATIONS	STANDARD SCORES			DISCREPANCY		Interpretation at +/− 1.50
	Actual	Predicted	Difference	PR	SD	SD (SEE)
Intra-Cognitive [Extended] Variations						
COMP-KNOWLEDGE (Gc)	97	93	4	63	+0.34	—
COMP-KNOWLEDGE (Ext)	97	93	4	65	+0.39	—
FLUID REASONING (Gf)	86	89	−3	36	−0.35	—
FLUID REASONING (Ext)	85	89	−4	34	−0.41	—
S-TERM WORK MEM (Gwm)	77	91	−14	10	−1.28	—
COG PROCESS SPEED (Gs)	81	95	−14	15	−1.04	—
AUDITORY PROCESS (Ga)	75	94	−19	6	−1.55	Weakness

Table 7.1 (continued)

| VARIATIONS | STANDARD SCORES | | | DISCREPANCY | | Interpretation at +/− 1.50 |
	Actual	Predicted	Difference	PR	SD	SD (SEE)
Intra-Cognitive [Extended] Variations						
L-TERM RETRIEVAL (*Glr*)	93	93	0	52	+0.05	—
VISUAL PROCESSING (*Gv*)	95	92	3	57	+0.17	—
QUANTITATIVE REASONING	92	89	3	61	+0.27	—
PERCEPTUAL SPEED	84	95	−11	20	−0.85	—
VOCABULARY	93	92	1	54	+0.09	—
PHONETIC CODING	96	94	2	54	+0.10	—
SPEED of LEXICAL ACCESS	86	96	−10	23	−0.73	—
Oral Vocabulary	88	92	−4	37	−0.34	—
Number Series	98	91	7	73	+0.62	—
Verbal Attention	95	93	2	56	+0.16	—
Letter-Pattern Matching	83	95	−12	19	−0.89	—
Phonological Processing	77	94	−17	9	−1.37	—
Story Recall	95	94	1	53	+0.08	—
Visualization	104	92	12	81	+0.88	—
General Information	104	94	10	78	+0.77	—
Concept Formation	75	92	−17	9	−1.36	—
Numbers Reversed	67	92	−25	2	−1.99	Weakness
Number-Pattern Matching	87	95	−8	28	−0.58	—
Nonword Repetition	82	95	−13	15	−1.04	—
Visual-Auditory Learning	94	94	0	52	+0.04	—
Picture Recognition	89	95	−6	34	−0.41	—
Analysis-Synthesis	89	92	−3	40	−0.24	—
Pair Cancellation	83	96	−13	17	−0.96	—
Picture Vocabulary	99	94	5	66	+0.41	—

look at the intra-cognitive variation procedure to see Jacob's relative strengths and weaknesses.

Now let us take at the various score profiles. We will delve into Jacob's referral concern and background *after* reviewing the *g* scores so you can generate hypotheses. It is not a concern if they do not match; most of the time, you will have this information in advance. However, by providing the detailed reason for referral and test behavior toward the end, you will be more likely to think about the various reasons as to why Jacob is showing the profile that he has without advance knowledge that might narrow your hypotheses.

So first we are going to look at the GIA. We can see that Jacob's GIA standard score (SS = 86) is in the low-average range. His Relative Proficiency Index (RPI) of 78/90 suggests limited to average proficiency. Now let us look at the *Gf-Gc* composite. It is 3 standard score points higher (SS = 89), but the *W* score is actually 1 point lower (as is the RPI). How can this be? Remember, standard scores and the RPI (based on the *W* score) are two different metrics. Although there is a difference of 6 percentile points, the proficiency is roughly the same when compared to the median student at his age.

DON'T FORGET

The standard score and RPI are two different scores that tell you two different things. They are not tied together. You can have an average standard score but an RPI that suggests limited proficiency or vice versa.

Let us also look at the tests that make up each. If we pull out our selective testing table, we can see that the GIA is made up of the first seven tests. The range of standard scores is 77 (Phonological Processing) to 104 (Visualization). As for Jacob's proficiency within these tasks, they range from a low of 33/90 (limited) for Letter-Pattern Matching to 92/90 (average) in Visualization. Think about that for a moment: Does anything come to mind immediately? Yes, Phonological Processing relies completely on information that is either processed auditorily or uses the phonological processes for the child to generate sounds. In contrast, Visualization relies primarily on Jacob's visual-spatial skills. Now before we even look at *Gf-Gc*, we can think about an interesting finding. Right now, it is fair to think of Phonological Processing as a potential deficit in auditory processing (we will double-check this in a bit), but why is the GIA then still so close to *Gf-Gc*? Yes, both Jacob's weakest and strongest scores are not included in the GIA. Remember, when you analyze the *Gf-Gc* cluster, you will also be losing measures of *Gv* and *Glr* in the analysis, and those may well be strengths of the child. Looking beyond the scores is critical.

DON'T FORGET

Looking beyond the scores is critical. Know what goes into each cluster, and see what differentiates the GIA from the *Gf-Gc* clusters.

So when we look at the tests, we have some that are in the average range of standard scores (Number Series, Verbal Attention, Visualization, and Story Recall) and some that are below the average range (Oral Vocabulary, Phonological Processing, and Letter-Pattern Matching.) In addition to being below average with regard to standard scores, Jacob's proficiency on all three tests is either limited or limited to average, indicating that he would find those tasks difficult or very difficult. So let us now look at the scores that make up the *Gf-Gc* Composite. We know Jacob has one low average score (Oral Vocabulary) and one solidly average score (Number Series). So now we put General Information in the mix, which is average, and Concept Formation, which is low. Another challenging conundrum! How is it that the score representing *Gc* gets larger and the score that represents *Gf* score (what was seemingly a better area for Jacob) gets weaker? We will analyze that a bit later, because we are still focused on clusters at this moment. Here is what we did find: We pulled out high and low scores in the GIA and we put in high and low scores into the *Gf-Gc*. Now it makes sense; we simply substituted scores of similar magnitude. Remember that you are not just deleting scores when analyzing the *Gf-Gc* scores, but you are substituting different ones. Only two tests are common to both the GIA and *Gf-Gc* cluster: Oral Vocabulary and Number Series.

At this point, you should have a solid footing on how some of Jacob's cognitive abilities are playing out. Now let us look at the CHC clusters. Our range of standard scores is a low of 75 in Auditory Processing (*Ga*) and a high of 95 in Visual Processing (*Gv*). When we look at the RPIs for our untimed tests, we see that *Ga* has a 57/90 and even *Gwm* has a 46/90, both of which suggest limited proficiency. The *Ga* score is not surprising, but the *Gwm* score is, because Jacob had an SS = 93 on Verbal Attention. We already know without looking at the score that Jacob struggled with Numbers Reversed. Overall, *Gc* really is not too bad—Jacob has what seems to be an appropriate vocabulary base. That is augmented by good *Glr*, indicating he is able to store information, particularly linguistic information, into long-term memory. Visually, he is stronger also. His processing speed, working memory capacity, and auditory processing tests are lower. At this point, you might be thinking about what type of academic areas Jacob may do well in and what areas are more difficult for him. However, there is an outlier: A standard score = 86 on Fluid Reasoning (*Gf*) and an SS = 85 on Fluid Reasoning—Extended. These scores do not fit so nicely and neatly into a cognitive profile that initially suggested potential decoding and spelling delays. Would you predict a math delay since *Gf* is lower? Not so fast; Jacob's Number Series is average. That is an initial insight that Jacob has skill with quantitative reasoning.

At this time, a profile of this child should be coming together in your mind. He has background knowledge, and his quantitative reasoning is good. He can learn new information and put meaning to it. Visuospatial skills are okay. He is not perceptually fast, and his working memory capacity is somewhat delayed, depending on the nature of the task. Auditory processing is going to be difficult. So far, much of the profile makes sense. But what do you make of that fluid reasoning? Perhaps the narrow ability clusters can provide more information.

When we look at Jacob's Perceptual Speed (P), that is somewhat lower, which is not a surprise. His vocabulary is satisfactory. (Note: You also need to administer Picture Vocabulary from the WJ IV OL to get this cluster score (see Table 7.2); you cannot get it from the WJ IV COG alone.) His score on Cognitive Efficiency is no surprise, as he clearly has deficits in *Gs* and *Gwm*, which comprise this cluster. So that leaves Quantitative Reasoning and Number Facility. Quantitative Reasoning is good, and the two tests that comprise this cluster almost overlap at 90% confidence. Number Facility—here Jacob struggles significantly.

Let us look further at the two tests that comprise the Number Facility cluster: Numbers Reversed and Number-Pattern Matching. A close look here is that Number-Pattern Matching is a bit below average but Numbers Reversed is very low. Although Jacob may have some difficulty with Number Facility (see his performance on Calculation and Math Facts Fluency later), it is also important to remember that he performed somewhat more strongly on Number-Pattern Matching than Letter-Pattern Matching. Furthermore, his limited proficiency on Number Facility seems to be most impacted by his poor performance in Numbers Reversed. (It is interesting to note that Jacob had the correct numbers, but they were often out of sequence.)

We have now finished our analysis at the cluster level. At this point, most things seem to make sense, but that lower Concept Formation and the lower Numbers Reversed seem to be in stark contrast to the other scores that make up their respective factors. This is why analysis at the test level is important. Although some argue that analysis beyond the cluster level is problematic (Watkins, Glutting, & Youngstrom, 2005), we would be remiss if we did not look at those areas more specifically. We will do that in a moment. But in a general way, let us look at tests that make up clusters with substantial differences.

For Comprehension-Knowledge (*Gc*), we see a 16-point difference between Oral Vocabulary and General Information and even an 11-point difference between Picture Vocabulary and Oral Vocabulary. Picture Vocabulary overlaps with both and is average, so we know Jacob's fund of information is developed similarly to his same-age peers. Oral Vocabulary is the lowest score of the three tests.

When we look at Fluid Reasoning (*Gf*), we see that Number Series is fine and Analysis-Synthesis seems to be an area of mild difficulty. Concept Formation stands as an outlier with absolutely no overlap of confidence intervals. (Number Series and Analysis-Synthesis also do not overlap.) We see no problem with overlap for *Glr* and can be confident that things are likely fine there. With regard to Cognitive Processing Speed (*Gs*), all tests overlap, which shows it is an area of some difficulty for Jacob. There is definitely a discrepancy between Picture Recognition and Visualization, and that may merit some further focus. Finally, we can see that Auditory Processing (*Ga*) is weak with overlapping confidence intervals between the tests that comprise this cluster.

Let's take a quick look at the intra-cognitive variation procedure. At the cluster level, he is noted to have a weakness in Auditory Processing (*Ga*). The difference between his predicted and actual score of 19 points indicates that only 6 percent of the population had that large of a difference or larger in the standardization sample. The difference is not only significant but it is also unusual. When we analyze at the test level, we can see that Numbers Reversed is significantly lower than expected … so much so that *only 2 percent of the population in the standardization sample* showed a difference that was similar or greater than 25 points. Take a moment and reflect … we did not even look at the intra-cognitive variations procedure until now. Yet we knew there was something unusual with Numbers Reversed by simply eyeballing the comparisons. This is what a skilled clinician can and will do.

Let us not leave the intra-cognitive variations procedure just yet. Just because it does not say "weakness" does not mean it is not a problem. The default is set to –1.5, meaning the percentage of the population who show that great of a difference or greater is set to around the 7th percentile. However, what was the other test that caught our attention? Yes, Concept Formation! Let us look at the variations table. The difference between expected and actual is not –1.5 standard deviations (*SD*) below but –1.36 *SD* below. There we see 9% of the population had a discrepancy that significant or greater. Just because the word *weakness* is not there does not mean that it is not an area of difficulty for the child. If you changed the setting to –1.3 *SD* from the default –1.5 *SD*, the word *weakness* would be listed. Good clinicians do not rely on labels from the scoring programs. Rather, they can compare and contrast strengths and weaknesses and ask further questions based on their own skills.

At this point, what do you want to know more about? You are probably asking yourself: What happened with Numbers Reversed and Concept Formation? From there, we need to look at test behavior, or our Level 1 analysis. We need to know what went wrong and why (and truthfully, we should be looking at Level 1 behavior for all of our tests; but right now, you should be asking yourself: What went wrong there?). Now you see why we did not start with the test behavior or background information: It would not have led you to wonder: What happened there?

Let us first review Concept Formation. According to the report, Jacob struggled with the complex directions in Concept Formation. He did not know what was being asked of him. Even when he understood the task for one moment, he would forget it the next. The examiner simplified the directions for him and scaffolded the task as a way to test the limits. Jacob then got many more items correct. The complexity did not interfere with Analysis-Synthesis as much until Jacob moved to three boxes. The answer was always there for him in the key. When the task became more complex, Jacob began to struggle. His teacher also noted that he can be successful in math, but he needs the directions laid out step by step. Jacob's Concept Formation score shows that he has limitations in verbal, language-based inductive reasoning.

So now we have a better sense of what is going on. Reasoning can be complex; once Jacob has to master additional steps, he struggles. Hopefully some interventions just entered your mind. Let us now turn to Numbers Reversed. The directions for Numbers Reversed are not complex (but we are willing to bet that was the first thing that came to your mind when you thought about it). So how is it possible that Jacob does well on a cognitively complex task like Verbal Attention but struggles on Numbers Reversed? A review of the report indicates that Jacob actually got many of the numbers correct, but they were out of order. Although Numbers Reversed does measure working memory capacity, processing of information must occur in the context of storage—this provides a clue to Jacob's performance on Numbers Reversed. In this case, when Jacob heard a 3-digit number, such as "5–4–2," he might say "2–5–4." He remembered the numbers, but his ability to transform the numbers into reversed order was affected. We might briefly want to think about the phonological loop, or the ability to hold the information we hear and maintain that in short-term memory. Interestingly, although Nonword Repetition loads onto the auditory processing cluster, it is also a measure of the efficiency of the phonological loop (see Chapter 4), and we know Jacob did not do well. This helps us to better understand the discrepancy between Verbal Attention and Numbers Reversed. (Administration of Memory for Words may have helped confirm this hypothesis as many of those words cannot be visualized and the individual must rely on the phonological loop.)

At this point, we may now have a better picture of Jacob's cognitive profile. The educational implications for Concept Formation and Numbers Reversed may be significant. We noticed two other possible outliers. One was Picture Recognition. There was nothing significant observed during administration of Picture Recognition. It is important to note that Jacob has mild attention concerns, and his focus during testing could have interfered with his performance. This leaves Oral Vocabulary. There is little qualitative information available about his performance on Oral Vocabulary, but the task requirements of Oral Vocabulary are more complex than General Information. To respond correctly to the antonyms subtest, the individual must have a conceptual understanding of the stimulus word before they can provide a word that expresses the opposite in meaning. When required to give synonyms, the individual must come up with a similar word even if they know the target word. This requires a well-established lexical network of closely associated words. Furthermore, Jacob's Comprehension-Knowledge (*Gc*) performance is only slightly below average when compared to same-age peers. He demonstrates limited-to-average performance on Oral Vocabulary, and General Information indicates his background knowledge is average.

Take a moment and reflect on what you have learned about Jacob by looking at his cognitive profile alone. Of course, we cannot get an entire picture from administration of the WJ IV COG (or any cognitive battery for that matter). We must look at other measures. The next section reviews Jacob's performance on the oral language and achievement portions, but they are not discussed in depth because the focus here is on the WJ IV COG. However, should the reader wish to know how the cognitive and oral language areas play into achievement, the next section should be helpful. At this point, however, let us recap. Jacob's overall cognitive ability is low average, as is his *Gf-Gc* Composite. However, we know that there are relative strengths and weaknesses present across the tests that comprise the GIA and the *Gf*-Gc clusters. The intra-cognitive variations procedure helps us to better discern where Jacob's personal strengths and weaknesses lie. Review of the tests does tell us which areas are stronger and which are weaker. However, the skill that separates the psychometrician from the clinician is the Level 1 analysis: how the individual responded to the various prompts and how the individual responds to limit testing.

Brief Look at Jacob's Complete Profile

Advanced interpretation of the various clusters and subtests for the WJ IV Tests of Oral Language and WJ IV Tests of Achievement is beyond the scope of this book. However, understanding how cognitive and oral language skills interact with achievement skills is important. Jacob's oral language and achievement scores are noted in Table 7.2.

As was highlighted earlier, Jacob's Picture Vocabulary score helped to provide a clearer picture that his language development skills are indeed where they should be. Interestingly, his ability with Sound Blending is strong, while Segmentation (his ability to break apart different words into sounds) is more impaired. The stronger auditory synthesis skill is actually not surprising given that he has been receiving an Orton-Gilingham approach to decoding when in remedial reading. Retrieval Fluency, which measures fluency of recall from long-term memory, is an area that is difficult for Jacob (although his fluency of recall is stronger when there is pictorial information).

Table 7.2 WJ IV OL and ACH Cluster and Test Scores for Jacob

			Woodcock-Johnson IV Tests of Oral Language		
CLUSTER/Test	W	RPI	SS (90% Band)	PR (90% Band)	Proficiency
PHONETIC CODING	495	85/90	96 (89–103)	39 (22–58)	Average
SPEED of LEXICAL ACCESS	491	71/90	86 (77–94)	17 (7–34)	Limited to Average
VOCABULARY	494	83/90	93 (86–101)	33 (17–52)	Average
Picture Vocabulary	499	89/90	99 (88–110)	47 (21–74)	Average
Segmentation	477	52/90	84 (77–92)	15 (6–30)	Limited
Rapid Picture Naming	496	78/90	94 (85–102)	34 (16–56)	Limited to Average
Sound Blending	512	97/90	113 (102–123)	80 (56–94)	Average to Advanced
Retrieval Fluency	485	62/90	76 (64–88)	5 (<1–21)	Limited

			Woodcock-Johnson IV Tests of Achievement Form A		
CLUSTER/Test	W	RPI	SS (90% Band)	PR (90% Band)	Proficiency
READING	465	17/90	73 (69–78)	4 (2–7)	Very Limited
BROAD READING	452	4/90	71 (66–76)	3 (1–5)	Very Limited
BASIC READING SKILLS	465	19/90	75 (71–79)	5 (3–9)	Very Limited
READING COMPREHENSION	478	50/90	77 (71–83)	7 (3–13)	Limited
READING FLUENCY	450	4/90	71 (64–78)	2 (<1–7)	Very Limited
MATHEMATICS	479	51/90	84 (79–89)	14 (8–24)	Limited
BROAD MATHEMATICS	475	37/90	80 (75–86)	9 (5–17)	Limited
MATH CALCULATION SKILLS	470	25/90	79 (72–85)	8 (3–16)	Limited
MATH PROBLEM SOLVING	480	54/90	83 (77–89)	13 (7–24)	Limited
WRITTEN LANGUAGE	478	48/90	83 (78–88)	13 (7–21)	Limited
BROAD WRITTEN LANGUAGE	479	51/90	82 (77–86)	11 (6–18)	Limited
BASIC WRITING SKILLS	461	13/90	71 (66–77)	3 (1–6)	Very Limited
WRITTEN EXPRESSION	490	79/90	92 (85–98)	29 (17–44)	Limited to Average
ACADEMIC SKILLS	461	12/90	71 (67–75)	3 (1–5)	Very Limited
ACADEMIC FLUENCY	459	8/90	73 (67–79)	4 (1–8)	Very Limited
ACADEMIC APPLICATIONS	486	70/90	88 (83–93)	21 (12–31)	Limited to Average
PHONEME-GRAPHEME KNOW	478	52/90	79 (73–86)	8 (4–17)	Limited
BRIEF ACHIEVEMENT	465	17/90	74 (70–78)	4 (2–7)	Very Limited
BROAD ACHIEVEMENT	469	23/90	75 (72–78)	5 (3–7)	Very Limited
Letter-Word Identification	454	5/90	72 (67–77)	3 (1–6)	Very Limited
Applied Problems	485	64/90	88 (80–96)	21 (9–38)	Limited
Spelling	458	8/90	70 (64–77)	2 (<1–6)	Very Limited
Passage Comprehension	476	41/90	80 (72–87)	9 (3–20)	Limited
Calculation	473	37/90	81 (75–88)	11 (5–22)	Limited
Writing Samples	498	91/90	101 (93–108)	52 (33–71)	Average
Word Attack	476	49/90	81 (73–89)	10 (4–23)	Limited
Oral Reading	473	35/90	79 (72–85)	8 (3–16)	Limited
Sentence Reading Fluency	426	0/90	71 (62–80)	3 (<1–9)	Extremely Limited
Math Facts Fluency	467	16/90	79 (69–88)	8 (2–22)	Very Limited
Sentence Writing Fluency	482	58/90	80 (70–91)	9 (2–28)	Limited
Reading Recall	480	59/90	79 (71–87)	8 (3–18)	Limited
Number Matrices	475	43/90	81 (73–90)	11 (4–24)	Limited
Editing	465	21/90	73 (65–82)	4 (1–11)	Very Limited
Spelling of Sounds	480	55/90	80 (71–89)	9 (3–24)	Limited

As can be seen, the more tests that are administered, the clearer the picture becomes for Jacob. Let us look at his achievement. Perhaps one of the most telling findings is how much stronger his application skills are compared to fluency and basic skills. This holds true across areas. Jacob seems able to bring his background knowledge skills and apply them in a compensatory way.

Two comparisons are especially noteworthy. One is to compare Reading Recall to Story Recall. Reading Recall is new to the WJ IV and basically requires the individual to read a passage and then remember and repeat what has been read. Notice how much weaker Jacob is when he has to read the passage rather than listen to it. The other significant finding is that Number Matrices is so low. Number Matrices is much like Number Series, but it is more complex because the solution to the problem must work both horizontally and vertically. Again, we can see the challenges when adding complexity. Jacob's ability to use his language and reasoning skills is stronger when presented with word problems. His lower Calculation score merits attention. Jacob was able to add, subtract, add with regrouping, and multiply with single-digit multipliers. He was unable to multiply with multidigit multipliers and could not regroup when subtracting. Upon reflection, both of those processes require multiple steps. Jacob may require some reteaching when regrouping when subtracting.

So now let us get to the most fascinating part of this case: the referral concern. Jacob was referred due to marked delays in reading and written expression, with writing being the most difficult area because of significant weaknesses with basic writing skills. His teacher indicated that if Jacob was able to dictate what he has learned, he has great ideas, but he cannot get them on paper. So why is his Written Expression score one of the strongest? His overall Written Expression standard score is 92 with a 101 in Writing Samples. The Writing Samples test requires Jacob to write short sentences to examiner-directed prompts. He does well. However, look at all of the other writing tests. Scores on Sentence Writing Fluency, Spelling, Editing, and Spelling of Sounds are all low. The examiner also followed up with the spontaneous composite *Test of Written Language–4th Edition* (Hammill & Larson, 2009) to confirm the issue with writing. Jacob again showed difficulty with the mechanics of writing (via the contrived writing) but had good ideas (via the spontaneous writing.)

Now we can see it all come together. We can see Jacob's learning disability in Basic Writing Skills and all reading areas due to his limitations in Auditory Processing (*Ga*) and Cognitive Processing Speed (*Gs*). There are some delays in math, but it is premature to say there's a definitive disability there. Jacob forgets some procedures and, as noted, needs things laid out step by step. Those are classroom-based interventions that can be delivered easily through a Response to

Intervention framework. However, Jacob requires specialized instruction in Basic Reading Skills (due to auditory processing deficits) and Reading Fluency (likely related to difficulty with accessing information quickly from long-term memory). His Reading Comprehension delays are more likely due to the deficits in Basic Reading Skills, which we can confirm from his stronger skills with background knowledge and even his stronger skills with his ideas in writing. However, Jacob will also need to receive specialized instruction with compensatory techniques to gain more meaning from text. He clearly requires direct specialized instruction with writing mechanics (spelling, capitalization, and punctuation), which can relate to those auditory processing difficulties and even difficulties with simultaneous storage and processing tasks (which have been shown through analysis of his test behavior and the greater difficulties noted with more cognitively complex tasks). Use of assistive technology to help him get his ideas in written form is also needed as Jacob has the skills but is unable to transfer that information to paper.

Now for the best part. Remember how we did not look at the intravariation procedure ahead of time, but we were able to figure Jacob out just through a clinical look? The same is true for the *Gf-Gc* Composite/Other Ability comparison procedure. See Jacob's relative strengths and weaknesses in comparison to his *Gf/Gc* Composite in Table 7.3.

You can see that the word "weakness" is written in the areas of Basic Reading Skills, Basic Writing Skills, and Reading Fluency when compared to the *Gf-Gc* Composite. We can see that Reading Comprehension is close (−1.3 *SD* below), but again, Jacob likely utilized his compensatory skills well.

DON'T FORGET

The strengths and weaknesses in the intravariation and comparison procedures are defaulted to +/−1.5 SD. Do not let the program make decisions for you ... you must use your own clinical skills to determine significant strengths and weaknesses.

Finally, let's look at the SAPT in Table 7.4.

We can see that more of our weak areas are somewhat close to where expected based on Jacob's closely related cognitive abilities, with the exception of Basic Writing Skills, which is actually much lower than expected. Nevertheless, we can see cognitive correlates that align with the academic weaknesses in almost every case.

It is hoped that, through analysis of Jacob's profile, you were able to identify where his strengths and weaknesses resided even before looking at his academic

Table 7.3 *Gf-Gc*/Other Ability Comparison Procedure for Jacob

COMPARISONS	Actual	Predicted	Difference	PR	SD	+/−1.50 SD (SEE)
Gf-Gc **Composite/Other Ability Comparisons**						
S-TERM WORK MEM (*Gwm*)	77	93	−16	9	−1.36	—
COG PROCESS SPEED (*Gs*)	81	94	−13	17	−0.97	—
PERCEPTUAL SPEED	84	94	−10	22	−0.79	—
SPEED of LEXICAL ACCESS	86	95	−9	26	−0.66	—
AUDITORY PROCESS (*Ga*)	75	93	−18	8	−1.42	—
PHONETIC CODING	96	94	2	56	+0.16	—
L−TERM RETRIEVAL (*Glr*)	93	94	−1	49	−0.03	—
VISUAL PROCESSING (*Gv*)	95	95	0	50	0.00	—
NUMBER FACILITY	75	93	−18	8	−1.39	—
COGNITIVE EFFICIENCY	73	94	−21	5	−1.62	Weakness
COG EFFICIENCY (Ext)	78	93	−15	12	−1.19	—
BRIEF ACHIEVEMENT	74	91	−17	4	−1.74	Weakness
BROAD ACHIEVEMENT	75	91	−16	6	−1.56	Weakness
READING	73	92	−19	4	−1.74	Weakness
BROAD READING	71	91	−20	3	−1.93	Weakness
BASIC READING SKILLS	75	92	−17	6	−1.53	Weakness
READING COMPREHENSION	77	92	−15	10	−1.30	—
READING FLUENCY	71	92	−21	3	−1.82	Weakness
MATHEMATICS	84	91	−7	25	−0.69	—
BROAD MATHEMATICS	80	91	−11	15	−1.06	—
MATH CALCULATION SKILLS	79	92	−13	13	−1.15	—
MATH PROBLEM SOLVING	83	91	−8	22	−0.78	—
WRITTEN LANGUAGE	83	92	−9	22	−0.78	—
BROAD WRITTEN LANGUAGE	82	91	−9	21	−0.80	—
BASIC WRITING SKILLS	71	91	−20	3	−1.87	Weakness
WRITTEN EXPRESSION	92	92	0	49	−0.03	—
ACADEMIC SKILLS	71	91	−20	3	−1.91	Weakness
ACADEMIC FLUENCY	73	93	−20	5	−1.66	Weakness
ACADEMIC APPLICATIONS	88	91	−3	37	−0.32	—
PHONEME-GRAPHEME KNOW	79	93	−14	13	−1.12	—

achievement. If we were to use the Response to Intervention process in isolation, it may have been more difficult to look at the various skills observed through controlled conditions. With practice and continued refinement of your analytic skills, you will be able to look at the skills of individuals through a refined lens.

CASE 2. DANIELLE—A DISABILITY-ATTENUATED GIA

Now we turn to a completely different case: that of Danielle. As with Jacob, we are going to look at all clusters, the differences of tests within those clusters, the

Table 7.4 Scholastic Aptitude/Achievement Discrepancy Procedure for Jacob

| COMPARISONS | STANDARD SCORES | | | DISCREPANCY | | Significant at +/− 1.50 |
	Actual SAPT	Predicted	Difference	PR	SD	SD (SEE)
Scholastic Aptitude/Achievement Comparisons						
READING	73	77	81	−8	25	−0.68	No
BROAD READING	71	77	81	−10	16	−0.99	No
BASIC READING SKILLS	75	83	87	−12	15	−1.05	No
READING COMPREHENSION	77	77	82	−5	35	−0.39	No
READING FLUENCY	71	77	82	−11	15	−1.05	No
MATHEMATICS	84	89	91	−7	23	−0.73	No
BROAD MATHEMATICS	80	89	91	−11	12	−1.16	No
MATH CALCULATION SKILLS	79	89	92	−13	10	−1.26	No
MATH PROBLEM SOLVING	83	79	84	−1	49	−0.03	No
WRITTEN LANGUAGE	83	82	85	−2	43	−0.19	No
BROAD WRITTEN LANGUAGE	82	82	85	−3	39	−0.27	No
BASIC WRITING SKILLS	71	82	86	−15	7	−1.50	Yes (−)
WRITTEN EXPRESSION	92	82	86	6	70	+0.51	No

intra-cognitive variation procedures, and the comparison procedures. Study the scores in Table 7.5 and start analyzing the profile in advance of providing any interpretive information. What does the GIA tell you? How about the *Gf-Gc* Composite? How about each CHC area? Do you see large differences between the tests that comprise each cluster, and, if so, what might the task demands say about Danielle? Go ahead and review the scores in Table 7.5.

So, as before, let us look at our GIA standard score first. As we can see, Danielle's overall GIA standard score is a 67, residing within the first percentile. As the WJ IV COG does assess overall cognitive ability, our first hypothesis is that this may be an individual who presents with an intellectual disability. Certainly, to confirm or refute this possibility, we would need to consider this within the whole context of the child, including analysis of classroom performance, past test scores, and adaptive behavior. We will review those factors after we have reviewed the cognitive profile.

Next, let us inspect the *Gf-Gc* composite. The standard score is somewhat higher (74), and the confidence bands have very little overlap to them, so there is a potential difference between the scores. Even more interesting, however, is the RPI. Notice how the RPI is *lower* for the *Gf-Gc* Composite, even though the standard scores are higher. Remember: Looking at the RPI provides a different set of information than the standard score provides. Nevertheless, one standard score is very low performance compared to same-age peers, while the other score, although low, may not suggest an intellectual disability. Which score should be

Table 7.5 Cluster and Test Scores with Intra-Cognitive Variations for Danielle

CLUSTER/Test	W	RPI	SS (90% Band)	PR (90% Band)	Proficiency
GEN INTELLECTUAL ABIL	486	51/90	67 (61–74)	2 (<1–4)	Limited
Gf-Gc COMPOSITE	486	50/90	74 (68–79)	4 (2–8)	Limited
COMP-KNOWLEDGE (Gc)	479	33/90	67 (59–74)	1 (<1–4)	Limited
COMP-KNOWLEDGE (Ext)	480	35/90	66 (60–73)	1 (<1–3)	Limited
FLUID REASONING (Gf)	493	67/90	87 (80–93)	19 (10–31)	Limited to Average
FLUID REASONING (Ext)	493	69/90	87 (81–92)	19 (11–30)	Limited to Average
S-TERM WORK MEM (Gwm)	489	60/90	82 (73–90)	11 (3–26)	Limited
COG PROCESS SPEED (Gs)	479	10/90	72 (63–81)	3 (<1–11)	Very Limited
AUDITORY PROCESS (Ga)	487	57/90	75 (68–82)	5 (2–12)	Limited
L-TERM RETRIEVAL (Glr)	479	50/90	63 (56–69)	<1 (<1–2)	Limited
VISUAL PROCESSING (Gv)	489	70/90	81 (72–90)	11 (3–25)	Limited to Average
QUANTITATIVE REASONING	497	78/90	92 (85–98)	29 (16–45)	Limited to Average
VOCABULARY	480	35/90	66 (58–73)	1 (<1–4)	Limited
COGNITIVE EFFICIENCY	490	41/90	80 (70–89)	9 (2–24)	Limited
Oral Vocabulary	479	31/90	65 (56–75)	1 (<1–4)	Limited
Number Series	501	83/90	96 (88–103)	38 (22–58)	Average
Verbal Attention	484	47/90	79 (69–89)	8 (2–24)	Limited
Letter-Pattern Matching	488	16/90	78 (66–90)	7 (1–25)	Very Limited
Phonological Processing	485	52/90	73 (63–83)	4 (<1–12)	Limited
Story Recall	474	38/90	59 (48–70)	<1 (<1–2)	Limited
Visualization	492	77/90	88 (78–97)	20 (7–42)	Limited to Average
General Information	480	36/90	75 (66–83)	5 (1–13)	Limited
Concept Formation	484	46/90	80 (73–88)	10 (4–21)	Limited
Numbers Reversed	493	71/90	89 (79–100)	24 (8–50)	Limited to Average
Nonword Repetition	488	62/90	84 (77–92)	15 (6–29)	Limited
Visual-Auditory Learning	485	62/90	78 (73–83)	7 (4–13)	Limited
Picture Recognition	487	61/90	82 (70–93)	11 (2–31)	Limited
Analysis-Synthesis	494	72/90	90 (83–98)	26 (13–45)	Limited to Average
Pair Cancellation	471	6/90	74 (63–84)	4 (<1–14)	Very Limited

VARIATIONS	STANDARD SCORES			DISCREPANCY		Interpretation at +/− 1.50 SD (SEE)
	Actual	Predicted	Difference	PR	SD	
Intra-Cognitive [Extended] Variations						
COMP-KNOWLEDGE (Gc)	67	80	−13	14	−1.08	—
COMP-KNOWLEDGE (Ext)	66	81	−15	12	−1.18	—
FLUID REASONING (Gf)	87	71	16	92	+1.39	—
FLUID REASONING (Ext)	87	71	16	93	+1.50	Strength
S-TERM WORK MEM (Gwm)	82	78	4	63	+0.33	—
COG PROCESS SPEED (Gs)	72	82	−10	24	−0.70	—
AUDITORY PROCESS (Ga)	75	77	−2	42	−0.21	—
L-TERM RETRIEVAL (Glr)	63	84	−21	4	−1.71	Weakness
VISUAL PROCESSING (Gv)	81	82	−1	48	−0.04	—
QUANTITATIVE REASONING	92	71	21	97	+1.89	Strength
VOCABULARY	66	79	−13	14	−1.10	—

(continued)

Table 7.5 (continued)

	STANDARD SCORES			DISCREPANCY		Interpretation at +/− 1.50 SD
VARIATIONS	Actual	Predicted	Difference	PR	SD	(SEE)
Oral Vocabulary	65	78	−13	13	−1.12	—
Number Series	96	72	24	98	+1.97	Strength
Verbal Attention	79	81	−2	44	−0.15	—
Letter-Pattern Matching	78	82	−4	37	−0.32	—
Phonological Processing	73	78	−5	35	−0.38	—
Story Recall	59	85	−26	2	−1.99	Weakness
Visualization	88	81	7	68	+0.47	—
General Information	75	83	−8	27	−0.63	—
Concept Formation	80	78	2	58	+0.20	—
Numbers Reversed	89	80	9	76	+0.72	—
Nonword Repetition	84	83	1	53	+0.08	—
Visual-Auditory Learning	78	87	−9	26	−0.65	—
Picture Recognition	82	88	−6	34	−0.42	—
Analysis-Synthesis	90	78	12	83	+0.96	—
Pair Cancellation	74	85	−11	19	−0.89	—

used? The score that should be used is the one that best presents whatever it is that is being sought. If there is interest in cognitive ability, being confident that the score is a true measure of cognitive ability and not a learning disability is important.

At this point, it is time to look at the broad abilities. The standard scores range from a low of 63 for Long-Term Storage and Retrieval (*Glr*) to a high of 87 for both the standard and extended Fluid Reasoning (*Gf*) clusters. What does this information tell you? Take some time and start to generate hypotheses.

Looking at the CHC cluster scores, it is clear that all of Danielle's scores are below average. When reviewing the narrow ability scores, we can see one score that is in the low end of the average range. Perhaps this provides more important consideration for the suspicion of an intellectual disability. Next, we want to look at the test scores and see if there are significant differences between them.

When we look at *Gc*, we can see that all tests that relate to this domain are weak. Even though General Information is somewhat stronger than Oral Vocabulary, enough to suspect a possible difference since the confidence bands do not overlap, both scores are weak. Even the Picture Vocabulary test from the WJ IV OL (see Table 7.6) is an area that is delayed, indicating that we can be confident that Danielle's skill with background knowledge is an area that is significantly delayed.

Danielle's *Gf* is limited to average, although the RPI does suggest she may find the tasks difficult. However, we need to take a closer look at the tests that comprise both *Gf* and *Gf*-EXT. Danielle's overall score in Number Series is solidly average, and the RPI suggests that she should find those tasks manageable. Her Concept Formation standard score is in the low-average range, but the 46/90 RPI suggests that she will likely find tasks involving verbal, language-based inductive reasoning very difficult. Conversely, Analysis-Synthesis is stronger. At this point, you will likely be saying "Sounds like Jacob!" And, indeed, Danielle presents somewhat of a similar profile here. There does seem to be some evidence that she can reason with numbers.

Looking at Short-Term Working Memory (*Gwm*), we see low-average standard scores, although the RPI of 60/90 indicates limited proficiency and suggests a cognitive limitation in this area; Danielle likely would have difficulty with tasks requiring an increased capacity of working memory. Looking at the tests that comprise this cluster, we see there is a notable but not significant difference between the two tests. Verbal Attention is in the low range of standard scores, and the RPI of 47/90 indicates limited proficiency. Numbers Reversed, however, is slightly below average, and the 71/90 score is almost at that critical 75/90 threshold, moving from frustration to instructional. Danielle was not administered Number-Pattern Matching, so we do not have an idea of her Number Facility, although Quantitative Reasoning does seem to be a relative strength. Conversely, trying to process and remember linguistic information as was required in Verbal Attention was not an easy task for her.

Cognitive Processing Speed (*Gs*) seems to be an area of cognitive limitation. It is one of Danielle's weaker areas; she did poorly with both Letter-Pattern Matching and Pair Cancellation. The nature of the stimulus did not seem to matter. We can see that she processes information more slowly than other individuals of her age.

Auditory Processing (*Ga*) is noted to be in the low range of standard scores and the RPI of 57/90 indicates a cognitive limitation and that those types of tasks are likely very difficult for Danielle. However, we can again see that there is a significant discrepancy in the standard scores that comprise the clusters. Her skills in Phonological Processing are weaker than in Nonword Repetition. Nevertheless, both areas are delayed, which is indicative of a deficit in this area.

Let us move to Visual Processing (*Gv*) next. We see the standard scores in the low-average range. However, the standard scores for both tests are higher than the composite. How can this be? Remember, when two scores move far below the mean, clusters are often lower. This is a statistical reality that is present in many tests and relates to the probability that a person will perform that far below the mean on both tests. Visualization skills, while noted to be in the low-average range of standard scores, are definitely an area of relative strength for her. Danielle's visual memory skills are limited.

Now let us look at *Glr*. Her standard score of 63 places her in less than the first percentile. Her RPI indicates that she would find tasks of encoding and retrieving information into and from long-term memory to be very difficult. We can see that the lower performance on Visual-Auditory Learning indicates she has a difficult time encoding new information into long-term memory. However, the key is with Story Recall, where Danielle's standard score is 59. The RPI suggests limited ability in this area. This is something that merits further exploring; what happened here? It turns out that Danielle misunderstood nearly every passage. One example is when she heard a passage about someone looking in an aquarium containing various marine life. It mentions a seahorse floating by. At the end of the passage, it indicates that that person felt like they were looking through enchanted glasses. When Danielle recalled the story, she said that this person saw a seahorse wearing the enchanted glasses. Based on what you have learned about this test in Chapter 4, it appears that Danielle has limitations in the ability to construct meaningful mental representations from orally imparted discourse. Think about this for just a moment and begin to consider what is going on given her profile.

Let us look at the intra-cognitive variations procedure next. The results should not be at all surprising. We see Danielle has a strength in the Number Series test. There are also areas that are stronger for Danielle even though they're not listed as strengths because they do not exceed the +1.5 *SD* level. We also see strength at the cluster level for Quantitative Reasoning. Only 3% of the population has a difference of 21 or more points between what they were expected to receive and what they actually received. So think for a moment: Are there achievement areas where you would expect Danielle to do well?

Now let us look at Danielle's weaknesses. *Glr* is a weakness primarily because of that very low Story Recall score, although Visual-Auditory Learning is also low. This is important because even though we know Danielle presents with global delays, these areas are still weak even compared to all of Danielle's other scores. Remember, the intra-cognitive variation procedure shows the individual's profile of strengths and weaknesses relative to the self.

DON'T FORGET

The intra-cognitive variation procedure is not about performing in the average range. It is a technique to show the individual's personal strengths and weaknesses when compared to the other scores they obtained.

We also remember that Danielle's Oral Vocabulary skills are also quite weak. At this point, you should have some idea of the achievement areas where Danielle may do better than others.

Brief Look at Danielle's Complete Profile

At this point, you probably have correctly concluded that Danielle does better with skills that do not rely on linguistic meaning (Number Series, Numbers Reversed) than those that do (Oral Vocabulary, Story Recall). Let's look at her oral language skills in Table 7.6.

The WJ IV OL is an important diagnostic supplement to the WJ IV COG. Because we know that Danielle's ability to store (encode) information into long-term memory is limited (limited *Glr*), we can also look at her speed of recall. We see the Speed of Lexical Access is also limited, with Retrieval Fluency being limited to average and Rapid Picture Naming being limited. This may be related to her very limited Cognitive Processing Speed (*Gs*).

Because Phonological Processing was an area of concern, it is important to look at the basic auditory processing skills as noted on the WJ IV OL. We see that Danielle can segment well (which may lead to greater skill in spelling), but blending is harder for her, which may relate to more delays with decoding.

Finally, we look at oral language. Note how both Picture Vocabulary and Oral Comprehension are low. Indeed, Danielle's background experience delays

Table 7.6 WJ OL Cluster and Test Scores for Danielle

CLUSTER/Test	W	RPI	SS (90% Band)	PR (90% Band)	Proficiency
ORAL LANGUAGE	478	31/90	65 (56–73)	<1 (<1–4)	Limited
BROAD ORAL LANGUAGE	481	39/90	65 (58–73)	1 (<1–3)	Limited
LISTENING COMP	481	39/90	65 (56–74)	<1 (<1–4)	Limited
PHONETIC CODING	491	71/90	87 (79–95)	19 (8–36)	Limited to Average
SPEED of LEXICAL ACCESS	492	61/90	80 (72–89)	9 (3–23)	Limited
VOCABULARY	480	35/90	66 (58–73)	1 (<1–4)	Limited
Picture Vocabulary	482	40/90	72 (61–83)	3 (<1–12)	Limited
Oral Comprehension	474	23/90	62 (51–73)	<1 (<1–4)	Very Limited
Segmentation	502	91/90	101 (93–109)	53 (32–73)	Average
Rapid Picture Naming	488	43/90	82 (73–92)	12 (4–29)	Limited
Understanding Directions	488	59/90	78 (68–88)	7 (2–21)	Limited
Sound Blending	479	37/90	74 (64–84)	4 (<1–14)	Limited
Retrieval Fluency	496	76/90	85 (74–96)	16 (4–39)	Limited to Average

are highlighted here, but what is really important is to see how low that Oral Comprehension score is. Danielle is showing real limitations with language comprehension. Do you see how this may be related to her limited ability on Story Recall? Now let us briefly look at academic achievement in Table 7.7.

Danielle's Basic Reading Skills are limited to average and are not unusual from a standard score point of view (SS of 89). Even the sound blending limitations did not seem to impact her decoding skills significantly. With regard to Reading Fluency and Reading Rate, those skills are noted to be very limited and extremely limited, with RPIs of 18/90 and 2/90, respectively. Note how her Reading Fluency proficiency is similar to her proficiency with Cognitive Processing Speed (*Gs*). Furthermore, when looking at her relative standing, her standard scores for Reading Fluency and Reading Rate are low, as is her Cognitive Processing Speed. Furthermore, her standard score for Speed of Lexical Access (i.e., the rate at which she retrieves information from long-term memory) is low average, also suggesting a delay. Consequently, her performance in this area makes sense.

So now we turn to our hypotheses with language. We would expect that with language delays, Reading Comprehension would be the most directly impacted. We can see that is very much the case. Danielle misunderstands what she reads as well as what she hears. We also predicted that math would likely be higher, given her higher skill with Quantitative Reasoning. We can see this is the case with Math Calculation Skills in the average range of standard scores. Although Math Problem Solving skills are limited, it is because she did poorly with Number Matrices (although she did do well with Applied Problems, which is surprising, given that there is an element of language comprehension). The reason was she became confused by the instructions for Number Matrices (remember that she did well with a similar test, Number Series).

So, is Danielle an individual with an intellectual disability? No, she has a *very severe* language processing deficit. In fact, her reason for referral is a three-year reevaluation. The development of her math abilities and quantitative reasoning abilities are not indicative of intellectual delay. As further evidence, she did receive a standard score of 84 (14th percentile) on the WISC–IV (Wechsler, 2003) three years earlier. The greater weakness on the WJ IV was likely because her difficulty with language comprehension was assessed more comprehensively in this evaluation. Although not assessed explicitly in this evaluation, Danielle generally showed age-appropriate skill to interact with others and engage in appropriate self-care skills, which is not indicative of significant delays with adaptive behavior.

Table 7.7 WJ IV ACH Cluster and Test Scores for Danielle

CLUSTER/Test	W	RPI	SS (90% Band)	PR (90% Band)	Proficiency
READING	482	32/90	77 (72–82)	7 (3–12)	Limited
BROAD READING	479	18/90	76 (71–82)	6 (2–11)	Very Limited
BASIC READING SKILLS	494	68/90	89 (84–94)	23 (15–35)	Limited to Average
READING COMPREHENSION	471	19/90	56 (49–63)	<1 (<1–<1)	Very Limited
READING COMP (Ext)	475	27/90	63 (57–68)	<1 (<1–2)	Limited
READING FLUENCY	479	18/90	79 (72–85)	8 (3–16)	Very Limited
READING RATE	456	2/90	75 (69–81)	5 (2–11)	Extremely Limited
MATHEMATICS	502	79/90	93 (88–98)	32 (20–46)	Limited to Average
BROAD MATHEMATICS	506	81/90	94 (89–99)	35 (24–47)	Limited to Average
MATH CALCULATION SKILLS	508	81/90	95 (90–100)	37 (25–51)	Limited to Average
MATH PROBLEM SOLVING	488	51/90	82 (76–88)	12 (6–22)	Limited
WRITTEN LANGUAGE	485	41/90	79 (74–84)	8 (4–15)	Limited
BROAD WRITTEN LANGUAGE	483	37/90	74 (69–79)	4 (2–8)	Limited
WRITTEN EXPRESSION	484	46/90	76 (68–83)	5 (2–13)	Limited
ACADEMIC SKILLS	493	52/90	85 (81–89)	15 (10–22)	Limited
ACADEMIC FLUENCY	488	33/90	81 (75–87)	10 (5–20)	Limited
ACADEMIC APPLICATIONS	486	51/90	78 (72–83)	7 (3–13)	Limited
ACADEMIC KNOWLEDGE	483	34/90	73 (67–79)	3 (1–8)	Limited
BRIEF ACHIEVEMENT	492	53/90	85 (81–89)	15 (10–22)	Limited
BROAD ACHIEVEMENT	489	45/90	80 (77–84)	10 (6–14)	Limited
Letter-Word Identification	494	57/90	88 (82–94)	21 (12–34)	Limited
Applied Problems	501	80/90	94 (87–101)	34 (18–54)	Limited to Average
Spelling	482	22/90	77 (72–83)	7 (3–13)	Very Limited
Passage Comprehension	470	14/90	63 (54–72)	<1 (<1–3)	Very Limited
Calculation	502	77/90	93 (87–100)	33 (18–50)	Limited to Average
Writing Samples	489	63/90	86 (80–93)	18 (9–33)	Limited
Word Attack	493	77/90	92 (83–100)	29 (13–49)	Limited to Average
Oral Reading	486	48/90	82 (75–88)	11 (5–21)	Limited
Sentence Reading Fluency	472	5/90	80 (72–89)	9 (3–22)	Very Limited
Math Facts Fluency	513	85/90	97 (90–104)	42 (25–62)	Average
Sentence Writing Fluency	478	30/90	66 (54–78)	1 (<1–7)	Limited
Reading Recall	472	27/90	57 (47–68)	<1 (<1–2)	Limited
Number Matrices	475	21/90	74 (66–82)	4 (1–12)	Very Limited
Word Reading Fluency	440	0/90	71 (63–80)	3 (<1–9)	Extremely Limited
Reading Vocabulary	484	48/90	77 (69–85)	6 (2–16)	Limited
Science	481	35/90	77 (67–86)	6 (1–18)	Limited
Social Studies	490	45/90	80 (71–90)	9 (3–25)	Limited
Humanities	478	23/90	72 (63–80)	3 (<1–9)	Very Limited

CASE 3. ARNOLD—ACCEPTING OR REJECTING THE NULL HYPOTHESIS

For our third and final case, let us review Arnold. Again, think about what each cluster and test score in Table 7.8 tells you.

Again, look at the GIA first. As can be seen, Arnold is performing in the average range of standard scores with an RPI that indicates average proficiency. As we look for overlap within the first seven tests, we can see that most of standard score confidence bands overlap, though there is an intra-cognitive strength with Verbal Attention. We also can see that Visualization is an area of difficulty for Arnold. Although there is one high and one lower score, most of the scores overlap, so the GIA seems to represent many of his skills. Remember, you will want to think of the task demands related to those strengths and areas of difficulty.

Next, we look at the *Gf-Gc* composite. The skill level is almost the same as the GIA, and when error is accounted for, the scores are practically interchangeable. Let us again look at scatter. We can see that while Oral Vocabulary and Number Series are similarly developed, General Information and Concept Formation are almost significantly discrepant. In fact, General Information is a bit better developed than Oral Vocabulary, and Concept Formation a bit less developed than Number Series. The confidence bands still overlap, but you still will want to think of the task demands.

Next, let us look at the CHC factors. Numbers Reversed was not administered for a reason that will be explained later, so there is no *Gwm* composite. Not surprisingly, Arnold's Comprehension-Knowledge (*Gc*) is fine, which we knew from analysis of the *Gf-Gc* composite. His Fluid Reasoning (*Gf*) is at the low end of the average range of standard scores, which we also knew from analysis of the *Gf-Gc* composite. Although there is a very slight difference between them, think about the task demands between Number Series and Concept Formation. If we look at the RPI for Concept Formation, we see that his proficiency is limited to average, given his RPI of 69/90, and that he would likely find those tasks difficult.

Looking next at Auditory Processing (*Ga*); Arnold's overall skill generally resides in the average range. The scores that comprise *Ga* are very close together, and the RPIs show average proficiency. No concerns are present here.

As we look into Cognitive Processing Speed (*Gs*), we see average proficiency. Although not significant, there is a notable difference between Letter-Pattern Matching and Pair Cancellation. Arnold may show some skill with orthography as only orthographically correct letter combinations will be part of the correct answer (i.e., each correct answer has a letter combination that can happen in combination, such as "ck," while impossible combinations, such as "qr," will never be

Table 7.8 Cluster and Test Scores with Intra-Cognitive Variations for Arnold

CLUSTER/Test	W	RPI	SS (90% Band)	PR (90% Band)	Proficiency
GEN INTELLECTUAL ABIL	498	87/90	95 (88–103)	38 (21–57)	Average
Gf-Gc COMPOSITE	494	82/90	92 (87–97)	30 (19–43)	Average
COMP-KNOWLEDGE (Gc)	498	88/90	97 (90–105)	43 (26–62)	Average
FLUID REASONING (Gf)	489	74/90	90 (84–96)	24 (14–38)	Limited to Average
COG PROCESS SPEED (Gs)	508	90/90	100 (90–110)	50 (25–75)	Average
AUDITORY PROCESS (Ga)	495	83/90	92 (85–99)	30 (16–48)	Average
L-TERM RETRIEVAL (Glr)	493	84/90	91 (84–99)	28 (14–47)	Average
VISUAL PROCESSING (Gv)	490	77/90	87 (78–95)	19 (8–38)	Limited to Average
PERCEPTUAL SPEED	507	92/90	102 (89–115)	55 (23–84)	Average
Oral Vocabulary	496	85/90	94 (85–104)	35 (16–59)	Average
Number Series	490	78/90	93 (86–101)	33 (17–53)	Limited to Average
Verbal Attention	513	97/90	114 (104–124)	82 (59–95)	Average to Advanced
Letter-Pattern Matching	521	96/90	106 (89–123)	66 (23–94)	Average to Advanced
Phonological Processing	495	83/90	92 (83–101)	29 (12–53)	Average
Story Recall	489	81/90	89 (78–101)	24 (7–52)	Limited to Average
Visualization	484	66/90	81 (71–90)	10 (3–26)	Limited
General Information	501	91/90	101 (92–109)	51 (30–73)	Average
Concept Formation	488	69/90	88 (82–95)	22 (11–37)	Limited to Average
Number-Pattern Matching	494	84/90	97 (85–109)	43 (17–73)	Average
Nonword Repetition	495	83/90	95 (87–102)	36 (20–55)	Average
Visual-Auditory Learning	496	87/90	96 (90–102)	39 (25–55)	Average
Picture Recognition	497	86/90	96 (86–106)	39 (17–65)	Average
Pair Cancellation	495	77/90	95 (86–103)	36 (18–57)	Limited to Average

VARIATIONS	STANDARD SCORES			DISCREPANCY		Interpretation at +/− 1.50 SD (SEE)
	Actual	Predicted	Difference	PR	SD	
Intra-Cognitive [Extended] Variations						
COMP-KNOWLEDGE (Gc)	97	96	1	54	+0.10	—
FLUID REASONING (Gf)	90	96	−6	29	−0.56	—
COG PROCESS SPEED (Gs)	100	96	4	62	+0.30	—
AUDITORY PROCESS (Ga)	92	96	−4	36	−0.37	—
L-TERM RETRIEVAL (Glr)	91	97	−6	31	−0.49	—
VISUAL PROCESSING (Gv)	87	99	−12	19	−0.87	—
PERCEPTUAL SPEED	102	96	6	68	+0.47	—
Oral Vocabulary	94	96	−2	44	−0.15	—
Number Series	93	97	−4	39	−0.29	—
Verbal Attention	114	94	20	94	+1.58	Strength
Letter-Pattern Matching	106	96	10	78	+0.76	—
Phonological Processing	92	96	−4	35	−0.37	—
Story Recall	89	98	−9	25	−0.67	—
Visualization	81	99	−18	9	−1.33	—
General Information	101	97	4	60	+0.26	—
Concept Formation	88	97	−9	25	−0.69	—

Table 7.8 (continued)

VARIATIONS	STANDARD SCORES			DISCREPANCY		Interpretation at +/− 1.50 SD (SEE)
	Actual	Predicted	Difference	PR	SD	
Intra-Cognitive [Extended] Variations						
Number-Pattern Matching	97	96	1	54	+0.11	—
Nonword Repetition	95	97	−2	42	−0.21	—
Visual-Auditory Learning	96	98	−2	44	−0.15	—
Picture Recognition	96	99	−3	41	−0.23	—
Pair Cancellation	95	97	−2	44	−0.16	—
Number Matrices	98	97	1	53	+0.08	—

part of the correct answer). Nevertheless, we see Arnold's performance is in the average to above-average range.

When reviewing Long-Term Storage and Retrieval (*Glr*) skills, we see that Arnold performs in the low end of the average range of standard scores. Although Story Recall is slightly below average, Visual-Auditory Learning is solidly average. The RPI for Story Recall is 1 point below the threshold between average and limited-to-average proficiency, suggesting it is not a significant concern. *Glr* skills are relatively intact.

Next we look at Visual Processing (*Gv*). Although the overall performance is within the low-average range of standard scores, there is a significant difference between the two tasks that relate to *Gv* performance. The Visualization RPI suggests that Arnold will have difficulty on tasks that relate to size and shape perception, part-to-whole analysis, and mentally transforming two- and three-dimensional images in space. His higher score on Picture Recognition is indicative of better visual memory skills. Think about the different task demands that are present on these two tasks.

Finally, although we do not have a *Gwm*, we must not ignore the Verbal Attention test score, as it is the highest. Think about what this tells you, and think about it in relation to the other tasks where Arnold excels and how this differs from where he struggles. So let us think about his higher ability with Verbal Attention, background knowledge, and visual memory. Let us also think about his lower ability with abstract reasoning (when numbers are not involved) and visuospatial analysis. We see that Arnold's performance on tasks is stronger when the information is more meaningful to him and is something to which he can relate.

As we look at the intra-cognitive variation procedures, we see that Verbal Attention stands as a strength. No other strengths and weaknesses are noted, but as clinicians, we can do more. At this time, Visualization should be in your mind as an area that was more difficult for Arnold. If we look at the intra-cognitive variations table, it is not listed as an intra-individual weakness, but the *SD* is −1.33, which corresponds to the 9th percentile. This means only 9% of the population had a difference of 18 or more points between what was expected and actually was obtained, which is uncommon. Clearly our additional focus on Visualization is not unfounded.

Brief Look at Arnold's Complete Profile

Okay, so now think: Where would you predict Arnold's academic strengths to reside? How about his weaknesses? Come up with some hypotheses, and let us then take a brief look at Arnold's achievement in Table 7.9.

Overall, we can see some areas that are in the average range of standard scores and some that are in the low-average range. Oral Reading does present as an area that is weak, but it is not significantly weaker than expected, given the GIA or *Gf-Gc* cluster. However, a close look at the RPIs does indicate there are academic areas where Arnold will struggle when compared to the average child his age. Nevertheless, when reviewing the composites, the lowest percentile rank is the 21st percentile, which does not present as exceptional when compared to the general population.

Reflect for a moment: Did you assume that Arnold was going to have a learning disability? Perhaps that lower Visualization score stayed in your mind. Arnold does not present with a learning disability. We always must remember that when doing an evaluation, we must always assume the null hypothesis—that nothing's wrong—and allow the data either to confirm or to refute the null. That is difficult to do in education when individuals are referred for a reason.

Arnold's case is unique. He previously received some outside assessment. As Numbers Reversed was already administered as part of the Wechsler scale, it was not repeated to avoid practice effects. Arnold also was noted to struggle in math in school. Despite this difficulty, we can see that Arnold's skills in math are not too bad, and actually, his reading skills are slightly weaker. Arnold does present with executive function deficits. Although he generally shows only mild delays on this assessment, he does show much more difficulty when asked to engage in connected writing.

The WJ IV works well as a power test. That is, it can show what an individual can and cannot do. We can see that Arnold is generally learning and his cognitive strengths and weaknesses relate to his academic strengths and weaknesses. Arnold's difficulties reside more with executive functioning and completion of longer tasks with multiple steps (such as engaging in a comprehensive writing

Table 7.9 WJ IV ACH Cluster and Test Scores for Arnold

CLUSTER/Test	W	RPI	SS (90% Band)	PR (90% Band)	Proficiency
READING	487	65/90	89 (84–93)	23 (14–33)	Limited
BROAD READING	486	62/90	90 (85–95)	25 (16–38)	Limited
BASIC READING SKILLS	483	57/90	87 (82–91)	19 (12–28)	Limited
READING COMPREHENSION	490	76/90	89 (83–95)	23 (13–37)	Limited to Average
READING FLUENCY	484	55/90	89 (82–96)	23 (12–39)	Limited
READING RATE	474	37/90	90 (84–97)	26 (14–42)	Limited
MATHEMATICS	490	75/90	92 (86–97)	29 (18–42)	Limited to Average
BROAD MATHEMATICS	490	71/90	90 (85–95)	26 (16–38)	Limited to Average
MATH CALCULATION SKILLS	488	64/90	90 (84–95)	24 (14–38)	Limited
MATH PROBLEM SOLVING	496	85/90	96 (90–102)	40 (26–55)	Average
WRITTEN LANGUAGE	488	68/90	89 (85–94)	24 (15–34)	Limited to Average
BROAD WRITTEN LANGUAGE	494	81/90	93 (89–98)	33 (23–44)	Limited to Average
WRITTEN EXPRESSION	500	90/90	100 (94–106)	50 (35–65)	Average
ACADEMIC SKILLS	484	55/90	86 (82–90)	18 (12–25)	Limited
ACADEMIC FLUENCY	494	76/90	94 (88–100)	34 (21–49)	Limited to Average
ACADEMIC APPLICATIONS	493	81/90	93 (88–98)	31 (21–44)	Limited to Average
BRIEF ACHIEVEMENT	487	62/90	88 (85–92)	22 (15–30)	Limited
BROAD ACHIEVEMENT	490	72/90	90 (87–94)	26 (20–33)	Limited to Average
Letter-Word Identification	483	53/90	88 (83–93)	22 (13–33)	Limited
Applied Problems	495	82/90	95 (87–102)	36 (20–56)	Average
Spelling	482	47/90	85 (80–91)	16 (9–27)	Limited
Passage Comprehension	490	75/90	91 (83–99)	28 (13–47)	Limited to Average
Calculation	486	66/90	90 (83–96)	24 (13–40)	Limited
Writing Samples	494	84/90	96 (90–102)	40 (26–55)	Average
Word Attack	482	61/90	85 (78–93)	17 (7–32)	Limited
Oral Reading	482	54/90	84 (78–90)	15 (7–26)	Limited
Sentence Reading Fluency	486	56/90	93 (84–102)	32 (15–54)	Limited
Math Facts Fluency	490	62/90	90 (82–99)	26 (12–47)	Limited
Sentence Writing Fluency	506	94/90	106 (97–115)	65 (41–85)	Average
Reading Recall	489	77/90	88 (81–96)	22 (10–39)	Limited to Average
Number Matrices	496	87/90	98 (90–106)	45 (26–64)	Average
Word Reading Fluency	462	22/90	88 (77–98)	20 (7–43)	Very Limited

piece). The WJ IV did well to retain the null hypothesis that math was not a significantly delayed area. However, the abstract nature of math may make new learning difficult for Arnold. Difficulty with initiation, task completion, and attending to the task for long periods of time are classroom-based concerns that need to be addressed but are not reflective of a deficit in the psychological processes that inhibit math ability. Rather they reflect executive function problems, which require a different focus.

CHAPTER SUMMARY

We have reviewed three different cases in this chapter. Through assessment of both the performances and the test behavior of the various individuals, we have been able to discern a child with a learning disability impacting writing, a child with a severe language comprehension learning disability, and a child with performance-based delays rather than significant innate learning delays. The ability to look at what each score suggests and view the patterns of test behavior to generate hypotheses is what separates the clinician from the psychometrician.

Appendix

The WJ IV *Gf-Gc* Composite and Its Use in the Identification of Specific Learning Disabilities

Fredrick A. Schrank, Kevin S. McGrew, and Nancy Mather

The authors of the *Woodcock-Johnson IV* (WJ IV; Schrank, McGrew, & Mather, 2014a) discuss the WJ IV *Gf-Gc* Composite, contrast its composition to that of the WJ IV General Intellectual Ability (GIA) score, and synthesize important information that supports its use as a reliable and valid measure of intellectual development or intellectual level. The authors also suggest that the associated WJ IV *Gf-Gc* Composite/Other Ability comparison procedure can yield information that is relevant to the identification of a specific learning disability (SLD) in any model that is allowed under federal Individuals with Disabilities Education Improvement Act (IDEA) of 2004 regulations.

The *Woodcock-Johnson IV Tests of Cognitive Abilities* (WJ IV COG; Schrank, McGrew, & Mather, 2014b) include a measure of intellectual development that is derived from Comprehension-Knowledge (*Gc*) and Fluid Reasoning (*Gf*) tests. This *Gf-Gc* Composite is a special-purpose measure of intellectual level based on four academically predictive tests representing the two highest-order (*g*-loaded or *g*-saturated) factors included in the Cattell-Horn-Carroll (CHC) theory of cognitive abilities (McGrew, 2005, 2009; McGrew, LaForte, & Schrank, 2014; Schneider & McGrew, 2012). The *Gf-Gc* Composite is highly correlated with general intellectual ability (*g*) as measured by the WJ IV COG General Intellectual Ability (GIA) score, as well as by other global indices of general intelligence. By design, the *Gf-Gc* Composite differs from broad-based measures of intellectual ability in an important way: Only *Gf* and *Gc* ability measures are included in the calculation of the score. Conceptually the *Gf-Gc* composite is analogous to the Wechsler General Ability Index (GAI), a composite score developed to remove the influence of working memory (*Gwm*) and processing speed (*Gs*) when estimating intelligence (Wechsler, 2008).

ORIGINS OF THE *GF-GC* COMPOSITE IN CONTEMPORARY CHC THEORY

The *Gf-Gc* Composite cluster name evokes an implicit reference to the work of Raymond Cattell, who posited the existence of two fundamentally different and distinguishable types of intellectual ability: fluid intelligence (*Gf*) and crystallized intelligence (*Gc*) (Cattell, 1941). The name of the cluster pays tribute to Cattell's seminal influence on CHC theory. His legacy factor analytic work laid a foundation for identifying all cognitive abilities subsequently classified within contemporary CHC theory (McGrew et al., 2014; Schneider & McGrew, 2012). The cluster name also suggests the primacy of *Gf* and *Gc* as the two most important cognitive abilities—those that are both historically and commonly associated with higher-level human cognition.

In contemporary CHC theory, *Gf* includes such abilities as abstract and inductive reasoning, deductive problem solving, and pattern recognition. *Gc* is associated with learned, acquired knowledge, particularly vocabulary knowledge and general information. By combining four of the most predictive and theoretically valid *Gf* and *Gc* tests into a single composite score, the *Gf-Gc* index represents, from roughly equal contributions, both the fundamental human capacity of reasoning via logic and the accumulation of knowledge from learning and experience.

The WJ IV authors do not suggest that other cognitive abilities are unimportant in understanding classroom performance nor do they imply that the *Gf-Gc* Composite is the best predictor of a wide variety of general life outcomes. However, the authors do suggest that *Gf* and *Gc* are the two primary cognitive abilities that may rely on other critical cognitive processes, storage and retrieval functions, or basic cognitive mechanisms to support their development and functioning. For example, *Gc* relies on Long-Term Retrieval (*Glr*) functions to access information from long-term memory. *Gf* is a complex, hierarchical cognitive ability that often utilizes one or more other cognitive processes to effect induction and deduction, including, in particular, Auditory Processing (*Ga*), Visual Processing (*Gv*), and Long-Term Retrieval (*Glr*). Cognitive Processing Speed (*Gs*) is a parameter of cognitive processing efficiency (Schneider & McGrew, 2012) that can facilitate complex cognitive performance when it is intact and automatic, but, when slow or impaired, can inhibit the completion of complex cognitive operations. Short-Term Working Memory (*Gwm*) is the active, conscious processing mechanism that both maintains and transforms information in immediate awareness so that reasoning has a venue for performance, and connections for encoding to stored acquired knowledge can occur. In contrast to *Gf* and *Gc*, the other broad cognitive abilities defined by CHC theory (*Glr*, *Ga*, *Gv*, *Gs*, and *Gwm*) are viewed as cognitive processes that can affect the development of the abilities to reason and acquire knowledge.

THE GENERAL INTELLECTUAL ABILITY (GIA) COMPARED TO THE *GF-GC* COMPOSITE

The WJ IV COG General Intellectual Ability (GIA) score is a measure of psychometric *g*, one of psychology's oldest and most well-researched constructs (Jensen, 1998). The existence of *g* was originally suggested by Galton (1869) and was later empirically established by Spearman (1904). Spearman's student, Raymond Cattell, "concluded that Spearman's *g* was best explained by splitting *g* into general fluid (g_f) and general crystallized (g_c) intelligence" (Schneider & McGrew, 2012, p. 102). More importantly, Cattell (1941) was able to explain how Spearman's *g* arose from interactions between the two "provincial powers" of *Gf* and *Gc*.

The best measure of *g* is based on the broadest spectrum of important cognitive abilities (Jensen, 1998). The WJ IV COG GIA score is derived from seven tests; each test represents the best single measure of one of seven broad CHC abilities. The GIA score is the best estimate of *g* available in the WJ IV as it meets Jensen's *psychometric sampling criterion*—"the particular collection of tests used to estimate *g* should come as close as possible, with some limited number of tests, to being a representative sample of all types of mental tests" (p. 85). Consequently, the WJ IV COG GIA score provides professionals with the best singular predictor—*across individuals*—of overall school achievement and other life outcomes that have some relationship to general intelligence.

Much like the construct of *g*, the WJ IV COG GIA score cannot be defined as a distinct cognitive ability because it is an amalgam of several important cognitive abilities, functions, or processes into a single-score index. Table A.1 contains the smoothed *g* weights for each of the seven tests included in the GIA score by technical age groups. A review of these weights suggests that at any one age, the component *Gf* and *Gc* tests combined contribute approximately 35% to the obtained GIA score. The remaining 65% of the obtained GIA score is based on

Table A.1 General Intellectual Ability Average (Smoothed) g Weights by Technical Age Groups

Test	CHC Domain	AGE								
		2	3	4	5	6	7	8	9	10
Oral Vocabulary	Gc	0.16	0.16	0.16	0.17	0.17	0.17	0.18	0.18	0.18
Number Series	Gf	0.18	0.18	0.18	0.18	0.18	0.18	0.18	0.18	0.18
Verbal Attention	Gwm	0.13	0.13	0.13	0.13	0.13	0.14	0.14	0.14	0.14
Letter-Pattern Matching	Gs	0.17	0.16	0.16	0.15	0.14	0.12	0.11	0.11	0.10
Phonological Processing	Ga	0.18	0.18	0.18	0.18	0.18	0.18	0.18	0.18	0.17
Story Recall	Glr	0.11	0.12	0.12	0.12	0.12	0.12	0.12	0.12	0.12
Visualization	Gv	0.07	0.07	0.07	0.08	0.08	0.09	0.10	0.10	0.11

Test	CHC Domain	AGE								
		11	12	13	14	15	16	17	18	19
Oral Vocabulary	Gc	0.18	0.18	0.18	0.18	0.18	0.18	0.18	0.18	0.18
Number Series	Gf	0.18	0.18	0.17	0.17	0.17	0.17	0.17	0.17	0.17
Verbal Attention	Gwm	0.14	0.14	0.14	0.14	0.14	0.14	0.14	0.14	0.14
Letter-Pattern Matching	Gs	0.10	0.10	0.10	0.10	0.11	0.11	0.11	0.11	0.11
Phonological Processing	Ga	0.17	0.17	0.17	0.17	0.17	0.17	0.17	0.17	0.17
Story Recall	Glr	0.11	0.11	0.11	0.11	0.11	0.11	0.11	0.11	0.11
Visualization	Gv	0.11	0.12	0.12	0.12	0.12	0.12	0.12	0.12	0.12

Test	CHC Domain	AGE							
		20–29	30–39	40–49	50–59	60–69	70–79	80+	Median
Oral Vocabulary	Gc	0.18	0.18	0.18	0.18	0.17	0.16	0.16	0.18
Number Series	Gf	0.16	0.16	0.15	0.15	0.15	0.15	0.15	0.17
Verbal Attention	Gwm	0.13	0.14	0.14	0.14	0.15	0.15	0.15	0.14
Letter-Pattern Matching	Gs	0.11	0.11	0.11	0.11	0.11	0.11	0.11	0.11
Phonological Processing	Ga	0.17	0.17	0.17	0.18	0.18	0.18	0.18	0.17
Story Recall	Glr	0.11	0.11	0.12	0.12	0.12	0.12	0.13	0.12
Visualization	Gv	0.13	0.12	0.12	0.12	0.12	0.12	0.12	0.12

the individual's performance on other tests that Schneider and McGrew (2012), drawing on a number of information processing models (e.g., Kyllonen, 2002; Woodcock, 1993), categorized as either sensory-motor domain-specific abilities or parameters of cognitive efficiency.[1]

In contrast, 50% of the *Gf-Gc* Composite is derived from two *Gc* tests (Oral Vocabulary and General Information), and the other 50% is derived from two *Gf* tests (Number Series and Concept Formation). When combined, *Gf* and *Gc* represent 100% of the *Gf-Gc* Composite. Although composed of only four tests, the *Gf-Gc* Composite yields highly stable scores, with reliability values comparable to

Table A.2 WJ IV Median Intellectual Ability Cluster Reliabilities

Cluster	Median r_{cc}
General Intellectual Ability (GIA)	0.97
Gf-Gc Composite (Gf-Gc)	0.96

the GIA score. The median *Gf-Gc* Composite reliability is .96 compared to the median GIA reliability of .97, as reported in Table A.2.

THE *GF-GC* COMPOSITE AS A MEASURE OF INTELLECTUAL DEVELOPMENT

The rationale for using only *Gf* and *Gc* tests to create an index of intellectual development has its basis in popular, theoretical, and empirically based notions of intelligence. A person's reasoning abilities and knowledge, particularly vocabulary knowledge and inductive reasoning, are the most common expressions of cognitive ability that laypersons observe or perceive and use—*consciously or not*—to gauge the intellectual level of another individual. For example, Sternberg, Conway, Ketron, and Bernstein's (1981) research found that implicit theories of intelligence held by both experts and laypersons typically include three abilities as the hallmarks of intelligence: problem solving abilities, verbal abilities, and social competence. Sternberg et al. (1981) noted that the problem solving and verbal facility abilities are similar to the Cattell (1941) and Horn (1991) constructs of fluid and crystallized intellectual abilities.

These common conceptualizations of intellectual ability are found among intelligence scholars as well. For example, 52 prominent intelligence scholars suggested that intelligence could be defined as "a very general mental capability that, among other things, involves the ability to reason, plan, solve problems, think abstractly, comprehend complex ideas, learn quickly, and learn from experience" (Gottfredson, 1997, p. 13). Although this definition does not suggest that intelligence is solely a function of *Gf* and *Gc*, the descriptive terms used imply that the *expression* of intelligence—in the classroom and in life—is heavily dependent on *Gf* and *Gc* abilities.

Empirical Research Supports *Gf* and *Gc* as the "King and Queen" of CHC Abilities

Gf, in particular, is often accorded special status as a proxy for general intelligence (*g*). The extant psychometric research reports that *Gf* and *g* are highly correlated, with some researchers suggesting that *Gf* may be isomorphic with *g* (Schneider & McGrew, 2012).[2] *Gc* abilities are also typically considered one of the two most important cornerstones of general intelligence (Hunt, 2000) as "almost any test involving cognition will involve *Gc* and *Gf*, to some degree" (Hunt, 2011, p. 103). To illustrate this idea, Carroll (1993) placed the broad stratum abilities of *Gf* and *Gc* in closest proximity to the stratum III general intelligence (*g*) factor in his three-stratum model figure to designate *Gf* and *Gc* as being more closely aligned with *g* than the other broad CHC abilities are, establishing their status as the "king and queen."

Table A.3 WJ IV Intellectual Ability Cluster Score Intercorrelations

	Ages 6 Through 8		Ages 9 Through 13		Ages 14 Through 19	
Cluster	GIA	*Gf-Gc*	GIA	*Gf-Gc*	GIA	*Gf-Gc*
General Intellectual Ability (GIA)	1		1		1	
Gf-Gc Composite (*Gf-Gc*)	0.84	1	0.84	1	0.88	1

Table A.4 Correlations between GIA, *Gf-Gc* Composite, and Reading Achievement Cluster Scores Across Five Age Groups

	Reading Achievement Clusters							
Ages Group and Predictor Cluster	Reading	Broad Reading	Basic Reading Skills	Reading Compre-hension	Reading Compre-hension— Extended	Reading Fluency	Reading Rate	Median
Ages 6–8 (*n* = 825)								
GIA	0.73	0.73	0.70	0.73	0.77	0.66	0.63	0.73
Gf-Gc Composite	0.72	0.70	0.66	0.70	0.74	0.62	0.55	0.70
Ages 9–13 (*n* = 1572)								
GIA	0.72	0.73	0.69	0.70	0.75	0.65	0.64	0.70
Gf-Gc Composite	0.71	0.72	0.63	0.69	0.74	0.63	0.58	0.69
Ages 14–19 (*n* = 1685)								
GIA	0.76	0.75	0.70	0.73	0.78	0.66	0.63	0.73
Gf-Gc Composite	0.75	0.74	0.66	0.72	0.78	0.65	0.58	0.72
Ages 20–39 (*n* = 1251)								
GIA	0.78	0.77	0.73	0.75	0.80	0.67	0.62	0.75
Gf-Gc Composite	0.77	0.74	0.68	0.74	0.80	0.64	0.54	0.74
Ages 40–90+ (*n* = 1146)								
GIA	0.80	0.79	0.75	0.77	0.82	0.71	0.68	0.77
Gf-Gc Composite	0.79	0.77	0.70	0.77	0.82	0.68	0.61	0.77

Summary correlations between the *Gf-Gc* Composite and GIA cluster scores in the WJ IV standardization sample are reported in Table A.3. As reported in McGrew et al. (2014), across all groups spanning ages six through late adulthood, the correlations range from .84 to .88 (median *r* = .88). These high correlations support the interpretation of the *Gf-Gc* composite as a strong proxy for general intellectual level. The median correlation of .88 indicates that, although highly related, the *Gf-Gc* composite and GIA cluster scores are not isomorphic—they share approximately 77% common variance. This supports the rationale of the *Gf-Gc* composite as an alternative index of intellectual level—an alternative that does not include the cognitive processing and efficiency variance that is present in the GIA.

As reported in Tables A.4 and A.5, compared to the GIA score, the *Gf-Gc* Composite sacrifices little in the way of validity when predicting the WJ IV Tests of Achievement (WJ IV ACH; Schrank, Mather, & McGrew, 2014a) reading and mathematics achievement clusters when these academic cluster scores do not also

Table A.5 Correlations Between GIA, *Gf-Gc* Composite, and Math Achievement Cluster Scores Across Five Age Groups

Ages Group and Predictor Cluster	Math	Broad Math	Calculation Skills	Math Problem Solving	Median
		Math Achievement Clusters			
Ages 6–8 (*n* = 825)					
GIA	0.75	0.76	0.73	0.74	0.74
Gf-Gc Composite	0.72	0.69	0.62	0.76	0.71
Ages 9–13 (*n* = 1572)					
GIA	0.77	0.78	0.73	0.76	0.76
Gf-Gc Composite	0.76	0.73	0.65	0.77	0.74
Ages 14–19 (*n* = 1685)					
GIA	0.80	0.80	0.75	0.80	0.80
Gf-Gc Composite	0.80	0.76	0.69	0.81	0.78
Ages 20–39 (*n* = 1251)					
GIA	0.79	0.79	0.74	0.81	0.79
Gf-Gc Composite	0.79	0.76	0.68	0.82	0.77
Ages 40–90+ (*n* = 1146)					
GIA	0.80	0.81	0.76	0.82	0.81
Gf-Gc Composite	0.82	0.79	0.72	0.83	0.80

include measures of speed or academic fluency. (The WJ IV ACH Reading, Basic Reading Skills, Reading Comprehension, Reading Comprehension-Extended, Mathematics, and Math Problem Solving clusters do not contain measures of speed or academic fluency.) McGrew et al. (2014) explained: "The GIA correlations are always slightly higher than the *Gf-Gc* Composite, but only by small and not practically relevant margins (.01 to .03). These findings support the use of the *Gf-Gc* Composite as a predictor of concurrent reading and math achievement" (p. 144).

Table A.6 contains the correlations of the GIA and *Gf-Gc* Composite with written language achievement. For written language, the GIA correlations are consistently higher than the *Gf-Gc* Composite, perhaps reflecting the relative importance of other CHC abilities in the prediction of written language performance. Even so, the *Gf-Gc* correlations with the written language measures remain moderate to moderately high and within an acceptable range for use as a predictor of written language achievement.

Table A.6 Correlations Between GIA, *Gf-Gc* Composite, and Writing Achievement Cluster Scores Across Five Age Groups

Ages Group and Predictor Cluster	Writing Achievement Clusters				
	Written Language	Broad Written Language	Basic Writing Skills	Written Expression	Median
Ages 6–8 (*n* = 825)					
GIA	0.74	0.75	0.73	0.70	0.73
Gf-Gc Composite	0.63	0.62	0.65	0.54	0.62
Ages 9–13 (*n* = 1572)					
GIA	0.73	0.75	0.74	0.67	0.74
Gf-Gc Composite	0.63	0.63	0.67	0.53	0.63
Ages 14–19 (*n* = 1685)					
GIA	0.76	0.77	0.76	0.70	0.76
Gf-Gc Composite	0.68	0.68	0.69	0.58	0.68
Ages 20–39 (*n* = 1251)					
GIA	0.74	0.76	0.76	0.68	0.75
Gf-Gc Composite	0.66	0.65	0.69	0.55	0.65
Ages 40–90+ (*n* = 1146)					
GIA	0.79	0.80	0.79	0.74	0.79
Gf-Gc Composite	0.71	0.70	0.72	0.63	0.71

Relationship of the GIA and *Gf-Gc* Composite to Other Intelligence Tests

Tables A.7–A.10 contain correlations of the WJ IV GIA and *Gf-Gc* Composite scores with several other commonly used full scale and subdomain intelligence indices. As shown in Table A.7, both the WJ IV GIA score and the *Gf-Gc* Composite are strongly correlated (.86 and .83) with general intellectual level as measured by the *Wechsler Intelligence Scale for Children–Fourth Edition* (WISC-IV; Wechsler, 2003) Full Scale IQ score. The pattern of GIA and *Gf-Gc* Composite scores with the WISC-IV index scores provides additional insights. The *Gf-Gc* Composite correlates slightly higher than the GIA score with the WISC IV Verbal Comprehension index (.79 and .74) and slightly lower than the GIA score with the WISC IV Perceptual Reasoning index (.73 and .74), suggesting similar levels of shared variance. The *Gf-Gc* Composite shows slightly lower correlations (than the GIA score) with the WISC-IV Working Memory index (.66 and .69) and notably lower correlations (than the GIA score) with the WISC-IV Processing Speed index (.44 and .57). This pattern of correlations with the WISC-IV indices supports the recommendation that the WJ IV *Gf-Gc* Composite is a valid measure of general intellectual level that can be expressed without a contribution from cognitive efficiency (*Gs* and *Gwm*) tests. A similar pattern of correlations can be found in Table A.8, which reports the correlations of .84 and .78 between the WJ IV GIA and *Gf-Gc* Composite scores and the *Wechsler Adult Intelligence Scale–Fourth Edition* (WAIS-IV; Wechsler, 2008) Full Scale IQ score and index scores.

Table A.7 Summary Statistics and Correlations for WJ IV COG Intellectual Ability Measures and WISC-IV Scales

| | | | WISC-IV Measures | | | | |
WJ IV Measures	Mean	SD	Full Scale IQ (*g*)	Verbal Compre-hension Index (*Gc*)	Perceptual Reasoning Index (*Gf/Gv*)	Working Memory Index (*Gwm*)	Processing Speed Index (*Gs*)
Cognitive Composite							
Clusters							
General Intellectual							
Ability (*g*)	107.2	14.2	0.86	0.74	0.74	0.69	0.57
Gf-Gc Composite	104.8	15.4	0.83	0.79	0.73	0.66	0.44
Mean			106.7	106.2	107.6	101.5	102.8
Standard Deviation			15.2	13.5	14.8	15.4	15.1

Note. *N* = 174 for all measures. Age range (years) 6–16, *M* 102, *SD* 2.6

Table A.8 Summary Statistics and Correlations for WJ IV COG Intellectual Ability Measures and WAIS-IV Scales

				WAIS-IV Measures			
WJ IV Measures	Mean	SD	Full Scale IQ (*g*)	Verbal Compre-hension Index (*Gc*)	Perceptual Reasoning Index (*Gv/Gf*)	Working Memory Index (*Gwm/Gq*)	Processing Speed Index (*Gs*)
Cognitive Composite Clusters							
General Intellectual Ability (*g*)	104.3	12.6	0.84	0.68	0.69	0.70	0.52
Gf-Gc Composite	105.0	13.8	0.78	0.69	0.63	0.61	0.41
Mean			107.1	105.8	106.0	103.2	107.6
Standard Deviation			14.1	14.1	14.5	15.1	15.0

Note. N = 177 for all measures. Age range (years) = 16–82, M = 37.1, SD = 14.3

Table A.9 Summary Statistics and Correlations for WJ IV COG Intellectual Ability Measures and SB-5 Scales

WJ IV Measures	Mean	SD	SB5 Full Scale IQ (*g*)
Cognitive Composite Clusters			
General Intellectual Ability (*g*)	97.8	17.2	0.80
Gf-Gc Composite	95.2	15.4	0.82
Mean			100.0
Standard Deviation			15.4

Note: N = 50 for all measures. Age range (years) = 6–16, M = 11.1, SD = 3.0

The correlations between the WJ IV COG intellectual ability measures and *Stanford-Binet Intelligence Scales, Fifth Edition* (SB5; Roid, 2003) Full Scale IQ scores presented in Table A.9 show strong relationships between the WJ IV GIA (.80) and *Gf-Gc* Composite (.82) scores and the SB5 Full Scale IQ score, provid-ing additional evidence that both the GIA and *Gf-Gc* Composite scores are valid measures of general intellectual level.

Table A.10 reports the correlations between the WJ IV COG intellectual ability scores and broad and narrow CHC factor scores and the *Kaufman Assessment Battery for Children–Second Edition* (KABC-II; Kaufman & Kaufman, 2004) index scores. Similar to the WISC-IV and WAIS-IV correlations, the GIA and *Gf-Gc* Composite clusters correlate at similar high levels (.77 and .71) with the KABC-II Fluid-Crystallized Index.[3] The *Gf-Gc* Composite cluster

Table A.10 Summary Statistics and Correlations for WJ IV COG Intellectual Ability Measures and KABC-II Scales

					KABC-II Measures				
WJ IV Measures	Mean	SD	Mental Processing Index	Fluid-Crystallized Index (*g*)	Sequential/*Gsm* Index	Simultaneous/*Gv* Index	Learning/*Glr* Index	Planning/*Gf* Index	Knowledge/*Gc* Index
GIA (*g*)	99.5	14.4	0.72	0.77	0.41	0.44	0.60	0.51	0.58
Gf-Gc Composite	97.2	14.8	0.57	0.71	0.33	0.33	0.50	0.41	0.78
Mean			99.7	100.3	100.1	98.0	99.7	102.8	101.6
Standard Deviation			13.6	12.7	14.4	14.9	14.6	15.3	13.0

Note. $N = 50$ for all measures. Age range (years) = 7–18, $M = 11.4$, $SD = 3.3$

correlates notably higher than the GIA cluster (.78 and .58) with the KABC-II Knowledge/*Gc* Index. This pattern is reversed, with the *Gf-Gc* Composite cluster correlating at a lower level than the GIA cluster (.41 and 51) with the KABC-II Planning/*Gf* index. McGrew et al. (2014) drew upon the Reynolds, Keith, Fine, Fisher and Low (2007) confirmatory analyses of the KABC-II standardization data to hypothesize that the lower correlations with the KABC-II Planning/*Gf* index may be due to the KABC-II index being a mixed measure of *Gf* and *Gv*. Of particular interest are the consistently lower correlations between the WJ IV *Gf-Gc* Composite and the KABC-II measures of processing than between the WJ IV GIA score and the KABC-II processing measures. The *Gf-Gc* Composite and GIA clusters correlate at .33 and .41 with the KABC-II Sequential/*Gsm* Index, at .33 and .44 with the KABC-II Simultaneous/*Gv* Index, and at .50 and .60 with the KABC-II Learning/*Glr* Index. The lower *Gf-Gc* Composite correlations with the KABC-II processing measures suggest that the WJ IV *Gf-Gc* Composite shares less variance with the KABC-II processing measures than does the WJ IV GIA score. This finding supports the interpretation of the WJ IV *Gf-Gc* Composite cluster as a proxy for general intelligence that is less influenced by cognitive processing abilities than is the WJ IV GIA cluster.

GF-GC COMPOSITE/OTHER ABILITY COMPARISON PROCEDURE IN SPECIFIC LEARNING DISABILITY DETERMINATION

In some cases, the GIA, or full scale intelligence score, may not provide the best description of attained intellectual level for an individual suspected of having a specific learning disability (SLD). This is particularly true when a significant limitation is present in one of the basic cognitive processes, storage and processing functions, or mechanisms of cognitive efficiency. Although these abilities contribute to the general intellectual ability score, they also can be identified as possible contributors to the disability itself. In such cases, the *Gf-Gc* Composite may be the preferred measure of intellectual development because it does not include any of the psychological processing abilities that might underlie a specific learning disability. The removal of processing mechanisms from the measure of intellectual development can help professionals isolate any specific cognitive limitations that may be related to learning difficulties and, thus, may be important in identifying the nature of the specific learning disability itself.

In the Individuals with Disabilities Education Improvement Act (IDEA) of 2004 reauthorization, the definition of *specific learning disability* (SLD) was maintained as "a disorder in one or more of the basic psychological processes involved in understanding or in using language, spoken or written, which ... may manifest itself in the imperfect ability to listen, think, speak, read well, or do mathematical calculations" (IDEA, 2004; 20 U.S.C. §1401 [30]). Examples of types of basic psychological processing disabilities contributing to SLD include weaknesses in aspects of phonological processing, orthographic processing, working memory, and processing speed. Essentially, these types of processing abilities support the ease and efficiency of symbolic learning, which is required in tasks like learning sound-symbol associations, memorizing the times tables, or writing the letters of the alphabet quickly. Problems in any one of these areas can affect an individual's development and performance in the basic academic skills of reading, writing, and/or mathematics. As Bateman (1992) observed, children with SLD have more trouble acquiring, applying, and retaining information than would be predicted on the basis of other information about the child.

Despite impairments in processing abilities, and in contrast to these abilities, students with SLD often have intact oral language and reasoning abilities. In fact, many have average or even above-average performance in verbal abilities (Orton, 1966). For example, in the case of students with reading disabilities or dyslexia, the most common type of learning disability, what distinguishes these individuals from other poor readers is that their listening comprehension abilities are higher than their ability to decode words (Rack, Snowling, & Olson, 1992). In discussing a common profile of students with dyslexia, Shaywitz (2003) described a "sea of strengths," where the students' reading/spelling problems are often surrounded by their strengths in vocabulary knowledge, language comprehension, and reasoning abilities. Thus, in cases involving the determination of SLD, it makes sense to compare the often intact *Gf-Gc* Composite with the individual's other, less efficient abilities, both in cognitive processing and academic achievement.

The *Gf-Gc* Composite can be compared to all other cognitive, language, and achievement clusters in the WJ IV that are not primarily measures of *Gf* or *Gc*. This comparison includes cognitive abilities representing the other broad domains of CHC theory (e.g., *Gwm, Glr, Ga, Gv, Gs*); many narrow ability clusters from the cognitive and oral language batteries (e.g., Perceptual Speed [P], Cognitive Efficiency, Quantitative Reasoning [RQ], Auditory Memory Span [MS], Number Facility [N], Phonetic Coding [PC], Speed of Lexical Access [LA]); and, importantly for SLD, measures of academic achievement. WJ IV Technical Manual (McGrew et al., 2014) Figure .1 portrays, in visual-graphic format, the complete set(s) of obtained cognitive, language, and achievement clusters that can be compared to the predicted scores based on an individual's *Gf-Gc* Composite score.

In the WJ IV, the *Gf-Gc* Composite/Other Ability comparison procedure is sometimes called a hybrid model because it employs the methodology of a traditional ability/achievement discrepancy procedure and presents any observed

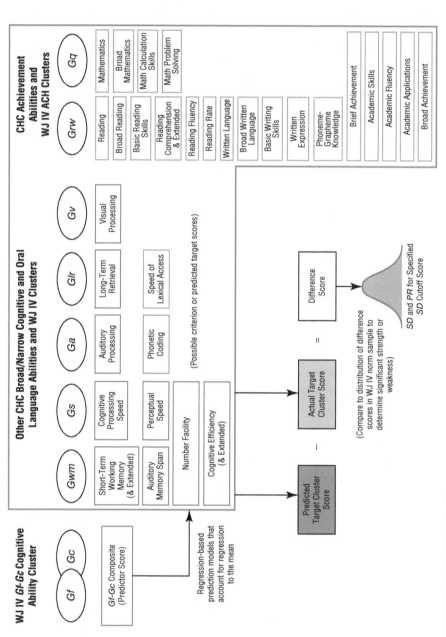

discrepancies as a profile of intra-individual strengths and weaknesses. If any cluster score is identified as discrepant, the target area is flagged as a strength or weakness relative to the person's level of intellectual development as defined by the *Gf-Gc* Composite. Discrepant clusters that are significantly higher than would be predicted by the *Gf-Gc* Composite are interpreted as relative strengths; discrepant clusters that are significantly lower than would be predicted by the *Gf-Gc* Composite are interpreted as relative weaknesses.

USE OF THE *GF-GC* COMPOSITE IN SLD-IDENTIFICATION MODELS

Based on guidance provided by the U.S. Department of Education Office of Special Education Programs (OSEP, 2006), schools are required to use one of the learning disability identification procedures provided in the Individuals with Disabilities Education Improvement Act (IDEA) of 2004 and the criteria issued by their state department of education. In general, three different alternatives for identification of a specific learning disability are permitted: (a) an ability/achievement discrepancy method, (b) a response-to-intervention (RTI) model, and (c) a research-based methodology that is typically operationalized as a pattern of strengths and weaknesses (PSW) model. In determining a specific learning disability, a comprehensive evaluation is required regardless of the model used by the school district or agency. The *Gf-Gc* Composite/Other Ability comparison procedure can provide information relevant to the identification of a SLD within the context of any of these models.

Ability/Achievement Discrepancy Model

Although school districts may now opt out of the traditional ability/achievement discrepancy requirement, assessment of intellectual development is specifically recognized. An ability/achievement discrepancy methodology is allowed and may provide information relevant to the identification of a SLD.

The ability/achievement discrepancy model has been validly criticized for several reasons, many of which are beyond the scope of this paper. However, two reasons are germane to the current discussion. First, the traditional ability/achievement discrepancy model places undo emphasis on a single score (the full-scale intelligence score used to predict achievement) for SLD identification and too little emphasis on understanding the nature of an individual's learning problems. Second, the commonly used full scale or general ability scores typically included tests of cognitive processing and efficiency that are often related to the individual's learning disability and, as a consequence, lower the score of the obtained general ability index. This second situation often causes individuals with identifiable learning disabilities in basic psychological processing to be ineligible for special services—an example of the paradoxical Catch-22.[4]

In many instances, the *Gf-Gc* Composite/Other Ability comparison procedure can circumvent the ability-achievement Catch-22 by minimizing the effects of a cognitive processing or efficiency disability from the index of intellectual development that is defined exclusively by the tests of *Gf* and *Gc*. The *Gf-Gc* Composite can be compared to IDEA-aligned measures of basic reading skills, reading fluency, reading comprehension, mathematics calculation, mathematics problem solving, and written expression from the *Woodcock-Johnson IV Tests of Achievement* (WJ IV ACH; Schrank, Mather, & McGrew, 2014a) and/or measures of oral expression and listening comprehension from the *Woodcock-Johnson IV Tests of Oral Language* (WJ IV OL; Schrank, Mather, & McGrew, 2014b), among other abilities from the cognitive processing and oral language domains that may be helpful in understanding the nature of an individual's learning problems.

Response-to-Intervention Model

The federal regulations allow schools to employ a process to determine whether an individual responds to scientific, research-based intervention as a part of the evaluation process. Response to intervention (RTI) is a school-wide intervention model intended to improve and expedite research-based educational service delivery through careful observation and measurement of outcomes. In this model, the individual's level of response to intervention can help determine whether the individual has a specific learning disability.

RTI procedures can provide valuable information as part of a comprehensive evaluation to determine whether a SLD exists. However, RTI is not a substitute for a comprehensive evaluation. A comprehensive evaluation must include a variety of assessment tools and strategies and cannot rely on any single procedure as the sole criterion for determining eligibility for services. When using the RTI model to determine whether a student has a SLD, the regulations specifically state that a team must consider, at a minimum, the relationship of the student's achievement to his or her intellectual level. In addition, the regulations respect the expertise of the professionals who hold the responsibility for conducting or contributing to the comprehensive evaluation to determine what additional information is relevant for disability determination and program planning.

The *Gf-Gc* Composite/Other Ability comparison procedure provides relevant information for the RTI evaluation team because it includes a measure of intellectual level devoid of measures of cognitive processing. The *Gf-Gc* Composite also can be compared to measures of academic achievement and other cognitive or cognitive-linguistic clusters that professional examiners or the evaluation team deem relevant to the evaluation.

Pattern of Strengths and Weaknesses Model

The U.S. Department of Education, Office of Special Education Programs (OSEP; OSEP 2006) issued guidance to clarify that a team may diagnose SLD when "the child exhibits a pattern of strengths and weaknesses in performance, achievement, or both, relative to age, State-approved grade-level standards, or intellectual development, that is determined by the group to be relevant to the identification of a specific learning disability, using appropriate assessments ... " (p. 2). This is often described as the pattern of strengths and weaknesses (PSW) model.

The *Gf-Gc* Composite and its related comparison procedure are well-suited for use in PSW models for a number of reasons. First, the *Gf-Gc* Composite provides a reliable and valid index of intellectual development derived exclusively from tests of fluid reasoning, verbal comprehension, and knowledge abilities, thus minimizing the impact of a psychological processing deficit in the obtained intellectual composite score. Second, the required pattern of strengths and weaknesses in achievement can be observed when comparing other clusters from the WJ IV COG, WJ IV OL, or the WJ IV ACH to the *Gf-Gc* Composite.

The OSEP guidelines yield to the clinical judgment of professionals and professional teams to determine what constitutes a pattern relevant to the identification of a SLD. The WJ IV can provide information that allows knowledgeable professionals working within PSW models to go beyond the minimal requirements and align the defining characteristic of SLD—a deficit in basic psychological processing—with the procedures to be used for identification. The *Gf-Gc* Composite/Other Ability comparison procedure allows areas of academic achievement and other cognitive and cognitive-linguistic processes to emerge as strengths or weaknesses relative to the overall index of *Gf* and *Gc* abilities in a single analysis. This procedure evaluates domain-specific achievement skills jointly with related cognitive and linguistic abilities, allowing patterns to emerge that may be particularly informative to understanding the nature of a SLD.

SUMMARY AND DISCUSSION

The theoretical foundation, predictive validity, concurrent validity, and reliability evidence summarized in this paper suggest that the WJ IV *Gf-Gc* Composite can be used as a measure of intellectual level or development. A review of the correlational evidence with part or factor scores obtained from the WJ IV standardization sample and other measures of global intelligence suggests that the *Gf-Gc* Composite score, when compared to the GIA cluster score, is less influenced by cognitive processing and cognitive efficiency abilities. By implication, when compared to the GIA cluster score and other full scale intelligence scores, an obtained *Gf-Gc* Composite score may be less attenuated by the effects of a cognitive processing or cognitive efficiency disability for some individuals, particularly those with a SLD.

The WJ IV authors propose two reasons why the *Gf-Gc* Composite can be useful in SLD identification. First, the relative influence of any functional limitations in one or more of the basic cognitive processes, storage and processing functions, or cognitive efficiency mechanisms is minimized in the *Gf-Gc* Composite. This is particularly useful when an individual has benefited from the investment of effort and experience in spite of limitations in *Gwm, Ga, Gv, Glr, Gs*, or any of their associated narrow abilities, such as perceptual speed, working memory capacity, or phonetic coding.

Second, the *Gf-Gc* Composite can be compared to levels of academic achievement as well as to measures of basic cognitive processes, storage and retrieval functions, mechanisms of cognitive efficiency, and/or critical cognitive-linguistic competencies. The *Gf-Gc* Composite/Other Ability comparison procedure yields a profile of cognitive, linguistic, and achievement abilities that may reveal a pattern of strengths and weaknesses relative to the *Gf-Gc* Composite. Based on the judgment of the evaluation team, an observed pattern may be relevant to the identification of a SLD. The *Gf-Gc* Composite and the related comparison procedure can be useful in any model of SLD identification that is allowed by IDEA (2004).

NOTES

1. Hunt (2011) similarly designates *Gf* and *Gc* as the primary cognitive abilities and all remaining CHC abilities as either measures of short- and long-term memory or abilities related to different sensory modalities.
2. The *Gf* = *g* hypothesis is not a unanimous position among intelligence scholars (see Ackerman, Beier, & Boyle, 2005; Kane, Hambrick, & Conway, 2005). Carroll (2003) believed that the available evidence was sufficient to reject the hypothesis that *Gf* = *g*.
3. The KABC-II provides two different global composite *g* scores based on two different theoretical models of intelligence—the Mental Processing Index and the Fluid-Crystallized Index. The Fluid-Crystallized Index is based on CHC theory and is the most appropriate score to compare to the WJ IV cognitive clusters.

4. From the novel of the same name by Heller (1961), a Catch-22 is a problem for which the only solution is denied by a circumstance inherent in the problem or by a rule; an illogical, unreasonable, or senseless situation where a solution to the problem is unattainable because the rules established to identify the problem prohibit it (Merriam-Webster, 2014). The analogy is appropriate to learning disabilities identification when, for example, a child's low achievement can be linked to an identified processing disability, but the child is denied special services because the processing disability is included in the measure of general intellectual development, which then reduces the likelihood of an ability/achievement discrepancy.

References

Adams, A. M., & Gathercole, S. E. (1995). Phonological working memory and speech production in preschool children. *Journal of Speech and Hearing Research, 38,* 403–414.

Adams, A. M., & Gathercole, S. E. (1996). Phonological working memory and spoken language development in young children. *Quarterly Journal of Experimental Psychology, 49*(A), 216–233.

Adams, A. M., & Gathercole, S. E. (2000). Limitations in working memory: Implications for language development. *International Journal of Language and Communication Disorders, 35,* 95–116.

Adams, M. J. (1990). *Beginning to read: Thinking and learning about print.* Cambridge, MA: MIT Press.

Ackerman, P. L., Beier, M. E., & Boyle, M. O. (2005). Individual differences in working memory within a nomological network of cognitive and perceptual speed abilities. *Journal of Experimental Psychology: General, 131,* 567–589.

Alloway, T. P. (2011). *Improving working memory: Supporting students' learning.* Thousand Oaks, CA: Sage.

Alloway, T. P. (2012). Can interactive working memory training improve learning? *Journal of Interactive Learning Research, 23,* 1–11.

Alloway, T. P., & Alloway, R. (2013). *The working memory advantage: Train your brain.* New York, NY: Simon & Schuster.

Alloway, T., & Archibald, L. (2008). Working memory and learning in children with developmental coordination disorder and specific language impairment. *Journal of Learning Disabilities, 41,* 251–262.

Alloway, T. P., Gathercole, S. E., Adams, A. M., & Willis, C. (2005). Working memory abilities in children with special educational needs. *Educational & Child Psychology, 22,* 56–67.

Altmann, G. T. (1999). *The ascent of Babel: An exploration of language, mind, and understanding.* New York, NY: Oxford University Press.

American Educational Research Association, American Psychological Association, & National Council on Measurement in Education. (2014). *Standards for educational and psychological testing.* Washington, DC: AERA.

Anders, P., & Bos, C. (1986). Semantic feature analysis: An interactive strategy for vocabulary development and text comprehension. *Journal of Reading, 9*(7), 610–616.

Anderson, J. R., & Mattessa, M. (1997). A production system theory of serial memory. *Psychological Review, 104,* 728–748.

Anderson, R. C. (1996). Research foundations to support wide reading. In V. Greaney (Ed.), *Promoting reading in developing countries* (pp. 55–77). Newark, DE: International Reading Association.

Anderson, R. C., & Nagy, W. E. (1991). Word meanings. In R. Barr, M. Kamil, P. Mosenthal, & P. D. Pearson (Eds.), *Handbook of reading research* (Vol. 2, pp. 690–724). New York, NY: Longman.

Anderson, R. C., & Nagy, W. E. (1992). The vocabulary conundrum. *American Educator, 16*, 14–18, 44–47.

Andrewes, D. (2001) *Neuropsychology: From theory to practice.* New York, NY: Psychology Press.

Anglin, J. M. (1993). Vocabulary development: A morphological analysis. *Monographs of the Society for Research in Child Development, 58*(10, Serial No. 238).

Apel, K. (2009). The acquisition of mental orthographic representations for reading and spelling development. *Communication Disorders Quarterly, 31*(1), 42–52.

Apel, K. (2010). Kindergarten children's initial spoken and written word learning in a storybook context. *Scientific Studies in Reading, 14*(5), 440–463. doi: http://dx.doi.org/10.1080/10888431003623496

Apel, K. (2011). What is orthographic knowledge? *Language, Speech, and Hearing Services in Schools, 42*, 592–603.

Archibald, L. M. D., & Gathercole, S. E. (2006). Short-term and working memory in specific language impairment. *International Journal of Language & Communication Disorders, 41*(6), 675–693.

Archibald, L. M. D., & Gathercole, S. E. (2007). Nonword repetition in specific language impairment: More than a phonological short-term memory deficit. *Psychonomic Bulletin & Review, 14*(5), 919–924.

Ashby, J. (2010). Phonology is fundamental in skilled reading: Evidence from ERPs. *Psychonomic Bulletin & Review, 17*, 95–100. http://dx.doi.org/10.3758/PBR.17.1.95

Ashby, J., Sanders, L. D., & Kingston, J. (2009). Skilled readers begin processing sub-phonemic features by 80 ms during visual word recognition: Evidence from ERPs. *Biological Psychology, 80*, 84–94. http://dx.doi.org/10.1016/j.biopsycho.2008.03.009

Ashcraft, M. H. (2002). *Cognition* (3rd ed.). Upper Saddle River, NJ: Prentice Hall.

Averbach, E., & Coriell, A. S. (1961). Short-term memory in vision. *Bell System Technical Journal, 40*, 309–328.

Averbach, E., & Sperling, G. (1961). Short term storage and information in vision. In C. Cherry (Ed.), *Information theory* (pp. 196–211). London, UK: Butterworth.

Baddeley, A. D. (1979). Working memory and reading. In P. A. Kolers, M. E. Wrolstad, & H. Bouma (Eds.), *Processing of visible language* (pp. 355–370). New York, NY: Plenum Press. http://dx.doi.org/10.1007/978-1-4684-0994-9_21

Baddeley, A. D. (1986). *Working memory.* London, UK: Oxford University Press.

Baddeley, A. D., Eldridge, M., & Lewis, V. (1981). The role of subvocalisation in reading. *Quarterly Journal of Experimental Psychology A: Human Experimental Psychology, 33*, 439–454. http://dx.doi.org/10.1080/14640748108400802

Baddeley, A. D., Gathercole, S. E., & Papagno, C. (1998). The phonological loop as a language learning device. *Psychological Review, 105*, 158–173.

Baddeley, A. D, & Hitch, G. (1974). Working memory. In G. A. Bower (Ed.), *The psychology of learning and motivation: Advances in research and theory* (Vol. 8, pp. 47–89). New York, NY: Academic Press.

Baddeley, A.D., & Hitch, G.J. (1994). Developments in the concept of working memory. *Neuropsychology, 8*, 485–493.

Baenninger, M., & Newcombe, N. (1989). The role of experience in spatial test performance: A meta-analysis. *Sex Roles, 20*(5–6), 327–344. http://dx.doi.org/10.1007/BF00287729

Baker, S., Simmons, D., & Kame'enui, E. (1998). *Vocabulary acquisition: Synthesis of the research*. Washington, DC: U.S. Department of Education, Office of Educational Research and Improvement, Educational Resources Information Center.

Barrouillet, P., & Camos, V. (2012). As time goes by: Temporal constraints in working memory. *Current Directions in Psychological Science, 21*(6), 413–419.

Barrouillet, P., Gauffroy, C., & Lecas, J.-F. (2008). Mental models and the suppositional account of conditionals. *Psychological Review, 115*, 760–771.

Barrouillet, P., Grosset, N., & Lecas, J.-F. (2000). Conditional reasoning by mental models: Chronometric and developmental evidence. *Cognition, 75*, 237–266.

Barrouillet, P., & Lucidi, A. (2011, November). *Individual differences in working memory: Where do they come from?* Paper presented at the 52nd annual meeting of the Psychonomic Society, Seattle, WA.

Barouillet, P., Portrat, S., & Camos, V. (2011). On the law relating processing to storage in working memory. *Psychological Review, 118*, 175–192.

Barsalou, L. W. (2008). Grounded cognition. *Annual Review of Psychology, 59*(1), 617–645.

Bartlett, F. (1932/1967). *Remembering: A Study in experimental and social psychology*. London, UK: Cambridge University Press.

Bateman, B. (1992). Learning disabilities: The changing landscape. *Journal of Learning Disabilities, 25*, 29–36.

Baumann, J. F., Edwards, E. C., Boland, E. M., Olejnik, S., & Kame'enui, E. J. (2003). Vocabulary tricks: Effects of instruction in morphology and context on fifth-grade students' ability to derive and infer word meanings. *American Educational Research Journal, 40*(2), 447–494.

Baumann, J. F., Kame'enui, E. J., & Ash, G. E. (2003). Research on vocabulary instruction: Voltaire redux. In J. Flood, D. Lapp, J. R. Squire, & J. M. Jensen (Eds.), *Handbook of research on teaching the English language arts* (2nd ed., pp. 752–785). Mahwah, NJ: Erlbaum.

Beard, R., Myhill, D., Riley, J., & Nystrand, M. (2009). *The Sage Handbook of Writing Development*. London, UK: Sage.

Beck, I. L., & McKeown, M. G. (2001). Text talk: Capturing the benefits of read aloud experiences for young children. *Reading Teacher, 55*, 10–20.

Beck, I. L., McKeown, M. G., & Kucan, L. (2002). *Bringing words to life: Robust vocabulary instruction*. New York, NY: Guilford Press.

Beckman, M. E., & Edwards, J. (2000). Lexical frequency effects on young children's imitative productions. In M. Broe and J. Pierrehumbert (Eds.), *Papers in laboratory phonology*, Vol. 5 (pp. 208–218). Cambridge, UK: Cambridge University Press.

Bentin, S., & Leshem, H. (1993). On the interaction between phonological awareness and reading acquisition: It's a two-way street. *Annals of Dyslexia, 43*, 125–148.

Bertling, J. P. (2012). *Measuring reasoning ability: Applications of rule-based item generation* (Unpublished doctoral dissertation). Westfälischen Wilhelms-Universität zu Münster.

Berninger, V. W., Whitaker, D., Feng, Y., Swanson, H. L., & Abbott, R. D. (1996). Assessment of planning, translating, and revising in junior high writers. *Journal of School Psychology, 34*(1), 23-52.

Biederman, I. (1987). Recognition-by-components: A theory of human image understanding. *Psychological Review, 94*, 115–147.

Biederman, I. (1990). Higher-level vision. In E. N. Osherson, S. M. Kosslyn, & J. M. Hollerbach (Eds.), *An invitation to cognitive science* (Vol. *2*, pp. 41–72). Cambridge, MA: MIT Press.

Biemiller, A. (2001). Teaching vocabulary: Early, direct, and sequential. *American Educator*, *25*(1), 24–28.

Bishop, D. V. M., North, T., & Donlan, C. (1996). Nonword repetition as a behavioural marker for inherited language impairment: Evidence from a twin study. *Journal of Child Psychology and Psychiatry*, *37*, 391–403.

Blachowicz, C., & Fisher, P. (2000). Vocabulary instruction. In M. L. Kamil, P. Mosenthal, P. D. Pearson, & R. Barr (Eds.), *Handbook of reading research*. (Vol. 3, pp. 503–523). Mahwah, NJ: Erlbaum.

Blevins, W. (2001). *Building fluency: Lessons and strategies for reading success*. New York, NY: Scholastic.

Brackett, J., & McPherson, A. (1996). Learning disabilities diagnosis in postsecondary students: A comparison of discrepancy-based diagnostic models. In N. Gregg, C. Hoy, & A. F. Gay (Eds.), *Adults with learning disabilities: Theoretical and practical perspectives* (pp. 68–84). New York, NY: Guilford Press.

Bradley, L., & Bryant, P. E. (1983, February 3). Categorizing sounds and learning to read: A causal connection. *Nature*, p. 419.

Brefczynski, J. A., & DeYoe, E. A. (1999). A physiological correlate of the "spotlight" of visual attention. *Nature Neuroscience*, *2*, 370–374.

Bridge, C. A., Winograd, P. N., & Haley, D. (1983). Using predictable materials vs. preprimers to teach beginning sight words. *Reading Teacher*, *36*(9), 884–891.

Broadway, J. M., & Engle, R. W. (2010). Validating running memory span: Measurement of working memory capacity and links with fluid intelligence. *Behavior Research Methods*, *42*, 563–570.

Brown, G. D., & Hulme, C. (1995). Modeling item length effects in memory span: No rehearsal needed? *Journal of Memory and Language*, *34*, 594–624.

Bowey, J. A. (1996). On the association between phonological memory and receptive vocabulary in five-year-olds. *Journal of Experimental Child Psychology*, *63*, 44–78.

Bowey, J. A. (1997). What does nonword repetition measure? A reply to Gathercole and Baddeley. *Journal of Experimental Child Psychology*, *67*, 295–301.

Bowey, J. A. (2001). Nonword repetition and young children's receptive vocabulary: A longitudinal study. *Applied Psycholinguistics*, *22*, 441–469.

Bunge, S. A., Mackey, A. P., & Whitaker, K. J. (2009). Brain changes underlying the development of cognitive control and reasoning. In M. S. Gazzaniga (Ed.), *The cognitive neurosciences* (4th ed., pp. 73–85). Cambridge, MA: MIT Press.

Bunting, M. Cowan, N., & Saults, J. S. (2006). How does running memory span work? *Quarterly Journal of Experimental Psychology*, *59*, 1691–1700.

Burgess, N. & Hitch, G. (1996). A connectionist model of STM for serial order. In S. Gathercole (Ed.), *Models of short-term memory* (pp. 51–72). Hove, UK: Psychology Press.

Campbell, T., & Fiske, D. (1959). Convergent and discriminant validation by multitrait-multimethod matrix. *Psychological Bulletin*, *56*, 81–105.

Canivez, G. L. (2008). Orthogonal higher order factor structure of the Stanford-Binet Intelligence Scales–Fifth Edition for Children and Adolescents. *School Psychology Quarterly*, *23*(4), 533–541. doi:10.1037/a0012884

Caplan, D. (1992). *Language: Structure, processing, and disorders.* Cambridge, MA: MIT Press.

Carlisle, J. F. (2004). Morphological processes influencing literacy learning. In C. A. Stone, E. R. Silliman, B. J. Ehren, & K. Apel (Eds.), *Handbook on language and literacy: Development and disorders* (pp. 318–339). New York, NY: Guilford Press.

Carroll, J. B. (1983). Studying individual differences in cognitive abilities: Through and beyond factor analysis. In R. F. Dillon (Ed.), *Individual differences in cognition* (Vol. 1, pp. 1–33). New York, NY: Academic Press.

Carroll, J. B. (1993). *Human cognitive abilities: A survey of factor-analytical studies.* New York, NY: Cambridge University Press.

Carroll, J. B. (1998). Human cognitive abilities: A critique. In J. J. McArdle & R. W. Woodcock (Eds.), *Human cognitive abilities in theory and practice* (pp. 5–24). Mahwah, NJ: Erlbaum.

Carroll, J. B. (2003). The higher-stratum structure of cognitive abilities: Current evidence supports *g* and about ten broad factors. In H. Nyborg (Ed.), *The scientific study of general intelligence: Tribute to Arthur R. Jensen* (pp. 5–21). New York, NY: Pergamon Press.

Carrow-Woolfolk, E. (1996). *Oral and written language scales: Written expression.* Torrance, CA: Western Psychological Services.

Castel, A. D., Pratt, J., & Drummond, E. (2005). The effects of action video game experience on the time course of inhibition of return and the efficiency of visual search. *Acta Psychologica, 119*(2), 217–230. http://dx.doi.org/10.1016/j.actpsy.2005.02.004

Cattell, R. B. (1941). Some theoretical issues in adult intelligence testing. *Psychological Bulletin, 38*, 592.

Cattell, R. B. (1943). The measurement of adult intelligence. *Psychological Bulletin, 40*, 153–193.

Cattell, R. B. (1963). Theory of fluid and crystallized intelligence: A critical experiment. *Journal of Educational Psychology, 54*, 1–22.

Cattell, R. B. (1987). *Advances in Psychology: Volume 35, Intelligence: Its structure, growth and action.* Amsterdam, the Netherlands: Elsevier.

Cattell, R. B., & Horn, J. L. (1978). A check on the theory of fluid and crystallized intelligence with description of new subtest designs. *Journal of Educational Measurement, 15*, 139–164.

Chace, K. H., Rayner, K., & Well, A. D. (2005). Eye movements and phonological parafoveal preview: Effects of reading skill. *Canadian Journal of Experimental Psychology/Revue canadienne de psychologie expérimentale, 59*, 209–217. http://dx.doi.org/10.1037/h0087476

Cicerone, K. D. (1996). Attention deficits and dual task demands after mild traumatic brain injury. *Brain Injury, 10*(2), 79–89.

Clark, J. M., & Paivio, A. (1991). Dual coding theory and education. *Educational Psychology Review, 3*, 149–210.

Coady, J. A., & Aslin, R. N. (2004). Young children's sensitivity to probabilistic phonotactics in the developing lexicon. *Journal of Experimental Child Psychology, 89*, 183–213.

Coady, J. A., & Evans, J. L. (2008). Uses and interpretations of non-word repetition tasks in children with and without specific language impairments (SLI). *International Journal of Language & Communication Disorders, 43*(1), 1–40.

Cohen, J. D., Dunbar, K., & McClelland, J. L. (1990). On the control of automatic processes: A parallel distributed processing account of the Stroop effect. *Psychological Review, 97*, 332–361.

Coluccia, E., & Louse, G. (2004). Gender differences in spatial orientation: A review. *Journal of Environmental Psychology, 24*, 329–340.

Conrad, N. J. (2008). From reading to spelling and spelling to reading: Transfer goes both ways. *Journal of Educational Psychology, 100*, 869–878. doi: http://dx.doi.org/10.1037/a0012544

Conti-Ramsden, G. (2003). Processing and linguistic markers in young children with specific language impairment (SLI). *Journal of Speech, Language, and Hearing Research, 46*, 1029–1037.

Conti-Ramsden, G, Botting, N., & Farragher, B. (2001). Psycholinguistic markers for specific language impairment (SLI). *Journal of Child Psychology and Psychiatry, 42*, 741–748.

Conti-Ramsden, G., & Hesketh, L. (2003). Risk markers for SLI: A study of young language-learning children. *International Journal of Language & Communication Disorders, 38*, 251–263.

Conway, A. R. A., Cowan, N., Bunting, M. F., Therriault, D. J., & Minkoff, S. R. B. (2002). A latent variable analysis of working memory capacity, short-term memory capacity, processing speed, and general fluid intelligence. *Intelligence, 30*, 163–183.

Conway, A. R. A., Kane, M. J., & Engle, R. W. (2003). Working memory capacity and its relation to general intelligence. *Trends in Cognitive Sciences, 7*, 547–552.

Conzelmann, K., & Süß, M.-H. (2015). Auditory intelligence: Theoretical considerations and empirical findings. *Learning and Individual Differences*, http://dx.doi.org/10.1016/j.lindif.2015.03.029

Cormier, D. C., Bulut, O., McGrew, K. S., & Frison, J. (2015). The role of Cattell-Horn-Carroll (CHC) cognitive abilities in predicting writing achievement during the school age years. Manuscript submitted for publication.

Cormier, D. C., McGrew, K. S., Bulut, O., & Funamoto, A. (2015). Exploring the relationships between broad Cattell-Horn-Carroll (CHC) cognitive abilities and reading achievement during the school-age years. Manuscript submitted for publication.

Cormier, D. C., McGrew, K. S., Bulut, O., & Singh, D. (2015). Predicting mathematics achievement from Cattell-Horn-Carroll (CHC) cognitive abilities. Manuscript submitted for publication.

Cornelissen, P., Bradley, L., Fowler, S., & Stein, J. (1994). What children see affects how they spell. *Developmental Medicine and Child Neurology, 36*(8), 716–726.

Cornelissen, P., & Hansen, P. (1998). Motion detection, letter position encoding, and single word reading. *Annals of Dyslexia, 48*(1), 155–188.

Cornelissen, P., Hansen, P., Hutton, J., Evangelinou, V., & Stein, J. (1998). Magnocellular visual function and children's single word reading. *Vision Research, 38*(3), 471–482.

Cornelissen, P. L., Kringelbach, M. L., Ellis, A. W., Whitney, C., Holliday, I. E., & Hansen, P. C. (2009). Activation of the left inferior frontal gyrus in the first 200 ms of reading: Evidence from magnetoencephalography (MEG). *PloS ONE, 4*, Article e5359. http://dx.doi.org/10.1371/journal.pone.0005359

Cornoldi, C., & Giofré, D. (2014). The crucial role of working memory in intellectual functioning. *European Psychologist, 19*(4), 260–268.

Cowan, N. (1988). Evolving conceptions of memory storage, selective attention, and their mutual constraints within the human information-processing system. *Psychological Bulletin, 104*, 163–191.

Cowan, N. (1995). *Attention and memory: An integrated framework.* New York, NY: Oxford University Press.

Cowan, N. (2001). The magical number 4 in short-term memory: A reconsideration of the mental storage capacity. *Behavioral and Brain Sciences, 24,* 87–185.

Cowan, N., Elliott, E. M., Scott Saults, J., Morey, C. C., Mattox, S., Hismjatullina, A., & Conway, A. R. (2005). On the capacity of attention: Its estimation and its role in working memory and cognitive aptitudes. *Cognitive Psychology, 51*(1), 42–100. http://dx.doi.org/10.1016/j.cogpsych.2004.12.001

Coyle, T. R. (2003). IQ, the worst performance rule, and Spearman's law: A reanalysis and extension. *Intelligence, 31,* 473–489.

Cunningham, A. E., & Stanovich, K. E. (1991). Tracking the unique effects of print. *Journal of Educational Psychology, 83,* 264–274.

Dahlin, E., Nelly, A. S., Larsson, A., Bäckman, L., & Nyberg, L. (2008). Transfer of learning after updating training mediated by the striatum. *Science, 320,* 1510–1512. http://dx.doi.org/10.1126/science.1155466

Daneman, M., & Carpenter, P. A. (1980). Individual differences in working memory and reading. *Journal of Verbal Learning and Verbal Behavior, 19,* 450–466.

Daneman, M., & Newson, M. (1992). Assessing the importance of subvocalization during normal silent reading. *Reading and Writing, 4,* 55–77. http://dx.doi.org/10.1007/BF01027072

Davidson, J., Elcock, J., & Noyes, P. (1996). A preliminary study of the effect of computer-assisted practice on reading attainment. *Journal of Research in Reading, 19*(2), 102–110.

Deary, I. J. (2000). *Looking down on human intelligence—From psychometrics to the brain.* Oxford, UK: Oxford University Press.

De Cruz, H. (2012). How do spatial representations enhance cognitive numerical processing? *Cognitive Processing, 13,* 137–140.

Dehn, M. J. (2008). *Working memory and academic learning: Assessment and intervention.* Hoboken, NJ: Wiley.

de Jong, P. F., Seveke, M. J., & van Veen, M. (2000). Phonological sensitivity and the acquisition of new words in children. *Journal of Experimental Child Psychology, 76,* 275–301.

De Koning, B. B., & van der Schoot, M. (2013). Becoming part of the story! Refueling the interest in visualization strategies for reading comprehension. *Educational Psychology Review, 25,* 261–281. doi: http://dx.doi.org/10.1007/s10648-013-9222-6

Demetriou, A., Christou, C., Spanoudis, G., & Platsidou, M. (2002). The development of mental processing: Efficiency, working memory, and thinking. *Monographs of the Society for Research in Child Development, 67* (Serial Number 268).

Desimone, R., & Duncan, J. (1995). Neural mechanisms of selective visual attention. *Annual Review of Neuroscience, 18,* 193–222.

Di Lollo, V. (1980). Temporal integration in visual memory. *Journal of Experimental Psychology: General, 109,* 75–97.

Dollaghan, C. A., Biber, M. E., & Campbell, T. F. (1995). Lexical influences on nonword repetition. *Applied Psycholinguistics, 16,* 211–222.

Dollaghan, C. A., & Campbell, T. F. (1998). Nonword repetition and child language impairment. *Journal of Speech, Language, and Hearing Research, 41,* 1136–1146.

Dumont, R. & Willis, J. O. (2014). Ten top problems with normed achievement tests for young children. Retrieved from http://www.myschoolpsychology.com/wp-content/uploads/2014/02/Ten-Top-Problems.pdf

Edwards, J. Beckman, M. E., & Munson, B. (2004). The interaction between vocabulary size and phonotactic probability effects on children's production accuracy and fluency in nonword repetition. *Journal of Speech, Language, and Hearing Research, 47*, 421–436.

Ekstrom, R. B., French, J. W., & Harman, M. H. (1979). Cognitive factors: Their identification and replication. *Multivariate Behavioral Research Monographs, 79*(2), 3–84.

Ellis Weismer, S., Tomblin, J. B., Zhang, X., Buckwalter, P., Chynoweth, J. G., & Jones, M. (2000). Nonword repetition performance in school-age children with and without language impairment. *Journal of Speech, Language, and Hearing Research, 43*, 865–878.

Engle, R. W. (2002). Working memory capacity as executive attention. *Current Directions in Psychological Science, 11*, 19–23.

Engle, R. W., & Kane, M. J. (2004). Executive attention, working memory capacity, and a two-factor theory of cognitive control. In B. Ross (Ed.), *The psychology of learning and motivation* (Vol. 44, pp. 145–199). New York, NY: Elsevier.

Eysenck, H. J. (1999). *Intelligence: A new look*. New Brunswick, NJ: Transaction.

Federation of American Scientists. (2006). *Summit on educational games: Harnessing the power of video games for learning*. Retrieved from http://www.fas.org/programs/ltp/policy_and_publications/summit/Summit%20on%20Educational%20Games.pdf

Feng, J., Spence, I., & Pratt, J. (2007). Playing and action video game reduces gender differences in spatial cognition. *Psychological Science, 18*(10), 850–855. http://www.psych.utoronto.ca/users/spence/Feng,%20Spence,%20&%20Pratt%20(in%20press).pdf

Flanagan, D. P., McGrew, K. S., & Ortiz, S. O. (2000). *The Wechsler intelligence scales and Gf-Gc theory: A contemporary approach to interpretation*. Boston, MA: Allyn & Bacon.

Flanagan, D. P., Ortiz, S. O., & Alfonso, V. (2013). *Essentials of Cross-Battery Assessment* (3rd ed.). Hoboken, NJ: Wiley.

Foreman, J., Gee, J. P., Herz, J. C., Hinrichs, R., Prensky, M., & Sawyer, B. (2004). Game-based learning: How to delight and instruct in the 21st century. *EDUCAUSE Review, 39*(5), 50–66. Retrieved from http://www.educause.edu/EDUCAUSE+Review/EDUCAUSEReviewMagazineVolume39/GameBasedLearningHowtoDelighta/157927

Frick, A., Möhring, W., & Newcombe, N. S. (2014). Development of mental transformation abilities. *Trends in Cognitive Sciences, 18*(10), 536–542.

Galton, F. (1869, 1978). *Hereditary genius: An enquiry into its laws and consequences*. London, UK: Collins.

Gathercole, S. E. (1995). Is nonword repetition a test of phonological memory or long-term knowledge? It all depends on the nonwords. *Memory and Cognition, 23*, 83–94.

Gathercole, S. E. (2006). Nonword repetition and word learning: The nature of the relationship. *Applied Psycholinguistics, 27*, 513–543.

Gathercole, S. E., & Adams, A. M. (1993). Phonological working memory in very young children. *Developmental Psychology, 29*, 770–778.

Gathercole, S. E., & Adams, A. M. (1994). Children's phonological working memory: Contributions of long-term knowledge and rehearsal. *Journal of Memory and Language, 33*, 678–688.

Gathercole, S. E., & Alloway, T. P. (2007). *Understanding working memory: A classroom guide.* York, UK: University of York. Retrieved from http://www.york.ac.uk/res/wml/Classroom%20guide.pdf

Gathercole, S.E., & Alloway, T. P. (2008). *Working memory and learning: A practical guide for teachers.* London, UK: Sage.

Gathercole, S. E., & Baddeley, A. D. (1989). Evaluation of the role of phonological STM in the development of vocabulary in children. *Journal of Memory and Language, 28,* 200–213.

Gathercole, S. E., & Baddeley, A. D. (1990). Phonological memory deficits in language-disordred children: Is there a causal connection? *Journal of Memory and Language, 29,* 336–360.

Gathercole, S. E., Hitch, G. J., Service, E., & Martin, A. J. (1997). Phonological short-term memory and new word learning in children. *Developmental Psychology, 33,* 966–979.

Gathercole, S. E., Service, E., Hitch, G. J., Adams, A. M., & Martin, A. J. (1999). Phonological short-term memory and vocabulary development: Further evidence on the nature of the relationship. *Applied Cognitive Psychology, 13,* 65–77.

Gathercole, S. E., Tiffany, C., Briscoe, J., Thorn, A. S. C., & the ALSPAC Team. (2005). Developmental consequences of phonological loop deficits during early childhood: A longitudinal study. *Journal of Child Psychology and Psychiatry, 46*(6), 598–611.

Gathercole, S. E., Willis, C., & Baddeley, A. D. (1991a). Differentiating phonological memory and awareness of rhyme: Reading and vocabulary development in children. *British Journal of Psychology, 82,* 387–406.

Gathercole, S. E., Willis, C. & Baddeley, A. D. (1991b). Nonword repetition, phonological memory, and vocabulary: A reply to Snowling, Chiat, and Hulme. *Applied Psycholinguistics, 12,* 375–379.

Gathercole, S. E., Willis, C., Emslie, H., & Baddeley, A. D. (1991). The influences of number of syllables and word-likeness on children's repetition of nonwords. *Applied Psycholinguistics, 12,* 349–367.

Gathercole, S. E., Willis, C., Emslie, H., & Baddeley, A. D. (1992). Phonological memory and vocabulary development during the early school years: A longitudinal study. *Developmental Psychology, 28,* 887–898.

Gathercole, S. E., Willis, C., Emslie, H., & Baddeley, A. D. (1994). The Children's Test of Nonword Repetition: A test of phonological working memory. *Memory, 2,* 103–127.

Gazzaniga, M. S., Irvy, R. B., & Mangun, G. R. (1998). *Cognitive neuroscience: The biology of the mind.* New York, NY: Norton.

Geary, D. C. (1990). A componential analysis of an early learning deficit in mathematics. *Journal of Experimental Child Psychology, 49,* 363–383.

Geary, D. C., & Brown, S. C. (1991). Cognitive addition: Strategy choice and speed-of-processing differences in gifted, normal, and mathematically disabled children. *Developmental Psychology, 27,* 398–406.

Geary, D. C., Brown, S. C., & Samaranayake, V. A. (1991). Cognitive addition: A short longitudinal study of strategy choice and speed-of-processing differences in normal and mathematically disabled children. *Developmental Psychology, 27,* 787–797.

Gee, J. P. (2003). *What video games have to teach us about learning and literacy.* New York, NY: Palgrave Macmillan.

Gerber, M. (1984). Techniques to teach generalizable spelling skills. *Academic Therapy, 20*(1), 49–58.

German, D. J. (2002a). A phonologically based strategy to improve word-finding abilities in children. *Communication Disorders Quarterly, 23*, 179–192.

German, D. J. (2002b). *Word finding intervention program* (2nd ed.). Austin, TX: Pro-Ed.

Gersten, R., Beckmann, S., Clarke, B., Foeggen, A., March, L., Star, J. R., & Witzel, B. (2009). *Assisting students struggling with mathematics: Response to Interventions (RtI) for elementary and middle schools* (MCEE 2009–4060). Washington, DC: National Center for Education Evaluation and Regional Assistance, Institute of Education Sciences, U.S. Department of Education. Retrieved from http://ies.ed.gov/ncee/wwc/pdf/practice_guides/rti_math_pg_042109.

Gersten, R., Ferrini-Mundy, J., Benbow, D., Clements, D. H., Loveless, T., Williams, V., Banfield, M. (2008). Report of the task group on instructional practices. In *National mathematics advisory panel, reports of the task groups and subcommittees* (pp. 45–53). Washington, DC: United States Department of Education.

Glazer, S. M. (1989). Oral language and literacy. In D. S. Strickland & L. M. Morrow (Eds.), *Emerging literacy: Young children learn to read and write* (pp. 16–26). Newark, DE: International Reading Association.

Goldstone, R. L., & Hendrickson, A. T. (2010). Categorical perception. *Wiley Interdisciplinary Reviews: Cognitive Science, 1*, 69–78. http://dx.doi.org/10.1002/ wcs.26

Gottfredson, L. (1997). Mainstream science on intelligence: An editorial with 52 signatories, history, and bibliography. *Intelligence, 24*, 13–23.

Graves, M. F. (2000). A vocabulary program to complement and bolster a middle-grade comprehension program. In B. M. Taylor, M. F. Graves, & P. van den Broek (Eds.), *Reading for meaning: Fostering comprehension in the middle grades* (pp. 116–135). Newark, DE: International Reading Association.

Graves, M. F., & Watts-Taffe, S. (2002). The role of word consciousness in a research-based vocabulary program. In A. Farstrup & S. J. Samuels (Eds.), *What research has to say about reading instruction* (pp. 140–165). Newark, DE: International Reading Association.

Gray, S. (2003). Diagnostic accuracy and test-retest reliability of nonword repetition and digit span tasks administered to preschool children with specific language impairment. *Journal of Communication Disorders, 36*, 129–151.

Green, C. S., & Bavelier, D. (2003). Action video game modifies visual selective attention. *Nature, 423*(6939), 534–537. http://dx.doi.org/10.1038/nature01647

Green, C. S., & Bavelier, D. (2007). Action-video-game experience alters the spatial resolution of vision. *Psychological Science, 18*(1), 88-94.

Greenleaf, R. K., & Wells-Papanek, D. (2005). *Memory, recall, the brain & learning*. Newfield, ME: Greenleaf & Papanek.

Gridley, B. E., Norman, K. A., Rizza, M. G., & Decker, S. L. (2003). Assessment of gifted children with the Woodcock-Johnson III. In F. A. Schrank & D. P. Flanagan (Eds.), *WJ III Clinical Use and Interpretation: Scientist-Practitioner Perspectives* (pp. 285–317). San Diego, CA: Academic Press.

Grudnik, J. L., & Kranzler, J. H. (2001). Meta-analysis of the relationship between intelligence and inspection time. *Intelligence, 29*, 523–535.

Gunderson, E. A., Ramirez, G., Beilock, S. L., & Levine, S. C. (2012). The relation between spatial skill and early number knowledge: The role of the linear number line. *Developmental Psychology, 48*(5), 1229–1241.

Gunn, B. K., Simmons, D. C., & Kame'enui, E. J. (1995). *Emergent literacy: A synthesis of the research*. Eugene, OR: National Center to Improve the Tools of Educators.

Hale, S., & Fry, A. F. (2000). Relationships among processing speed, working memory, and fluid intelligence in children. *Biological Psychology, 54*, 1–34.

Halford, G. S., Wilson, W. H., & Phillips, S. (1998). Processing capacity defined by relational complexity: Implications for comparative, developmental, and cognitive psychology. *Behavioral and Brain Sciences, 21*, 803–864.

Hambrick, D. Z., & Altmann, E. M. (2015). The role of placekeeping ability in fluid intelligence. *Psychonomic Bulletin & Review, 22*, 1104–10. http://dx.doi.org/http://www.ncbi.nlm.nih.gov/pubmed/25504456

Hammill, D., & Larsen, S. (2009). *Test of Written Language* (4th ed.). Austin, TX: Pro-Ed.

Hannon, B., & Daneman, M. (2014). Revisiting the construct of "relational integration" and its role in accounting for general intelligence: The importance of knowledge integration. *Intelligence, 47*, 175–187.

Hardiman, M. M. (2003). *Connecting brain research with effective teaching*. Lanham, MD: Rowman & Littlefield Education.

Hart, B., & Risley, T. R. (1995). *Meaningful differences in the everyday experience of young American children*. Baltimore, MD: Paul Brookes.

Hart, B., & Risley, T. R. (2003). The early catastrophe: The 30 million word gap by age 3. *American Educator, 22*, 4–9.

Hatcher, P. J., Hulme, C., & Ellis, A. W. (1994). Ameliorating early reading failure by integrating the teaching of reading and phonological skills: The phonological linkage hypothesis. *Child Development, 65*, 41–57.

Hayakawa, S. I. (1939, 1978). *Language in thought and action*. San Diego, CA: Harcourt Brace Jovanovich.

Hegarty, M., & Waller, D. A. (2005). Individual differences in spatial abilities. In P. Shah & A. Miyake (Eds.). *The Cambridge handbook of visuospatial thinking* (pp. 121–169). New York, NY: Cambridge University Press.

Heller, J. (1961). *Catch-22*. New York, NY: Simon & Schuster.

Herman, P. A., Anderson, R. C., Pearson, P. D., & Nagy, W. E. (1987). Incidental acquisition of word meanings from expositions with varied text features. *Reading Research Quarterly, 23*, 263–284.

Hickin, J., Best, W., Herbert, R., Howard, D., & Osborne, F. (2002). Phonological therapy for word-finding disorders: A re-evaluation. *Aphasiology, 16*, 1087–1114.

High/Scope Educational Research Foundation. (2003). *Classification, seriation, and number*. Ypsilanti, MI: High/Scope Press.

Hintzman, D. L. (1978). *The psychology of learning and memory*. San Francisco, CA: Freeman.

Holmes, V. M., Malone, A. M., & Redenbach, H. (2008). Orthographic processing and visual sequential memory in unexpectedly poor spellers. *Journal of Research in Reading, 31*, 136–156. doi: http://dx.doi.org/10.1111/j.1467–9817.2007.00364.x

Holzman, T. G., Pellegrino, J. W., & Glaser, R. (1983). Cognitive variables in series completion. *Journal of Educational Psychology, 75*, 603–618.

Horn, J. L. (1968). Organization of abilities and the development of intelligence. *Psychological Review, 75*, 242–259.

Horn, J. L. (1991). Measurement of intellectual capabilities: A review of theory. In K. S. McGrew, J. K. Werder, & R. W. Woodcock, *WJ-R technical manual* (pp. 197–232). Itasca, IL: Riverside.

Horn, J. L. (1994). The theory of fluid and crystallized intelligence. In R. J. Sternberg (Ed.), *The encyclopedia of human intelligence* (pp. 433–451). New York, NY: Macmillan.

Horn, J. L., & Stankov, L. (1982). Auditory and visual factors of intelligence. *Intelligence, 6*, 165–185.

Horohov, J. E. & Oetting, J. B. (2004). Effects of input manipulations on the word learning abilities of children with and without specific language impairment. *Applied Psycholinguistics, 25*, 43–65.

Hutchison, K. A. (2007). Attentional control and the relatedness proportion effect in semantic priming. *Journal of Experimental Psychology: Learning, Memory, and Cognition, 33*, 645–662.

Hunt, E. (1980). Intelligence as an information-processing concept. *British Journal of Psychology, 71*, 449–474.

Hunt, E. (2000). Let's hear it for crystallized intelligence. *Learning and Individual Differences, 12*(1), 123–129.

Hunt, E. (2011). *Human intelligence*. New York, NY: Cambridge University Press.

Individuals with Disabilities Education Improvement Act of 2004 (IDEA), Pub. L. No. 108–446, 118 Stat. 2647 (2004). Amending 20 U.S.C. §§ et seq.

Irwin, D. E., & Yeomans, J. M. (1986). Sensory registration and informational persistence. *Journal of Experimental Psychology: Human Perception and Performance, 12*, 343–360.

Jaffe, L. E. (2009). *Development, interpretation, and application of the W score and the relative proficiency index* (Woodcock-Johnson III *Assessment Service Bulletin* No. 11). Itasca, IL: Riverside. http://www.riverpub.com/products/wjIIIComplete/pdf/WJ3_ASB_11.pdf

Jared, D., Levy, B. A., & Rayner, K. (1999). The role of phonology in the activation of word meanings during reading: Evidence from proofreading and eye movements. *Journal of Experimental Psychology: General, 128*, 219–264.

Jensen, A. R. (1998). *The g factor*. Westport, CT: Praeger.

Jones, A. C., Folk, J. R., & Rapp, B. (2009). All letters are not equal: Subgraphemic texture in orthographic working memory. *Journal of Experimental Psychology: Learning, Memory, and Cognition, 35*, 1389–1402. doi: http://dx.doi.org/10.1037/a0017042

Jones, G., Gobet, F. & Pine, J. M. (2007). Linking working memory and long-term memory: A computational model of the learning of new words. *Developmental Science, 10*(6), 853–873.

Just, M. A., & Carpenter, P. A. (1985). Cognitive coordinate systems: Accounts of mental rotation and individual differences in spatial ability. *Psychological Review, 92*(2), 137–172. http://dx.doi.org/10.1037/0033-295X.92.2.137

Kail, R V. (1991). Developmental change in speed of processing during childhood and adolescence. *Psychological Bulletin, 109*, 490–501.

Kail, R. V. (1992). Processing speed, speech rate, and memory. *Developmental Psychology, 28*, 899–904.

Kail, R. V. (2000). Speed of information processing: Developmental change and links to intelligence. *Journal of School Psychology, 38*, 51–61.

Kail, R. V., & Ferrer, E. (2007). Processing speed in childhood and adolescence: Longitudinal models for examining developmental change. *Child Development, 78*, 1760–1770.

Kail, R. V., & Park, Y. (1992). Global developmental change in processing time. *Merrill-Palmer Quarterly*, *38*(4), 525–541.

Kane, M. J., Brown, L. E., Little, J. C., Silvia, P. J., Myin-Germeys, I., & Kwapil, T. R. (2007). For whom the mind wanders, and when: An experience-sampling study of working memory and executive control in daily life. *Psychological Science*, *18*, 614–621.

Kane, M. J., Conway, A. R. A., Hambrick, D. Z., & Engle, R. W. (2007). Variation in working memory capacity as variation in executive attention and control. In A. R. A. Conway, C. Jarrold, M. J. Kane, A. Miyake, & J. Towse, *Variation in working memory* (pp. 21–48). NY: Oxford University Press. http://englelab.gatech.edu/2007/kaneconwayhambrickengle2007chapter.pdf

Kane, M. J., Hambrick, D. Z., & Conway, A. R. A. (2005). Working memory capacity and fluid intelligence are strongly related constructs: Comment on Ackerman, Beier, and Boyle (2005). *Psychological Bulletin*, *131*, 66–71.

Katz, L. (1977). Reading ability and single-letter orthographic redundancy. *Journal of Educational Psychology*, *69*(6), 653–659.

Kaufman, A. S., & Kaufman, N. L. (2004). *Kaufman Assessment Battery for Children* (2nd ed.). San Antonio, TX: Pearson.

Keith, T. Z., & Reynolds, M. (2010). Cattell-Horn-Carroll abilities and cognitive tests: What we've learned from 20 years of research. *Psychology in the Schools*, *47*(7), 635–650.

Kennison, S. M., Fernandez, E. C., & Bowers, J. M. (2014). The roles of semantic and phonological information in word production: Evidence from Spanish-English bilinguals. *Journal of Psycholinguist Research*, *43*, 105–124.

Kintsch, W. (1988). The role of knowledge in discourse comprehension: a construction integration model. *Psychological Review*, *95*, 163–182. doi: http://dx.doi.org/10.1037/0033-295X.95.2.163

Kintsch, W. (1998). *Comprehension: A paradigm for cognition*. Cambridge, UK: Cambridge University Press.

Klatt, D. H. (1979). Speech perception: A model of acoustic-phonetic analysis and lexical access. *Journal of Phonetics*, *7*, 279–312.

Klauer, K. J., & Phye, G. D. (2008). Inductive Reasoning: A Training Approach. *Review of Educational Research*, *78*(1), 85-123.

Klauer, K. J., Willmes, K., & Phye, G. D. (2002). Inducing inductive reasoning: Does it transfer to fluid intelligence? *Contemporary Educational Psychology*, *27*, 1–25.

Klingberg, T. (2009). *The overflowing brain: Information overload and the limits of working memory*. (N. Betteridge, Trans.). New York, NY: Oxford University Press.

Klingberg, T. (2014). Childhood cognitive development as a skill. *Trends in Cognitive Sciences*, *18*(11), 573–579.

Korzybski, A. (1933, 2000). *Science and sanity: An introduction to non-Aristotelian systems and general semantics*. New York, NY: Institute of General Semantics.

Kosslyn, S. M., Alpert, N. M., & Thompson, W. L. (1995). Identifying objects at different levels of hierarchy: A positron emission tomography study. *Human Brain Mapping*, *3*, 107–132.

Kosslyn, S. M., & Thompson, W. L. (2000). Shared mechanisms in visual imagery and visual perception: Insights from cognitive neuroscience. In M. S. Gazzaniga (Ed.), *The new cognitive neurosciences* (2nd ed., pp. 975–985). Cambridge, MA: MIT Press.

Kroesbergen, E. H., & Van Luit, J. E. H. (2003). Mathematical interventions for children with special educational needs. *Remedial and Special Education, 24*, 97–114.

Kyllonen, P. C. (2002). *g*: Knowledge, speed, strategies, or working-memory capacity? A systems perspective. In R. J. Sternberg & E. L. Grigorenko (Eds.), *The general factor of intelligence: How general is it?* (pp. 415–465). Mahwah, NJ: Erlbaum.

LaBerge, D. (2000). Networks of attention. In M. S. Gazzaniga (Ed.), *The new cognitive neurosciences* (2nd ed., pp. 711–724). Cambridge, MA: MIT Press.

LaForte, E. M., McGrew, K. S., & Schrank, F. A. (2014). *WJ IV Technical Abstract* (Woodcock-Johnson IV *Assessment Service Bulletin No. 2*). Itasca, IL: Riverside.

Leinenger, M. (2014). Phonological coding during reading. *Psychological Bulletin, 140*(6), 1534–1555. http://dx.doi.org/10.1037/a0037830

Levy, B. A. (1978). Speech processing during reading. In A. M. Lesgold, J. W. Pellegrino, S. D. Fokkema, & R. Glaser (Eds.), *Cognitive psychology and instruction* (pp. 123–151). New York, NY: Plenum Press. http://dx.doi.org/10.1007/978-1-4684-2535-2_14

Liberman, I. Y., Shankweiler, D., & Liberman, A. M. (1989). The alphabetic principle and learning to read. In Shankweiler, D., & Liberman, I. Y. (Eds.), *Phonology and reading disability: Solving the reading puzzle* (pp. 1–33). Ann Arbor, MI: University of Michigan Press.

LINKS. (2002). http://www.linkslearning.k12.wa.us/reading_links/readingmanuals/PhonemicAwarenessFACILITATOR.pdf

Logie, R. H., Della Sala, S., Laiacona, M., & Chalmers, P. (1996). Group aggregates and individual reliability: The case of verbal short-term memory. *Memory and Cognition, 24*, 305–321.

Luck, S. J., & Vogel, E. K. (1997). The capacity of visual working memory for features and conjunctions. *Nature, 390*, 279–281.

Lubinski, D. (2010). Spatial ability and STEM: A sleeping giant for talent identification and development. *Personality and Individual Differences, 49*, 344–351.

Lukatela, G., Lukatela, K., & Turvey, M. T. (1993). Further evidence for phonological constraints on visual lexical access: TOWED primes FROG. *Perception & Psychophysics, 53*(5), 461–466.

Lukatela, G., & Turvey, M. T. (1994a). Visual lexical access is initially phonological: 1. Evidence from associative priming by words, homophones, and pseudohomophones. *Journal of Experimental Psychology: General, 123*, 107–128. http://dx.doi.org/10.1037/0096-3445.123.2.107

Lukatela, G., & Turvey, M. T. (1994b). Visual lexical access is initially phonological: 2. Evidence from phonological priming by homophones and pseudohomophones. *Journal of Experimental Psychology: General, 123*, 331–353. http://dx.doi.org/10.1037/0096-3445.123.4.331

Lundberg, I., Frost, J., & Peterson, O. (1988). Effects of an extensive program for stimulating phonological awareness in preschool children. *Reading Research Quarterly, 23*(3), 263–284.

Macdonald, M. C., & Christiansen, M. H. (2002). Reassessing working memory: Comment on Just and Carpenter (1992) and Walters and Caplan (1996). *Psychological Review, 109*, 35–54.

Mackey, A. P., Hill, S. S., Stone, S. I., & Bunge, S. A. (2010). Differential effects of reasoning and speed training in children. *Developmental Science, 14*(3), 582–590.

Mahncke, H. W., Bronstone, A., & Merzenich, M. M. (2006). Brain plasticity and functional losses in the aged: Scientific bases for a novel intervention. In A. R. Moller (Ed.), *Progress in brain research: Reprogramming the brain* (Vol. 157, pp. 81–109). Amsterdam, the Netherlands: Elsevier.

Majerus, S., Van Der Linde, M., Mulder, L., Meulemans, T., & Peters, F. (2004). Verbal short-term memory reflects the sublexical organization of the phonological language network: Evidence from an incidental phonotactic learning paradigm. *Journal of Memory and Language, 51*, 297–306.

Manning, B., & Payne, B. (1996). *Self-talk for teachers and students: Metacognitive strategies for personal and classroom use.* Boston, MA: Allyn & Bacon.

Markovits, H., & Barrouillet, P. (2002). The development of conditional reasoning: A mental model account. *Developmental Review, 22*, 5–36.

Martin, A. (2009). Circuits in mind: The neural foundations for object concepts. In M. S. Gazzaniga (Ed.), *The cognitive neurosciences* (4th ed., pp. 1031–1045). Cambridge, MA: MIT Press.

Martin, A. (1998). The organization of semantic knowledge and the origin of words in the brain. In N. Jablonski & L. Aiello (Eds.), *The origins and diversifications of language* (pp. 69–98). San Francisco, CA: California Academy of Sciences.

Marzano, R. J., Pickering, D. J., & Pollock, J. E. (2001). *Classroom instruction that works.* Alexandria, VA: Association for Supervision and Curriculum Development.

Mather, N., & Jaffe, L. (2015). *Woodcock-Johnson IV: Recommendations, reports, and strategies.* Hoboken, NJ: Wiley.

Mather, N., & Wendling, B. J. (2014). *Examiner's manual. Woodcock-Johnson IV tests of cognitive abilities.* Itasca, IL: Riverside.

Mather, N., & Wendling, B. J. (2015). *Essentials of WJ IV tests of achievement.* Hoboken, NJ: Wiley.

Mathias, J.L., & Wheaton, P. (2007). Changes in attention and information-processing speed following severe traumatic brain injury: A meta-analytic review. *Neuropsychology, 21*(2), 212–223.

McAuliffe, C. (2003). *Visualizing topography: Effects of presentation strategy, gender, and spatial ability* (Doctoral dissertation). Available from ProQuest Dissertations and Theses database (UMI No. 3109579).

McCusker, L. X., Hillinger, M. L., & Bias, R. G. (1981). Phonological recoding and reading. *Psychological Bulletin, 89*, 217–245. http://dx.doi.org/10.1037/0033-2909.89.2.217

McFall, R. M. (1991). Manifesto for a science of clinical psychology. *Clinical Psychologist, 44*, 75–88.

McFall, R. M. (2000). Elaborate reflections on a simple manifesto. *Applied and Preventive Psychology, 9*, 5–21.

McGrew, K. S. (1994). School psychologists vs. school proceduralists: A response to Willis and Dumont. *Communiqué, 22*(8), 13–15.

McGrew, K. S. (2005). The Cattell-Horn-Carroll (CHC) theory of cognitive abilities. Past, present and future. In D. P. Flanagan & P. L. Harrison (Eds.), *Contemporary intellectual assessment. Theories, tests, and issues* (pp.136–202). New York, NY: Guilford Press.

McGrew, K. S. (2009). Editorial. CHC theory and the human cognitive abilities project. Standing on the shoulders of the giants of psychometric intelligence research. *Intelligence, 37*, 1–10.

McGrew, K. S. (2012, September). *Implications of 20 years of CHC cognitive–achievement research: Back-to-the-future and beyond CHC*. Paper presented at the Richard Woodcock Institute, Tufts University, Medford, MA.

McGrew, K. S., & Flanagan, D. P. (1998). *The intelligence test desk reference (ITDR): Gf-Gc cross-battery assessment*. Boston, MA: Allyn & Bacon.

McGrew, K. S., LaForte, E. M., & Schrank, F. A. (2014). *Technical manual. Woodcock-Johnson IV*. Itasca, IL: Riverside.

McGrew, K. S., & Wendling, B. J. (2010). Cattell-Horn-Carroll cognitive-achievement relations: What we learned from the past 20 years of research. *Psychology in the Schools, 47*, 651–675.

McGrew, K. S., Werder, J. K., & Woodcock, R. W. (1991). *Technical manual. Woodcock-Johnson Psycho-Educational Battery–Revised*. Itasca, IL: Riverside.

Medina, J. (2008). *Brain rules: 12 Principles for surviving and thriving at work, home, and school*. Seattle, WA: Pear Press.

Melby-Lervag, M., Lyster, S., & Hulme, C. (2012). Phonological skills and their role in learning to read: A meta-analytic review. *Psychological Bulletin, 138*(2), 322–352.

Merriam-Webster.com. (2014). Catch-22. Retrieved December 6, 2014 from http://www.merriam-webster.com/dictionary/catch%2022

Metsala, J. L. (1999). Young children's phonological awareness and nonword repetition as a function of vocabulary development. *Journal of Educational Psychology, 91*, 3–19.

Metsala, J. L., & Walley, A. C. (1998). Spoken vocabulary growth and the segmental restructuring of lexical representations: Precursors to phonemic awareness and early reading ability. In J. L. Metsala & L. C. Ehri (Eds.), *Word recognition in beginning literacy* (pp. 89–120). Mahwah, NJ: Erlbaum.

Michas, I. C., & Henry, L. A. (1994). The link between phonological memory and vocabulary acquisition. *British Journal of Developmental Psychology, 12*(2), 147–164. doi: 10.1111/j.2044–835X.1994.tb00625.x

Miellet, S., & Sparrow, L. (2004). Phonological codes are assembled before word fixation: Evidence from boundary paradigm in sentence reading. *Brain and Language, 90*, 299–310. http://dx.doi.org/10.1016/S0093-934X(03)00442-5

Miller, E. K., & Cohen, J. D. (2001). An integrative theory of prefrontal cortex function. *Annual Review of Neuroscience, 24*, 167–202.

Miyake, A., Friedman, N. P., Emerson, M. J., Witzki, A. H., Howerter, A., & Wager, T. D. (2000). The unity and diversity of executive functions and their contributions to complex "frontal lobe" tasks: A latent variable analysis. *Cognitive Psychology, 41*, 49–100.

Miyake, A., & Shah, P. (1999). *Models of working memory: Mechanisms of active maintenance and executive control*. New York, NY: Cambridge University Press.

Moats, L. C. (2001). Overcoming the language gap. *American Educator, 25*(5), 8–9.

Moats, L. C. (2004). *Speech to print: Language essentials for teachers*. Baltimore, MD: Paul H. Brookes.

Moats, L. C. (2009). *Spellography for teachers. How English spelling works* (2nd ed., Vol. 3). Boston, MA: Sopris West.

Moje, E. B., Ciechanowski, K. M., Kramer, K., Ellis, L., Carrillo, R., & Collazo, T. (2004). Working towards third space in content area literacy: An examination of everyday funds of knowledge and discourse. *Reading Research Quarterly, 39*(1), 38–69.

Moll, K., & Landerl, K. (2009). Double dissociation between reading and spelling deficits. *Scientific Studies of Reading, 13*, 359–382.

Mosier, C. I. (1943). On the reliability of a weighted composite. *Psychometrika, 8*, 161–168.

Mueller, S. T. (2002). *The roles of cognitive architecture and recall strategies in performance of the immediate serial recall task* (Unpublished doctoral dissertation). University of Michigan, Ann Arbor.

Munson, B. (2001). Phonological pattern frequency and speech production in adults and children. *Journal of Speech, Language, and Hearing Research, 44*, 778–792.

Munson, B., Kurtz, B. A., & Windsor, J. (2005). The influence of vocabulary size, phonotactic probability, and word-likeness on nonword repetitions of children with and without specific language impairment. *Journal of Speech, Language, and Hearing Research, 48*, 1033–1047.

Muter, V., Hulme, C., Snowling, M., & Taylor, S. (1997). Segmentation, not rhyming predicts early progress in learning to read. *Journal of Experimental Child Psychology, 65*, 370–396.

Nagy, W. E. (2005). Why vocabulary instructions needs to be long-term and comprehensive. In E.H. Hiebert & M.L. Kamil (Eds.), *Teaching and learning vocabulary: Bringing research to practice* (pp. 27–44). Mahwah, NJ: Erlbaum.

Nagy, W. E., & Scott, J. A. (2000). Vocabulary processes. In M. L. Kamil, P. Mosenthal, P. D. Pearson, & R. Barr (Eds.), *Handbook of reading research* (Vol. 3, pp. 269–284). Mahwah, NJ: Erlbaum.

Nation, K., & Snowling, M. J. (1998). Semantic processing and the development of word recognition skills: Evidence from children with reading comprehension difficulties. *Journal of Memory and Language, 39*, 85–101.

National Council of Teachers of Mathematics. (2000). *Principles and Standards for School Mathematics*. Reston, VA: Author.

National Institute for Literacy. (2008). *Developing early literacy: Report of the early literacy panel: A scientific synthesis of early literacy development and implications for intervention*. Jessup, MD: Author.

National Institute of Child Health and Human Development. (2000). *Report of the National Reading Panel: Teaching children to read: An evidence-based assessment of the scientific research literature on reading and its implications for reading instruction*. Washington, DC: Author.

National Reading Panel. (2000). *Teaching children to read: An evidence-based assessment of the scientific research literature on reading and its implications for reading instruction*. Washington, DC: National Institute of Child Health and Human Development.

Neisser, U. (1967). *Cognitive psychology*. New York, NY: Appleton–Century–Crofts.

Nelson, M. A. (2009). *Exploring the relationships among various measures of processing speed in a sample of children referred for psychological assessments* (Unpublished doctoral dissertation). University of Virginia. UMI Microform 3348732.

Neubauer, A. C. (1997). The mental speech approach to the assessment of intelligence. In J. Kingma & W. Tomic (Eds.), *Advances in cognition and educational practice: Reflections on the concept of intelligence* (pp. 149–174). Greenwich, CT: JAI Press.

Newcombe, N. S. (2010). Picture this: Increasing math and science learning by improving spatial thinking. *American Educator, 34*, 29–35, 43. http://dx.doi.org/10.1037/A0016127

Newcombe, N. S., Uttal, D. H., & Sauter, M. (2013). Spatial development. In P. D. Zelazo (Ed.), *The Oxford handbook of developmental psychology, Vol. 1: Body and mind*. Oxford, UK: Oxford University Press.

Niileksela, C. R., Reynolds, M. R., Keith, T. Z., & McGrew, K. S. (2016). A special validity study of the WJ IV: Acting on evidence for specific abilities. In D. P. Flanagan and V. C. Alfonso (Eds.), *WJ IV clinical use and interpretation: Scientist-practitioner perspectives.* (pp. 65–106). San Diego, CA: Academic Press.

Nisbett, R. (2009). *Intelligence and how to get it: Why schools and cultures count*. New York, NY: Norton.

Oakhill, J., Hartt, J., & Samols, D. (2005). Levels of comprehension monitoring and working memory in good and poor comprehenders. *Reading and Writing, 18*(7–9), 657–686. doi: http://dx.doi.org/10.1007/s11145-005-3355-z

Oberauer, K. (2002). Access to information in working memory: Exploring the focus of attention. *Journal of Experimental Psychology: Learning, Memory, and Cognition, 28*, 411–421.

Oberauer, K. (2009). Design for a working memory. In B. H. Ross (Ed.), *Psychology of learning and motivation: Advances in research and theory* (Vol. 51, pp. 45–100). San Diego, CA: Academic Press.

Oberauer, K., & Hein, L. (2012). Attention to information in working memory. *Current Directions in Psychological Science, 21*(3), 164–169.

Oberauer, K., & Kliegel, R. (2006). A formal model of capacity limits in working memory. *Journal of Memory and Language, 55*, 601–626.

Oberauer, K., Süß, H-M., Schultze, R., Wilhelm, O., & Wittman, W. W. (2000). Working memory capacity—facets of a cognitive ability construct. *Personality and Individual Differences, 29*, 1017–1045.

Oberauer, K., Süß, H. M., Wilhelm, O., & Wittman, W. W. (2008). Which working memory function predicts intelligence? *Intelligence, 6*, 641–652.

O'Brien, B. A., Wolf, M., Miller, L. T., Lovett, M. W. & Morris, R. (2011). Orthographic processing efficiency in developmental dyslexia: An investigation of age and treatment factors at the sublexical level. *Annals of Dyslexia, 61*(1), 111–135. http://dx.doi.org/10.1007/s11881-010-0050-9

Ofiesh, N. S. (2000). Using processing speed tests to predict the benefit of extended test time for university students with learning disabilities. *Journal of Postsecondary Education and Disability, 14*, 39–56.

Orton, J. (1966). The Orton-Gillingham approach. In J. Money (Ed.), *The disabled reader: Education of the dyslexic child* (pp. 119–145). Baltimore, MD: Johns Hopkins University Press.

Paivio, A. (2006). *Mind and its evolution: A dual coding theoretical interpretation*. Mahwah, NJ: Erlbaum.

Palincsar, A. S., & Brown, A. L. (1984). Reciprocal teaching of comprehension-fostering and comprehension-monitoring activities. *Cognition and Instruction, 2*, 117–175.

Pammer, K., Lavis, R., Hansen, P., & Cornelissen, P. L. (2004). Symbol-string sensitivity and children's reading. *Brain and Language, 89*, 601–610.

Patterson, K., Nestor, P. J., & Rogers, T. T. (2007) Where do you know what you know? The representation of semantic knowledge in the human brain. *Nature Reviews Neuroscience, 8*(12), 976–987.

Pedhazur, E. J. (1997). *Multiple regression in behavioral research: Explanation and prediction* (3rd ed.). Fort Worth, TX: Harcourt Brace.

Perfetti, C. A. (1998). Learning to read. In P. Reitsma & L. Verhoeven (Eds.), *Literacy problems and interventions* (pp. 15–48). Dordrecht, the Netherlands: Kluwer.

Perfetti, C. A. (2007). Reading ability: Lexical quality to comprehension. *Scientific Studies of Reading, 11*, 357–383.

Perfetti, C. A., & Hart, L. (2001). The lexical quality hypothesis. In L. Verhoeven, C. Elbro, & P. Reitsma (Eds.), *Precursors of functional literacy* (pp. 189–214). Philadelphia, PA: John Benjamins.

Phye, G. D. (1989). Schema training and transfer of an intellectual skill. *Journal of Educational Psychology, 81*, 347-352.

Phye, G. D. (1997). Inductive reasoning and problem solving: The early grades. In G. D. Phye (Ed.), *Handbook of academic learning: The construction of knowledge* (pp. 451-457). San Diego: Academic Press.

Pittelman, S. D., Heimlich, J. E., Berglund, R. L., & French, M. P. (1991). *Semantic feature analysis: Classroom applications*. Newark, DE: International Reading Association.

Pollatsek, A., Lesch, M., Morris, R. K., & Rayner, K. (1992). Phonological codes are used in integrating information across saccades in word identification and reading. *Journal of Experimental Psychology: Human Perception and Performance, 18*, 148–162. http://dx.doi.org/10.1037/0096-1523.18.1.148

Posner, M. I. (1978). *Chronometric explorations of mind*. Hillsdale, NJ: Erlbaum.

Posner, M. I., & DiGirolamo, G. J. (2000). Attention in cognitive neuroscience: An overview. In M. S. Gazzaniga (Ed.), *The new cognitive neurosciences* (2nd ed., pp. 623–631). Cambridge, MA: MIT Press.

Posner, M. I., & Petersen, S.E. (1990). The attention system of the human brain. *Annual Review of Neuroscience, 13*, 25–42.

Pressley, M. (1990). *Cognitive strategy instruction that really improves children's academic performance*. College Park, MD: University of Maryland, College of Education.

Race, E. A., Kuhl, B. A., Badre, D., & Wagner, A. D. (2009). In M. S. Gazzaniga (Ed.). *The cognitive neurosciences* (4th ed., pp. 705–723). Cambridge, MA: MIT Press.

Rack, J. P., Snowling, M. J., & Olson, R. K. (1992).The nonword reading deficit in developmental dyslexia: A review. *Reading Research Quarterly, 27*(1), 28–53.

Ramani, G. R., & Siegler, R. S. (2005). *It's more than just a game: Effects of children's board games play on the development of numerical estimation*. Poster presented at the biennial meeting of the Society for Research in Child Development, Atlanta, GA.

Rasch, G. (1960). *Probabilistic models for some intelligence and attainment tests*. Copenhagen, DK: Danish Institute for Educational Research.

Rauth, J., & Stuart, R. (2008, July). *Sound instruction: Phonemic awareness in kindergarten and first grade*. Presentation at the 5th Annual National Reading First Conference, Nashville, TN.

Reams, R., Chamrad, D., & Robinson, N. M. (1990). The race is not necessarily to the swift: Validity of the WISC–R bonus points for speed. *Gifted Child Quarterly, 34*, 108–110.

Reynolds, M. R., & Keith, T. Z. (2007). Spearman's law of diminishing returns in hierarchical models of intelligence for children and adolescents. *Intelligence, 35*(1), 267–281.

Reynolds, M. R., Keith, T. Z., Fine, J. G., Fisher, M. E., & Low, J. A. (2007). Confirmatory factor structure of the Kaufman Assessment Battery for Children–Second Edition: Consistency with Cattell-Horn-Carroll theory. *School Psychology Quarterly*, *22*(4), 511–539.

Reynolds, M., & Niileksla, C. (2015), Test review: Woodcock-Johnson IV Tests of Cognitive Ability. *Journal of Psychoeducational Assessment*, *33*(4) 381–390.

Richards, T. L., Berninger, V. W., & Fayol, M. (2009). fMRI activation differences between 11-year-old good and poor spellers' access in working memory to temporary and long-term orthographic representations. *Journal of Neurolinguistics*, *22*, 327–353. doi: http://dx.doi.org/10.1016/j.jneuroling.2008.11.002

Roid, G. H. (2003). *Stanford Binet Intelligence Scales* (5th ed.). Austin, TX: Pro-Ed.

Rutter, M. (1981). Psychological sequelae of brain damage in children. *American Journal of Psychiatry*, *138*(12), 1533–1544.

Sadoski, M. Paivio, A. (2001). *Imagery and text: a dual coding theory of reading and writing*. Mahwah, NJ: Erlbaum.

Samuels, S. J., & Flor, R. (1997). The importance of automaticity for developing expertise in reading. *Reading and Writing Quarterly*, *13*, 107–122.

Schneider, W. J., & McGrew, K. S. (2012). The Cattell-Horn-Carroll model of intelligence. In D. P. Flanagan & P. L. Harrison (Eds.), *Contemporary intellectual assessment: Theories, tests, and issues* (3rd ed., pp. 99–144). New York, NY: Guilford Press.

Schrank, F. A., & Dailey, D. (2014). *Woodcock-Johnson Online Scoring and Reporting* [Online format]. Itasca, IL: Riverside.

Schrank, F. A., Mather, N., & McGrew, K. S. (2014a). *Woodcock-Johnson IV Tests of Achievement*. Itasca, IL: Riverside.

Schrank, F. A., Mather, N., & McGrew, K. S. (2014b). *Woodcock-Johnson IV Tests of Oral Language*. Itasca, IL: Riverside.

Schrank, F. A., McGrew, K. S., & Mather, N. (2014a). *Woodcock-Johnson IV*. Itasca, IL: Riverside.

Schrank, F. A., McGrew, K. S., & Mather, N. (2014b). *Woodcock-Johnson IV Tests of Cognitive Abilities*. Itasca, IL: Riverside.

Schrank, F. A., McGrew, K. S., & Mather, N. (2015a). *The WJ IV Gf-Gc composite and its use in the identification of specific learning disabilities* (Woodcock-Johnson IV Assessment Service Bulletin No. 3). Itasca, IL: Riverside.

Schrank, F. A., McGrew, K. S., & Mather, N. (2015b). *Woodcock-Johnson IV Tests of Early Cognitive and Academic Development*. Itasca, IL: Riverside.

Schrank, F. A., & Wendling, B. J. (2015a). *WJ IV Interpretation and Instructional Interventions Program*. Itasca, IL: Riverside.

Schrank, F. A., & Wendling, B. J. (2015b). *Manual and Checklists. WJ IV Interpretation and Instructional Interventions Program*. Itasca, IL: Riverside.

Seidel, K. (2007). *Social intelligence and auditory intelligence—Useful constructs?* (Doctoral dissertation, Otto von Guericke Universität Magdeburg, Germany). Retrieved from http://edoc2.bibliothek.uni-halle.de/hs/content/titleinfo/1229

Sengpiel, F., & Hubener, M. (1999). Visual attention: Spotlight on the primary visual cortex. *Current Biology*, *9*, 318–321.

Shaywitz, S. (2003). *Overcoming dyslexia: A new and complete science-based program for overcoming reading problems at any level*. New York, NY: Knopf.

Shea, D. L., Lubinski, D., & Benbow, C. P. (2001). Importance of assessing spatial ability in intellectually talented young adolescents: A 20-year longitudinal study. *Journal of Educational Psychology, 93*(3), 604–614. http://dx.doi.org/10.1037/0022-0663.93.3.604

Shipstead, Z., Lindsey, D. R. B., Marshall, R. L., & Engle, R. W. (2014). The mechanisms of working memory capacity: Primary memory, secondary memory, and attention control. *Journal of Memory and Language, 72*, 116–141.

Shriffin, R. M. (1970). Memory search. In D. A. Norman (Ed.), *Models of human memory* (pp. 375–447). New York, NY: Academic Press.

Shriffin, R. M., & Atkinson, R. C. (1969). Storage and retrieval processes in long-term memory. *Psychological Review, 79*, 179–193.

Sims, V. K., & Mayer, R. E. (2002). Domain specificity of spatial expertise: The case of video game players. *Applied Cognitive Psychology, 16*, 97–115.

Sinatra, R. C., Berg, D., & Dunn, R. (1985). Semantic mapping improves reading comprehension of learning disabled students. *Teaching Exceptional Children, 17*(4), 310–314.

Slattery, T. J., Pollatsek, A., & Rayner, K. (2006). The time course of phonological and orthographic processing of acronyms in reading: Evidence from eye movements. *Psychonomic Bulletin & Review, 13*, 412–417. http://dx.doi.org/10.3758/BF03193862

Slowiaczek, M. L., & Clifton, C., Jr. (1980). Subvocalization and reading for meaning. *Journal of Verbal Learning & Verbal Behavior, 19*, 573–582. http://dx.doi.org/10.1016/S0022-5371(80)90628-3

Snow, C. E., Burns, M. S., & Griffin, P. (1998). *Preventing reading difficulties in young children.* Washington, DC: National Academy Press.

Sorby, S. A. (2009). Educational research in developing 3-D spatial skills for engineering students. *International Journal of Science Education, 31*, 459–480.

Spearman, C. (1904). General intelligence, objectively determined and measured. *American Journal of Psychology, 15*, 201–293.

Spear-Swerling, L., & Sternberg, R. J. (1994). The road not taken: An integrative theoretical model of reading disability. *Journal of Learning Disabilities, 27*, 91–103.

Sperling, G. (1960). The information available in brief visual presentations. *Psychological Monographs, 74*(Whole No. 498), 1–29.

Squire, L. R., & Schacter, D. L. (2003). *Neuropsychology of memory* (3rd ed.). New York, NY: Guilford Press.

Stahl, S. A. (1999). *Vocabulary development.* Cambridge, MA: Brookline Books.

Stahl, S. A. (2005). Four problems with teaching word meanings (and what to do to make vocabulary an integral part of instruction). In E. H. Hiebert and M. L. Kamil (Eds.), *Teaching and learning vocabulary: Bringing research to practice* (pp. 95–114). Mahwah, NJ: Erlbaum.

Stankov, L., & Horn, J. L. (1980). Human abilities revealed through auditory tests. *Journal of Educational Psychology, 75*(4), 471–490.

Stanovich, K. E. (1994). Romance and reality. *Reading Teacher, 4*, 280–290.

Sternberg, R. J., Conway, B. E., Ketron, J. L., & Bernstein, M. (1981). People's conceptions of intelligence. *Journal of Personality and Social Psychology, 41*(1), 37–55.

Stevens, S. S. (1951). *Handbook of experimental psychology.* New York, NY: Wiley.

Stieff, M. (2007). Mental rotation and diagrammatic reasoning in science. *Learning and Instruction, 17*, 219–234.

Stieff, M., Dixon, B. L., Ryu, M., Kumi, B. C., & Hegarty, M. (2014). Strategy training elim-
inates sex differences in spatial problem solving in a STEM domain. *Journal of Educational
Psychology, 106*(2), 390–402.

Stigler, J. W., Lee, S. Y., & Stevenson, H. W. (1986). Digit memory in Chinese and English:
Evidence for a temporally limited store. *Cognition, 23*, 1–20.

Strickland, D. S. (1991). Emerging literacy: How young children learn to read. In B. Persky &
L. H. Golubchick (Eds.), *Early childhood education* (2nd ed., pp. 337–344). Lanham, MD:
University Press of America.

Swanson, H. L., & Berninger, V. W. (1996). Individual differences in children's working memory and writing skill. *Journal of Experimental Child Psychology, 63*, 358-385.

Tallal, P., Miller, S. L., Bedi, G., Byma, G., Wang, X., Nagarajan, S. S., … Merzenich, M.
(1996). Language comprehension in language-learning impaired children improved with
acoustically modified speech. *Science, 5*(271), 81–84.

Taylor, H. G., Lean, D., & Schwartz, S. (1989). Pseudoword repetition ability in
learning-disabled children. *Applied Psycholinguistics, 10*, 203–219.

Temple, C. M. (1991). Procedural dyscalculia and number fact dyscalculia: Double dissociation in developmental dyscalculia. *Cognitive Neuropsychology, 8*, 155–176

Templeton, S., Bear, D. R., Invernizzi, M., Johnston, F., Flanigan, K., Townsend, D. R., …
Hayes, L. (2015). *Vocabulary their way: Word study with middle and secondary students*
(2nd ed.). Boston, MA: Pearson.

Tomeson, M., & Aarnoutse, C. (1998). Effects of an instructional program for deriving word
meanings. *Educational Studies, 24*, 107–128.

Tomic, W., & Klauer, K. J. (1996). On the effects of training inductive reasoning: How
far does it transfer and how long do the effects persist? *European Journal of Psychology of
Education, 11*(3), 283-299.

Tommasi, L., & Laeng, B. (2012). Psychology of spatial cognition. *WIREs Cognitive Science,
3*, 565–580. doi: 10.1002/wcs.1198

Torgesen, J. K. (1997). The prevention and remediation of reading disabilities: Evaluating
what we know from research. *Journal of Academic Language Therapy, 1*, 11–47.

Torgesen, J. K., Wagner, R. K., Rashotte, C. A., Rose, E., Lindamood, P., Conway, T., &
Garvan, C. (1999). Preventing reading failure in young children with phonological pro-
cessing difficulties: Group and individual responses to instruction. *Journal of Educational
Psychology, 91*, 579–593.

Troia, G. A. (1999). Phonological awareness intervention research: A critical review of the
experimental methodology. *Reading Research Quarterly, 34*, 28–52.

Tulvig, E. (1972). Episodic and semantic memory. In E. Tulvig & W. Donaldson (Eds.),
Organization of memory. Oxford, UK: Oxford University Press.

Tulvig, E. (1985). How many memory systems are there? *American Psychologist, 40*, 385–398.

Tzuriel, D., & Egozi, G. (2010). Gender differences in spatial ability of young children: The effects of training and processing strategies. *Child Development, 81*(5),
1417–1430.

Unsworth, N. (2015). Consistency of attentional control as an important cognitive trait:
A latent variable analysis. *Intelligence, 49*, 110–128.

Unsworth, N., & Engle, R. W. (2006). Simple and complex memory spans and their relation
to fluid abilities: Evidence from list-length effects. *Journal of Memory and Language, 54*,
68–80.

Unsworth, N., & Engle, R.W. (2007a). Individual differences in working memory capacity and retrieval: A Cue-dependent search approach. In J. S. Nairne (Ed.), *The foundations of remembering: Essays in Honor of Henry L. Roediger III* (pp. 241—258). New York, NY: Psychology Press.

Unsworth, N., & Engle, R.W. (2007b). The nature of individual differences in working memory capacity: Active maintenance in primary memory and controlled search from secondary memory. *Psychological Review, 114*(1), 104–132.

Unsworth, N., & Spillers, G. J. (2010). Working memory capacity: Attention, memory, or both? A direct test of the dual component model. *Journal of Memory and Language, 62,* 392–406.

U.S. Department of Education, Office of Special Education Programs. (2006). *Topic Briefs: IDEA regulations: Identification of specific learning disabilities.* http://idea.ed.gov/explore/view/p/%2Croot%2Cdynamic%2CTopicalBrief%2C23%2C

Uttal, D. H., Meadow, N. G., Tipton, E., Hand, L. L., Alden, A. R., Warren, C., & Newcombe, N. S. (2013). The malleability of spatial skills: A meta-analysis of training studies. *Psychological Bulletin, 139*(2), 352–402. doi:10.1037/a0028446

Utall, D. H., Miller, D. I., & Newcombe, N. S. (2013). Exploring and enhancing spatial thinking: Links to achievement in science, technology, engineering, and mathematics? *Current Directions in Psychological Science, 22*(5), 367–373.

van den Broek, P. (1989). Causal reasoning and inference making in judging the importance of story statements. *Child Development, 60,* 286–297. doi: http://dx.doi.org/10.2307/1130976

van den Broek, P. (1997). Discovering the cement of the universe: The development of event comprehension from childhood to adulthood. In P. van den Broek, P.W. Bauer, & T. Bourg (Eds.), *Developmental spans in event comprehension and representation* (pp. 321–342). Mahwah, NJ: Erlbaum.

Van Orden, G. C. (1987). A ROWS is a ROSE: Spelling, sound, and reading. *Memory & Cognition, 15,* 181–198. http://dx.doi.org/10.3758/BF03197716

Van Orden, G. C., & Goldinger, S. D. (1994). Interdependence of form and function in cognitive systems explains perception of printed words. *Journal of Experimental Psychology: Human Perception and Performance, 20,* 1269–1291.

Van Orden, G. C., & Goldinger, S. D. (1996). Phonological mediation in skilled and dyslexic reading. In C. H. Chase, G. D. Rosen, & G. F. Sherman (Eds.), *Developmental dyslexia: Neural, cognitive and genetic mechanisms* (pp. 185–223). Timonium, MD: York Press.

Verhoeven, L., & Perfetti, C. (2008). Advances in text comprehension: Model, process, and development. *Applied Cognitive Psychology, 22,* 293–301.

Vermeer, A. (2001). Breadth and depth of vocabulary in relation to L1/L2 acquisition and frequency of input. *Applied Psycholinguistics, 22,* 217–234.

Vock, M., Preckel, F., & Holling, H. (2011). Mental abilities and school achievement: A test of a mediation hypothesis. *Intelligence, 39,* 357–369.

Vogel, E. K., Woodman, G. F., & Luck, S. J. (2001). Storage of features, conjunctions, and objects in visual working memory. *Journal of Experimental Psychology: Human Perception & Performance, 27,* 92–114.

Wagner, R. K., Torgesen, J. K., Laughon, P., Simmons, K., & Rashotte, C. A. (1993). The development of young readers' phonological processing abilities. *Journal of Educational Psychology, 85,* 1–20.

Wagner, R. K., Torgesen, J. K., & Rashotte, C. A. (1994). The development of reading-related phonological processing abilities: New evidence of bi-directional causality from a latent variable longitudinal study. *Developmental Psychology, 30*, 73–87.

Walczyk, J. J., Wei, M., Griffith-Ross, D. A., Goubert, S. E., Cooper, A. L., & Zha, P. (2007). Development of the interplay between automatic processes and cognitive resources in reading. *Journal of Educational Psychology, 99*(4), 867–887.

Wai, J., Lubinski, D., & Benbow, C. P. (2009). Spatial ability for STEM domains: Aligning over 50 years of cumulative psychological knowledge solidifies its importance. *Journal of Educational Psychology, 101*(4), 817–835. http://dx.doi.org/10.1037/a0016127

Wang, P.L. (1987). Concept formation and frontal lobe function: The search for a clinical frontal lobe test. In E. Perecman (Ed.), *The frontal lobes revisited*. New York, NY: IRBN Press.

Watkins, M. W., Glutting, J. J., & Youngstrom, E. A. (2005). Issues in subtest profile analysis. In D. P. Flanagan & P. L. Harrison (Eds.), *Contemporary intellectual assessment: Theories, tests, and issues* (2nd ed., pp. 251–268). New York, NY: Guilford Press.

Wechsler, D. (2002). *Wechsler Preschool and Primary Scale of Intelligence* (3rd ed.). San Antonio, TX: Pearson.

Wechsler, D. (2003). *Wechsler Intelligence Scale for Children* (4th ed.). San Antonio, TX: Pearson.

Wechsler, D. (2008). *Wechsler Adult Intelligence Scale* (4th ed.). San Antonio, TX: Pearson.

Wending, B. J. (2014). *Examiner training workbook. Woodcock-Johnson IV Tests of Cognitive Abilities*. Itasca, IL: Riverside.

Willis, J. O., & Dumont, R. P. (1994). Reaction to McGrew: In God we trust, all others bring your data. *Communiqué, 22*(8), 13–15.

Willis, J. O., & Dumont, R. (2002). *Guide to identification of learning disabilities* (3rd ed.). Peterborough, NH: Author.

Wilson, M. (2002). Six views of embodied cognition. *Psychonomic Bulletin and Review, 9*(4), 625–636.

Wheat, K. L., Cornelissen, P. L., Frost, S. J., & Hansen, P. C. (2010). During visual word recognition, phonology is accessed within 100 ms and may be mediated by a speech production code: Evidence from magnetoencephalography. *Journal of Neuroscience, 30*, 5229–5233. http://dx.doi.org/10.1523/JNEUROSCI.4448–09.2010

Wheatley, G. (1996). *Quick draw: Developing spatial sense in mathematics*. Tallahassee, FL: Florida Department of Education.

Wright, B. D., & Stone, M. H. (1979). *Best test design*. Chicago, IL: MESA Press.

Wolfe, P. (2001). *Brain matters*. Alexandria, VA: Association for Supervision and Curriculum Development.

Wolter, J. A., & Apel, K. (2010). Initial acquisition of mental graphemic representations in children with language impairment. *Journal of Speech, Language, and Hearing Research, 53*, 179–195. doi:10.1044/1092-4388(2009/07-0130)

Woltz, D. J. (1988). An investigation of the role of working memory in procedural skill acquisition. *Journal of Experimental Psychology: General, 117*, 319–331.

Wong, B. Y. L., Harris, K. R., Graham, S. & Butler, D. L. (2003). Cognitive strategies instruction: Research in learning disabilities. In H. L. Swenson, K. R. Harris, & S. Graham (Eds.), *Handbook of learning disabilities* (pp. 383–402). New York, NY: Guilford Press.

Woodcock, R. W. (1956). *Construction and evaluation of a test for predicting success in remedial reading* (Unpublished doctoral dissertation). University of Oregon, Eugene.

Woodcock, R. W. (1958). An experimental prognostic test for remedial readers. *Journal of Educational Psychology, 49*, 23–27.

Woodcock, R. W. (1990). Theoretical foundations of the WJ-R measures of cognitive ability. *Journal of Psychoeducational Assessment, 8*, 231–258.

Woodcock, R. W. (1993). An information processing view of *Gf-Gc* theory. In *Journal of Psychoeducational Assessment Monograph Series: Woodcock-Johnson Psycho-Educational Battery–Revised* (pp. 80–102). Cordova, TN: Psychoeducational Corporation.

Woodcock, R. W., & Johnson, M. B. (1977). *Woodcock-Johnson Psycho-Educational Battery*. Itasca, IL: Riverside.

Woodcock, R. W., & Johnson, M. B. (1989a). *Woodcock-Johnson Psycho-Educational Battery–Revised*. Itasca, IL: Riverside.

Woodcock, R. W., & Johnson, M. B. (1989b). *Woodcock-Johnson Psycho-Educational Battery–Revised Tests of Achievement*. Itasca, IL: Riverside.

Woodcock, R. W., & Johnson, M. B. (1989c). *Woodcock-Johnson Psycho-Educational Battery–Revised Tests of Cognitive Ability*. Itasca, IL: Riverside.

Woodcock, R. W., McGrew, K. S., & Mather, N. (2001a). *Woodcock-Johnson III*. Itasca, IL: Riverside.

Woodcock, R. W., McGrew, K. S., & Mather, N. (2001b). *Woodcock-Johnson III Tests of Cognitive Abilities*. Itasca, IL: Riverside.

Woodcock, R. W., McGrew, K. S., Mather, N., & Schrank, F. A. (2003). *Woodcock-Johnson III diagnostic supplement to the Tests of Cognitive Abilities*. Itasca, IL: Riverside.

Woodcock, R. W., McGrew, K. S., Schrank, F. A., & Mather, N. (2001, 2007). *Woodcock-Johnson III Normative Update*. Itasca, IL: Riverside.

Yonelinas, A. P. (2002). The nature of recollection and familiarity: A review of 30 years of research. *Journal of Memory and Language, 46*, 441–517.

Zhang, W., & Luck, S. J. (2009). Sudden death and gradual decay in visual working memory. *Psychological Science, 20*, 423–428. doi:http://dx.doi.org/10.1111/j.1467-9280.2009.02322.x

Zhou, R., & Black, I. B. (2000). Development of neural maps: molecular mechanisms. In M. S. Gazzaniga (Ed.), *The new cognitive neurosciences* (2nd ed., pp. 213–221). Cambridge, MA: MIT Press.

Zwaan, R. A., Langston, M. C., & Graesser, A. C. (1995). The construction of situation models in narrative comprehension: An event-indexing model. *Psychological Science, 6*, 292–297. doi: http://dx.doi.org/10.1111/j.1467-9280.1995.tb00513.x

Zwaan, R. A., & Radvansky, G. A. (1998). Situation models in language comprehension and memory. *Psychological Bulletin, 123*, 162–185. doi: http://dx.doi.org/10.1037/0033-2909.123.2.162

Zwaan, R. A., & Taylor, L. J. (2006). Seeing, acting, understanding: Motor resonance in language comprehension. *Journal of Experimental Psychology: General, 135*(1), 1–11.

About the Authors

Fredrick A. Schrank, PhD, ABPP, is the senior author of the Woodcock-Johnson IV. He is a licensed psychologist and a board-certified specialist in school psychology from the American Board of Professional Psychology. A past president of the American Academy of School Psychology, Dr. Schrank obtained a PhD from the University of Wisconsin–Madison. His professional interests include neurocognitive interpretation and intervention.

Scott L. Decker, PhD, is an associate professor and Director of the Applied Cognitive Neuropsychology Lab in the Department of Psychology at the University of South Carolina. His research focuses on the assessment of children with learning and attention problems. Dr. Decker's current research explores the correspondence between measures of brain activity with cognition. Additionally, his research examines cognitive predictors of academic achievement.

John M. Garruto, DEd is a school psychologist in central New York and an adjunct professor at SUNY Oswego. He sits on the executive board for the New York Association of School Psychologists as Research Chair, as an at-large member for the Ethics and Professional Practices Committee of the National Association of School Psychologists, and is also a trainer for the WJ IV suite of assessments. He received his Doctor of Education degree from Indiana University of Pennsylvania. His interests relate to the cognitive and neuropsychological assessment of learning disabilities and the professional practice of school psychology.

About the Contributors

Melanie A. Bartels Graw is an education and publishing consultant. She formerly served as the publisher of the Woodcock-Muñoz Foundation Press and was Senior Director of Clinical Product Development at Riverside Publishing Company.

Robert Walrath, PsyD is Director, Doctoral Program in Counseling and School Psychology, Rivier University.

John O. Willis, EdD, SAIF, Department of Education, Rivier University.

Ron Dumont, EdD, NCSP, is Director, School of Psychology, Fairleigh Dickinson University.

Index